Moroccan Foreign Policy under Mohammed VI, 1999–2014

This book presents a comprehensive survey of Moroccan foreign policy since 1999. It considers the objectives, actors and decision-making processes involved, and outlines Morocco's foreign policy activity in key areas such as the international management of the Western Sahara conflict and relations with the other states of North Africa, relations with the European Union, especially France and Spain, and relations with the United States and the Middle East. The book links the behaviour and discourses analysed to differing conceptions of Morocco's national role on the international scene – champion of national territorial integrity, model student of the EU and good ally of the United States – and shows how these competing approaches to the country's foreign policy enjoy different degrees of domestic consensus, and result in different degrees of legitimation for the regime.

Irene Fernández-Molina is a Lecturer in Middle East Politics at the University of Exeter, United Kingdom.

Durham modern Middle East and Islamic world series
Series Editor: Anoushiravan Ehteshami
University of Durham

1 **Economic Development in Saudi Arabia**
   Rodney Wilson, with Abdullah Al-Salamah, Monica Malik and Ahmed Al-Rajhi

2 **Islam Encountering Globalisation**
   Edited by Ali Mohammadi

3 **China's Relations with Arabia and the Gulf, 1949–1999**
   Mohamed Bin Huwaidin

4 **Good Governance in the Middle East Oil Monarchies**
   Edited by Tom Pierre Najem and Martin Hetherington

5 **The Middle East's Relations with Asia and Russia**
   Edited by Hannah Carter and Anoushiravan Ehteshami

6 **Israeli Politics and the Middle East Peace Process, 1988–2002**
   Hassan A. Barari

7 **The Communist Movement in the Arab World**
   Tareq Y. Ismael

8 **Oman – The Islamic Democratic Tradition**
   Hussein Ghubash

9 **The Secret Israeli–Palestinian Negotiations in Oslo**
   Their success and why the process ultimately failed
   Sven Behrendt

10 **Globalization and Geopolitics in the Middle East**
   Old games, new rules
   Anoushiravan Ehteshami

11 **Iran–Europe Relations**
   Challenges and opportunities
   Seyyed Hossein Mousavian

12 **Islands and International Politics in the Persian Gulf**
   The Abu Musa and Tunbs in strategic perspective
   Kourosh Ahmadi

13 **Monetary Union in the Gulf**
   Prospects for a single currency in the Arabian Peninsula
   Emilie Rutledge

14 **Contested Sudan**
   The political economy of war and reconstruction
   Ibrahim Elnur

15 **Palestinian Politics and the Middle East Peace Process**
Consensus and competition in the Palestinian Negotiation Team
Ghassan Khatib

16 **Islam in the Eyes of the West**
Images and realities in an age of terror
Edited by Tareq Y. Ismael and Andrew Rippin

17 **Islamist Extremism in Kuwait**
From the Muslim Brotherhood to Al-Qaeda and other Islamist political groups
Falah Abdullah al-Mdaires

18 **Iraq, Democracy and the Future of the Muslim World**
Edited by Ali Paya and John Esposito

19 **Islamic Entrepreneurship**
Rasem N. Kayed and M. Kabir Hassan

20 **Iran and the International System**
Edited by Anoushiravan Ehteshami and Reza Molavi

21 **The International Politics of the Red Sea**
Anoushiravan Ehteshami and Emma C. Murphy

22 **Palestinian Christians in Israel**
State attitudes towards non-Muslims in a Jewish State
Una McGahern

23 **Iran–Turkey Relations, 1979–2011**
Conceptualising the dynamics of politics, religion and security in middle-power states
Suleyman Elik

24 **The Sudanese Communist Party**
Ideology and party politics
Tareq Y. Ismael

25 **The Muslim Brotherhood in Contemporary Egypt**
Democracy defined or confined?
Mariz Tadros

26 **Social and Gender Inequality in Oman**
The power of religious and political tradition
Khalid M. Al-Azri

27 **American Democracy Promotion in the Changing Middle East**
From Bush to Obama
Edited by Shahram Akbarzadeh, James Piscatori, Benjamin MacQueen and Amin Saikal

28 **China–Saudi Arabia Relations, 1990–2012**
Marriage of convenience or strategic alliance?
Naser M. Al-Tamimi

29 **Adjudicating Family Law in Muslim Courts**
Cases from the contemporary Muslim world
Edited by Elisa Giunchi

30 **Muslim Family Law in Western Courts**
Edited by Elisa Giunchi

31 **Anti-Veiling Campaigns in the Muslim World**
Gender, modernism and the politics of dress
Edited by Stephanie Cronin

32 **Russia–Iran Relations Since the End of the Cold War**
Eric D. Moore

33 **Islam and Pakistan's Political Culture**
Farhan Mujahid Chak

34 **Iraq in the Twenty-First Century**
Regime change and the making of a failed state
Tareq Y. Ismael and Jacqueline S. Ismael

35 **Islamism and Cultural Expression in the Arab World**
Abir Hamdar and Lindsey Moore

36 **The Emerging Middle East–East Asia Nexus**
Edited by Anoushiravan Ehteshami and Yukiko Miyagi

37 **Islamism and Globalisation in Jordan**
Daniel Atzori

38 **The Military in Post-Revolutionary Iran**
The evolution and roles of the Revolutionary Guard to the Military in post-revolutionary Iran
Hesam Forozan

39 **Moroccan Foreign Policy under Mohammed VI, 1999–2014**
Irene Fernández-Molina

Moroccan Foreign Policy under Mohammed VI, 1999–2014

Irene Fernández-Molina

LONDON AND NEW YORK

First published 2016
by Routledge
2 Park Square, Milton Park, Abingdon, Oxon OX14 4RN

and by Routledge
711 Third Avenue, New York, NY 10017

Routledge is an imprint of the Taylor & Francis Group, an informa business

© 2016 Irene Fernández-Molina

The right of Irene Fernández-Molina to be identified as the author of this work has been asserted by her in accordance with sections 77 and 78 of the Copyright, Designs and Patents Act 1988.

All rights reserved. No part of this book may be reprinted or reproduced or utilised in any form or by any electronic, mechanical, or other means, now known or hereafter invented, including photocopying and recording, or in any information storage or retrieval system, without permission in writing from the publishers.

Trademark notice: Product or corporate names may be trademarks or registered trademarks, and are used only for identification and explanation without intent to infringe.

British Library Cataloguing in Publication Data
A catalogue record for this book is available from the British Library

Library of Congress Cataloging in Publication Data
Molina, Irene Fernández, 1980– author.
Moroccan foreign policy under Mohammed VI, 1999–2014 / Irene Fernández Molina.
  pages cm. – (Durham modern Middle East and Islamic world series ; 39)
  Includes bibliographical references and index.
  1. Morocco–Foreign relations–21st century. 2. Morocco–Politics and government–1999– 3. Mohammed VI, King of Morocco, 1963– I. Title. II. Series: Durham modern Middle East and Islamic world series ; 39.
  DT326.3.M65 2016
  327.64–dc23   2015019534

ISBN: 978-1-138-79661-4 (hbk)
ISBN: 978-1-315-75779-7 (ebk)

Typeset in Times New Roman
by Wearset Ltd, Boldon, Tyne and Wear

Printed and bound in Great Britain by
TJ International Ltd, Padstow, Cornwall

Contents

List of figures x
List of tables xi
Acknowledgements xii

Introduction and analytical framework 1
Research question and hypotheses 2
The analysis of the foreign policies of Arab countries, the Maghreb and Morocco 7
From the domestic sources of foreign policy to constructivism through role theory 10
Methodology and sources 15
Structure of the book 17

1 Objectives, actors and decision-making under Mohammed VI 19
A 'new' approach: 'economic diplomacy' and reform of the foreign service 21
Changes at the monarchical and security core of decision-making 29
The subsidiary role of the government, the parliament and the consultative councils 34
Political parties and civil society actors in the periphery 41

2 The tribulations of a 'territorial champion': the international management of a changing Western Sahara conflict 46
Domestic and international progress of the 'third way' approach 49
Morocco's rejection of the Baker Plan II and the ensuing strategic crisis 54

viii *Contents*

The 'reconciliation' strategy and the Autonomy Plan 61
Returning on the defensive in the face of a transformed conflict 66

3 The Sisyphean game of Maghrebi integration and normalisation with Algeria 76
Historicist, economistic, security and social discourses on regional cooperation 79
The vicissitudes of bilateral relations with Algeria 82
Newly dashed expectations after the Arab Spring 93

4 A 'model student' in search of a differentiated relationship with the EU 96
Morocco's superficial but effective socialisation by the EU 101
An exemplary performance in the Euro-Mediterranean Partnership 105
A self-interested welcome to differentiation within the European Neighbourhood Policy 114
Weighing up the costs and benefits of cooperation on migration 118

5 Moments of truth and paybacks: from the Advanced Status to the Arab Spring 127
Steering the Union for the Mediterranean towards Morocco's preferences 128
Intergovernmental dynamics and 'rhetorical action' in pursuit of an Advanced Status 131
'Business as usual' after (and despite) the Arab Spring 146

6 The unbalanced postcolonial triangle with France and Spain 157
An exceptional socioeconomic and elite interdependence with France 158
From paternalism to a pragmatic and economistic turn 162
The duality of increased cooperation and territorial obstacles with Spain 170
From the 2001–2003 conflict spiral to the repairing of bilateral relations 174

7 An uneasy loyalty: remaining a 'good ally' of the United States in times of Middle East turmoil 188
Morocco's multifaceted participation in the War on Terror after 9/11 191

*The BMENA initiative and the hosting of the Forum for the
   Future 195*
*Strengthening economic ties through highly 'political' aid and
   trade 198*
Security cooperation in a reshaped Maghreb-Sahel region 204
Lobbying in Washington over the Western Sahara issue 207

Conclusions 212

References 220
Index 249

Figures

1.1	Organisation chart of the Ministry of Foreign Affairs and Cooperation	25
3.1	Military expenditure in Morocco and Algeria in constant (2011) US$ million, 1999–2013	92
3.2	Military expenditure in Morocco and Algeria as percentage of GDP, 1999–2013	92
6.1	Total value of Moroccan trade with France and Spain, 1999–2012 (US$ million)	159
6.2	Share of France and Spain in Morocco's total trade, 1999–2012 (%)	160
6.3	FDI flows in Morocco originating from France and Spain, 2001–2011 (US$ million)	161

Tables

1.1	Embassies/missions of Morocco abroad, 2014	29
2.1	Chronology of Morocco's *domestic* and international management of the Western Sahara conflict, 1999 onwards	48
4.1	Perception of the EU within Moroccan public opinion	98
4.2	Perception of Morocco's relations with the EU within Moroccan public opinion	98
4.3	EU financial assistance to Morocco under MEDA Programmes and the ENPI	117
4.4	European Neighbourhood and Partnership Instrument (ENPI) – Commitments in National Indicative Programmes for Morocco, 2007–2010 and 2011–2013	118

Acknowledgements

This book is part of the results of the research project 'New Spaces, Actors and Instruments in Spain's External Relations with the Arab and Muslim world' (CSO2011-29438-C05-02), funded by the Spanish Ministry of Economy and Competitiveness.

In its first life it was a PhD thesis which I defended at the Universidad Complutense de Madrid in 2013 and which was awarded a PhD special prize. This would not have been possible without the four-year PhD research fellowship granted to me by this university, and the institutional and academic support from its Department of Public International Law and International Relations (International Studies). My thanks in particular to the inspiring late professor Roberto Mesa, who encouraged me to undertake this journey, Isabel Castaño, who took over as my supervisor, the members of my thesis jury and my fellow PhD candidates during all those years.

I am indebted for their time and kindness to many academics who provided me with hints, guidance, advice or criticism during the long process of research design, documentary collection and fieldwork, including the members of the Moroccan and French centres that hosted me as a visiting researcher – Institut Marocain des Relations Internationales (IMRI, Casablanca), Centre Jacques Berque pour le Développement des Sciences Humaines et Sociales au Maroc (CJB, Rabat) and Institut de Recherche sur le Monde Arabe et Musulman (IREMAM, Aix-en-Provence) – as well as the Workshop on International Mediterranean Studies (TEIM) of the Universidad Autónoma de Madrid and the Spanish Forum of Researchers on the Arab and Muslim World (FIMAM).

From the latter Spanish academic community I have to particularly acknowledge Miguel Hernando de Larramendi for showing a generosity which is out of this world; the other enthusiastic members of the research projects in which I have had the chance to participate at the Universidad de Castilla-La Mancha: Irene González, Aurèlia Mañé, Bárbara Azaola and Ana Planet; the founders of TEIM Election Watch: Luciano Zaccara and Rafael Bustos; my companions in electoral adventures in Morocco: Bernabé López García, Raquel Ojeda and Said Kirhlani; and other scholars who have helped me in different ways, such as Laura Feliu, Thierry Desrues, Eduard Soler, Isaías Barreñada, María Angustias

Parejo, Inmaculada Szmolka, Victoria Veguilla, Ángela Suárez Collado and Montserrat Emperador. Outside academia, I am also grateful to Emilio Cassinello and Haizam Amirah Fernández, for inviting me to participate respectively in the Task Force on Western Sahara of Search for Common Ground (SFCG) and Centro Internacional de Toledo para la Paz (CITpax), and the Working Group on the Maghreb and Spanish–Moroccan Relations at Real Instituto Elcano.

From my second academic life at the College of Europe, Natolin (Warsaw) campus, I owe special thanks to my colleagues from the European Neighbourhood Policy Chair, Tobias Schumacher, Michał Natorski, Dimitris Bouris, Maja Olszewska, Andriy Tyushka, Angelos Katsaris and Roxana Barbulescu, who have provided me with feedback on different chapter drafts, moral support and unrepeatable moments (especially in Tunis!), as well as to other Natolin colleagues and the students I have taught and supervised, from whom I have learnt so much. Other academics and researchers with whom I have had the pleasure of collaborating in recent projects and publications are Yahia H. Zoubir, Greg White, Daniela Huber, Lorenzo Kamel, Marco Pinfari, Justine Louis and Intissar Fakir. Isabelle Werenfels, Gerd Nonneman, Nora El Qadim, Luis Martinez and Rachid El Houdaïgui also expressed interest in my work when we met at different conferences and seminars.

When it comes to the book itself, I would like to express my appreciation to the hundreds of officials, diplomats, politicians, civil society activists, academics, thinktankers and journalists I have interviewed at different times in Morocco, with special sympathy for those fighting in one way or another for a fairer and democratic future; to the professors from the universities of Rabat, Casablanca, Mohammedia and Ifrane who discussed my project and shared their ideas with me, in particular Abdelwahab Maalmi, El Hassan Bouqentar, Mohammed Madani and Mohamed Darif; and to the friends from Rabat, chiefly Marie and Virginia. My incomparable Arabic teacher from the Languages Institute of the Universidad de Sevilla, Kadhim Alshameary, the administrators and *stagiaires* with whom I worked more closely at the European Parliament in 2012 – especially Stefan Krauss – and other people I have met more recently for different research or academic projects in Madrid, Brussels, Laayoune, Algiers and Tunis have also made a huge contribution to this endeavour without knowing it.

I am also deeply grateful to Anoush Ehteshami, who offered me the possibility of publishing this book with Routledge within the Durham Modern Middle East and Islamic World Series, and to Thomas Roberts and Pamela Lalonde for the language editing support.

A more personal thank you goes to all my family, especially to my grandparents for believing in me disproportionately as only grandparents do; to my parents, for supporting me since I was a child in all my decisions and more or less foolish projects, including my subsequent migrations to Seville, Paris, Madrid, Rabat, Brussels, Warsaw and Exeter; and to my two brothers, for being my brothers. To my friends from Seville, for listening to me and distracting me from my responsibilities during hard times, above all to three who have long since moved away, Rafa, Patricio and Alicia, and to Fernando and Paco. And from Madrid, to Vicky and Carlos, who hospitably sheltered me at different times in Cuatro Caminos and Legazpi.

To all the brave people I have met everywhere.

And to Miguel, the bravest, for the Scottish and Polish adventures.

Introduction and analytical framework

Much of the interest of this book lies precisely in the very reasons that advised against writing it. 'It is not possible to research the foreign policy of Morocco', was the encouraging warning with which a Moroccan expert received the author in late 2007 when she was about to embark on the main part of the fieldwork, documentary collection and interviews for her PhD thesis. Regardless of whether this might have been a self-interested opinion or well-meaning advice about the foreseeable hurdles that awaited her, the sentence was to haunt her over the following years. Another reason for doubt was the relevance of a study focusing on the early years of the reign of King Mohammed VI, given that all commentators generally agreed on the diagnosis of overall continuity with the later foreign policy of Hassan II. Moroccan foreign policy was certainly not an overwhelming source of novelty and surprises. Indeed, this foreign policy was also to stay the course amidst the widespread political transformations unleashed across the region since 2011, sitting, in a way, in the eye of the Arab Spring storm. Similarly, it was not altered either by the fact that, during this period, for the first time, a politician who was not directly appointed by the King and who was, moreover, a member of the Islamist Justice and Development Party (PJD) became the Moroccan foreign minister. In general, the dilemma of political change and continuity is pervasive in Morocco like nowhere else, with all of its analytical elusiveness and grey zones (Zerhouni, 2006: 11–25).

In fact, rather than insisting on the quest for dazzling breaks and novelties under Mohammed VI's reign, the core research problem to be investigated focused on the run-of-the-mill and *grey* reasons that could account for such outstanding Moroccan stability and persistence, both externally and internally. Foreign policy itself seems to be at least part of the secret. Two connected puzzles call for attention in this regard. The first one is the paradox of the unpredictable predictability – so to speak – of Moroccan foreign policy, most notably in times of flux and turmoil such as the Arab Spring. The fact that Rabat's foreign policy behaviour barely changed in 2011 despite unprecedented and pressing transformations within the regional environment as well as some new apparent domestic constraints (Hernando de Larramendi and Fernández-Molina, 2015) seems at first sight to be counter-intuitive.

2 Introduction and analytical framework

The second question mark concerns the contribution of Moroccan foreign policy to continuity and stability in Moroccan domestic politics and, by extension, to authoritarian resilience. Recent literature comparing the dissimilar outcomes of the Arab Spring protests across different political systems has attributed the lower level of strife and greater regime resilience witnessed in the Arab monarchies to the relatively stronger traditional legitimacy and societal support supposedly enjoyed by them (Barany, 2013). However, especially in the cases of Morocco and Jordan, this cultural explanation for the 'new monarchical exceptionalism' does not appear sufficient if it is not coupled with domestic institutional and political factors – a greater level of political liberalisation and reliance on cross-cutting coalitions – and, not least, a 'permissive international environment', including the 'backing of foreign patrons' (Yom and Gause, 2012; Gause, 2013; Barari, 2015).

The purpose of this book is to contribute to achieving a deeper understanding of these international factors of the Moroccan regime's resilience. Yet, as suggested by Jean-François Bayart's (2000) theory of 'extraversion', instead of limiting the analysis to the usual North-South perspective, it conversely places the focus on the *agency* of the Rabat authorities, their capacity for adaptation to the external environment and their 'extraordinary ability to secure the world's indulgence' (Amar, 2009: 10). Indeed, the top three priorities for this state's foreign policy since the 1990s have been: first, the international promotion of the 'democratising' image of Morocco – or at least the idea of a 'Moroccan exception' within a regional context marked by greater political instability and/or authoritarianism; second, the continuous strengthening and preservation of privileged bilateral relations with the European Union (EU); and third, the international recognition and *legalisation* of Rabat's de facto annexation of Western Sahara. These three priorities are closely connected and dependent on one another, as well as being vital for the monarchy's ongoing legitimacy and stability. Another crucial commonality lies in the fact that their accomplishment is ultimately a matter of external recognition. Considerable success has been achieved in this regard in the relations with the EU, as is evident from Morocco's securing of Advanced Status in 2008 and EU post-Arab Spring *rewards* comparable to those obtained by Tunisia since 2011 (Biscop *et al.*, 2012: 32; Behr, 2012: 21). By contrast, international recognition has never been complete and satisfactory for Rabat on the Western Sahara issue, which is considered to be the only foreign policy area where Morocco's proficient 'international political marketing' has failed in recent times (interview with Mohammed Madani, 5 June 2013).

Research question and hypotheses

The general aim of this book is to present an empirical study of Moroccan foreign policy since the accession of King Mohammed VI to the throne in 1999, maintaining a holistic and cross-cutting perspective, whilst paying special attention to foreign policy's entanglement with domestic politics. The starting premise is thus the deep interconnection between these two spheres, which is

Introduction and analytical framework 3

strongly at odds with the rigid separation often postulated by realism in International Relations (IR). Whilst the latter dichotomy is generally regarded as outdated today, its analytical futility does not appear any clearer than in the countries of the global South (Braveboy-Wagner, 2003: 15–16). Put in structuralist, core-periphery terms, 'foreign policy outside the core is more likely to be a tool to achieve domestic goals than a means to the outcomes emphasised by realism'. In the periphery, the abstraction of 'national interest' becomes all the more elusive and the states' external action becomes 'an indispensable tool for meeting state imperatives: capital accumulation, state legitimacy, social stability, and government maintenance' (Moon, 1995: 198).

The theoretical foundations upon which the empirical work is based bring together elements of, on the one hand, liberal/pluralistic approaches to Foreign Policy Analysis (FPA) focusing on the interaction between internal and foreign policies – or the so-called 'domestic sources' of foreign policy – and, on the other hand, constructivist scholarship which highlights the social and ideational aspects of such interplay, i.e. those falling beyond strictly rational and material interests. The *bridge* allowing both strands of theory to be integrated is role theory as applied to FPA.

The liberal/pluralistic emphasis can be found in the view that the Moroccan state is fragmented and penetrated, and not a unitary and impermeable actor, which stresses the importance of the state-society relationship in foreign policy in a similar manner to domestic politics. According to Ilham Rifai (2005: 56), any state-centric explanation of Morocco's 'national interest' that does not take account of the societal input remains incomplete. This is reflected in the attention paid to all domestic actors within Moroccan foreign policy, irrespective of their uneven level of influence, i.e. not only those located at the core of decision-making structures but also those occupying subordinate and marginalised positions. Despite the ongoing centralisation of decision-making processes, the political liberalisation underway since the 1990s has increased their 'vulnerability, permeability or sensitivity' to the influence of non-governmental or 'private' actors (Charillon, 2006: 4; El Houdaïgui, 2006: 1, 5). Another important reference are the works of Joe D. Hagan (1995, 1987) on domestic political constraints on foreign policy, such as the games of building policy coalitions and retaining political power, the characteristics of opposition and the ensuing strategies followed by leaders in managing foreign policy (accommodation, mobilisation and insulation). Some of the author's Moroccan interlocutors questioned the application of a liberal/pluralistic approach to what continued to be largely an authoritarian state: 'You speak of Morocco as if it were a democratic country in which political parties are really foreign policy actors'. In fact, according to Hagan, differences in foreign policymaking between democratic and authoritarian regimes need to be relativised: 'Political conflict within the regimes of authoritarian political systems can be rather intense and foreign policy decision-making highly political' (1987: 342).

The constructivist component of this research lies in the importance attached to identity-related factors resulting from social interaction and socialisation which determine the definition/construction processes of Moroccan foreign policy 'interests'. These include the actors' perceptions and understandings of the outer world along with their own self-understandings (Hasenclever *et al.*, 1997: 188), the prevailing discourses in society which 'reflect and shape beliefs and interests' (Walt, 1998: 40–41) as well as *norms* of behaviour established by the latter (Barnett, 1998). Foreign policy in particular has an inherently close and co-constitutive relationship with state and national identity:

> As it is practised, and by virtue of the fact that it deals with difference, foreign policy constructs national political identity. Foreign policy is then an identity-making tool that erects boundaries between the self and the other, defining in the process what are national interests.
> (Messari, 2001a: 227)

The following chapters will show how Moroccan foreign policy discourse and behaviour are primarily constrained by the weighty importance of the *norm* concerning national territorial integrity and the 'Moroccanity' of Western Sahara, although other secondary role conceptions also come with a normative load and exert a non-negligible influence. In addition, constructivism is also the most suitable perspective for approaching Morocco's growing interest and involvement in the foreign image policies and public diplomacy (Régragui, 2013).

Building on these theoretical underpinnings, this book's central research question revolves around the *functionality* of Moroccan foreign policy in terms of the legitimation of the regime in the Mohammed VI era: Does it (still) contribute to the continuity of the established political system and ruling elite? Does it (still) bring about a 'national consensus' in a general fashion? The existing literature has uniformly portrayed this foreign policy, from independence to the present day, as an indispensable and virtually foolproof tool for legitimising the monarchy in the face of latent domestic political conflict. In this sense, it is implicitly or explicitly argued that the exploitation of certain identity-related *norms* and discourses prevailing within national political culture, especially those of a nationalist nature, favours consensus among various political actors and helps neutralise spontaneous or organised opposition to the regime (Dalle, 2004: 767), all of which is largely in line with Hagan's strategy of 'mobilisation' (1995: 129–130). According to this view, and as far as the connection between state formation and foreign policy is concerned, Morocco can be argued to have evolved over the years from a 'domestic vulnerability model' – in which foreign policy works as an instrument of domestic survival and legitimation for the incumbent regime – to a 'leadership-dominant model' – in which the leader faces fewer internal constraints (Hinnebusch and Ehteshami, 2002: 10–11). This process was arguably facilitated by the Moroccan monarchy/authorities' resort to what neoclassical realists Michael Mastanduno, David A. Lake and G. John Ikenberry call 'external extraction' ('accumulating resources from outside [their] borders that can be of use in achieving domestic objectives') and 'external validation' ('utilising their status as authoritative international representatives of the nation-state to enhance their domestic political positions'), especially in times during which political instability was increasing at home (1989: 464–466).

Without denying the soundness of this widespread view, the purpose of this study is to provide a less mechanistic interpretation by also considering a possible gradual decline in the mobilising and legitimising effectiveness of Moroccan foreign policy since the 1990s and under Mohammed VI's reign, as two new trends developed. First, the Moroccan nationalist discourse no longer fully satisfied some actors and parts of public opinion whose ideological references became increasingly pluralistic, as opposition discourses from pro-democracy and/or Islamist spheres gained ground. Second, the Rabat authorities appeared to become increasingly torn between the contradictory stances of making concessions to these emerging sensibilities and meeting the requirements of Morocco's 'pro-Western' (pro-U.S.) alignment, which especially affected relations with the Middle East. Broadly speaking, for decades it has been argued that the main source of instability in the Middle East and North Africa is the contradiction between the constraints imposed by the region's international dependence and the Arab-Islamic supra-state identity enduring across it: 'Foreign policies which are considered to sacrifice identity and autonomy in exchange for the satisfaction of an increasingly interventionist American hegemon entail growing legitimacy costs, preventing the congruence between identity and interests that stability requires' (Hinnebusch, 2005: 254–255). With specific reference to this country, Raffaella A. Del Sarto suggests that the 'parameters of Moroccan foreign policy' might be affected by domestic developments such as political liberalisation and the emergence of Islamism:

> Against the backdrop of political liberalisation, and given the persistence of internal and external pressures, it remains to be seen whether the Moroccan monarchy will continue to be able to master the political identity game – the rules of which seem to be changing.
>
> (2006: 192)

This would explain the more frequent domestic use of strategies of 'accommodation' (bargaining and controversy avoidance, low-risk political behaviour) and 'insulation' (suppression of the opposition) (Hagan, 1995: 128–132).

This empirical study is based on three hypotheses which relate different levels of domestic functionality of Moroccan foreign policy to normative *national role conceptions* (Holsti, 1970) guiding the latter in its most significant areas:

- 1: The most significant areas of Moroccan foreign policy between 1999 and 2014 can be divided into two categories according to their domestic functionality:
    - Those that continue to be globally consensual and conducive to the legitimation and resilience of the regime include territory-related issues, such as the international management of the Western Sahara conflict and tensions with neighbouring Algeria and Spain – still a breeding

ground for nationalism and strategies of mobilisation – as well as relations with the EU – a vital source of external economic extraction and political validation which enables strategies of accommodation to be pursued.
– Those that bring about domestic dissent and even episodic destabilisation comprise relations with the U.S. and the Middle East, where foreign policy behaviour accordingly fluctuates between strategies of accommodation and insulation.

- 2: The two main national role conceptions that underlie foreign policy discourse and behaviour during these years – *champion of national territorial integrity* and *model student of the EU* – reflect the structural tension between a realist/geopolitical/territorial and a liberal/pragmatic/economistic definition of Moroccan national interests, which sometimes entails role conflict.
- 3: The roles of *champion of national territorial integrity* and *model student of the EU* largely correspond to the category of consensual and functional foreign policy areas, which tips the scales overall in favour of the continuing domestic functionality of Moroccan foreign policy.

As regards the time frame of the study, the choice of the dynastic succession as a starting point and defining, almost intuitive landmark is justified by the central and hegemonic role historically played by the head of state in the design and implementation of Morocco's foreign policy. The closed nature of this decision-making system is coupled with the usual importance of leadership, personality and charisma as foreign policy resources. Moreover, 1999 is also an inevitable turning point in the discourses of domestic political actors and, not least, in the international community's perceptions of this country. At this point in time, Mohammed VI was viewed as one of a new generation of Arab leaders who were supposed to have more reformist leanings (Droz-Vincent, 2004: 971–972), a cohort of 'heirs' in search of legitimacy in the face of the twofold challenge of domestic reform and continuity in external orientations (Charillon, 2002: 592–594). In the realm of foreign policy, the succession at the top of the regime roughly coincided with Morocco's abandonment of the roadmap towards a referendum on self-determination in the Western Sahara conflict – a disengagement which was initially tacit and only became an explicit official position from 2003 – and the entry into force (in March 2000) of the bilateral Association Agreement between Morocco and the EU. The latter development turned into the starting point for the search for a special relationship or Advanced Status with the EU. The major juncture in Morocco's relations with the U.S. and the Middle East, however, would not arrive until two years later, with the terrorist attacks of 11 September 2001, the declaration of the War on Terror, and the ensuing shift in Washington's foreign policy approach and priorities in this region.

From a domestic perspective, the period from 1999 to 2014 in Morocco included a first phase of political opening and liberalisation, which prolonged the experience of governmental alternation (*alternance*) from the last years of Hassan II's era, and a second phase starting in 2002–2003 involving a regression of civil rights and freedoms along with apparent authoritarian consolidation (Feliu and Parejo, 2013). Third, superficial as it might have been, a second 'transition' with implications for foreign policy (Omar Saghi in *Tel Quel*, 19 May 2014) followed the Arab Spring protests led in Morocco by the 20 February Movement (Desrues, 2013; Hoffmann and König, 2013) and the constitutional reform subsequently launched by King Mohammed VI (Maghraoui, 2011; Fernández-Molina, 2011b; Benchemsi, 2012). Even though they did not result in democratisation, all of the processes of political liberalisation launched by the Moroccan regime during these years had an effect on foreign policy decision-making. Limited as it might have been, they have involved an increase in the level of participation, the role of the opposition and the relevance of coalition-building dynamics, the weight of non-state actors, the influence of interest groups and public opinion and, broadly speaking, the domestic constraints exerted on the *central decision-making unit* (El Houdaïgui, 2003a: 27–29).

The analysis of the foreign policies of Arab countries, the Maghreb and Morocco

Research on international relations within the Mediterranean basin has increased considerably since the 1990s,[1] although has generally retained a markedly North–South perspective (Nonneman, 2005: 1). The fact that FPA has only been applied to these countries in a limited number of cases is indicative of the fact that southern/Arab states continue to be treated as passive objects much more often than as active subjects or agents. FPA having since its birth been character-ised by its U.S. origins and been only slowly transplanted to European academia, it was not until the 1970s that Bahgat Korany *discovered* the foreign policies of the Third World as an object of analysis, drawing attention to the 'under-developed study of underdeveloped countries' from this viewpoint (Korany, 1983: 465).

Later on, the mainstream of FPA gradually started to recognise the difficulty of making general statements about foreign policy applied to all of the world's states in a universal and uniform fashion. A significant leap forward came in the 1990s with the so-called *second generation* of FPA, whose proponents distin-guished between 'two parallel international universes' – the advanced industrial-ised countries, and non-Western and developing countries – where the objectives and instruments of foreign policy differed (Neack *et al.*, 1995: 39–44). One of their arguments was that 'realism fares less well the further it is removed from the Eurocentric core and the national security issue area where it was born' (Moon, 1995: 188). At the same time, when looking at the periphery, this group of authors rejected both the usual tendency to overrate the weight of the person-ality of authoritarian leaders and the extreme structuralism underlying interpreta-tions of these countries' foreign policies as simply a result of their subordinate status within the international system: 'Third World foreign policy processes are as complex as those in the rest of the world' (Neack et al., 1995: 202). Avoiding these two extremes in the agency-structure dilemma, five factors were considered as possible reasons as to why the foreign policy patterns of 'developing' states should differ from those of developed states: the former's the dependent position, their relative lack of resources, their lower levels of state formation and legitimacy, their greater susceptibility to the influence of transnational identities and their location in generally less stable environments (Nonneman, 2005: 9–10).

As far as the Arab and/or Middle Eastern and North African states are concerned, the main books which have presented a systematic and theoretically informed study of their foreign policies since the 1990s are those edited by Bahgat Korany and Ali E. Hillal Dessouki (1991; 2009), Raymond Hinnebusch and Anoushiravan Ehteshami (2002) and Gerd Nonneman (2005). Whilst connected by a common thread and often speaking to each other, their analytical frameworks rely on dissimilar theoretical perspectives.[2] Noting that the global system provides Arab foreign policies with more constraints than opportunities, Korany and Dessouki opted for a modified dependency approach which prioritised macro or structural lenses and highlighted these states' subordinate position within the international chessboard. They argued that the most important changes they witness, even domestically, are ultimately determined by external forces. At the same time, these authors showed an awareness of the drawbacks of an excessive structuralism, which is better equipped to explain general dynamics of development/underdevelopment than the specific functioning of foreign policies, and which tends to generalise and treat all dependent countries uniformly (Korany and Dessouki, 1991: 30–31). Accordingly, they qualified and modified some aspects of dependency theory, recognising the importance of domestic sources of foreign policy and certain specificities of the Arab region such as the shared Islamic religious identity, considerable cultural and linguistic homogeneity, interference by the Israeli–Palestinian conflict and the concentration of oil resources (Korany and Dessouki, 1991: 32–37; 2009: 46–52).

In the early 2000s, the working hypotheses of Hinnebusch and Ehteshami were closer to the realist mainstream of IR theory, since they assumed that insecurity and power are the prevailing factors which shape foreign policies in this region. Their premises were that, first, 'in the Middle East the state is the main actor in foreign policy' and, second, 'a built-in feature of a state system, anarchy, has generated profound insecurity and a pervasive struggle for power'. However, these two authors also embraced theoretical impurity by advocating 'a modified form of realist theory'. Admittedly, realism has certain limitations in explaining international dynamics within a region where, first, the system of states is 'still in the process of consolidation'; second, late economic development and dependency within the world capitalist system constrain state sovereignty (structuralist correction); third, interactions are also conditioned by identity-related factors such as transnational ideologies (constructivist correction); and fourth, states are 'not unitary and impermeable, as realism assumes, but fragmented and penetrated' (liberal/pluralistic correction) (Hinnebusch and Ehteshami, 2002: 1–2).

Meanwhile, Nonneman opted from the outset for a paradigmatic synthesis and 'a complex model of international politics' combining elements of realist thinking – both in its neorealist and neo-classical versions – with constructivism's emphasis on cultural and ideational factors and the structuralist ideas of centre-periphery, dependency and limited state autonomy. His liberal/pluralistic view of the state, which highlighted the complexity of decision-making, the interplay between foreign and domestic policies, and the constraints imposed by structural conditions, led this author to advocate 'multi-level and multi-causal' explanations of foreign policy (Nonneman, 2005: 7–9, 14–17). Given this eclectic theoretical proposal, along with his recognition of the difficulty of generalising and the importance of incorporating context at all times, Nonneman's work was much aligned with the spirit of the *second generation* of FPA.

Alongside these three seminal collective works and a more recent contribution by Hassan Hamdan al-Alkim (2011), other studies have addressed the foreign policies of this region by focusing on the role of non-state actors (El Houdaïgui, 2006) and the foreign policies' growing 'privatization' or sensitivity to their influence (Charillon, 2006). Some have even tried to disentangle the elusive weight of the religious factor, questioning whether Islam as such casually determines the external behaviour of these states, or is rather used as a legitimising or justificatory discourse, along with the extent to which it influences the images and perceptions of incumbent political leaders and enables some religious institutions to play a role in the implementation of foreign policy (Dawisha, 1983; Riziki Mohamed, 2005).

Narrowing down the perspective, IR and FPA production focusing on the Maghreb countries is notably scarce and, in most cases, exclusively empirical. Noteworthy contributions include the books on the foreign policies of Algeria and Tunisia by Nicole Grimaud (1984, 1995) and Abdelaziz Chneguir (2004) as well as the comparative theses by Nicole Kasbaoui (1978) and Abderrahman Belgourch (2001). Intra-Maghrebi relations and the evolution of the Arab Maghreb Union (AMU) have been examined at various stages by Mary-Jane Deeb (1989, 1993), Robert A. Mortimer (1999), Yahia H. Zoubir (2000, 2004) and Miguel Hernando de Larramendi (2008). Attempts at theorising inter-state dynamics within this sub-regional system have led to realist readings (Hami, 2003) and works which relate the emergence of the AMU integration project with domestic security threats perceived by the Maghrebi regimes in the 1990s (Mezran, 1998). This region's integration into the international system has been analysed by Laura Feliu (2001) and Khadija Mohsen-Finan (2011). Other than this, a special mention needs to be made of the studies devoted to the Western Sahara conflict, which appears to be the touchstone for intra-regional relations (Hodges, 1983; Zoubir and Volman, 1993; Mohsen-Finan, 1997; Shelley, 2004; Zunes and Mundy, 2010; Jensen, 2012; Boukhars and Roussellier, 2013).

In the case of Morocco, several observers have highlighted the 'serious lack of research and studies on foreign policy' (Belhaj, 2009: 31), which is regarded as a proof that, for a long time, 'the question of Morocco's place in the world did not give rise to much debate, [and was] the very example of a non-issue'

(Benjelloun, 2002: 116). Historical studies include the books by Charles-André Julien (1978), Albdelhadi Tazi (1989), Thérèse Benjelloun (1991), and Saïd Ihraï and Amina Aouchar (1991). The main reference monographs on the post-colonial period are those by Saïd Ihraï (1986), Abdelkhaleq Berramdane (1987), Miguel Hernando de Larramendi (1997)[3] and Rachid el Houdaïgui (2003a). These are supplemented by books which also provide a comprehensive view such as the ones by El Hassane Bouqentar (2002) and Abdessamad Belhaj (2009), and a number of university dissertations (El Hassane, 1984; Zouitni, 1986, 1998; Naciri, 1994; Benaomari, 1995; Najih, 1984; Cheikh, 1987; Et-Tajani, 1984; Boussaid, 1990; Hami, 1984, 2005; Barre, 1988; Guessous, 1983). The void to be filled is much larger in English-speaking international academia, which has long surrendered to post-colonial legacies in blatantly neglecting Moroccan foreign policy, apart from exceptions such as the book chapters by I. William Zartman (1983, 2001), Michael J. Willis and Nizar Messari (2003), Jennifer Rosenblum and I. William Zartman (2009) and Daniel Zisenwine (2013).

As regards the Moroccan foreign policy during the most recent period, i.e. Mohammed VI's reign, the only comprehensive monograph is El Hassane Bouqentar (2014). The remaining available literature is limited to mostly unpublished university dissertations focusing on specific aspects (Benmoussa, 2003; Belalami, 2006; Bennis, 2008), synthesis articles or chapters in edited volumes (Willis and Messari, 2003; Abouddahab, 2006; Rosenblum and Zartman, 2009; El Houdaïgui, 2010; Bouqentar, 2010; Maalmi, 2012; Hernando de Larramendi, 2012a; Zisenwine, 2013), and relatively influential journalistic works on bilateral relations with France (Tuquoi, 2006; Tuquoi and Amar, 2012), Algeria (Dekkar, 2013) and Spain, some of which are more rigorous (Cembrero, 2006) whilst others amount to little more than pamphleteering (Dahbi, 2011). This is the gap that this book seeks to fill, building mainly on the aforementioned works on Hassan II's period by Hernando de Larramendi (1997) and El Houdaïgui (2003a), thus trying to contribute to empirical accumulation which is often non-existent in IR and FPA on the Maghreb (Belgourch, 2001: 18).

From the domestic sources of foreign policy to constructivism through role theory

The aim of highlighting the *agency* element when examining Morocco's place in the world leads naturally into FPA. The coordinates that locate FPA within the broader picture of IR are the primacy of the interstate component and the analytical priority of agency over structure. Its first advantage is that, while subscribing to the movement for the recovery of the state as an analytical category (Evans *et al.*, 1983), it replaces the realist view of the state as a unitary and rational actor by the idea of a 'fragmented actor': opening the *black box* of the state enables a multitude of disparate political actors, interests and processes that coexist inside it to be discovered. Second, as argued by one of its initiators in the 1960s, James N. Rosenau, FPA is a 'bridging discipline' connecting different levels of analysis, from the individual to the international system (Hermann *et al.*, 1987: 1–2), which can also serve as a passage between IR and area studies and enable the development of – forgiving the oxymoron – 'single country theories' (Hermann *et al.*, 1987: 59–64).

Valerie M. Hudson highlights as the main advantages of FPA its capacity of meaningfully integrating theories at different levels of analysis, incorporating a stronger concept of agency into IR theory, overcoming natural law-like generalisations about state behaviour (Hudson, 2005: 3–5), breaking with the monolithic view of the state as a unitary actor and the abstraction of 'national interest', accepting the limits of rationality in decision-making processes, seeking greater concreteness in theory and thoroughly working on the 'specification of the situation' and the context (Hudson and Vore, 1995: 210–211). Margot Light emphasises the FPA's ability to translate abstract theory into concrete problems, to connect the micro level (domestic politics) and the macro level (the international system) and to bring IR closer to other social sciences (Groom and Light, 1994: 94). More specifically, out of all the different strands of FPA developed since the 1950s, this book combines elements of the liberal/pluralistic and constructivist approaches, which are linked together by means of role theory.

The liberal/pluralistic exploration of the interplay between internal and foreign policies – the domestic sources of foreign policy – was pioneered as early as the 1960s by Rosenau's 'linkage' theory (1969) and gained momentum in the next decade when different authors theorised the domestic determinants of foreign policy and international politics. Whereas neo-Weberian Peter J. Katzenstein (1976) and Stephen D. Krasner focused their attention on the internal institutional setting, others attached greater relevance to the processes of coalition-building and consensus-building affecting foreign policy (Gourevitch, 1978). Both perspectives were to converge in mixed approaches such as that of Robert D. Putnam (1988), who popularised the metaphor of 'two-level games' in order to stress the critical importance of domestic ratification for any international negotiation – and not only in democratic countries. According to him, the likeliness of such ratification and the size of the acceptable win-set are conditioned by internal factors such as the distribution of power, preferences and possible coalitions (Gourevitch's perspective) along with the structure of political institutions (Katzenstein's perspective). Meanwhile, neoclassical realists Mastanduno, Lake and Ikenberry considered the two facets of state action when identifying internal strategies (mobilisation and resource extraction) which serve international goals (acquisition of power and wealth) and, conversely, international strategies (external extraction and validation) aimed at achieving domestic objectives (control of resources and legitimation of rulers) (1989: 461–466).[4]

Elaborating on these works, Hagan assumed from the outset that domestic political imperatives behind foreign policy are twofold, involving multiple arenas of opposition, that their effects are contingent and depend on the leaders' strategic choices, and that their consequences are 'subtle' because they are neither the sole nor the most decisive foreign policy determinant. The duality of

12 Introduction and analytical framework

domestic imperatives results from the existence of two simultaneous political games, i.e. building policy coalitions, whereby leaders seek domestic support for any external initiative, and retaining political power, which pushes them to pursue foreign policies with low internal cost (Hagan, 1995: 121–127). Other related factors are the characteristics of political opposition, which can originate from divisions within the ruling elite stemming from personality, factional and bureaucratic differences; legislative or other non-executive institutional actors; politically active segments of society such as interest groups; and the broader mass public, either in the form of public opinion or as general civil unrest (Hagan, 1987: 343). Faced with these constraints, state leaders can opt for three basic strategies when managing foreign policy: accommodation, mobilisation and isolation (Hagan, 1995: 127–132). Last but not least, Hagan has also criticised the conventional distinction between open and closed systems contending that, far from being limited to democracies, the aforementioned phenomena occur across all the different types of political systems (Hagan, 1987: 340–342, 1995: 121).

Some of these liberal/pluralistic approaches had a particular impact on authors interested in the foreign policies of peripheral or Third World states, whose leaders or governments often tend to be authoritarian and weak in terms of domestic legitimacy. One of the most influential contributions in this regard was Steven R. David's (1991) theory of 'omnibalancing', which explains how Third World leaders are impelled to seek an overall balance between various domestic and external threats in order to ensure their own survival, and how the former threats can weigh as much or more than the latter – contrary to what realism might suggest – in determining international alignment.[5] However, the common feature and liability of this large school of FPA is its distinctly rationalist outlook, which leaves out of the picture all of the ideational and identity-related factors that are not reducible to rational choice.

Arguably, the best way to overcome the limitations of such narrow rationalism is by integrating elements of constructivism into FPA. Constructivism is a meta-theoretical framework encompassing different theoretical and empirical options which share the belief that the ontological and epistemological foundations of IR should be primarily social and ideational in nature (Wendt, 1995: 73–74). For its proponents, the existence of social facts such as political actors and institutions inevitably depends on human consciousness and language, as well as social interaction. Agents and structures co-constitute each other throughout all of these social dynamics (Adler, 2002: 100–101). Building on these premises, IR constructivists engaged in a shift 'from a stress on the capabilities of states, or the distribution of power as a structural property of the system, to a stress on the identity of states' (Kubálková, 2001: 33). As a result, according to Steve Smith, 'social construction and foreign policy analysis look made for one another' (in Kubálková, 2001: 38). A number of authors have similarly highlighted the potential of constructivism for the analysis of issues related to identity and social understandings, which feature nowadays among the most pressing problems for FPA (White, 1999: 55–57; Hudson, 2005: 18–19; Kubálková,

2001: 227–236, 268–270). However, the truth is that this school's rapprochement to the study of foreign policy has not been an easy road.

The potential contribution of constructivism to FPA was for quite some time overshadowed by the hegemony of the mainstream version of Alexander E. Wendt, which was openly unconcerned by everything that happened inside states (Hasenclever *et al.*, 1997: 188). Although, in his early works, this author had advocated the need to theorise the state as an agent, explaining its action in terms of both its social structural context and its internal organisational structure (Wendt, 1987: 365–366), and had stated that 'the raw material out of which members of the state system are constituted is created by domestic society before states enter the constitutive process of international society' (Wendt, 1992: 402), his *Social Theory of International Politics* ended up giving priority to the systemic perspective and deliberately neglecting the pole of agency, to the point of challenging structural realism with a so-called 'structural idealism' (Wendt, 1999: 1). Critics of Wendt have noted that his version of constructivism precludes any connection with FPA, since his anthropomorphic notion of the state as an international actor – a unitary and 'pre-social' actor to which intentionality can be attributed as if it were a 'person' (Wendt, 1999: 193–198, 215–224, 243) – does not leave room for internal influences or factors: 'The actors are the states-as-persons, and there is no need to look into the black box of the foreign policy process' (Kubálková, 2001: 51). Hence, different voices have for years been calling for the 'domestication' of constructivism (Ozkececi-Taner, 2005: 271), i.e. an opening up of this approach to domestic politics and non-state actors, a journey into the micro ('go micro') inside the *black box* where national preferences are forged (Adler, 2002: 109–110).

For the purposes of this book, the chosen *bridge* or passage into the domestic sphere which allows integrating constructivism and liberal/pluralistic FPA is role theory. Reviving Kal J. Holsti's ground-breaking attempt to import role theory into the FPA literature through the concept of *national role conceptions* (Holsti, 1970), a group of authors has recently vindicated role theory as a means of achieving a synthesis between the U.S. FPA tradition, which is more focused on agency, and European constructivist IR scholarship, which prioritises structure and system-level factors – and thus, at the same time, further integrating agency and structure within the analysis (Thies and Breuning, 2012; Harnisch, 2012). One of the strengths of this dialogue lies in its questioning of the extent to which foreign policy roles actually enjoy domestic consensus, instead of taking for granted that such consensus exists both vertically (between elites and masses) and horizontally (among the elites themselves). The consideration of the mass-elite nexus and intra-elite conflict leads to a deeper examination of 'contested roles' at the vertical level, which reveal a disconnect between the positions of leaders and public opinion, and at the horizontal level, which stem from disagreements over foreign policy between governing elites and political opposition, within governing (multiparty) coalitions, within small decision-making and advisory groups or across bureaucratic agencies (Cantir and Kaarbo, 2012: 6–16). This and other concordant contributions also discuss the possibility of 'role conflict' between different role conceptions included in a role-set which originate each from disparate domestic or international institutional sources, or were formulated in changing temporal contexts. Role conflict can bring about foreign policy dysfunctions but is also understood as an inevitable incentive for foreign policy change (Cantir and Kaarbo, 2013: 467–468, 2012: 10–11; Aggestam, 2006: 23). One last useful concept proposed by Cristian Cantir and Juliet Kaarbo is that of the 'strategic use of roles', that is, the 'actors' conscious use of national role conceptions to achieve particular policy, political, or personal goals' (2012: 19).

One final element of this book's theoretical framework, which has been applied specifically to the analysis of Moroccan foreign policy towards the EU, is the concept of international socialisation. Starting from a general understanding of socialisation as 'a process of inducting actors into the norms and rules of a given community', whose ultimate end is, in principle, the internalisation of these norms by the actor and a behavioural switch 'from a logic of consequences to a logic of appropriateness' (Checkel, 2006: 5–6), international socialisation has been defined as 'the process that is directed toward a state's internalisation of the constitutive beliefs and practices institutionalised in its international environment' (Schimmelfennig, 2000: 111–112). It involves a structurally asymmetric relationship between two distinct actors, namely the 'socialisation agency' and the 'external state' to be socialised, which are in this case, respectively, the EU and Morocco. The extent and nature of the changes achieved allows for the distinction of two types of socialisation, i.e. 'adoption of new roles' vs. 'changes in values and interests' (Checkel, 2006: 9, 6). As regards the process of knowledge acquisition or *learning* necessary in order for the socialised actor to respond appropriately to external expectations, this dichotomy is reminiscent of the classical opposition between simple vs. complex learning, or adaptation vs. learning, whereby the former changes only the actor's political means while the latter transforms also its identities and interests (Knopf, 2003: 189; Wendt, 1999: 327, 333).

Of particular interest for the analysis here presented is Frank Schimmelfennig's theoretical proposal on international socialisation, which, in order to overcome the limits of both rational institutionalism (assumptions of egoism and instrumentalism) and sociological/constructivist approaches (neglect of strategic action and domestic factors), bridges the gap between the two perspectives using the concept of international legitimacy.[6] On the one hand, the structure, or international setting, is viewed through a sociological lens, as a 'normatively institutionalised' environment where value-based norms constrain the states' behaviour. On the other hand, the agents, or states involved, are portrayed as basically selfish, rational and cost-benefit calculating actors. Yet obtaining international legitimacy is the main purpose of their instrumental action, which means that they are impelled to credibly live up to the social norms and 'standards of legitimacy' of their institutionalised external environment. The emphasis is on the fact that this behaviour works 'without the assumption of genuine ideational commitment and changes in the logic of action' (Schimmelfennig, 2000: 116). International legitimacy represents a valuable resource for the socialised state and its leaders. Its concrete benefits include enhancing the state's security and autonomy, facilitating material gratifications such as development aid or military assistance, and reinforcing the domestic legitimacy and rule. In other words, international legitimacy contributes both to economic 'external extraction' and political 'external validation' (Mastanduno *et al.*, 1989: 464–466).

Methodology and sources

As far as the empirical component of this research is concerned, the author's journey encountered a categorical barrier from the outset: the general paucity of information on political processes in Morocco turned into the proverbial opacity and secrecy in the realm of foreign policy (Hami, 2003: 85). Obstacles on the collection of primary material included the general absence of organised and open archives and the difficulty, if not impossibility, of accessing internal documentation from the Ministry of Foreign Affairs and Cooperation and other state institutions. This complicated the mere basic verification of evidence and reconstruction of factual accounts, not to mention any chance of penetrating deep into the policymaking and decision-making processes behind the scenes of Moroccan foreign policy. The documentary material available was largely limited to public speeches, statements and releases, which entailed the risk that the resulting analyses turned out to be 'superficial' (Zouitni, 2003: 70) or 'an exhausting riddle game' (Daoud, 2007: 313).

Making somehow a virtue out of necessity, although this book does not engage extensively with the methodology of discourse analysis (Milliken, 1999), it pays special attention to discursive production and practices, i.e. the manner in which discourses on Moroccan foreign policy are shaped and circulate, the identity of the authorised voices and the audiences they address, the kind of impact achieved inside and outside the country's borders, and the extent to which competition exists between hegemonic and alternative or peripheral discourses (Larsen, 1997: 20–22, 25). The primary source needed to analyse the hegemonic 'enunciation of the political' (Bayart, 1985) continues to be royal speeches, which reflect the perceptions and views of the dominant player in the system – the core of the *central decision-making unit* – and define the broad outlines of state action, with obvious *performative* implications (Hernando de Larramendi, 1997: 83–84; El Houdaïgui, 2003a: 103–104; Belhaj, 2009: 99). The most significant of King Mohammed VI's addresses as regards foreign policy are those delivered each year on the Throne Day (30 July), the anniversary of the so-called Revolution of the King and the People (20 August) and the commemoration of the Green March (6 November), in addition to international events, state visits abroad and receptions of foreign leaders. Second, another official source that has been extensively employed in this research consists in public documents from the Ministry of Foreign Affairs and Cooperation (official statements, press releases, speeches and interviews, *dossiers* on international events held in Morocco).[7]

Third, outside the official sphere, the most valuable and recurrently cited primary sources are articles from Moroccan newspapers, chiefly – for practical reasons – French-speaking weeklies and the organs usually labelled as the 'independent press' (*Le Journal, Le Journal Hebdomadaire, Tel Quel, Lakome* and *Demain Online*). Many of the print or online media included in the latter category, which had the merit of offering more professional journalistic coverage of topical issues, and of even filling some of the gaps in the production of contemporary history on Morocco (Stora, 2002: 75–80), have unfortunately ceased to be published – and disappeared from the internet – during these years as a result of the regime's judicial harassment. Other useful albeit less critical publications have been the daily newspapers *Aujourd'hui le Maroc* and *Le Matin*, the business papers *L'Économiste* and *La Vie Éco*, and the weekly *Maroc Hebdo International*. These media sources are combined with dispatches from the Moroccan official news agency, Maghreb Arab Press (MAP), and Agence France-Presse, as well as press reviews from the French embassy to Morocco and translations from Al Fanar.[8] Another precious source of material that became unexpectedly available during the research process were the confidential diplomatic 'cables' from the U.S. embassy in Rabat released by Wikileaks between 2010 and 2011, and the internal documents from the Moroccan foreign ministry which were disseminated by the anonymous hacker 'Chris Coleman' in late 2014. The countless press articles and institutional press releases or statements used are not listed in the book's final references, but simply referenced within the text with the name of the publication/institution (the French acronym MAEC in the case of the foreign ministry) and the date.

Finally, these variegated documentary sources are supplemented by more than 100 semi-structured interviews with actors and observers of Moroccan foreign policy which were conducted by the author during several fieldwork stays in Rabat and Casablanca in February 2006, September–December 2007, June 2009, November 2011 and June 2013, as well as a trip to Brussels in May 2014. The interviewees include Moroccan diplomats and officials from the Ministry of Foreign Affairs and Cooperation, representatives from all of the major political parties in parliament as well as some extra-parliamentary organisations, members of parliament and officials from the House of Representatives, civil society activists from associations engaged in one way or another with foreign policy or international affairs, academics, thinktankers and journalists. Needless to say, many other interview attempts or requests were unsuccessful. In view of this fact, it cannot be said that the finally resulting corpus is exhaustive, systematic or homogeneous – a common problem among researchers who have used this method in a country like Morocco (Catusse, 1999: 61–63; Sater, 2007: 17).

On the other hand, the obstacles of fieldwork, its ins and outs and anecdotes, are extremely significant in themselves. The often untold negotiation process leading to the 'opening up of the field' for the researcher reveals as much or more about the dynamics of Moroccan political life than the conventional results that are usually published through academic channels. This negotiation is influenced by variables such as the immediately relevant situation of each interlocutor and his/her organisation within the national political scene, as well as his/her perception of the researcher, who is often 'assimilated to other figures: agent of the information services, spokesperson, journalist, expert, pollster' (Bennani-Chraïbi, 2010: 108). In the author's case, along with distrust arising from the (semi)authoritarian context, the lack of transparency of the foreign ministry and the concurrent political games of different actors, fieldwork had to face the additional limitations imposed by her own status as a young foreign woman in a markedly patriarchal cultural context and a distinctly male professional area – both in Morocco and in Europe – such as foreign policy and diplomacy. This entailed a continuing effort to assert herself, be taken seriously and avoid patronising attitudes (Catusse, 1999: 60–62).[9]

Structure of the book

The conceptual thread upon which this book is structured is comprised of the main national role conceptions formulated in, or underlying, Moroccan foreign policy from 1999 to 2014. In proportion to their respective weight in foreign policy discourse and behaviour during these years, the roles that receive comparatively more attention are those of *champion of national territorial integrity* and *model student of the EU*, both of which correspond to foreign policy areas that are hypothesised here to be globally consensual and functional in terms of their legitimation of the regime. At the same time, these two prevailing roles result in a structural tension between realist/geopolitical/territorial and liberal/pragmatic/economistic approaches to Moroccan foreign policy, which is reflected in the two major parts into which the book is divided.

As a necessary introduction, Chapter 1 discusses the foreign policy objectives declared by King Mohammed VI upon his accession to the throne, including innovations such as the promotion of *economic diplomacy* and the reform of the foreign ministry and service. These attempts at economistic and technocratic modernisation are compared with the continuing hegemony of the King behind the scenes over highly centralised decision-making processes, despite subtle variations at sub-systemic level. Chapter 2 analyses Morocco's international management of the Western Sahara conflict as the paramount territorial issue in which the role of *champion of national territorial integrity* is ingrained whilst, paradoxically, success ultimately depends on external recognition, which has forced this country to maintain other more cooperative roles vis-à-vis the international community – involving some degree of role conflict. A four-stage chronology is proposed for the period 1999–2014 based on the evolving interplay between the *domestic* and international management of this 'Sahara question' by the Rabat authorities, and the parallel *inward turn* of the conflict itself. Chapter 3 examines how Morocco's ambivalent foreign policy towards Algeria and the Maghreb has reflected a role conflict between the domestically defined conception of this country as *territorial champion*, which entailed controlled rivalry and periodic declaratory escalations with the eastern neighbour, and external (European and U.S.) expectations about the promotion of Maghrebi regional integration, which led to recurring calls for the 'normalisation' of bilateral relations.

Chapters 4 and 5 address how Morocco's priority role as *model student of the EU*, involving exemplary behaviour at both bilateral and multilateral (Euro-Mediterranean) level, has been put to strategic use and exploited by Rabat as a means for achieving differentiated and privileged treatment from Brussels, as was symbolically enshrined by the Advanced Status obtained in 2008. Morocco's outstanding pro-European foreign policy activism is explained as a case of superficial but effective international socialisation, which has not resulted in any deep change in political interests, values and identity but has brought substantial benefits in terms of legitimation or external validation for the Rabat authorities. Chapter 6 disentangles the contents of the *intergovernmental advantage*, which is the second key factor behind Morocco's advantageous treatment from the EU, reviewing how Moroccan foreign policy has reactively approached bilateral relations with France and Spain since 1999. Whereas unparalleled postcolonial symbiosis has ensured an extraordinarily intense and stable alliance with France, leading Morocco destined to play an unstated or implicit role of *good son*, relations with Spain have featured a permanent duality and conflict between the roles of *good neighbour* and *territorial champion*.

Chapter 7 deals with the only priority area of Moroccan foreign policy under Mohammed VI that has at times aroused significant domestic dissent, i.e. relations with the U.S. The War on Terror declared following the 9/11 attacks brought to the fore Morocco's longstanding role as *good U.S. ally*, leading to a visible strengthening of bilateral ties at all levels, although also caused this role to clash overtly with Morocco's Arab-Muslim identity and deep-rooted role as *pan-Islamic leader*, especially when stances on or involvement in Middle East conflicts were at stake.

Notes

1 For a comprehensive overview of international relations in the Middle East, see Fawcett (2013) and Ismael and Perry (2014).
2 This theoretical foundation distinguishes these works from other purely empirical edited volumes as the one by L. Carl Brown (2001).
3 Translated into Arabic in Hernando de Larramendi (2005).
4 See also Halliday (1994: 84–86).
5 For an argument along the same lines concerning 'peripheral states', see Moon (1995: 192–195).
6 In general, the dichotomy between socialisation and rational choice appears to be largely artificial. Even acting as a tough negotiator that is apparently guided only by rational choice implies an effective socialisation of the practices or rules of the game of such bargaining.
7 Most of them are/were accessible in both Arabic and French on the website of the foreign ministry, www.maec.gov.ma (accessed on 31 August 2011) and, since October 2011, www.diplomatie.ma (accessed on 31 January 2015).
8 www.boletin.org (accessed on 31 January 2015).
9 Quotations from both primary sources and secondary academic literature in different languages have been translated into English by the author, who assumes full responsibility for any errors.

1 Objectives, actors and decision-making under Mohammed VI

Within the domestic sphere, what Morocco witnessed in July 1999 can be viewed, according to the classification proposed by Joe D. Hagan, as a 'regime change involving a change in the effective head of state, but no change in the basic political make-up of the ruling group' (1987: 347). This concept of regime change does not necessarily involve a systemic change or transition, but also includes 'change within a given type of political regime' (Albrecht and Schlumberger, 2004: 387). Overall, discontinuity in Moroccan foreign policy under Mohammed VI was to be less marked on an internal level than it was to be in terms of regional and international constraints, since the latter two environments were significantly disrupted from late 2001 onwards as a consequence of the 9/11 attacks. In other words, the origin of the perceptible changes would be more often exogenous than endogenous.

Morocco was not the only Arab country to undergo succession of the head of state at this point in time. Along with King Hassan II, King Hussein of Jordan and the Syrian President Hafez al Assad died in 1999–2000. The three of them were among the oldest and most charismatic Arab leaders, and were considered to be the most skilled in the arts of diplomacy. The three of them – including also the republican president – were *dynastically* succeeded by their sons, who were around 40 years old at the time. In these circumstances, it was logical to wonder about the implications of 'heritage' in the realm of foreign policy, where the particular 'inside-outside game' which had hitherto guaranteed the survival of these regimes was played out, even more so considering the closed nature of their decision-making systems and the importance of leadership, personality and charisma as foreign policy resources, both externally and domestically. The new political leaders seemed to have fairly limited margin for manoeuvre, as they faced somehow paradoxical external expectations, i.e. pushing through substantial internal reforms while maintaining continuity in their countries' external orientations (Charillon, 2002). Mohammed VI's distinct choice of continuity in foreign affairs can be explained both by the structural constraints on his action imposed by the regional and international context, and by his own inability – lack of experience, resources or authority – to change the course followed by the state administration and his inherited circle of advisors. A third factor could be that his pressing need for legitimation dissuaded him from straying from the path traced by his predecessor, which had been endorsed by a relative domestic consensus. In that case, continuity would largely result from adjusting foreign policy behaviour and discourse to already settled identity-related *norms* for reasons of 'self-image' and 'self-preservation' (Barnett, 1998: 11–12).

Following his succession to the throne, various observers highlighted the lack of training, experience and 'lust for power' of the new King, whom his father had kept away from the tasks of government (Dalle, 2004: 22, 632). Despite Hassan II's simultaneous efforts to turn his offspring into a 'diplomat king' in his image and likeness, as was evident from his education – law studies, master's thesis on the Arab-African Union between Morocco and Libya (1984–1986) (Ben El Hassan Alaoui and Chraïbi, 1985), traineeship at the European Commission and PhD thesis on cooperation between the European Economic Community (EEC)/European Union (EU) and the Arab Maghreb Union (AMU) (Ben El Hassan Alaoui, 1994) – the image that Mohammed VI at first projected was one of frivolity and a lack of interest in state affairs.

Mohammed VI's inaugural speech concerning foreign policy was given in late April 2000 on the occasion of the National Day of Moroccan Diplomacy, and is a highly revealing source for analysing the main functions assigned by this King to foreign policy as well as his conception of the diplomatic apparatus. It unsurprisingly started with a reference to the past: in order to contribute to 'the greatness [*grandeur*], glory, splendour and prosperity we want for our people', foreign policy should honour the kingdom's magnified diplomatic tradition and the legacy of the previous monarch. Building on this, and assuming the 'interdependence of internal and external issues' which characterised the era of globalisation, the King provided an indicative definition of foreign policy as a 'prolongation' of domestic politics and highlighted the necessary contribution of the former to achieving the overall goals of the state. Conversely, and symbiotically, he also advocated capitalising in the area of international relations on the new image of 'democratic and modernist Morocco' (Sehimi, 2003: 109). The general objectives of Moroccan foreign policy were formulated as follows:

- International recognition of Morocco's de facto control over Western Sahara: 'enshrining Morocco as a country that has regained its territorial integrity'.
- Extension of domestic policies and contribution to the 'objectives of the general policy of the state'.
- Promotion of economic development: 'exploiting the opportunities for expansion and fruitful exchange offered at external level'.
- Integration of Morocco into the globalised economy: 'taking best advantage of globalisation [*mondialisation*], integrating into the global economy, while reducing its negative impact on our development'.
- Diversification of Morocco's external relations into new regions (America, Asia): 'exploring new spaces for economic cooperation'.
- Maintaining Morocco's traditional role as regional stabiliser: 'consolidating Morocco's position as a pioneering regional pole and a factor of stability

and peace within its Maghreb, Arab, Islamic, Euro-Mediterranean, African and American environment'.
- Promoting Morocco's image in the eyes of the international community: 'its diplomacy must now be mobilised in order to capitalise on the new image [...] of a democratic and modernist Morocco, which is mobilised around its sovereign, an example of moderation and tolerance'.

(Speech by Mohammed VI, Rabat, 28 April 2000)

A second key royal speech on foreign policy was delivered in August 2002, on the forty-ninth anniversary of the Revolution of the King and the People. Within a regional and international context which had been deeply disrupted in the aftermath of 9/11, the arguments of Mohammed VI on the feedback between foreign and domestic policies remained the same: 'The degree of democratic development of a state is nowadays a determining factor for its international standing; and its ability to cope with these challenges has become dependent on the effectiveness of its diplomatic action' (speech by Mohammed VI, Tangier, 20 August 2002). The continuity of this basic approach was again made clear two years later, with just the addition of growing concern for global security and the fight against terrorism (speech by Mohammed VI, Rabat, 30 July 2004).[1]

A 'new' approach: 'economic diplomacy' and reform of the foreign service

These defining royal speeches reflected what were purportedly the two major innovations envisaged by Mohammed VI in the realm of foreign policy, which were closely connected to each other: paying greater attention to the 'economic dimension' of foreign policy and reforming the foreign service in order to set up an 'efficient' diplomacy with 'renewed structures'. In subsequent years, indeed, the extension of a new economistic official discourse into various foreign policy areas was coupled with attempts to develop and promote a new technocratic foreign policy elite – although tangible results were at most limited.

Whilst the assignment of economic functions to diplomatic missions abroad was far from a novelty in historical terms, at the turn of the millennium Moroccan decision-makers showed an increasing awareness of the huge challenges that the national economy was facing as a result of its liberalisation, opening up and integration into the global system. In terms of trade alone, this country had shifted in just two decades from strong protectionism to an earnest strategy of trade opening and diversification by all means (Escribano, 2007: 188–193; Abouddahab, 2010b). Accordingly, new demands were placed on so-called *economic diplomacy*, both at macro level – relations with multilateral economic institutions – and micro level – support for the internationalisation of Moroccan companies and national exports, attraction of foreign direct investment and contribution to the development of priority sectors such as tourism. The context within which this new leitmotif became widespread was marked by the diversification of the actors involved in external relations, the loss of the monopoly in this area by the Ministry of Foreign Affairs and Cooperation, the increasing participation of economic and technical ministries, the development of parallel diplomacy and the improvement of information and communication media for all parties (Belalami, 2006: 1–8, 79).

Against this background, it was at the beginning of Mohamed VI's reign that *economic diplomacy* was enshrined as an official foreign policy priority, as the economistic and technocratic leanings of the Rabat authorities became also increasingly explicit (El Messaoudi and Bouabid, 2007; Tozy, 2008). In accordance with a 'royal project' defined by the 'primacy of economics over politics',[2] foreign policy officials started to shape an allegedly depoliticised and pragmatic economistic discourse, which was applied with different variations to relations with the EU, Maghrebi regional integration, the kingdom's positions within the Arab League and its alliance with the Gulf countries, and its proclaimed *new African policy*. The foreign minister appointed in April 1999, Mohamed Benaissa, claimed in the National Day of Moroccan Diplomacy in 2004 that 'three quarters' of the activities of his department concerned economic issues (MAEC, 19 April 2004). This 'priority' of *economic diplomacy* was reaffirmed once again by deputy minister Youssef Amrani in 2012 (MAEC, 15 February 2012).[3]

On the other hand, various political actors of different persuasions had pointed out the need to restructure the Moroccan Ministry of Foreign Affairs and Cooperation, including both the central administration and the foreign service, since the late 1990s – not long after the 1995 reform (decree 2-94-864, 20 January 1995) which 'created' this ministry under its current denomination, fixing its organisational structure and regulating its functions (Janati-Idrissi, 1999: 126–130). This was also one of the concerns of the nascent independent press. For example, in 1999 *Le Journal* published an investigation revealing the high levels of inefficiency and corruption within the Moroccan embassy in Washington, which had until that time been headed by Benaissa himself, and its negligence in defending the Moroccan positions on the Western Sahara conflict before a crucial body such as the United States Congress (*Le Journal*, 30 October–5 November 1999; Amar, 2009: 151). Within ordinary political debate, some of the responsibility for the dysfunctions of Moroccan foreign policy was attributed to 'the weakness, even decadence, of the diplomatic service': 'This body is appointed on the basis of patronage and favouritism, not competition' (Abouddahab, 2006: 63). Recurrently highlighted deficiencies included the lack of resources, arbitrary criteria for accessing the diplomatic career and the inadequate training of the latter's members. Moreover, until 2011 ambassadors were appointed directly by the King, without any government involvement (Abouddahab, 2006: 72–73).[4]

Discontent also became visible within the foreign ministry itself. Evidence of this was the *white paper* anonymously circulated by a dozen senior diplomats in December 2002, following the confirmation that Benaissa would remain at the head of this ministry under the new government of Driss Jettou (2002–2007). The document, copies of which were sent to Jettou, the Directorate-General for Studies and Documentation (DGED, the external intelligence agency) and the

King's entourage, railed against Benaissa's management and denounced with facts, figures and names the incompetence, disorganisation and abundant irregularities which plagued the daily operations of this department. Its authors ended up asking for a parliamentary investigation to be launched. The reasons for their rebellion could be found in their proximity to Abdellatif Filali, former prime minister (1994–1998) and Benaissa's predecessor in this portfolio (1971–1972, 1985–1999)[5] as well as the expectations raised by the speech on the reform of diplomacy given by Mohammed VI in August of the same year (*Le Journal Hebdomadaire*, 7–13 December 2002).

In fact, the official response to widespread dissatisfaction with the performance of the Moroccan foreign ministry and service came in the form of two royal speeches in April 2000 and August 2002. The first of them, already mentioned above, proposed some of the objectives of the envisaged reorganisation of the foreign ministry, according to a model of 'centralised planning and decentralised implementation' of foreign policy (El Houdaïgui, 2010: 317–320): improving its coordination capacity, both within the central government and with the diplomatic missions; enabling the involvement of all kinds of parliamentary, associative, economic, cultural and media actors in tasks of parallel diplomacy; and enhancing the role of the ambassadors, imposing higher demands in terms of competence and capacity for initiative (speech by Mohammed VI, Rabat, 28 April 2000). Two years later, Mohammed VI announced major changes in both the central structures of the foreign ministry and its peripheral administration:

> We have issued Our High Instructions to ensure the upgrading [*mise à niveau*], modernisation and reorganisation of our diplomatic apparatus. The procedure envisaged for implementing this reform must affect the structures of the Ministry of Foreign Affairs and Cooperation, its mission of driving, coordination and follow up, as well as the actions and working methods of our diplomatic and consular representations.

The stated aim was to achieve a diplomatic service that was 'more active and enterprising, rational and persuasive', 'forceful and offensive without being aggressive', by 'renewing its tools and means of action' (speech by Mohammed VI, Tangier, 20 August 2002). The new economic imperatives were the most frequently repeated justification for the changes announced. At the same time, some observers drew attention to the temporal proximity between this speech and the Perejil crisis with Spain in July 2002, which had provoked harsh domestic and foreign criticism of the management of Moroccan foreign policy.

The reforms launched in November 2002 within the Ministry of Foreign Affairs focused on four key areas: modernisation of budget management and accounting; introduction of new technologies (computers, internet) and bringing the administration closer to citizens (establishment of regional delegations aimed at migrants); enhancement of the *economic diplomacy* (appointment of a new cohort of economic advisors with demonstrated training and experience to 40 embassies and consulates) (Belalami, 2006: 22, 54–55, 116); and, above all, a change in the approach to the management of human resources.[6] The latter objective encompassed measures such as the reform of the status of diplomatic and consular personnel, the introduction of more defined and objective criteria for appointments and promotions, the systematisation of public examinations and the codification of rules for destinations abroad. Overall, it was intended to enhance the value of professional qualifications and encourage competitiveness and performance within the diplomatic and administrative staff of the ministry. For this purpose, the recruitment policy was planned until 2010, internal promotion mechanisms were reactivated and the system of remuneration (allowances, compensations, etc.) was improved (*Maroc Hebdo International*, 3–9 December 2004). For critics, however, all this was nothing more than a 'réformette' which avoided addressing the root problems (*Le Journal Hebdomadaire*, 7–13 December 2002).

Evidence of attempts to implement some of these measures included the publication of a 'Guide of the Moroccan diplomat' in 2009 (MAEC, 2009) and a 'Charter of values of the Moroccan diplomat' in 2011, the latter highlighting the importance of 'patriotism', 'dignity', 'openness', 'communication' and 'professionalism' (MAEC, 2011). Later on, after the constitutional reform of July 2011, a new decree concerning the powers and the organisation of the foreign ministry was adopted, the main novelty of which was the addition of a new Directorate-General for Economic Promotion, Cultural Action and Public Diplomacy to the two existing directorate-generals dedicated to bilateral and multilateral relations (decree 2–11–428, 6 September 2011; MAEC, 7 July 2011; *Hespress*, 11 July 2011).[7]

Training a new technocratic foreign policy elite

In terms of human resources, one of the pending issues on which the King had placed greater emphasis in his speech given in August 2002 was the improvement of mechanisms for selecting and training the diplomatic staff.[8] The three most ambitious initiatives in this area were the launch of the Master of Arts in International Studies and Diplomacy (MAISD) at Al Akhawayn University in Ifrane (AUI) in 2000, the creation of the Moroccan Royal Academy of Diplomacy (MoRAD) at the same location in 2004 and the replacement of the latter by the Moroccan Academy of Diplomatic Studies (AMED) in Rabat, which was eventually inaugurated in April 2011. It was highly significant that the first two of these projects were located in and devised jointly with AUI, a private institution founded in 1993 offering undergraduate studies in English based on the U.S. system which had maintained from the outset a policy of collaboration (mainly on training) with various ministries (Benali, 1999: 178). This gave clear indications of the type of new technocratic foreign policy elite that was envisaged at this point in time by the Rabat authorities, which was somehow expected to overcome postcolonial attachment and socialisation, being less French-speaking and French-oriented than the existing one.[9]

The MAISD programme actually came into existence two years before the 2002 royal speech. It was devised jointly by the president of this university and

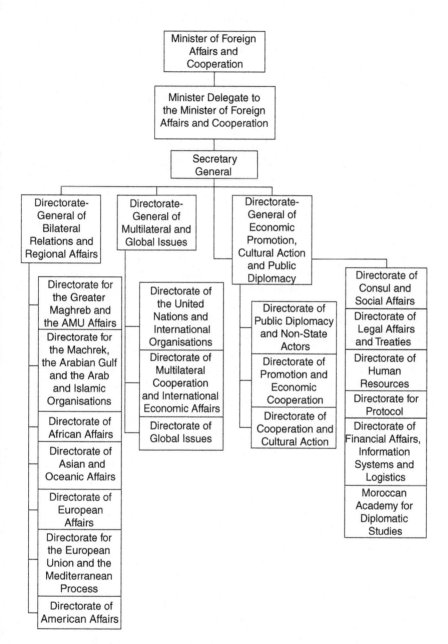

Figure 1.1 Organisation chart of the Ministry of Foreign Affairs and Cooperation.

foreign minister Benaissa with an objective that transcended purely academic education, i.e. training future Moroccan diplomats. The choice of AUI to host this experiment was not unrelated to the pro-U.S. connections and leanings of Benaissa, who had previously served as ambassador to Washington and was convinced of the need to transcend the traditional *francophone* bias of Moroccan diplomacy. Foreign ministry support consisted, first, in the direct financing of the programme during its first six years of life (2000–2006) and the granting of scholarships to some of its students. Second, the MAISD faculty and students were frequently invited to attend events held at the ministry in Rabat, whilst the ministry in turn supported and actively participated in various conferences organised by the AUI. Some of these events, such as those dedicated to Morocco's bilateral relations with the U.S. (January 2002) (Ouaouicha *et al.*, 2003), Saudi Arabia (April 2002) (Ouaouicha and Aboussaid, 2003) and South Africa (July 2002) (Mills, 2002), visibly fulfilled functions of parallel and public diplomacy.

Third, although there was no specific commitment of recruitment, all of the first cohort of MAISD graduates were immediately hired by the ministry and, in subsequent years, some were selected for internships. According to some accounts, some of them had to face mistrust due to their U.S.-style education, their alleged pro-U.S. tendencies, the elitist image of their university (Benali, 1999) or their critical approaches to Moroccan foreign policy. Some sources consider such resistance to have had a sociolinguistic dimension and attributed them mainly to the 'francophone elite' which had traditionally dominated the foreign ministry. Others mention 'bureaucratic resistance' or 'mid-level reluctance to change', for fear of being ousted or deprived of opportunities for promotion due to competition from younger generations: 'The further up you go in the ministry, the more reform-oriented it is. The closer to the "middle ego", the more hostility towards reform you find' (confidential interviews, November 2008). In any case, out of the 50 people who graduated from the MAISD between 2000 and 2008, around half were to continue working in the foreign ministry.

The second chapter of the cooperation between the foreign ministry and AUI was the temporary establishment at this university of what was then called the Moroccan Royal Academy of Diplomacy (MoRAD). Mohammed VI himself gave the official starting signal during a visit to Ifrane in late August 2004. According to minister Benaissa, this ambitious initiative was launched within the framework of the royal guidelines established in the speeches of April 2000 and August 2002, and was aimed at 'strengthening the Moroccan diplomatic service by providing it with competent officials [*cadres*] able to negotiate and manage international files in a professional manner'. More specifically, the aim was for new staff joining the ministry to undergo basic theoretical and practical training in the centre for at least one year. Two additional objectives were to offer training to serving Moroccan diplomats and to organise training sessions for 'friendly countries' in order to raise awareness of Morocco (i.e. public diplomacy) (MAEC, 30 August 2004; Belalami, 2006: 53, 55, 152).[10] In practice, what started at this point in time was only the training of the first promotion of the

MoRAD, which was made up of 16 trainees selected by the ministry. According to the ministry, this was only a temporary solution, since the final headquarters of the diplomatic academy was still awaiting construction (MAP, 31 August 2004). In the end, only two cohorts graduated from AUI. This programme was suspended in 2006, just before it was announced that the academy would be transferred to Rabat to facilities annexed to the building occupied by the ministry, which would henceforth have exclusive control over it. According to some sources, this decision represented a victory for the sectors within the foreign ministry that were most reform-averse and hostile to AUI.

This marked the start of the MoRAD's replacement by a Rabat-based and renamed Moroccan Academy of Diplomatic Studies (AMED). The prestigious Diplomatic Academy of Vienna was commissioned with carrying out a feasibility study funded by the UN Development Programme (UNDP) in order to shape the new training project. The resulting curriculum, which also benefited from contributions from the UN Institute for Training and Research (UNITAR) and staff from the foreign ministry, was presented in May 2007. The start of courses was initially scheduled for September 2008 (MAEC, 7 May 2007; *Aujourd'hui Le Maroc*, 18 May 2007; *Maroc Hebdo International*, 25–31 May 2007), yet it was later postponed several times pending completion of the building. The foreign ministry's budget for 2009 allocated 13 million dirhams to this project (*Al Masaa*, 19 November 2008). Eventually, the Moroccan government approved the decree creating the AMED in March 2011 after which it was inaugurated with great fanfare in late April (MAEC, 26 April 2011; *Al Ahdath Al Maghribia*, 27 April 2011).

The main objective of AMED, which was presented as an initiative of the new foreign minister Taieb Fassi Fihri (*L'Économiste*, 27 April 2011), continued to be to increase the competence and professionalism of Moroccan diplomats. Yet now, although basic courses were offered on the history of Moroccan foreign policy, international relations and international law, emphasis was placed on more practical knowledge and skills: the procedures of diplomatic and consular action, negotiation techniques, management methods, protocol and languages. In parallel, AMED was to strengthen international cooperation, building contacts with various diplomatic institutes from Africa and Asia (interview with Driss Boufekar, 17 June 2009). For example, a cooperation memorandum was signed with the Chinese diplomatic institute in late 2012 (MAEC, 3 December 2012) and the fourth cohort to graduate from AMED (2014) included for the first time ten young diplomats from francophone West African countries (MAEC, 10 February 2014). As regards the EU, the AMED project also featured in the negotiations concerning the EU–Morocco Advanced Status, the Joint Document on which envisaged the possibility of promoting a partnership between the Royal Academy of Diplomatic Studies of Morocco [sic] and the College of Europe (EU–Morocco Association Council, 2008a: 13), as previously proposed by the Moroccan negotiators (EU–Morocco Working Group on the Advanced Status, 2008: 16).

The renewal of the ambassador corps

Discourse and training initiatives aside, overall, in the years following the promising 2002 royal speech on the reform of the foreign ministry and service, actually significant effects appeared to be rather thin on the ground. The main tangible change that occurred during this period was an extensive renovation of the ambassador corps. Mohammed VI's appointments showed, first, a greater attention to African and Latin American countries, which was not unrelated to the old diplomatic competition with the Polisario Front for international recognition (or withdrawal of recognition) of the Sahrawi Arab Democratic Republic (SADR) (*Al Watan al An*, 3 December 2007). The second aim was to encourage the renewal and rejuvenation of the diplomatic corps, co-opting also figures from the political parties of the historical opposition, academia and civil society. For example, out of the 25 ambassadors appointed in November 2008, 19 were first-time appointees and the average age (53 years) was well below that of the outgoing officials (61). The list included well-known politicians from the Socialist Union of Popular Forces (USFP), the Party of Progress and Socialism (PPS) and the Istiqlal Party (PI), plus a female academic and a former dissident (MAP, 8 November 2008; *Al Quds al Arabi*, 10 November 2008; *L'Économiste*, 10 November 2008).

Third, the fact that five out of the 25 ambassadors appointed on this occasion were women revealed a political will to promote women's access to this masculine professional realm – which represented an invaluable asset for Morocco's image abroad (*Al Sabah*, 24 November 2008).[11] In any case, beyond the new faces, the criteria for accessing the diplomatic career had not ceased to be arbitrary and were often marked by patronage (*Al Watan al An*, 9 December 2010). As *Al Watan al An* (3 December 2007) wondered: 'Does Morocco choose an ambassador for his political allegiance to power, for his loyalty to a particular party in government, for his aptitude and experience or in order to send him away from Morocco?'

Special mention should be made of another new policy promoted from 2006–2007 onwards by the Ministry of the Interior – which was often mired in controversy and irregularities: incorporating unionist Sahrawis and Polisario defectors into Moroccan embassies abroad or the foreign ministry itself. The appointment of Ahmed Lekhrif (PI) as secretary of state for Foreign Affairs in September 2007 fell within this approach, but ended up with the removal from office of this lifelong unionist Sahrawi only a year later. The royal decision was officially justified by Lekhrif's recent acquisition of Spanish nationality, thanks to the new opportunities offered by Madrid to persons born in Western Sahara up to 1975 – a policy rejected outright by the Rabat authorities (*El País*, 23 December 2008; *Aujourd'hui Le Maroc*, 24 December 2008) – although others attributed it to his contacts with members of his family belonging to the Polisario Front (*Al Ousboue*, 2 February 2009). Even more controversial and awkward for the Spanish government was the choice of Ahmed Ould Souilem as the new ambassador to Madrid, a recent returnee from the Sahrawi refugee camps in

Tindouf (Algeria) who had been one of the Polisario's founders and had served as representative of the SADR in many countries before going over to Morocco in July 2009 (*Jeune Afrique*, 30 May–5 June 2010; *El País*, 27 June 2010; *Al Watan al An*, 9 December 2010).[12]

Other than this, the number of Moroccan embassies or missions abroad (92 in 2014) continued to appear out of proportion to the political and economic capacities of this country, according to observers who insisted on the need to streamline it. Except for some 20 genuinely active representations, the rest were located in countries in which Morocco had no vital interests and were maintained for essentially 'political' reasons linked to the Western Sahara conflict (Belalami, 2006: 130, 149; *Tel Quel*, 11–17 April 2009).

Changes at the monarchical and security core of decision-making

Verifiable information is much scarcer when it comes to changes behind the scenes which affected the formulation and decision-making processes of Moroccan foreign policy after Mohammed VI's accession to the throne. Domestic critics have often linked structural deficiencies such as the lack of a coherent or unified strategy within this foreign policy – which was supposedly the source of its 'ambiguity', 'instability', 'indecision', 'wait-and-see attitude' (*attentisme*), 'bandwagoning' (*suivisme*), 'lack of autonomy' and 'foreign dependence' – with the democratic deficit within decision-making, which was monopolised in practice by a restricted group of individuals absolutely lacking in transparency. In fact, this was nothing but the projection of the concentration of power that characterised the Moroccan political system also internally (Abouddahab, 2006: 59–63, 73).

Arguably, various features of neopatrimonialism remained present there: the personal control of the state and its resources by the leader and his entourage, which was built on virtually family-based criteria; the privatisation and personalisation of political power; and, above all, the prevalence of informal, poorly institutionalised governance methods. In other words, networks of personal relationships carried more weight than formal institutions or organisations (Zubaida,

Table 1.1 Embassies/missions of Morocco abroad, 2014

Region	Embassies/missions
Europe	27
Sub-Saharan Africa	19
Arab countries	18
Asia-Pacific	13
America	11
International organisations	4
Total	92

Source: www.diplomatie.ma.

1990: 61; Saaf, 1991: 73–74). If the overall political tendency during the first decade of Mohammed VI's reign was increased interventionism by and public visibility of head of state, the areas traditionally considered as the monarchy's 'reserved domain' (*domaine réservé*) were particularly affected (*Le Journal Hebdomadaire*, 13–19 October 2007). This 'mode of governance which [remained] still very empirical, erratic, centralised and personalised' (Desrues, 2006: 244) could have different effects on foreign policy behaviour. For example, according to Jennifer Rosenblum and I. William Zartman, 'this semi-collegial policymaking system discourages bold initiatives and has led to a conservative policy bent, and also to some missed opportunities' (2009: 331). Furthermore, it also greatly complicated the task of foreign diplomats accredited to Rabat. 'Nobody knows exactly where decisions are made and whom one should address himself to', complained an ambassador in 2000 (Garçon, 2000: 431).

On the other hand, the persistence of royal supremacy and neopatrimonial practices did not prevent more subtle movements at sub-systemic level, or regime changes without democratisation (Albrecht and Schlumberger, 2004), which affected foreign policy decisions and can be analysed – with the due caution dictated by the paucity of data – from the viewpoint of the bureaucratic approach to Foreign Policy Analysis (FPA) (Hill, 2003: 85–96). Regarding actors included in the core or *central decision-making unit* (El Houdaïgui, 2003a: 27–29), the most noteworthy changes were the successive alterations in the balance of power within the circle of the King's advisors (both official and unofficial), a temporary increase in the political influence of certain senior army officers (until 2005) and the open involvement of the DGED in the implementation of foreign policy, playing a role that reached far beyond intelligence tasks proper. Within the *subordinate decision-making unit*, the monopoly of the interior ministry over the management of the Western Sahara issue came to an end, thereby expanding the powers of the foreign ministry in this area, and significant functions of parallel and public diplomacy were assigned to some consultative councils placed under the King's direct authority.

The unchallenged hegemony of the King over the design and implementation of Moroccan foreign policy was part of the legacy of Hassan II's reign, after which 'no party openly [questioned] the monarch's central symbolic role or even his special privileges in foreign relations and defence' (Leveau, 2000: 123). The doctrinal foundation on which this dominance rested was the assumption that foreign affairs belonged to the *reserved domain* of the monarchy, which was forged during the state of emergency (1965–1970) and inspired by the model of French presidentialism. This served as an extra-constitutional and extra-legal justification for the palace's disproportionate powers in foreign policy, and resulted in the unwritten practice of considering the corresponding government portfolio – alongside Interior, Justice and Islamic Affairs – as one of the *ministries of sovereignty* whose heads were directly appointed by the King (El Maslouhi, 1999; Zouitni, 2003). In legal terms, both the Moroccan Constitution of 1996 and its predecessors enshrined the religious authority of the King, designating him as the symbol and the person ultimately responsible for national sovereignty and unity (article 19). His powers included the ability to declare war, after consulting the government and informing parliament (articles 66 and 74), the signature and ratification of international treaties and the appointment of Moroccan ambassadors to foreign countries or international organisations (article 31). These came in addition to defence powers as the supreme commander of the army (article 30) and the presidency of the Council of Ministers (article 25).

By and large, according to the classification of foreign policy *ultimate decision units* proposed by Margaret G. Hermann, Charles F. Hermann and Joe D. Hagan (in Hermann, Kegley and Rosenau, 1987: 309–336), King Mohammed VI was to behave overall as a 'sensitive predominant leader', i.e. one who showed contextual sensitivity and was 'externally penetrable', whose clear-cut hegemony did not exclude exogenous influences. One of the outward manifestations of the royal prominence was the extraordinary political significance attached to the King's speeches, in the times both of Hassan II and Mohammed VI (Hernando de Larramendi, 1997: 83–84; El Houdaïgui, 2003a: 103–104; Belhaj, 2009: 99). Historically, these addresses had always worked as *speech acts* with a widely assumed *performative* dimension, thus demanding discourse analysis.[13] Another highly symbolic task related to the implementation of foreign policy was the King's official trips and visits abroad. Over the nine years between his accession to the throne and July 2008, Mohammed VI travelled officially as head of state on a total of 85 occasions (*La Vie Éco*, 25 July 2008), with Saudi Arabia, France, the United Arab Emirates and the U.S. as the most frequent destinations (*Al Watan al An*, 3 December 2007). His successive 'African tours' in June 2004, February–March 2005, February 2006, March 2013 and February–March 2014 – mainly to francophone Western and Central African countries – were also presented as being of the utmost importance (*Alif Post*, 18 February 2014). In everyday practice, his most incisive competence was probably the 'power of appointment', which included, among others, the foreign minister, the ambassadors and the heads of the intelligence services (Brouksy, 2014: 68–69). On the other hand, it was in times of crisis when it became more evident that key decisions could only be made by the King in person, whilst he could never be held politically accountable for them (Brouksy, 2014: 115).

Paradoxically, this symbolic hegemony and practical concentration of powers in the figure of the King coexisted with an apparent personal lack of interest for international political issues (Dalle, 2004: 737; Maalmi, 2012: 783; Zisenwine, 2013: 71). This was at least the perception that became widespread within the Moroccan independent press from 2006–2007 onwards. Compared to the indefatigable activism displayed by Hassan II, Mohammed VI's repeated absences from international high-level events – the summit on the tenth anniversary of the Euro-Mediterranean Partnership (EMP, Barcelona, 2005), the Franco-African summits in Bamako (2005) and Cannes (2007), the Euro-African Ministerial Conference on Migration and Development (Rabat, 2006), the launch of the Union for the Mediterranean (UfM, Paris, 2008) and all of the Arab League summits held during these years – as well as receptions of foreign dignitaries visiting Rabat, led to talk of a 'withdrawal' of Morocco from the international scene (Tuquoi, 2006: 203–205). According to *Le Journal Hebdomadaire* (19–25 July 2008), 'Mohammed VI's attitude [contrasted] with that of Hassan II, who participated in major meetings and took the opportunity to try to give Morocco a leadership role, if only at Arab level'. Another alternative explanation was that the King was deliberately stepping back in order to show that not all foreign policy decisions depended directly on him, just as his physical presence was not indispensable at all events (*Tel Quel*, 19–25 July 2008). The same debate resurfaced in 2013–2014, after Mohammed VI snubbed the Turkish prime minister Recep Tayyip Erdoğan during the latter's visit to Rabat in June 2013 and cancelled his announced trips to New York – where he was scheduled to deliver a speech at the UN General Assembly – Russia and China in the autumn of 2014 (*Orilla Sur*, 4 December 2014).

Some of these absences were made up for by more or less well-known members of the royal family who, without occupying any official position, acted as de facto advisors or envoys of the head of state (*Al Ayam*, 2 February 2009). The most active by far was Prince Moulay Rachid, Mohammed VI's younger brother and second in line to the throne, who was to become the Moroccan monarchy's surrogate face at international meetings requiring representation at the highest level.[14]

Outside the family sphere, whilst maintaining the same tenor of informal relationships rooted in trust, one of the main loci of the *central decision-making unit* of Moroccan foreign policy was the circle of Mohammed VI's advisors. This group included both the members of the Royal Cabinet, which had been relatively institutionalised and stable since the previous reign, and a more variable number of informal advisors chosen from the King's closest companions. In addition to its old role as a *shadow cabinet* which closely supervised the activities of the government (Dalle, 2004: 453–454), the Royal Cabinet worked as a space for co-opting elites with an increasingly technocratic profile. Although the trend over the first decade of the new reign was towards less direct interference of the Royal Cabinet in government tasks, its members maintained 'influence' (Mohamed Tozy in *Tel Quel*, 20–26 September 2008) and de facto control over the many royal commissions, consultative councils and foundations which reported directly to the palace. At the same time, if only for generational reasons, the six advisors who formed the Royal Cabinet in the early years of Mohammed VI's reign, mostly inherited from Hassan II, had lost standing compared to the new King's intimate friends – old classmates from the Royal College – who were exercising growing ascendancy over him (*Le Journal Hebdomadaire*, 4–10 July 2009). Chief among the latter were Fouad Ali El Himma, secretary of state (1999–2002) and later deputy minister of the Interior (2002–2007), Mounir Majidi, personal secretary of the King (2000–), and Yassine Mansouri, head of the DGED (2005–). Mohamed Rochdi Chraibi, the director of the Royal Cabinet, was the only advisor to belong simultaneously to both circles, official and unofficial, from the outset (*Le Journal Hebdomadaire*, 26 April–2 May 2008; Brouksy, 2014: 142–145).

This balance of power was to be altered in 2011 in the wake of the Arab Spring protests and the Moroccan constitutional reform, when Mohammed VI expanded the Royal Cabinet by appointing a number of prominent figures, including Abdellatif Menouni, legal scholar and former president of the Consultative Commission for the Reform of the Constitution (2011); Mostapha Sahel, former interior minister (2002–2006) and ambassador to the UN (2006–2008) and France (2009–2011); and Omar Azziman, former minister of Justice (1997–2002), ambassador to Spain (2004–2010) and president of the Consultative Council on Human Rights (CCDH, 2002–2004) and the Consultative Council on Regionalisation (2010–2011). Both Sahel and Azziman had relevant diplomatic experience which could turn into influence over foreign policy decision-making. Most significantly, the 'King's friend' El Himma joined them after his political adventure as leader of the loyalist Party Authenticity and Modernity (PAM, 2008–2011) (MAP, 7 December 2011). The last three appointments were made against the backdrop of the victory of the Justice and Development Party (PJD) in the legislative elections of November 2011 and the formation of a coalition government led for the first time by these Islamists, which the reinforced Royal Cabinet seemed to be tasked with overseeing, as in Hassan II's times. The return of the *shadow cabinet* created a barely disguised duality in the Moroccan executive power (*Jeune Afrique*, 14 December 2011).

As far as the army was concerned, the death of Hassan II enabled a thaw in relations between the Palace and the Royal Armed Forces (FAR), which had been marked by mistrust since the attempted coups in 1971 and 1972. In the early years of the new reign, the dismissal of the previously omnipotent interior minister Driss Basri and the removal of many of his men within the state administration sparked speculation of a rise in the political influence of the military leadership, albeit only temporary (López García, 2000: 180). Following their rehabilitation, generals such as Housni Benslimane and Abdelhak Kadiri could aspire to fill the power vacuum. The former was indeed appointed as head of security at the palace, whilst the latter kept his position as head of the DGED. Another military official, General Hamidou Laanigri, was appointed as head of the Directorate for Territorial Surveillance (DST), the domestic intelligence agency, in September 1999 (Dalle, 2001; Vermeren, 2004: 270). These senior army officers were routinely consulted by the King (Garçon, 2000: 431) and had personal political and economic interests which made their behaviour unpredictable. An indication of their influence at this point in time was the fact that Mohammed VI himself had to deny it: 'The army has no political role. Its power stems from royal power. And I do not need the army to do politics' (interview with Mohammed VI in *Le Figaro*, 4 September 2001).

In any case, the army's apparent political ascendancy was merely ephemeral. A new trend towards the demilitarisation of the security and intelligence services was observed from 2005 onwards. The most telling measures announced during that year were the appointments of Mansouri and Abdellatif Hammouchi to head the DGED and DST respectively. Whereas, on the one hand, these moves responded to the new U.S. demands for cooperation in the fight against Islamist terrorism (Desrues, 2007: 283), on the other they helped to reinforce direct control of the security apparatus by the King and his associates (*Tel Quel*, 24 December 2005–6 January 2006; *Le Journal Hebdomadaire*, 26 April–2 May 2008).

In fact, the decline in the influence of the military within the *central decision-making unit* was offset by the growing involvement of Moroccan intelligence services in foreign policymaking. More specifically, the external intelligence agency DGED acquired an unprecedented role in this domain under Mansouri's direction, creating an anomalous situation of dual leadership with the foreign ministry. The fact that the DGED's network of overseas agents included members of the Moroccan diplomatic corps was certainly not a novelty. What seemed more unusual was that its new director officially acted as one of the top officials in charge of the international management of the Western Sahara issue and a regular member of the delegations sent to international negotiations on an equal footing with successive foreign ministers, Benaissa and Fassi Fihri (*Tel Quel*, 4–10 October 2008). Mansouri was present throughout almost every stage of the ambitious diplomatic campaign organised to promote the Moroccan Autonomy Plan for the disputed territory in February–April 2007 – especially in visits to key countries (the U.S., France, Spain, the United Kingdom and Russia) and to the UN headquarters – and also during the four rounds of negotiations with the Polisario Front held in Manhasset from June 2007 to March 2008 (*Aujourd'hui Le Maroc*, 1 October 2008). He was also instrumental in the Moroccan campaign to counter a report on Western Sahara by Human Rights Watch which advocated expanding the mandate of the UN Mission for the Referendum in Western Sahara (MINURSO) to human rights monitoring (*Tel Quel*, 20–26 December 2008).

The existence of a strategy to enhance coordination between the foreign ministry and the DGED was disclosed in news reports from late 2009, which mentioned plans to extend this cooperation beyond central structures to the entire network of Moroccan embassies abroad (*Al Masaa*, 16 October 2009). This was also corroborated to some extent by a significant portion of the documents leaked in the autumn of 2014 by a hacker hiding behind the nickname of 'Chris Coleman', comprised of emails of DGED agents and collaborators inside and outside Morocco. Among other things, many of these contained strong evidence that the DGED had been bribing journalists and thinktanks in France, the U.S. and Italy to write papers in favour of Moroccan positions on the Western Sahara conflict (*Orient XXI*, 15 December 2014; *Le Monde*, 2 January 2015).

The subsidiary role of the government, the parliament and the consultative councils

In contrast to this, the Moroccan government and parliament were definitely placed within the *subordinate decision-making unit*, which exerts a limited influence on foreign policy on the basis mainly of technical and organisational resources (El Houdaïgui, 2003a: 29). As a rule, these two institutions were less full-blown foreign policy actors capable of mobilising resources to achieve their objectives and enjoying a minimum of autonomy in decision-making, as rather largely *agents* following instructions from above (Hill, 2003: 75). Their functions involved more administration, management and implementation than a proper executive or oversight role.

In the case of the government, impotence was virtually structural, both de jure and de facto: the limited extent of its constitutional powers and its dependence on the King – who appointed and could dismiss the prime minister and other ministers (article 24) and chaired the Council of Ministers (article 25) – was coupled with the close daily monitoring of various ministries by royal advisors. In the foreign policy realm, the old and untouchable doctrine of *reserved domain* also remained in force (El Maslouhi, 1999; Zouitni, 2003). Against this backdrop, the first years of Mohammed VI's reign coincided with the peaking, since post-independence, of the Moroccan government's quest for autonomy and attempted resistance to the *reserved domain* in foreign policy (interview with Abdelwahab Maalmi, 16 October 2007). In the words of Rachid el Houdaïgui, this was a stage of 'de facto reintegration of foreign policy into the "shared domain"' (2003a: 191). Even with all of its limitations, the *alternance* government led by Abderrahmane Youssoufi (USFP, 1998–2002) had eked out unusual room for manoeuvre in this area (El Houdaïgui, 2003a: 201–203, 197; Janati-Idrissi, 1999). The trend towards increasing participation in foreign policy decision-making by the government and the prime minister was maintained upon Mohammed VI's accession to the throne (Zouitni, 2001: 38).

However, relations between the government and the palace started to deteriorate in 2000 due, among other things, to disagreements relating to foreign policy. The final blow was struck in July 2002 by the crisis provoked by the occupation of the islet of Perejil, during which the Youssoufi government was entirely sidelined and informed of key decisions only after the fact. The minister of Territorial Planning and senior USFP leader Mohamed El Yazghi vehemently expressed the discontent of his fellow government members during an unprecedentedly tense Council of Ministers, in which the King invited him to 'reread the constitution' (Dalle, 2004: 742–743; Planet and Hernando de Larramendi, 2006: 420; Abouddahab, 2006: 63; Tuquoi, 2006: 80; Cembrero, 2006: 44). This was one of the most awkward moments which this cabinet was forced to confront. By comparison, the subsequent governments of Driss Jettou (technocrat, 2002–2007) and Abbas El Fassi (PI, 2007–2011) were to display reduced aspirations for autonomy and to be less willing to assert their powers in foreign affairs vis-à-vis the monarchy. This withdrawal and subordination was most obvious under the El Fassi cabinet, whose head summarised his role in this area as 'representing His Majesty in various summits' and receiving foreign leaders at the request of the King (*Jeune Afrique*, 28 September 2008).

New expectations for a *comeback* by the Moroccan government in the foreign policy arena were created in 2011–2012 as a result of the post-Arab Spring constitutional reform and the formation of a coalition cabinet led by Islamist Abdelilah Benkirane (PJD). Whilst it did not result in any structural change in the distribution of powers, the new constitution adopted in July 2011 put an end to the 'sacred' character of the figure of the King – who still remained above the law as 'inviolable' (article 46) – and slightly cut back his powers in favour of the government. A provision was introduced whereby the head of government was to be appointed from within the political party receiving the most votes in parliamentary elections (article 47), although the King continued to preside over the Council of Ministers (article 48). This Council gained powers such as the power to declare war (article 49). Within the old *reserved domain* of foreign policy, there were two main novelties: an increase in the categories of international treaties requiring parliamentary approval prior to signature and ratification by the King – treaties of peace or of union, treaties concerning border delimitation, commercial treaties, treaties committing the finances of the state or requiring legislative measures, treaties concerning the rights and freedoms of citizens (article 55) – and specification of the rule that the appointment of ambassadors by the King (article 55) should occur 'at the proposal of the head of government and at the initiative of the minister concerned' (article 49). In addition, a new High Security Council was envisaged for coordinating of the country's domestic and external security under the presidency of the King (article 54) (interview with Hassan Bouqentar, 5 June 2013).[15]

In practice, the extents of these and other constitutional changes were dependent on subsequent legislative development in the form of organic laws, which was almost paralysed in 2012–2013. Another factor that could determine the actual division of labour between the monarchy and the government was the personality and desire for autonomy of the head of government. Benkirane was a highly popular politician with outstanding communication skills, whose media exposure at times even outweighed that of the King (interview with Mohammed Madani, 5 June 2013), which could presage a new stage of *shared domain* in foreign policy akin to that witnessed with the Youssoufi government. However, Benkirane soon publicly admitted his subordinate status, commenting that 'in Morocco the head of the government has some power, but His Majesty is the supreme master of this power' (*El País*, 20 May 2012). One of the most visible moments of tension between his cabinet and the King occurred following the military overthrow of President Mohammed Morsi in Egypt in July 2013. Whilst Mohammed VI promptly congratulated the new interim Egyptian president, Adly Mansour, the Moroccan government limited itself to acknowledging the events through a neutral communiqué of the foreign ministry (MAEC, 3 July 2013) and the PJD's party organs and members of parliament condemned what they regarded as a 'coup' (Hernando de Larramendi and Fernández-Molina, 2015). After three years in office, assessments of the role of the Benkirane government in Moroccan foreign policy were fairly negative and highlighted its failure to 'launch any external initiative, leaving the field of diplomacy to the royal institution' (*Alif Post*, 28 November 2014).

All of these *external* constraints limiting the agency of the Moroccan government in foreign policy decision-making were coupled with an *internal* anomaly concerning the Ministry of Foreign Affairs and Cooperation. The holder of this portfolio, who was appointed directly by the King and enjoyed his confidence, could in practice have greater access to information and influence than his theoretical superior, the prime minister (Zouitni, 2003: 72, 2001: 34–35). At the same time, the first two men to hold this position under Mohammed VI's reign, Mohamed Benaissa (1999–2007) and Taieb Fassi Fihri (2007–2011), had very different profiles and de facto political status. Both being career diplomats, the former was a holdover from the last years of Hassan II, whilst the latter belonged to the circle of close associates and friends of the new King. Therefore, even when he was officially still only the *number two* of the foreign ministry – as secretary of state (1999–2004) and later deputy minister (2004–2007) – this francophone technocrat already acted as the supreme authority, bypassing his hierarchical superior, who was in turn increasingly discredited and marginalised. The division of labour during the eight years of this duumvirate can be summarised as follows: 'Fassi Fihri oversees the important aspects of foreign relations – relations with the U.S., France, and the Sahara. Benaissa handles the administration and finances of the foreign ministry and is its senior roving diplomat' (Rosenblum and Zartman, 2009: 332). Fassi Fihri's promotion to the position of minister in 2007 was to clarify the chain of command somehow.

The situation changed substantially when the PJD took up governmental office in December 2011. Under the Benkirane cabinet, the foreign ministry was for the first time no longer headed by a royal appointee, and was led by the former secretary-general of the Islamist party, Saad-Eddine El Othmani. This politician initially displayed noteworthy activism and aspirations for some independence (*Al Akhbar al Youm*, 11 January 2012; *Tel Quel*, 28 March 2012). However, the monarch's reluctance to withdraw from this portfolio was evident from gestures such as a hasty round of ambassadorial appointments shortly before the new cabinet took up office and Fassi Fihri's transfer to the Royal Cabinet in order to reinforce it as *shadow cabinet* (*Maghreb Confidentiel*, 19 January 2012). Within the ministry itself, the King relapsed into the old hierarchical duality by appointing as deputy minister Youssef Amrani,[16] an EU-oriented career diplomat who enjoyed his confidence. As a result, El Othmani's room for manoeuvre was visibly limited. His personal determination to prioritise the revitalisation of bilateral relations with Algeria was soon thwarted (interview with Abdelwahab Maalmi, 7 June 2013) and he himself admitted internal tensions with Amrani during the crisis over the enlargement of the MINURSO mandate in April 2013 (*Al Tajdid*, 5 June 2013; interview with Mohammed Madani, 5 June 2013).

In October 2013, the cabinet reshuffle provoked by the PI's exit from the ruling coalition and the need to replace it with the National Rally of Independents (RNI), an old allied party of the monarchy, forced the PJD to resign the foreign ministry. El Othmani was replaced by the RNI leader, Salaheddine Mezouar, while another member of the latter party with a very distinct and purposeful profile, the young female unionist Sahrawi Mbarka Bouaida, was appointed deputy minister (*Lakome*, 10 October 2013). Overall, technocrats and men close to the palace once again controlled most of the key government posts, to the detriment of the PJD (Desrues, 2014: 265–267). Amrani was promoted to the Royal Cabinet, from which position at the palace he continued to represent Morocco at relevant international events, sidelining the government, as occurred for example in the 2015 Munich Security Conference (*Yabiladi*, 10 February 2015).

The Moroccan parliament was even more politically powerless. Not only had the 1996 constitution maintained its inherent subordination to monarchical authority, but a general sense of crisis surrounding the principle of political representation and representative institutions spread during the first decade of Mohammed VI's reign. The practical limitations on the political input of the House of Representatives (lower house) and the House of Councillors (upper house) were further accentuated by the lack of internal resources. Ultimately, as Saloua Zerhouni notes, this was 'more a space for "doing politics" than for "producing politics"' (2008: 217). At the same time, some indications of institutional development were observed at this stage, albeit in relative terms, based on the emergence of a 'nascent parliamentary culture', a sense of corporate identity and a willingness to assert and exercise constitutional functions of legislation, control and budget approval (Denoeux and Desfosses, 2007).

With regard to foreign policy, the marginal position of the legislature was well grounded both in legal texts and political practice (Zouitni, 2001: 28–33). The deficiencies in parliamentary oversight, propositions and debate on foreign policy remained a key feature under Mohammed VI. Any criticism of government officials by members of parliament – in oral or written questions, or in relation to the presentation of the government's programme, the annual approval of the budget of the foreign ministry or parliamentary investigations – was hampered by the ongoing consideration of the foreign ministry as a *ministry of sovereignty*. The Committee on Foreign Affairs, National Defence and Islamic Affairs of the House of Representatives was by far the least important in terms of the number of members (31 compared to 60 for most other five committees) and its chair was not one of the most coveted positions. This could be due to the fact that the three political areas it covered were part of the *reserved domain* of the monarchy, that is 'a field of (in)action at least unexpected' (*Tel Quel*, 13–19 December 2008).

Parliament was relatively more involved in foreign economic policymaking. On the one hand, this resulted from the 1996 constitutional obligation to approve by law any international treaty including a financial commitment for the state prior to ratification (article 31) – although, in practice, the government enjoyed some discretion in this regard. On the other hand, under Mohammed VI it became the norm during negotiations concerning relevant economic and trade agreements for members of parliament to be briefed and consulted by government officials, usually within the framework of the Committee on Foreign Affairs, as well as for oral questions to be answered in both houses of parliament. The negotiations that aroused the greatest parliamentary involvement and debate were those concerning the 2004 Free Trade Agreement with the U.S. and the 2006 fisheries agreement with the EU, although the former was more controversial (interview with Mohamed Benyahia, 19 October 2007). In such cases, the limits on the participation of members of parliament were largely due to the technical complexity of the issues in play, the lack of sufficient intervention and control instruments, a shortage of information on the progress of negotiations and the necessary pace and discretion of these conversations (Belalami, 2006: 46–48).

At the same time, constraints on the legislative, oversight and control functions of the Moroccan parliament in the foreign policy domain contrasted with its much-publicised activism in the area of parliamentary diplomacy. Since Hassan II's times, there had been a notable tradition of bilateral relations with foreign parliaments and participation in multilateral interparliamentary fora, as well as the dispatch of delegations abroad to promote Moroccan official positions, especially on the Western Sahara conflict. The plural and cross-party composition of delegations enhanced the regime's image by providing it with a certain 'democratic label' (Hernando de Larramendi, 1997: 149–166; El Houdaïgui, 2003a: 66–69, 75–76).[17] Along the same lines, Mohammed VI was to seek support from elected Moroccan representatives in order to project and defend the kingdom's interests internationally through 'parliamentary diplomacy conducted with professionalism' (speech by Mohammed VI, Rabat, 12 October 2007). The person responsible for representing the House of Representatives in international forums or foreign countries was its president, a position held by Abdelwahed Radi (USFP) between 1997 and 2007, and again in 2010–2011 (interview with Abdelwahed Radi, 3 December 2007). Different observers have highlighted the Moroccan parliament's particular dynamism during these years within networks and fora related to the EMP (IEMed, 2009: 129) and with regard to external economic issues (Belalami, 2006: 45). Still, in practice, limited parliamentary autonomy and the weakness of political parties in Morocco did not allow for the added value that parliamentary diplomacy was generally supposed to bring in terms of representativeness and pluralism. Parliamentary diplomacy worked as 'some kind of relay' (Zouitni, 2001: 29) for official guidelines from the government and, above all, the palace.

Other less conventional institutional actors which acquired an unprecedented role in Moroccan foreign policy under Mohammed VI were the consultative councils (Fernández-Molina, 2011a). Reporting directly to the palace and controlled by various royal advisors, these advisory bodies formed part of the *subordinate decision-making unit* similarly to the government and the parliament, which they often outweighed, however, in terms of public international presence. Mohammed VI recovered and strengthened this sui generis mode of governance already employed in the previous reign, which met his needs for domestic and international legitimation and suited his technocratic leanings. The common objective of these institutions, which lacked any organic relationship with either the government or the parliament, was to manage certain strategic matters of state in a consensual and depoliticised manner, prioritising the participation of civil society and 'experts' over widely discredited political parties. The promotion of civil society and a 'participatory approach' were part and parcel of an internationally valued discourse on democratisation on which this regime sought to capitalise.[18] At the same time, this governance mode was also in keeping with the 'consensus game' orchestrated from above which had historically dominated Moroccan politics (El Mossadeq, 1995). It prioritised consultation and intercession – the Islamic *shura* – over political representation, thus contributing to the existence of a 'deactivated political sphere' (Tozy, 1991: 165) and further undermining the government and parliament (Madani, 2006: 129).

As far as foreign policy is concerned, three consultative councils were particularly relevant between 1999 and 2014: two of them created during these years – the Royal Consultative Council for Saharan Affairs (CORCAS, 2006) and the Council for the Moroccan Community Abroad (CCME, 2007) – and another dating back to 1990, which was now reformed and revitalised – the Consultative Council on Human Rights (CCDH). The latter was to be transformed into the National Council on Human Rights (CNDH) and acquired greater formal independence in the 2011 constitutional reform. Externally, these consultative councils acted primarily as instruments of parallel diplomacy, i.e. actors not dependent on the government/executive but operating according to the guidelines of, or in coordination with, official foreign policy actors. Sometimes they also assumed functions of public diplomacy, understood as 'the process whereby governments bypass their equivalents in another country and target the wider political process, including civil society' (Hill, 2003: 279). Their ambiguous political nature allowed them to present themselves as non-governmental actors, despite their effective subordination to the monarchy, and to address their messages to wider international audiences, which transcended the purely governmental sphere and included foreign civil society, media and public opinion. That is why consultative councils played a role throughout all vital areas of Moroccan foreign policy at this stage: the Western Sahara issue (Autonomy Plan), relations with the EU (Advanced Status) and the promotion of the 'democratising' image of Morocco abroad.

The CCDH participated in Morocco's relations with three crucial international actors: the UN, backing official positions within the Human Rights Council; the EU, launching a National Action Plan on Human Rights and Democracy at the time of the Advanced Status negotiations; and the U.S., 'selling' the Moroccan *transitional justice* and national reconciliation process after the conclusion of the work of the Equity and Reconciliation Commission (IER) (*Jeune Afrique*, 1–7 July 2007; Amar, 2009: 259; Brouksy, 2014: 169). Another unwritten mission of the CCDH and its successor, the CNDH, was to act as interlocutors with international human rights NGOs and to defend the Moroccan authorities against criticisms from these groups concerning ongoing violations, especially with regard to the Western Sahara territory. In the case of the CORCAS, alongside propaganda campaigns against the Polisario Front, 'diplomatic' activities were to attain an almost official status. This council was associated with the ambitious governmental campaign to promote Rabat's Autonomy Plan for Western Sahara in early 2007 (interview with CORCAS member, 7 June 2013) as well as the subsequent Manhasset negotiations – yet not without misgivings on the part of the U.S. ambassador to Rabat (Amar, 2009: 267). Meanwhile, the CCME was expected to contribute to turning organisations and networks of the Moroccan diaspora into 'Morocco's mouthpiece abroad' (Abouddahab, 2010a: 369–370), or 'important relays [*relais*] for the external projection of the country' 'at a time of parallel diplomacies' (Comité Directeur du Rapport, 2006: 36, 79), in line with the new fashionable concepts of *diaspora diplomacy* and 'immigrant lobbying' (Kalpakian, 2006: 59).

Political parties and civil society actors in the periphery

Finally, the *marginalised decision-making unit* of Moroccan foreign policy includes political parties, employers' organisations and other civil society actors with an accessory role or circumstantial influence in this area (El Houdaïgui, 2003a: 27–29). Despite the persistent centralisation of decision-making processes, nongovernmental foreign policy actors have in the last two decades witnessed a 'gradual dynamisation' in various Arab countries, especially those, such as Morocco, where political liberalisation has gone further (El Houdaïgui, 2006: 1, 5). Whilst organisations of this type did not abandon their peripheral position, there was certainly a relative increase in the 'vulnerability, permeability or sensitivity of decision-making processes [...] to the views, actions and mobilisations of private actors' (Charillon, 2006: 4) and therefore some decline in the 'Arab states' ability to control the tensions between the internal and the external' (El Houdaïgui, 2006: 9).

In the case of Moroccan political parties, no substantial changes were observed in their contribution to foreign policymaking under Mohammed VI's reign. They continued to be largely confined to their historical functions as mouthpieces for official positions and discourse within international fora which were deemed to be close to them ideologically and, at domestic level, intermediaries between the regime and civil society when it was necessary to seek support from the latter. Episodes of criticism or opposition to the King's decisions by the parties related to the old National Movement (PI, USFP, PPS) had been the exception rather than the rule under Hassan II (Hernando de Larramendi, 1997: 140–142, 146).[19] Still, during both periods, the parties' limited opportunities to gain real *power* and to participate directly in decision-making through the national representative institutions (government and parliament) did not prevent them from asserting their demands and exerting some influence on the core decision-makers. Various authors have described these parties as 'simple intercessors in a completely closed political field' where they 'do not actually access more than the institutional threshold of consultation' (Santucci, 2006: 101, 107), although they have also highlighted their ability to 'put pressure on the existing government through mobilising public opinion on particular issues' (Willis, 2002a: 18–19). This means that, in practice, their performance and contribution to Moroccan foreign policy has resembled what is generally expected from pressure groups or lobbies, and has also not been too different from that of civil society associations (interview with Mohamed Darif, 30 October 2007; Daoud,

2007: 406). Depending on the circumstances, this could either enhance or constrain the state's official foreign policy orientations and guidelines established from the palace.

In addition, Moroccan political parties maintained their own foreign relations with fellow organisations from other countries, as well as within fora such as the Socialist International (USFP), the Centrist Democrat International (PI) or the General Congress of Arab Parties. Nevertheless, the messages conveyed during these contacts, especially on the Western Sahara issue, remained largely in keeping with official guidelines, which turned them into yet another form of parallel diplomacy. Even the Islamist PJD, which initially appeared to be an 'original' and 'atypical' force within the Moroccan political landscape (Mohsen-Finan and Zeghal, 2006: 79–80), hardly deviated from proclaimed 'national consensuses' during its time in opposition (Fernández-Molina, 2007) and later in government.

By contrast, various Moroccan civil society actors displayed a greater willingness to play a distinct role in foreign policymaking, or at least to maintain independent positions, irrespective of their influence. As on the domestic level (Catusse and Vairel, 2003: 85), the most politically significant sectors pursuing a discernible foreign policy discourse were three in number, namely the employers' organisations, certain human rights associations and the fraction of the Islamist movement that had not become institutionalised as a political party. The main organisation representing Moroccan businessmen, the General Confederation of Moroccan Entrepreneurs (CGEM), had emerged in the 1990s as a 'developmental business association' (Cammett, 2007: 1891) and had expressed a certain desire for autonomy from the regime until it ended up being recognised as a legitimate political actor (Catusse, 1999). It was then formally associated with the making and implementation of Moroccan foreign economic policy. From 2000s onwards, the CGEM set up an International Department, opened a permanent representation in Brussels and signed a memorandum of cooperation with the foreign ministry in order to coordinate the action of Moroccan businessmen and diplomats abroad (MAEC/CGEM, 2001; *La Vie Économique*, 28 March–3 April 2003; Belalami, 2006: 22, 62–63). In 2004, the CGEM considered itself to be fully incorporated into the 'club of economic diplomacy' (*CGEM Infos*, 10 September 2004), after playing an unprecedentedly prominent role in the free trade negotiations with the U.S. and Turkey. It also carved out a niche for itself in Morocco's relations with the EU (EU–Morocco Association Council, 2008a: 6), the Middle East, Latin America and Asia, as well as in Mohammed VI's *new African policy*, in all of which areas official discourse insisted on strengthening the economic dimension. After Mohammed VI's tour of Western Africa in February–March 2014, a Public-Private Joint Committee was established by the foreign ministry and the CGEM in order to follow up on the implementation of the economic agreements and projects which had been launched (*Le Matin*, 19 March 2014; *Aujourd'hui Le Maroc*, 4 April 2014; MAEC, 23 July 2014).

In another vein, the Moroccan human rights movement had historically been characterised by the fact that its work often bordered on political activism

(Rollinde, 2002; Feliu, 2004a). In particular, the Moroccan Association for Human Rights (AMDH) stood out under Mohammed VI's reign as a full-blown political actor occupying a core position within the opposition to the regime (*Le Journal Hebdomadaire*, 6–12 October 2007). In the foreign affairs domain, it presented itself as part of the 'anti-imperialist network' focusing on 'solidarity with the Palestinian and Iraqi people, and all peoples subject to the torments of imperialist domination, but also the fight against all forms of imperialist existence and domination here in our country' (*Attadamoun*, April 2008, January 2009). As a result, along with different Islamist and leftist groups, the AMDH was one of the leading organisations behind the protests witnessed in Morocco throughout these years relating to the Israeli–Palestinian conflict (autumn 2000, April 2002, June–July 2006, December 2008–January 2009), the wars in Iraq (February–March 2003) and Lebanon (July–August 2006) and U.S. foreign policy in the region (November 2004, February 2006) (interview with Abdelhamid Amine, 31 October 2007; interviews with Mohamed El Boukili, 20, 22 February 2006; interview with Abderrazak Drissi, 11 June 2009). These demonstrations had the peculiar feature of drawing much larger crowds than those that focused on strictly domestic issues, and revealed a 'paradoxical phenomenon of intense politicisation of ordinary citizens at transnational scale' (Bennani-Chraïbi, 2008: 147).

The most representative organisation from the non-institutionalised Moroccan Islamist movement was Al Adl wal Ihsan. Founded in the 1980s by charismatic dissident ideologist Abdessalam Yassine and never officially recognised by the Rabat authorities, it was often considered – and presented itself – as the most powerful and uncompromising force of opposition to the regime (Zeghal, 2005; Maddy-Weitzman, 2003). Its vision of Moroccan foreign policy and international affairs, which also strayed from the official discourse and the prevailing national consensus, was marked by the centrality of 'Muslim issues' proclaimed by Yassine (Belhaj, 2009: 153). A Support Committee for the Causes of the Ummah, reporting to the Political Circle, dealt with these priority matters and organised activities devoted, for example, to the Israeli–Palestinian conflict and the Iraq war (interview with Aziz Oudouni and Merieme Yafout, 4 December 2007). However, this ideology-driven concern coexisted with Al Adl's pragmatic interest in asserting itself as an interlocutor and partner of the EU and the U.S. Some of the visible figures of the movement proved to be fully aware of the debate underway in Western foreign ministries on the benefits and drawbacks of engaging 'moderate' Islamists in Arab countries. They accordingly emphasised the need for the EU to seek out new partners in southern Mediterranean countries, complaining that EU democracy assistance in Morocco was 'missing the real vectors of society' (Khakee, 2010: 10), while by contrast praising U.S. 'pragmatism'. Contacts with Washington and its embassy in Rabat were not a taboo for this organisation, which was 'open to dialogues with all parties'. Closer to home, these Islamists decried the 'chauvinism' of Moroccan official discourse on the Western Sahara conflict and relations with Algeria (interview with Nadia Yassine, 5 November 2007), but avoided taking a clear stance on the fundamental problem (Belhaj, 2009: 156).[20]

In addition to these general-purpose associations, other Moroccan civil society actors had a specific interest in various foreign policy and international affairs, including universalistic, migration, EU-related and pan-Arab issues, the Western Sahara conflict, relations with neighbouring Algeria and Spain, and even Judeo-Amazigh friendship. Furthermore, following the recommendations of the semi-official report on the fiftieth anniversary of Moroccan independence (Comité Directeur du Rapport, 2006: 55), there was great enthusiasm surrounding the creation of thinktanks dedicated to a greater or lesser extent to foreign policy (*Tel Quel*, 19–25 July 2008). The best known, listed according to their respective dates of creation, were the Club of Political Analysis (Rabat, 2001), linked to the USFP; the Moroccan Institute of International Relations (IMRI, Casablanca, 2004); the Moroccan Interdisciplinary Centre for Strategic and International Studies (CMIESI, Fes, 2007); the Royal Institute for Strategic Studies (IRES, Rabat, 2007), directly dependent on the palace (*Tel Quel*, 11–17 April 2009); and the Amadeus Institute (Rabat, 2008), chaired by Brahim Fassi Fihri, the son of the then foreign minister (*Maghreb Confidentiel*, 18 February 2010).

In sum, this chapter has highlighted the contrast between, on the one hand, the innovations announced by King Mohammed VI upon his succession to the throne concerning the prioritisation of the 'economic dimension' of foreign policy and the modernisation of the foreign ministry and service – including the training of a new technocratic elite and the renewal of the ambassador corps – and, on the other hand, the essential continuity in foreign policy decision-making processes, which have remained marked by the symbolic and practical hegemony of the King and various features of neopatrimonialism. Sub-systemic changes at the core of decision-making have included alterations in the balance of power within the circle of royal advisors, a temporary influence of top army officers and the open involvement of the external intelligence agency in the implementation of foreign policy, while the Moroccan government and parliament have maintained a subordinate and dependent role in what is still regarded as the *reserved domain* of the monarchy. This combination of traditional legitimising doctrines and practices with a streamlined economistic and technocratic façade appears to be the secret of the modernisation and international adaptation of Moroccan authoritarianism in the twenty-first century.

Notes

1 For a gloss by a pro-regime newspaper on Mohammed VI's vision of 'internal and external policies' as 'two sides of the same coin', and the 'permanent constructive dialectic' between both of them, see *Le Matin* (30 July 2009).
2 In the words of Fouad Ali El Himma, as reported in Brouksy (2014: 152).
3 See also Dafir and Haoudi (2014) and Dafir (2014).
4 See the 'sociology of Moroccan diplomacy' offered by Riziki Mohamed (2014).
5 See his memoirs in Filali (2008).
6 According to minister Benaissa, there were three lines of action: organisation and modernisation of the methodology for diplomatic action, management and restructuring of human resources, and restructuring of the ministry itself (MAEC, 19 April 2004).

7 The Moroccan foreign ministry's growing interest in public diplomacy started to be observed in 2008 (Régragui, 2013: 75–77).
8 According to Jennifer Rosenblum and I. William Zartman, the royal dominance in the realm of foreign policy largely explains 'why Morocco has not contributed international statesmen to world diplomacy as have some other global south countries' (2009: 331).
9 On the 'pro-American illusion' of part of the Moroccan elites and resistances to it by others, see Omar Saghi's blog, http://omarsaghi.com, 9 December 2014 (accessed on 9 December 2014).
10 Mohammed VI's Latin American tour in November and December 2004 led to the signing of cooperation agreements between the MoRAD and the diplomatic institutes of countries such as Brazil or Argentina (Vagni, 2010: 116, 143; MAEC, 17 April 2006).
11 The ambassadorial appointments in January 2009 and August 2010 included again some women and political party representatives (*Aujourd'hui Le Maroc*, 23 January 2009; *Jeune Afrique*, 25–31 January 2009; *Al Sabah*, 19 August 2010).
12 Another former Polisario leader was appointed to the embassy in Mexico in 2011 (*ABC*, 31 July 2011).
13 For an analysis of Mohammed VI's speeches on Moroccan foreign policy and the indications they contain concerning this policy's frame of reference (historical, identity and current sources), the roles played on the international stage and the tasks of the diplomatic service, see El Houdaïgui (2010).
14 See Moulay Rachid's blog, which provides information concerning all of his official activities from 2006 to 2008: http://princemoulayrachid.blogspot.com (accessed on 30 November 2008).
15 See *Al Ahdath Al Maghribia* (24 June 2011), Maghraoui (2011: 695–696), Madani *et al.* (2012), Bendourou *et al.* (2014).
16 See Youssef Amrani's website: www.youssef-amrani.ma (accessed on 28 February 2015).
17 See also Chambre des Représentants (1990).
18 See Youssef Amrani in IEMed (2009: 88).
19 On the participation of Moroccan political parties in foreign policy in times of Hassan II, see Ihraï (1986), Cheikh (1987) and Najih (1984).
20 On Nadia Yassine's role as 'ambassador' or unofficial international spokeswoman of the movement, see Belhaj (2009: 153–158, 268).

2 The tribulations of a 'territorial champion'
The international management of a changing Western Sahara conflict

When examining Morocco's foreign policy behaviour over the years, the Western Sahara conflict invariably appears as the ultimate core issue, with the international recognition and *legalisation* of Rabat's de facto annexation of the former Spanish colony representing the final goal. This is more than a foreign policy issue in the strict sense of the term: it is a politically existential question which is deeply rooted in the Moroccan political culture and is perceived in this country as being primarily a domestic matter. In practice, the complexity of the 'Sahara question' has always resulted from the Moroccan authorities' need to manage it simultaneously on two fronts, the *domestic* and the international. At the *domestic* level, Rabat has had to rule over an occupied territory which has been fully incorporated into its administrative structures as its 'Southern provinces' since 1976–1979, even though international law and the United Nations (UN) regarded (and regards) it as a non-self-governing territory awaiting decolonisation. Externally, Western Sahara has been a cross-cutting and almost ubiquitous issue on the Moroccan foreign policy agenda (Zartman, 2013: 55): even when it was not directly at issue in conversations or dealings with other states or international organisations, it could be indirectly discerned in the background of the relations conducted with these actors in various areas. Moreover, each international actor's support for the Moroccan positions on this conflict, by design or by default, appeared to be the acid test – a necessary and often even sufficient condition – for its good relations with Rabat.

The main research question examined in this chapter is how Moroccan foreign policy has reacted to the *inward turn* of the Western Sahara conflict since the turn of the millennium, assuming the dialectic between the *domestic* and international management of this issue by the Rabat authorities. The starting premise is that the key to analysing Morocco's performance in the Western Sahara conflict lies in the interplay, or permanent dialectic, between its *domestic* and international management, all the more so as, from the year 2000 onwards, the perceived centre of gravity of the conflict has moved – or returned – *inwards* to the heart of the disputed land out of which it originated. This domestic-international duality has also been reflected in the national role conceptions (Holsti, 1970) underpinning Moroccan foreign policy. First and foremost, the Western Sahara issue was at this point in time the main *raison d'être* for

Morocco's inveterate role as *champion of national territorial integrity*. Yet at the same time, Morocco's ultimate dependence on external recognition in order to legalise its control over this territory forced it to play much more cooperative roles vis-à-vis different international partners, such as *model student* of the European Union (EU), *good son* of France, *good neighbour* of Spain and *good ally* of the United States: 'Regarding this issue, Morocco tries to achieve two goals. Being fully part of the concert of nations and asserting its sovereignty over what the community of nations calls Western Sahara' (*Lakome*, 30 April 2013). Arguably, albeit to different and varying extents, there has always been degree of role conflict (Cantir and Kaarbo, 2013: 467–468, 2012: 10–11; Aggestam, 2006: 23) between a domestically defined (*ego*) national role conception (*territorial champion*) and externally set (*alter*) role expectations (*good student/ally*). This accounts for the swings between various roles which can be observed in Moroccan foreign policy on the Western Sahara issue: especially in times of crisis, this state can easily switch from the role of 'pampered child of the international community to the unenviable status of spoiler' (*Le Journal Hebdomadaire*, 25–31 October 2003).

A spatial and scalar shift which occurred gradually in the Western Sahara conflict from 2000 onwards added further complexity and compelling force to this equation. Change emerged from underneath a stalled *diplomatic* surface, as a result of a strategic reorientation and reshaping of the Sahrawi party. Its strategy evolved 'from one based on armed struggle and diplomacy conducted by the Polisario, to one based on civilian-led nonviolent resistance led by Sahrawis living inside the occupied territory' (Stephan and Mundy, 2006: 2). Parallels with the Palestinian movement's shift from exile to the Israeli-occupied territories in the 1980s with the First Intifada (1987), as well as with the South African anti-apartheid struggle, have also been highlighted (Barreñada, 2012; Zunes and Mundy, 2010: 163–164). At the very least, the realisation that internal Sahrawi pro-independence activists had become 'key players' in the conflict posed problems for all the parties (interview with Mohammed Madani, 5 June 2013). Stretching the argument, this spatial shift might even have involved a more essential transformation or change in the nature of the conflict according to conventional conflict typologies, i.e. a de facto partial evolution from the category of decolonising war of 'national liberation' or 'extra-systemic war' to what increasingly displays features of a 'state-nation war' or 'complex intra-state war' in a former colonial state carried out by 'identity' or 'communal' groups, 'often with the purpose of secession of separation from the state' (Holsti, 1996: 21; Singer, 1996: 43, 47). To be sure, the original decolonisation component of the Western Sahara issue remains fully valid and relevant, both de jure and de facto, but this does not detract from the interest in analysing its recent development *concurrently* as that of an identity/secession conflict (Ramsbotham *et al.*, 2011: 76).

While Morocco's *domestic* policies of *reconciliation* towards the population of the occupied territory largely complied with international expectations, they accidentally created opportunities for an *inward turn* of the conflict, which would eventually change the diplomatic game and place renewed strain on the Moroccan foreign policy. Based on this circularity between Moroccan actions at both levels and the succession between virtuous circles and vicious circles for this country's interests, it is possible to distinguish between four stages since 1999.[1] The first of them involved a period of relative political opening and decrease in repression in the territory controlled by Rabat, which was related to internal and international progress of the idea of autonomy under Moroccan sovereignty, or *third way* (1999–2003). The second stage was marked by a crisis within the Moroccan international negotiation strategy caused by the rejection of the Baker Plan II, which led to an explicit and definitive abandonment of the roadmap towards a referendum on self-determination (2003–2006). In the third stage, a policy of integration or *reconciliation* aimed at the Sahrawi population was implemented, which helped Rabat to regain the international initiative by promoting its new Autonomy Plan for the disputed territory (2006–2008). Finally, a new tightening up of the *domestic* management of the occupied territory was coupled with a strong setback for Moroccan positions on international level (2009 onwards).

From the viewpoint of Moroccan foreign policy, this timeline alternates between on the one hand 'offensive' stages during which Morocco actively promoted its positions, ensuring that its role of *territorial champion* was compatible with that of a *good student* of the international community (1999–2003 and 2006–2008), and on the other hand 'defensive' stages, during which the harmony between these roles was jeopardised and the *territorial champion* even turned into a *spoiler* on the international level (2003–2006 and 2009–2014).

Table 2.1 Chronology of Morocco's *domestic* and international management of the Western Sahara conflict, 1999 onwards

Stage	'Domestic' management	International/foreign policy management	
1999–2003	Political opening and decrease in repression; domestic progress of the *third way* approach	International progress of the *third way* approach (Baker Plans I and II)	Offensive
2003–2006	Impasse; emergence of internal Sahrawi activism	Spoiling of Baker Plan II; crisis of Moroccan negotiation strategy	Defensive
2006–2008	Policy of integration and *reconciliation* – (Re)creation of CORCAS – Autonomy Plan	International promotion and success of the Autonomy Plan	Offensive
2009–	New tensions in domestic governance and peaks of repression	Reduction of international advantage; crises with UN, U.S., European Parliament, etc.	Defensive

Domestic and international progress of the *'third way'* approach

With hindsight, the overall approach that has defined Moroccan foreign policy regarding the Western Sahara issue since Mohammed VI's accession to the throne has been the abandonment of the roadmap towards a referendum on self-determination for the Sahrawi people. This principle had been formally accepted by King Hassan II as a way for conflict resolution back in 1981, putting an end to the strategy of the 'closed issue' (1976–1981), and was enshrined by the UN Settlement Plan signed by both parties in 1991 at the time of the ceasefire declaration. Based on the uncertain premise of voluntary cooperation between the two parties (Jensen, 2012: 33), the implementation of this peace plan repeatedly ran up against the issue of determining the referendum electorate, on which Morocco and the Polisario Front had reached no prior agreement and asserted irreconcilable claims. The never-ending difficulties of defining who is a 'true Sahrawi' and/or a 'native' of the former Spanish colony (Jensen, 2012: 1; Daadaoui, 2008: 154–155; Veguilla 2012: 211–221) was coupled with both sides' political manipulation of the voter identification process – which had been originally conceived of as an 'innocuous' technical procedure (Jensen, 2012: 29–30, 49). Even the Houston Accords devised in 1997 by James Baker, the new personal envoy of the UN Secretary-General for Western Sahara (1997–2004), were of little use in overcoming the deadlock in the organisation of the referendum. In the absence of military operations, the battle had shifted to the issue of voter lists (Mohsen-Finan, 1997: 182).

Morocco's disengagement from the Settlement Plan roadmap was already being hinted at by some observers barely a year after Mohammed VI's ascent to the throne (Mezran, 2000), even though this was still far from being acknowledged as an official position to the international community. In the eyes of the outside world, the commitment was being formally kept through the UN-led peace process and voter identification. The latter concluded in 1999, and its result was very different from that expected by Rabat (*Le Journal*, 23–29 January 1999). Out of the 195,589 applications received, only 86,412 names were listed in the provisional electoral roll issued between July 1999 and January 2000, which represented a very limited increase on the 72,370 from the revised 1974 Spanish census. The list left out virtually all members of the three contested tribal groups (H41, H61 and J51/52) which Morocco had intended to add in order to secure a favourable electorate; more than 131,000 appeals were lodged (Jensen, 2012: 89–90). Against this backdrop, the double talk by the Rabat authorities was barely able to conceal the strategic change in course underway. While the interior ministry persisted in talking about the appeals submitted to the Identification Commission of the UN Mission for the Referendum in Western Sahara (MINURSO), the minister of Habous and Islamic Affairs assured the national press that 'the referendum [was] over [*le référendum est fini*] and the bay'a[2] linking the King of Morocco and the Sahrawis [prevailed] over the referendum' (*Le Journal*, 6–12 November 1999).

Alongside this adverse situation on the international level, in the first months of Mohammed VI's reign there were also some novel *domestic* developments within the Western Sahara territory under Rabat's control. The first of them was the cycle of protests that erupted in Laayoune in the autumn of 1999. The accession to the throne of the new monarch in Rabat opened up a window of opportunity which enabled small-scale Sahrawi protests to intensify. In September, the disproportionate repression of a peaceful sit-in of Sahrawi students expressing social demands (scholarships and transport subsidies) eventually led to violent riots lasting for several weeks. The first demonstrators were joined by unemployed Sahrawi graduates, former political prisoners or 'disappeared' persons and workers from the phosphate mines. In addition, it was more surprising and worrying for the Rabat authorities that the protest's supporters also included some impoverished Moroccan/northerner settlers from the outskirts of Laayoune and ethnic Sahrawis living in the southern regions of Morocco, outside the disputed territory (Shelley, 2004: 115–121; Smith, 2005: 557; Stephan and Mundy, 2006: 11–13). This brought to the fore long-simmering socioeconomic grievances that had gone unnoticed for years in the occupied territory, as well as a potential reshaping of fluid social and identity cleavages.

The new King and other Moroccan authorities provided a multifaceted response to this crisis. First, a new discourse began to take shape that interpreted Sahrawi protests as exclusively stemming from socioeconomic grievances, thus stripping them off any 'political' (i.e. pro-independence) content.[3] The national media received governmental instructions to avoid portraying any expression of frustration or dissatisfaction as a sign of support for 'separatism': 'One can be Moroccan and be in rage [*en colère*] and one can also get indignant and protest being Moroccan' (*Le Journal*, 6–12 November 1999, 2–8 October 1999).[4]

Second, the brutal repression of the demonstrations in Laayoune led to the dismissal of Hassan II's powerful interior minister, who had hitherto been the main architect of *domestic* Western Sahara policy, Driss Basri. This involved an unheard-of official recognition of 'mistakes in the governmental action in the Sahara' and the need to 'hold accountable those responsible' (*Le Journal*, 6–12 November 1999). By extension, the fall of this major player was interpreted as evidence of a comprehensive rethinking of the Moroccan strategy in this area, and the end of a 'system' that had failed in its use of both the 'stick' (harsh repression) and the 'carrot' (governance of the territory, economic investments, etc.) (*Le Journal*, 2–8 October 1999). This was presented as the start of a new era of conciliation – or 'reconciliation' – between the Moroccan authorities and the population of Western Sahara, which was to be marked by the 'abandonment of the security-based approach' (Bouqentar, 2010: 328) and a 'policy of appeasement on the ground' (Sater, 2010: 130). Immediate actions in this direction included the establishment of a Royal Commission for the Monitoring of Saharan Affairs, which brought together local elected representatives and civilian and military appointees, the first task of whom was to hear complaints concerning the repression of recent protests.

Third, a more gradual but crucial transformation on Moroccan domestic level came with the progress made by the idea of a *third way* (autonomy under

Moroccan sovereignty) towards the resolution the Western Sahara conflict. The exact genealogy of this novel formula is difficult to determine. Different sources attribute its authorship (or resurrection) alternatively to the U.S. diplomacy under the Bill Clinton administration (specifically, to the Assistant Secretary of State for Near Eastern Affairs, Martin Indyk), to the UN Secretary-General Kofi Annan and his personal envoy, James Baker (Zoubir and Benabdallah-Gambier, 2004: 54–56; Theofilopoulou, 2006: 7–9, 16), or even to the Rabat authorities themselves (*Le Journal Hebdomadaire*, 19–25 July 2003). The fact is that this approach brought together the preferences of, on the one hand, the UN Secretary-General and the main international powers and, on the other hand, the Moroccan authorities. The former were increasingly convinced that the Settlement Plan was not viable, and were hence reluctant to enforce it. The latter were rapidly dissociating themselves from the referendum roadmap, frustrated by the results of the voter identification, having lost the only top official who could have been capable of controlling (or rigging) the results of such election – the dismissed Basri (Mundy 2007; ICG 2007b: 14; Amar, 2009: 103) – and being alarmed by the outbreak of protests in the disputed territory. Therefore, Morocco's foreign policy roles as *territorial champion* and *good student* of the international community became increasingly compatible, thus enabling an 'offensive bargaining strategy' (Zartman, 2013: 66–68) to be pursued.

The young independent Moroccan press played a central role in promoting the *third way* within a rapidly expanding public sphere. The weekly *Le Journal* acted almost as a thinktank in advocating and disseminating this novel approach well before it was adopted as the Moroccan official position and supported by the international community (Amar, 2009: 185).[5] The penetration of the idea into the state's decision-making structures and diplomacy only became official at a meeting between the parties held in Berlin in September 2000 when, under pressure from Baker's team (Zunes and Mundy, 2010: 222),[6] the country's representatives for the first time stated their willingness to engage in 'a sincere and frank dialogue' with the Polisario Front with the prospect of a 'decentralisation' for Western Sahara.[7] This meant that the taboo had been broken on negotiating directly with what was euphemistically called 'the other party' for fear that any official contact with it represented a sign of recognition (although, behind the scenes, there had already been several meetings of this kind since 1997). This announcement was also preceded by the relaunch of the old idea of decentralisation in the royal speech on Throne Day (speech by Mohammed VI, Rabat, 30 July 2000; *Le Journal*, 7–13 October 2000). In this way, the *domestic* management of the Western Sahara issue was placed at the service of its international management.

Le Journal immediately applauded a twofold change in strategy, which it was argued would bring many benefits to Rabat on international level (ingratiating Morocco with Baker, making it easier for the U.S. and France to defend Moroccan interests) and, at home, could even represent 'an opportunity for democracy' (*Le Journal*, 7–13 October 2000). By contrast, the Moroccan political parties were initially puzzled and responded with ultranationalist reflex positions to the political U-turn in which they had barely been involved. Even those which were part of the governmental coalition had not been sufficiently briefed.[8]

On the international level, consideration of alternatives to the Settlement Plan began to be hinted at in the reports of the UN Secretary-General in 2000 (UNSC, S/2000/461, 22 May 2000), although without making any reference to the *third way* or presenting any definite proposal. The Security Council seconded Annan's call to 'explore all ways and means' to resolve the conflict, overcoming the 'multiple problems relating to the implementation of the Settlement Plan' (UNSC, S/RES/1301, 31 May 2000). Morocco seized the opportunity to move its new approach forward and, according to some sources, presented an initial autonomy proposal to the UN in March 2001.[9] The first tangible result of all these exploratory manoeuvres was the Framework Agreement on the Status of Western Sahara, also known as Baker Plan I, which Annan's personal envoy presented to the parties in May of that year and the Security Council discussed a month later. Some reports noted that the plan's content was directly inspired by the previous Moroccan draft (*Afrol News*, 27 June 2001; Callies de Salies, 2003: 169; Zoubir and Benabdallah-Gambier, 2004: 57). However, its originality lay in maintaining the aim of holding a referendum after a transitional period of up to five years during which an autonomy formula would be applied. In other words, it was supposed to be a mixed solution combining elements of the now Rabat-promoted *third way* (autonomy) and the legal requirements for self-determination for the Saharawi people provided in the Settlement Plan (referendum).

Having been conceived of as a mere framework (preliminary) agreement intended to serve as a basis for negotiation between the parties, the Baker Plan I only delineated the broad outlines of temporary autonomy for Western Sahara under Moroccan sovereignty and the general conditions applicable to the referendum which would determine the final status of the territory. The autonomy formula was based on three pillars: first, power-sharing between the autonomous Authority of Western Sahara (exclusive competence over local governmental administration, territorial budget, law enforcement, internal security, the economy, infrastructure, social welfare, culture and education) and the Moroccan state (exclusive competence over foreign relations, national security and external defence, control over firearms and the 'preservation of the territorial integrity against secessionist attempts'); second, the legal relationship between the two levels (all laws passed or implemented by the autonomous Authority had to 'respect and comply with the Constitution of the Kingdom of Morocco'); and third, the separation of powers within the autonomous Authority and the mode of election or appointment to its corresponding bodies (Executive, Assembly, courts). The final referendum would be held within five years of the date on which implementation of the plan started and all persons who had been full-time residents of the territory for the preceding one year would be qualified to vote (UNSC, S/2001/613, 20 June 2001, annex I). The most significant omission was that the question to be voted on – and the inclusion of independence among the options – was not specified (Zunes and Mundy, 2010: 223). This ambiguity, together with the large scope of the final electorate, considerably biased the plan in favour of Morocco.

Morocco immediately expressed its in-principle agreement with the Baker Plan I: the temporary autonomy formula proposed fitted in with its view of the *third way* and the conditions of the final referendum were vague enough to allow it to be turned into a simple confirmatory act that would permanently validate such provisional solution. Conversely, the Polisario Front and Algeria rejected the plan outright, arguing that it was unbalanced and biased toward integration, ignoring the principle of self-determination in breach of Baker's own mandate (UNSC, S/2001/613, 20 June 2001, annexes II and IV). The UN Security Council did not approve it but quite clearly 'encouraged' the parties 'to discuss the draft Framework Agreement and to negotiate any specific changes they would like to see in this proposal, as well as to discuss any other proposal for a political solution' (UNSC, S/RES/1359, 29 June 2001). At this point, Mohammed VI became so optimistic as to state that he had 'settled the Sahara issue' (interview with Mohammed VI in *Le Figaro*, 4 September 2001) – shortly before travelling to the territory himself for the first time.

In fact, the diplomatic battle had only begun. The Polisario and Algeria deployed all means at their disposal to halt the Baker Plan I, taking special advantage of the marked U.S. rapprochement with Algiers occurring in parallel (in June 2001, Abdelaziz Bouteflika became the first Algerian President to visit Washington in 16 years, and in addition returned only four months later) (*Le Journal Hebdomadaire*, 21–27 July 2001). Morocco's measures to try to save this plan in extremis included the King's call for 'all stakeholders' to 'show a positive attitude toward this path that [had] enjoyed international unanimity' (speech by Mohammed VI, Rabat, 6 November 2001). There was a discreet meeting in Washington between foreign minister Mohamed Benaissa and U.S. President George W. Bush, while networks of 'informal diplomacy' were also activated (*Le Journal Hebdomadaire*, 10–16 November 2001).

However, none of the actors involved changed its stance. After using up the additional five months granted in order to continue exploring this solution and find a compromise between the parties, the UN Secretary-General submitted a new report to the Security Council in which he acknowledged that the Baker Plan I was not feasible and proposed four alternatives: resuming attempts to implement the Settlement Plan (but this time 'without requiring the concurrence of both parties'), revising the Baker Plan I taking account of the concerns expressed by Algeria and the Polisario (now also 'on a non-negotiable basis'), exploring the possibility of partitioning the disputed territory or simply recognising the UN's failure to solve this conflict and terminating MINURSO (UNSC, S/2002/178, 19 February 2002; Mohsen-Finan, 2002: 9–11). In the end, the most significant novelty was the suggestion that it was necessary to move from a consensus-based and non-binding settlement approach to an enforced solution (Theofilopoulou, 2006: 10–11; Jensen, 2012: 97–98).

Morocco's rejection of the Baker Plan II and the ensuing strategic crisis

The path eventually chosen by the UN was to revise the Baker Plan I and to prepare a new proposal for a political solution whilst, significantly, ruling out the possibility of imposing it on the parties in the event that they did not consent to it. The second version of this mixed plan involving temporary autonomy and a final referendum, which was much more polished and detailed from a legal standpoint, was drafted by the UN Secretary-General's personal envoy in the utmost confidentiality. It was not unveiled to the public until May 2003, when Annan included it in his report to the Security Council. What was now called the Peace Plan for Self-Determination of the People of Western Sahara – a significant change of title – and informally known as Baker Plan II involved an agreement between Morocco and the Polisario Front which should also be signed by neighbouring countries Algeria and Mauritania as well as the UN itself.

The transitional power-sharing between the autonomous Western Sahara Authority and the Moroccan state included two lists of issues under each authority's exclusive competence that were identical to those of the Baker Plan I except for three significant limitations for Rabat: first, Morocco's control over firearms in the territory should not prevent 'the duly authorised use of weapons by the law enforcement authorities of the Western Sahara Authority'; second, Morocco's 'right to preserve territorial integrity' should 'not authorise any action whatsoever that would prevent, suppress, or stifle peaceful public debate, discourse or campaign activity, particularly during any election or referendum period'; and third, Morocco's authority over foreign relations should be exercised 'in consultation with the Western Sahara Authority'. A second novel provision was the establishment, within the Western Sahara Authority, of a Supreme Court that should 'have jurisdiction to adjudicate the compatibility of any law of Western Sahara with this plan' and 'be the final authority in interpreting the law of Western Sahara'. This was coupled with a new reference to overall legal consistency with 'internationally recognised human rights standards' – ahead of the Moroccan constitution's guarantees.

Finally, the conditions applicable to the final referendum to be held four or five years after the plan took effect were defined more precisely. The vote should be 'organised and conducted' by the UN and include the two options provided for in the Settlement Plan (independence and integration into Morocco) plus any other agreed by the parties. The electorate would consist of adults identified as being qualified to vote in 1999 by MINURSO's Identification Commission, those included in the repatriation list of the United Nations High Commissioner for Refugees (UNHCR) or persons continuously resident in Western Sahara since 30 December 1999, with no possibility of appeal (UNSC, S/2003/565, 23 May 2003, annex II).

Overall, the arrangement for provisional power-sharing between the two authorities and the electorate for the final vote had hardly changed between the Baker Plan I and the Baker Plan II, although the latter was more balanced and stipulated, as a critical difference, that the UN Secretary-General would have authority to issue binding interpretations in the event of disagreement between the parties (Jensen, 2012: 101): 'Unlike the settlement plan, it does not require the consent of both parties at each and every stage of implementation' (UNSC, S/2003/565, 23 May 2003: 10). Before disclosing and submitting the new proposal to the Security Council, the UN personal envoy had discussed it in confidence with the parties and the neighbouring countries. King Mohammed VI received Baker for this purpose in January 2003. At the time, foreign minister Benaissa said that Morocco would examine the initiative with 'constructive spirit' and 'full readiness' to cooperate with the UN (MAEC, 14 January 2003). Rabat's acceptance of this plan was almost taken for granted, given its similarities with the Baker Plan I, the imprint of the Moroccan idea of the *third way* and, above all, the establishment of a broad electorate for the final referendum, as this country had always demanded.

However, surprisingly, Morocco was quick to express its misgivings, as officially reflected in the 'observations' submitted to the UN in the spring of 2003. The main aim of this document was 'to avoid any confusion between this political solution, or "third way", and the Settlement Plan'; that is, to re-establish 'the initial architecture of the political solution: a viable alternative to the options set out in the Settlement Plan' (UNSC, S/2003/565, 23 May 2003, annex III: 24). Therefore, Rabat objected to the very essence of Baker's plans as mixed or intermediate proposals falling between the *third way* (autonomy) and the Settlement Plan (referendum). The aspects that were problematic for this country were, according to the document submitted to the UN:

- General issues: the very title of the Baker Plan II (mentioning 'self-determination' but not 'political solution') and its structure; the conditions governing its entry into force.
- Regarding the final referendum: the choices available for the vote, which were taken in principle from the Settlement Plan; the conditions for intervention by the UN and its relationship with the Moroccan authorities; certain criteria used to define the electorate; the conditions under which the results would be respected.
- Regarding the transitional autonomy formula: the one-year period allowed for the election of the executive and legislative bodies of the 'local authority', which might create a 'legal vacuum or lacuna' in the administration of the territory; the exception to the 'prohibition of secessionist activities' regarding 'speeches and declarations during the election period'; the exception regarding the use of arms by the 'local authority' in law enforcement; the use of the expression 'foreign relations of Western Sahara'; the relationship between the directly elected chief executive and the legislative body; the legal 'subsidiarity principle' in favour of the 'local authority'; the 'advanced federal model' inspiring the judicial power of this authority, which was 'difficult to apply in Morocco, a country whose judicial system is unified and centralised'; the degree of independence of a Supreme Court of

Western Sahara whose members would be designated by the territory's executive and legislature; guarantees concerning respect for internationally recognised human rights standards; the system governing the election of the chief executive and the assembly of the 'local authority', based on a more limited electorate than that of the final referendum; judicial guarantees for these elections.
- Other issues: the conditions governing any change in the status of the territory; the release of prisoners of war and political prisoners; the reduction and confinement of troops following the plan's entry into force; the Secretary-General's binding authority to interpret the plan.

(UNSC, S/2003/565, 23 May 2003, annex III)

In April, Prime Minister Driss Jettou engaged in a consultation exercise with the main political parties represented in parliament in order to present the outlines of the Baker Plan II and the official Moroccan position. The parties' reaction was unanimous: closing ranks around a decision in which they had not participated, they all considered the UN proposal to be inadmissible simply on the grounds that it questioned Morocco's 'national sovereignty' or 'territorial integrity' (i.e. by including independence as an option in the final referendum). By contrast, contrary to the positions in 2000, the prospect of autonomy for Western Sahara within the context of a global decentralisation of the Moroccan state now seemed to have been generally accepted. A new national consensus had emerged around the *third way* (no to a referendum, yes to autonomy) as was shown by the statements of the Istiqlal Party (PI) and the Justice and Development Party (PJD) (*Le Journal Hebdomadaire*, 19–25 April 2003).[10] Once again however, the vagueness of the parties' arguments proved that they were only superficially aware of what was at stake in international negotiations concerning Western Sahara, which continued to be treated in Morocco as the exclusive domain (*domaine réservé*) of the monarchy. A more substantial and original contribution to the public debate at this stage came from civil society and, more specifically, the Collectif Sahara-Maghreb, which advocated a win–win solution for the Western Sahara conflict based on the democratisation, decentralisation and regional integration of the Maghreb states (Collectif Sahara-Maghreb, 2003; interview with Driss Moussaoui, 21 February 2006).

The day of reckoning that would test the firmness of Morocco's rejection of the Baker Plan II came in June 2003, shortly before it was due to be discussed at the UN Security Council, when the Polisario Front unexpectedly changed its stance and agreed to the proposal (three months before it had expressed an in-principle disagreement). This diplomatic bombshell, which had been brought about as a result of Algerian and Spanish pressure on the Front's leadership (Hernando de Larramendi, 2008: 191; Smith, 2005: 552), was interpreted as an attempt to turn the tables and isolate Rabat, placing it in an awkward position in the eyes of the international community – an area in which it had steadily kept the initiative in previous years (*Le Journal Hebdomadaire*, 19–25 July 2003). The usual *good student* had suddenly become a *spoiler* blocking efforts at conflict resolution. The Moroccan resolve to maintain its refusal to the end also provoked surprise domestically: 'The Baker Plan II is far from being the worst thing that can happen to us. Why then allow the Polisario and Algeria to seize the opportunity and confine ourselves to the same old fearful attitude that blocks everything?' (Abraham Serfaty in *Le Journal Hebdomadaire*, 19–25 July 2003).

In fact, leaving aside the battery of official objections or 'observations' submitted to the UN, Morocco's staunch denial appeared to be driven by less rational political fears and even an unconfessed *fear of peace*. Rationally, the Baker Plan II seemed to be overall favourable to Moroccan interests, mainly due the broad electorate established for the final referendum, which included all persons who had continuously resided in the Western Sahara territory over the past four years, regardless of their geographical or tribal origin, and thus a large number of Moroccan/northerner settlers who, 'except for surprises', should support integration into Morocco (*Le Journal Hebdomadaire*, 19–25 July 2003). Less rationally, the Rabat authorities feared that a victory by Polisario officials in the first elections to the Western Sahara Authority (Zunes and Mundy, 2010: 230), coupled with the restrictions on Moroccan powers provided for under this plan's autonomy formula (inability to prevent public debate, establishment of a Supreme Court of Western Sahara, legal precedence of international human rights standards) would lead to a loss of control over the territory during the transitional stage and the risk of victory for the independence option in the final referendum (Hernando de Larramendi, 2008: 191–192). Arithmetically, the latter scenario could only come to pass in the event that northerner settlers endorsed the 'separatist theses', either due to deep dissatisfaction with the regime in Rabat or under the influence of the new autonomous institutions and the Sahrawis newly returned from exile in the Polisario-ruled Tindouf refugee camps (*Le Journal Hebdomadaire*, 8–14 November 2003).[11] These concerns had been aggravated by surveys conducted in the major cities of Western Sahara at the end of Hassan II's reign (Mohsen-Finan, 2010: 560) and some northerners' support for the Sahrawi protests in Laayoune in 1999 (Smith, 2005: 557). Furthermore, the fact that the final referendum was to be organised and conducted by the UN ruled out any possibility of controlling or rigging its results, as Basri had apparently intended in the 1990s. The Moroccan deputy foreign minister, Taieb Fassi Fihri, went as far as to say unofficially that the Baker Plan II was a 'scheduled march towards independence' (Tuquoi, 2006: 99).[12]

As of June 2003, and following the surprising acceptance of Baker Plan II by the Polisario Front, Morocco's foreign policy strategy consisted in resisting repeated international pressure to review its position and virtually 'pleading' with the UN Security Council members – starting with France and the U.S. – not to approve this proposal in a form that enabled it to be enforced against the wishes of the parties (Zoubir and Benabdallah-Gambier, 2004: 68). U.S. diplomats simply did not understand why Morocco blocked the plan in such an uncompromising way: 'The categorical rejection expressed by Mohamed Benaissa remains an enigma', said a member of team of the U.S. ambassador to the UN, John D. Negroponte. Negroponte circulated a forceful first draft resolution which stated that the Security Council 'endorsed' the Baker Plan II and urged the parties to 'fully cooperate' with the Secretary-General and his personal envoy, which was perceived in Morocco as a 'surprising turnaround' or even a 'stab in the back' from Washington (*Le Journal Hebdomadaire*, 19–25 July 2003).

In the end, thanks mainly to the help of France, Morocco was able to water Resolution 1495 down significantly: although the Baker Plan II was described as an 'optimum political solution', the text that was finally adopted unanimously on 31 July did not 'endorse' but merely 'supported' it (UNSC, S/RES/1495, 31 July 2003). The resolution also specified that it fell under Chapter VI of the UN Charter, which deals with non-binding means for the peaceful settlement of disputes, such as mediation and good offices (Jensen, 2012: 102). The effect of all of this was to give the Baker Plan II political endorsement but no legally binding force. Ambassador Negroponte himself said at the meeting that this resolution '[represented] a considered recommendation of the Council to the parties and neighbouring States but [did] not constitute an imposition.'[13] Rabat expressed 'satisfaction' that the final decision '[enshrined] the sacred and fundamental principle whereby nothing can be implemented if it has not been first negotiated and accepted by the parties' (MAEC, 1 August 2003). In any case, the Security Council's unanimous support for the Baker Plan II represented an unprecedented setback for Moroccan foreign policy, whose decision-makers were accused by the national independent press of incompetence and 'lack of an articulated vision' (*Le Journal Hebdomadaire*, 19–25 July 2003).

Morocco continued to avoid responding to Resolution 1495 in the following months, despite growing pressure from the UN Secretary-General who imposed an ultimatum, setting the end of the year as a deadline for Rabat's acceptance and implementation of the Baker Plan II (UNSC, S/2003/1016, 16 October 2003). This earned Annan harsh criticism from the Moroccan permanent representative to the UN, Mohammed Bennouna, who accused him of having 'deviated from his neutrality and objectivity' by ignoring the fact that compliance with the resolution could not be imposed on the parties, in a letter sent to the president of the Security Council and Ambassador Negroponte (MAEC, 2003a, 22 October 2003, 28 October 2003). The following speech by Mohammed VI on the anniversary of the Green March was to insist again on the Secretary-General's 'inappropriate interpretation' of Resolution 1495 (speech by Mohammed VI, Rabat, 6 November 2003).

Morocco was certainly confronted for some time with the spectre of international isolation and U.S. incomprehension due to its rejection of the Baker Plan II. Independent domestic voices heightened their criticism and wondered about possible 'collateral damage' due to the fact that, in 'in neglecting the UN, Moroccan diplomacy [had] pretended to ignore the U.S. position' (*Le Journal Hebdomadaire*, 25–31 October 2003). Yet in the end, these were nothing but temporary predicaments, since both Paris and Washington came to Morocco's assistance by reiterating the dismissal of any 'imposed solution'. Statements were made to this effect both by President Jacques Chirac and the U.S. Assistant

Secretary of State for Near Eastern Affairs, William J. Burns, during their trips to Morocco in October 2003 (AFP, 28 October 2003). President Bush had also offered similar guarantees to Mohammed VI during their meeting at the UN General Assembly in September (Jensen, 2012: 103). The healthy status of relations between Morocco and the U.S. was amply demonstrated the following year. Furthermore, in mid-2004, shortly after the UN Secretary-General reaffirmed in a new report that the Baker Plan II continued to be 'the best political solution to the conflict' (UNSC, S/2004/325, 23 April 2004),[14] his personal envoy Baker resigned from his position. Although a communiqué of the Moroccan foreign ministry officially 'regretted' this decision (MAEC, 12 June 2004), the Rabat authorities could not hide their enthusiasm for what they saw as a victory for their positions. According to minister Benaissa himself, 'the resignation of [...] Mr. James Baker is the result of the tenacity of the Moroccan diplomacy and its rejection of certain principles which threaten Morocco's territorial integrity' (MAEC, 12 June 2004).

At this point (2003–2004) a new phase in the Western Sahara conflict started, which was marked by the stagnation of UN initiatives to find a political solution. In order to compensate for its blocking of the Baker Plan II and to regain the initiative on international level, Morocco was obliged to put forward a credible alternative proposal, which necessarily entailed a stage of redefinition of its strategy. The novelty was that, from this moment on, the Rabat authorities would openly advocate a permanent autonomy solution excluding the holding of a self-determination referendum, i.e. which constituted a final result and not a mere transitional formula (Hernando de Larramendi, 2010): 'The Kingdom of Morocco cannot agree to a transitional period, marked by uncertainty as to the final status of the territory. [...] The final nature of the autonomy solution is not negotiable' (UNSC, S/2004/325, 23 April 2004, annex I: 10–11). The tacit abandonment of the referendum roadmap, which had marked Moroccan foreign policy since Mohammed VI's accession to the throne, now became explicit.

An initial attempt to advance in the direction of autonomy came with the 'Contribution of the Kingdom of Morocco to the negotiation of a mutually acceptable political solution to the Sahara issue', which deputy foreign minister Fassi Fihri presented to the UN in December 2003. This non-paper included

> A project for a statute of autonomy for the Region of the Sahara which is constructive and capable of favouring the conclusion of a final and realistic agreement, allowing thus the populations of the Sahara to freely and democratically manage their own affairs, within respect for the sovereignty of the Kingdom of Morocco, its territorial integrity and its national unity.
> (MAEC, 2003b)

Under this hypothetical statute, which was to be submitted to a referendum and subsequently annexed to the Moroccan constitution, the power-sharing arrangements between the bodies of the 'Sahara Region' (Regional Legislative Assembly, Executive and local courts) and the Moroccan state were inspired by those contained in the Baker plans, but were far more conservative in terms of self-governance for Western Sahara: the proposal would significantly reduce the autonomy of the judiciary in the territory; eliminate the restrictions on Morocco's powers under the Baker Plan II regarding the preservation of territorial integrity, control over firearms and the foreign relations of the territory; and, even more significantly, assign management of strategic natural resources and the media to the Rabat government. For this reason, Baker rejected the document and asked Morocco to review it. A second, almost identical proposal suffered the same fate in April 2004 (Zunes and Mundy, 2010: 236–237). Over the following years, some of the major international allies of Morocco – such as France, the U.S. and Spain – encouraged the Rabat authorities to develop a more viable and 'credible' version of their autonomy project that was capable of receiving their support (ICG, 2007b: 6).[15]

In parallel, during this phase of impasse and redefinition of their strategy at international level (2003–2006), the Moroccan authorities witnessed some profound political transformations in the disputed territory which were to complicate their future *domestic* and international management of the Western Sahara issue. However stuck or 'frozen' negotiations concerning conflict resolution might have been on the diplomatic level, there was no status quo whatsoever on the ground (Barreñada, 2012). A strategic reorientation and reshaping of the Sahrawi party (broadly speaking) was underway, as nonviolent resistance (Mundy and Zunes, 2014; Dann, 2014) and protests inside the Moroccan-occupied territory gradually gained prominence, received international recognition and thus became central to the conflict. This *inward turn* of the conflict not only put renewed strain on Rabat's *domestic* governance of its 'Southern provinces', but also unprecedentedly complicated Moroccan foreign policy. The organisational basis for this emerging internal Sahrawi activism was provided by civil society organisations that operated without legal recognition and focused on the field of human rights, which were showing increasingly open pro-independence stances and connections with the Polisario Front – albeit emphasising their organisational autonomy. The two leading groups created during those years were the Sahrawi Association of Victims of Gross Human Rights Violations Committed by the Moroccan State (ASVDH) and the Collective of Sahrawi Defenders of Human Rights (CODESA). Most worrying for Rabat, the framing of their struggle in universalistic terms allowed them to achieve considerable international visibility, recognition and legitimisation (Brouksy, 2008).

Paradoxically enough, the breeding ground for this internal pro-independence Sahrawi activism could be found to a considerable extent in Morocco's own policies of liberalisation, memory and *reconciliation* which, since the 1990s, had opened up several windows of opportunity (as unintended consequences) through which this budding movement sought to evolve and become empowered. Chief among them were, in Mohammed VI's times, the new memory policies and the conciliatory approach to Western Sahara following his accession to the throne and the Laayoune protests in 1999, the development of an autonomy plan for the disputed territory and the flawed experience of *transitional justice* led by the Equity and Reconciliation Commission (IER) in 2004. All of these partial measures of recognition, which sought to give international and domestic credibility to the *third way* – and to convince the Sahrawis of the benefits of integration into Morocco – could also backfire for Moroccan interests (Fernández-Molina, 2015), as was clear from the protests cycle that was dubbed the Sahrawi Intifada in the spring of 2005.

In late May 2005, following its violent break-up by the Moroccan police, a small rally in Laayoune opposing the transfer of a Sahrawi prisoner sparked off an unprecedented cycle of demonstrations, repression and riots (Smith, 2005: 545–546, 558; Solà-Martín, 2007: 402; Mundy, 2007). In addition to the role played by emerging Sahrawi groups such as the ASVDH, four things were new in this episode: the magnitude of the protests in terms of numerical participation, extension over time and geographical scope (they spread to other Western Saharan cities, ethnic Sahrawi communities in southern Morocco and Sahrawi students in Moroccan universities), the open use of pro-independence symbols and slogans rarely displayed before in the occupied territory, the prominent involvement of Sahrawi youths and high school students, and the unusual level of attention received from the international community due to the new opportunities for communication opened up by mobile phones and the internet (Gimeno, 2013: 23).

The 'reconciliation' strategy and the Autonomy Plan

In any case, it was from 2006 onwards that the Moroccan authorities fully engaged with the *reconciliation* strategy towards the Sahrawi population, which coincided with their attempt to regain the offensive on international level following the retreat and uncertainty caused by the rejection of the Baker Plan II. At this stage, the novelties in Rabat's management of the conflict at *domestic* and international level – the resurrection of the Royal Consultative Council for Saharan Affairs (CORCAS) and the launch of what was supposed to be the final Autonomy Plan for the territory – were once again intertwined.

The CORCAS was one of the consultative councils under the immediate authority of the King – lacking any structural relationship with the Moroccan government and parliament – which Mohammed VI had promoted since his accession to the throne (Fernández-Molina, 2011a). In fact, it was not a new institution but the resurrection of a long-inactive body set up by Hassan II in 1981. Its activity as of 2006 was to be twofold, involving domestic and international aspects. First, this council's (re)creation could not be dissociated from the preparation of the new Autonomy Plan, to which it actively contributed and devoted several extraordinary sessions (MAP, 26 May 2006, 16 December 2006; El Messaoudi and Bouabid, 2008: 11–12). Subsequently, the CORCAS was to take on functions of parallel and even official diplomacy: in 2007 and 2008, it was placed at the service of the governmental campaign to promote the Autonomy Plan[16] and the subsequent negotiations with the

Polisario Front in Manhasset (New York). Indeed, one of the arguments used by Morocco to defend its project was 'the extension of the space of participation to the management of local affairs and the emergence of new elites capable of taking on responsibilities' (speech by Mohammed VI, Laayoune, 25 March 2006).

As regards the drafting of the Autonomy Plan in question, it had been announced in a royal address in November 2005 and presented as 'a broad process of dialogue and consultation with political and social actors' (speech by Mohammed VI, Rabat, 6 November 2005). In order to regain the initiative in the eyes of the international community, the Moroccan authorities intended to count on the collaboration of all national forces in order to devise a second proposal for a permanent autonomy solution which was more solid and streamlined than the one from December 2003. The political parties also engaged with this process by offering some suggestions (El Messaoudi and Bouabid, 2008: 9–10; interview with Réda Benkhaldoun, 10 January 2007) and participated in a preliminary diplomatic campaign to publicise the ongoing work in October 2006 (*L'Économiste*, 18 October 2006, 31 October 2006). The project drafted by the CORCAS was presented to the King in December. A Moroccan delegation travelled to France, Spain, the U.S., the United Kingdom, Germany and Russia in order to provide verbal information concerning its contents (MAEC, 5 February 2007, 8 February 2007), shortly before it was presented to the UN Secretary-General, Ban Ki-moon, and the members of the Security Council in March and April 2007.

The Autonomy Plan was, in principle, a document conceived of as a basis for negotiation in subsequent direct talks between the two parties, the result of which would be submitted to a referendum involving the (unspecified) 'populations concerned'. This was how it sought to formally comply with the international law requirements for self-determination (Solà-Martín, 2007: 402–403). The hypothetical power-sharing outlined between the 'Sahara Autonomous Region' and the Moroccan state, and the political institutions of the former did not differ significantly from those of the Moroccan proposal from 2003, although the list of issues under Rabat's 'exclusive competence' was less exhaustive this time. The main novelties in 2007 were the removal of any indication or assumption that the autonomy formula would be temporary,[17] which implied greater distancing from Baker's plans, and the introduction of the Sahrawi tribes, for the first time, into a mixed mode of election for the autonomous regional parliament ('made up of members elected by the various Sahrawi tribes, and of members elected by direct universal suffrage, by the Region's population') (MAEC, 2007).[18]

In sum, in the wake of such a long drafting process, the Autonomy Plan presented did not meet the expectations of the countries that had encouraged and supported Morocco most in this endeavour, since it did not include any substantial advance or incentive capable of persuading the Polisario Front. This dissatisfaction was evident in an informal meeting convened by the political counsellor of the Spanish embassy in Rabat with his counterparts from the U.S., France, the

United Kingdom and Germany in March 2007, coinciding with the presentation of the Moroccan plan to the UN Secretary-General. According to a U.S. diplomatic cable that came to light later:

> The energy of the initiative, however, did not appear to be matched by any apparent breakthrough on the substance of autonomy that could convince the other side. The broad outlines of the autonomy plan [...] suggested Rabat would retain full control, and did not go far beyond what was in the 2003 plan.
> (U.S. Embassy in Rabat, cable 07RABAT494, 19 March 2007)[19]

In their public declarations, by contrast, the U.S. officials chose to praise the Moroccan initiative as a point of departure for new direct negotiations.

In parallel, one month previously Rabat had set in motion a monumental diplomatic and image-boosting campaign aiming at promoting its autonomy proposal throughout the world (*Jeune Afrique*, 22–28 April 2007). Its primary targets, which were visited by Moroccan delegations in February, were the countries considered to be key players in the resolution of the conflict, namely the permanent members of the Security Council (France, the U.S., the United Kingdom, Russia),[20] the old colonial power (Spain, which, along with the four countries mentioned above, formed the Group of Friends of Western Sahara at the UN) and the then President of the Council of the EU (Germany). Directly after this, within barely two months, a flurry of official trips followed to the Arab states deemed to be closest to Moroccan positions (Saudi Arabia, United Arab Emirates, Bahrain, Kuwait, Egypt, Yemen, Jordan, Oman), the Maghreb (Mauritania, Libya, Tunisia) and Senegal, Latin America (Argentina, Brazil, Paraguay, Chile, Peru, Colombia, Mexico), China and other countries from Europe (Belgium, Portugal, Italy) and Africa (Ghana, Congo Brazzaville).

The composition of the Moroccan delegations was highly revealing of the importance attached to the different groups of countries and the real decision-making hierarchy within this country's foreign policy. The strategic destinations (UN, key countries, Maghreb and Senegal, Europe) were assigned to a trio of the King's closest companions which included Fouad Ali El Himma, deputy minister of the Interior, Taieb Fassi Fihri, deputy minister of Foreign Affairs, and Yassine Mansouri, head of the Directorate-General for Studies and Documentation (DGED), the external intelligence agency. These men were accompanied on a case-by-case basis by the minister of the Interior, Chakib Benmoussa (key countries, Maghreb and Senegal, Europe) or the chairman of the CORCAS, Khalihenna Ould Errachid (UN). Fassi Fihri and Mansouri alone took care of China and the African countries. The latter also travelled to most of the Arab countries with the royal advisor Mohammed Moatassim. Finally, foreign minister Benaissa was left with only the Latin American capitals, also supported by Spanish-speaking Ould Errachid. The monarchy's direct control over the Western Sahara issue and the consequent marginalisation of the government were once again demonstrated. Abbas El Fassi, who was at the time secretary-general of the PI and minister, stated that the government did not know anything about the delegations sent abroad by the King (Martinez, 2008: 15).

Within the U.S., the Moroccan diplomatic campaign was reinforced by a significant investment in lobbying firms specialising in influencing Congress, estimated to be around $3.4 million in 2007 and 2008 (*ProPublica*, 18 August 2009). Considerable efforts were also made in terms of online propaganda, with the internet turning into a new battlefront with the Polisario (*Le Journal Hebdomadaire*, 14–20 June 2008), as well as the publication of apparently academic books which were ultimately intended to shore up Rabat's official positions regarding the Western Sahara conflict, and were widely disseminated by the Moroccan embassies (Cherkaoui, 2007; El Ouali, 2007; Védie, 2008).

U.S. support was crucial to the achievement of Morocco's chief objective: to change the course of the UN-led negotiation process and steer it towards direct talks with the Polisario Front in which autonomy – and not a self-determination referendum – was the priority option on the table. Morocco's bet was paid off. Adopting the same language as the Bush Administration, in April 2007 the Security Council praised the 'serious and credible Moroccan efforts to move the process forward towards resolution', and called on the parties to 'enter into negotiations *without preconditions* in good faith, taking into account the developments of the last months' (UNSC, S/RES/1754, 30 April 2007, emphasis added). Resolution 1754 marked a turning point in the UN's approach to the Western Sahara conflict, since it confirmed the break with Baker's view, and backed direct negotiations upon new bases (Bouqentar, 2010: 329–330; ICG, 2007b: ii, 8–9; *L'Économiste*, 2 May 2007, 3 May 2007; *Jeune Afrique*, 6–12 May 2007). The following resolutions 1783 (UNSC, S/RES/1783, 31 October 2007), 1813 (UNSC, S/RES/1813, 30 April 2008) and 1871 (UNSC, S/RES/1871, 30 April 2009) also followed the same lines. In sum, the Autonomy Plan enabled Moroccan foreign policy to regain an 'offensive stance' (Bouqentar, 2010: 331) and reconcile the role of *good student* of the international community with that of *territorial champion*, finding 'a favourable echo in the international political and normative discourse' (El Houdaïgui, 2010: 316).

The immediate consequence of this change of course were the four rounds of direct negotiations between Morocco and the Polisario which were held in Manhasset (New York) between June 2007 and March 2008 under the auspices of the UN Secretary-General.[21] In the end, all of these efforts resulted in a new failure, as neither of the two parties yielded at all from its initial position. The stalemate in the process led the Secretary-General's personal envoy, Peter van Walsum (2005–2008), to acknowledge at a closed meeting with the Security Council in April 2008 that, in his opinion, 'an independent Western Sahara [was] not an attainable goal'. To Morocco's satisfaction, his recommendation was to urge the parties to negotiate '*without preconditions* on the temporary assumption that there will not be a referendum with independence as an option' (*PR Newswire*, 24 April 2008; MAP, 22 April 2008, emphasis added).[22] This statement provoked a real diplomatic earthquake, as the Polisario accused Van Walsum of having deviated from neutrality, and the mandate of this personal envoy was not renewed in the end. The Moroccan Ministry of Foreign Affairs vehemently protested this last UN decision in a letter sent to the UN Secretary-General in which it was claimed that the Security Council had 'confirmed the pre-eminence of the Moroccan autonomy initiative' (MAEC, 1 September 2008).[23]

In any case, judging by the poor results from the first four rounds, the negotiation process had reached a new deadlock. No attempts were made to revive it until August 2009 when, at the request of the Council Security (UNSC, S/RES/1871, 30 April 2009; MAEC, 2 May 2009), the new UN personal envoy, Christopher Ross, organised a more informal and restricted meeting in Durnstein (Vienna) (MAEC, 8 August 2009; MAP, 12 August 2009). At the same time, a report on Western Sahara presented by the Special Political and Decolonisation Committee of the UN General Assembly (UN General Assembly, A/RES/63/105, 18 December 2008) was welcomed by Morocco as evidence of 'a significant change in the treatment of this issue within this Committee', which had always been a stronghold for the right of self-determination, and the reconciliation of its doctrine with the approach of the Security Council (MAEC, 28 October 2008, 12 November 2008): 'The treatment of the Sahara issue has witnessed a qualitative breakthrough within the UN, as demonstrated by the change of discourse, language and terminology' (MAEC, 23 October 2008).

Altogether, it seems indisputable that the Autonomy Plan enabled Moroccan foreign policy to achieve some notable successes between 2006 and 2008. The main instructions and arguments received by the Moroccan diplomats in this context can be summarised as follows:

- Mastering the content of the Autonomy Plan and communicating its political, security and humanitarian importance in terms of: political stability in the Maghreb, realisation of the principle of self-determination (which should not presuppose independence), contribution to international security by addressing growing security threats in the Sahel and Saharan areas and support for unity instead of division and the 'balkanisation' in the Arab world.
- Openness to civil society in the state of destination, in order to counteract an increasingly active 'separatist lobby' which would no longer be limited to Spain but also present in different parts of Europe.
- Recognition of the role of the Moroccan community abroad in promoting Moroccan positions on Western Sahara.

(*Al Ittihad al Ishtiraki*, 10 February 2010)

The impact of the Moroccan Autonomy Plan on the other party to the conflict was also noteworthy, as was demonstrated by the Polisario Front's intensifying threats to resume armed struggle in 2007 and 2008 – as if it had to remind the international community of its very existence. The tensest episode on the ground occurred in late 2007, following the Polisario's much-publicised decision to hold its twelfth congress in Tifariti, a small town in the narrow strip of Western Sahara outside the berm controlled by this movement ('liberated territory').

The Moroccan reaction was reflected in two letters addressed to Ban Ki-moon by the Moroccan permanent representative to the UN and the new foreign minister Fassi Fihri, which condemned the passivity of MINURSO and urged the UN to 'take the necessary measures to tackle these dangerous and provocative actions that [threatened] peace and stability in the region' (MAEC, 12 December 2007; *Jeune Afrique*, 13–19 January 2008).[24] This diplomatic escalation was to continue over the following months, when plans were announced to establish the permanent parliament of the Sahrawi Arab Democratic Republic (SADR) in Tifariti (*Le Journal Hebdomadaire*, 8–14 March 2008) and the Association for Moroccan Sahara (ASM) even called for a protest march to this city – which did not take place in the end though (*Tel Quel*, 26 January–1 February 2008).

Returning on the defensive in the face of a transformed conflict

However, mainly since 2009, Morocco was to lose much of the diplomatic advantage gained with the Autonomy Plan and went back on the defensive in the Western Sahara conflict in different ways. The situation seemed to be swiftly 'darkening' for Moroccan interests (interview with Abdelhamid El Ouali, 7 June 2013). This change of course was provoked by changes in the international situation which somehow converged with the ongoing strategic reorientation and reshaping of the Sahrawi party – the latter dynamic resulting at this stage in a visible reconnection between *internal* Sahrawi activists from the occupied territory and the Polisario Front. At international level, the first setback for Rabat was Van Walsum's replacement as the UN Secretary-General's personal envoy by the American Christopher Ross (MAEC, 13 January 2009), who stopped giving explicit precedence to the autonomy solution as the basis for direct negotiations between the parties. The Moroccan authorities were also suspicious of him for having previously served as U.S. ambassador to Algeria (U.S. Embassy in Rabat, cable 08RABAT832, 5 September 2008; cable 09RABAT179, 27 February 2009). This was coupled with the uncertainty elicited by the coming to power in Washington of Barack Obama, a Democratic president whose future position on the Western Sahara conflict was still in doubt. In addition to the initial ambiguity of the statements made by his administration – in which a certain division of labour could be found between the President and a seemingly more pro-Moroccan Secretary of State Hillary Clinton – the Rabat authorities had to come to terms with the idea that previous steadfast, almost unconditional, U.S. support could no longer be taken for granted (*Al Ousboue Assahafi*, 11 December 2008; *Le Reporter*, 13 July 2009).

At the same time, inter-Sahrawi reconnection allowed the other party to seize the initiative for the first time since 2003, overcoming the phase of lethargy, confusion and strategic crisis in which it had been engulfed following Morocco's Autonomy Plan and subsequent diplomatic offensive (*Tel Quel*, 10–16 November 2007). The budding Tindouf-Laayoune alliance was formalised in September 2009 by a pioneering official visit to the Tindouf camps by seven *internal*

Sahrawi human rights activists from ASVDH and CODESA (among others), who were arrested on their return to Laayoune amid a climate of Moroccan patriotic outrage and virulent attacks by the media and political parties. As a result, Rabat's management of the Western Sahara issue started to appear increasingly reactive and edgy at both *domestic* and international level. At home, the effectiveness of the previous years' *reconciliation* strategy towards the Sahrawis – including the performance of the CORCAS – began to be questioned (*Al Watan Al An*, 5 May 2011). A repressive turn was announced in Mohammed VI's speech on the anniversary of the Green March, which seemed to be a warning to the *internal* Sahrawi activists:

> There is no more room for ambiguity or duplicity: either a citizen is Moroccan or he is not. Gone are the days of double games and evasion. [...] Either one is a patriot or one is a traitor. There is no golden mean between patriotism and treason. One cannot enjoy the rights of citizenship and renounce them at the same time by conspiring with the enemies of the homeland.
> (Speech by Mohammed VI, Rabat, 6 November 2009)

The most immediate consequence of Morocco's stronger grip on the occupied territory's activists was the crisis that broke out in mid-November 2009 when Aminatou Haidar (CODESA) was denied entry to Laayoune from abroad and unlawfully expelled to the Canary Islands. In fact, according to documents revealed afterwards, at this stage the Moroccan authorities were prepared to deport her at the slightest provocation. This extreme decision, for which the King was personally responsible, ended up seriously compromising Morocco's relations with Spain, as the Madrid government had not weighed up the political consequences of accepting such illegal expulsion. Haidar protested with a hunger strike, attracting great international attention and sympathy. High-level diplomatic intervention by the U.S. (Secretary of State Hillary Clinton) and France (President Nicolas Sarkozy) was needed to break Rabat's initial firmness and ensure her return home (Brouksy, 2014: 129–132). The U.S. embassy described this crisis as a 'a disastrous episode' for the Moroccan government, 'which drew dangerously close not only to perpetrating a case of forced exile, but also to badly jeopardising its relationships with Spain and other allies through its belligerent handling of the case and some stunningly maladroit diplomacy' (U.S. Embassy in Rabat, cable 09RABAT990, 18 December 2009). It was evident that Morocco's behaviour no longer corresponded to that expected from a *good student/ally*.

This trend of problematic *domestic* management of Western Sahara with problematic implications for the Moroccan foreign policy was to be prolonged one year later, when the establishment of the Sahrawi protest camp of Gdeim Izik, on the outskirts of Laayoune, led to the largest protest cycle ever seen inside the Moroccan-controlled territory. Although, at first, the camp's founders seemed to be primarily motivated by socioeconomic grievances – protest against an irregular distribution of plots of land by the city council – and avoided explicit Sahrawi nationalist or pro-independence symbols, the pro-independence framing prevailed in the Rabat authorities' reading of the situation. Therefore, even though a basic agreement had been reached between the Moroccan Ministry of Interior and the protesters, the camp was forcibly dismantled by the Moroccan security forces overnight, provoking chaos and deadly clashes (López García, 2011; Gómez Martín, 2012). The ex post justification was that 'the exploitation of social demands served outside political agendas seeking to generate violence and thus to internationalise and perpetuate the camp' (parliamentary report quoted in *Au Fait Maroc*, 13 January 2011).[25] Again, this crisis episode did nothing but increase the international recognition of *internal* Sahrawi activism and the arrival of foreign observers and supporters in Laayoune (Gimeno, 2013: 40), to the detriment of Morocco's standing.

By and large, the growing tensions and peaks of repression in Morocco's *domestic* management of the Western Sahara issue had a negative impact on its international management: they pushed Moroccan foreign policy into a vicious circle in which the credibility of the Autonomy Plan and international advantage achieved in 2006–2008 dwindled. Conversely, the Sahrawis of both Tindouf and Laayoune seized this window of opportunity by pursuing two novel international/diplomatic strategies which placed the focus on the occupied territory's specific problems: the demand to extend MINURSO's mandate to human rights monitoring and the questioning of the legality of the exploitation of Western Sahara's natural resources by Morocco. In this way, they managed to put unprecedented strain on Morocco's relations with, respectively, the UN and the U.S., on the one hand, and the EU, on the other.

The establishment of a human rights monitoring mechanism in Western Sahara – by either enlarging MINURSO's mandate or setting up a regional office of the UN's Office of the High Commissioner for Human Rights (OHCHR) – was first put on the table by the OHCHR in 2006 (HRW, 19 June 2009), following the lead of international human rights NGOs. This idea was to become the main bone of contention within UN Security Council debates on Western Sahara from 2009, backed by the U.S. and the United Kingdom, subsequently gaining greater momentum in the wake of the Gdeim Izik protest and the regional wave of uprisings of the so-called Arab Spring. Its advocates expected that it could help create opportunities to break the impasse within the peace process by increasing this conflict's visibility and changing its underlying dynamics. As far as MINURSO was concerned, the addition of competence over human rights would simply redress an anomaly and bring its mandate into line with those of most post-Cold War UN peacekeeping missions (Capella, 2011). Facing Moroccan interlocutors, it was sympathetically claimed that the acceptance of human rights monitoring in the territory under Moroccan control would ultimately serve Rabat's interests by giving credibility to its Autonomy Plan, since 'human rights protection is inherent to autonomy' (Khakee, 2014). However, Morocco staunchly opposed this initiative, arguing that it would create two 'parallel jurisdictions' in Northern and 'Southern' Morocco, weaken Morocco's authority and complicate the maintenance of public order in the disputed territory, exert a 'pull effect' on pro-independence activists, 'denature' the allegedly 'regional' character of the conflict and lead to a 'Timorisation' of the Sahara issue.[26]

Against this new background, a first serious *multilateral* crisis between Morocco and the UN broke out in the spring of 2012 which led Rabat to withdraw confidence from the UN Secretary General's personal envoy Ross. The alarm bells had started to ring for the Moroccan authorities this year for two reasons: the unprecedented criticism of their behaviour in Ban Ki-moon's report and the predictable attempts to extend MINURSO's mandate during its annual renewal by the Security Council in April. The report included complaints concerning obstacles to the daily work of MINURSO personnel in Moroccan-controlled Western Sahara and indications of violations of the confidentiality of their communications with the UN headquarters in New York (UNSC, S/2012/197, 5 April 2012: 10, 19). This last objection was interpreted as a thinly veiled accusation of espionage. An immediate protest lodged by the Moroccan representatives forced the removal of a paragraph from an earlier draft referring to 'police surveillance' and 'close monitoring' of the UN personnel's movements (Reuters, 12 April 2012; *Yabiladi*, 12 April 2012; *Lakome*, 13 April 2012). Meanwhile, the demands to extend MINURSO's mandate seemed to be strengthened by the Secretary-General's call for 'further and more focused engagement' with human rights issues, as well as the personal envoy's insistence that 'it was vital for the UN and the international community as a whole to have access to reliable, independent information on developments in both Western Sahara and the refugee camps', and hence that 'MINURSO personnel should enjoy full freedom of movement and outreach' (UNSC, S/2012/197, 5 April 2012: 21, 5).

The Moroccan reaction to these adverse developments at UN level involved three moves. First, foreign minister Saad-Eddine El Othmani toured the capitals of the permanent members of the Security Council before the meeting scheduled in April (*Al Akhbar al Youm*, 11 April 2012). Second, once this UN body approved the extension of MINURSO ultimately without any significant changes (UNSC, S/RES/2044, 24 April 2012), the same minister once again emphasised 'Morocco's concerns regarding the content of this report, attempts at denaturing MINURSO's mandate and the obstacles hindering the negotiation process' in a meeting with Ban Ki-moon (MAEC, 10 May 2012).[27] Third, the Moroccan government surprisingly announced the decision to withdraw confidence from Ross, in a unilateral attempt to end his mediation in the Western Sahara conflict which was justified for three reasons: the 'stalemate in the negotiation process' ('instead of focusing on substantive issues [...], discussions get lost in the consideration of secondary issues'), the 'deviations noted in the last report of the Secretary-General' and the 'unbalanced and biased line of conduct' observed in 'actions, statements and initiatives of the personal envoy' (MAEC, 17 May 2012). This 'risky' decision was not without domestic controversy. An opposition leader accused El Othmani of pushing Morocco into a crisis with the UN without having previously consulted with key national political stakeholders (*Al Akhbar al Youm*, 1 June 2012). In fact, the reality was that such an important initiative on the *national question* could only come from the King himself, as the foreign minister himself later admitted (interview with Réda Benkhaldoun, 6 June 2013; interview with Hassan Bouqentar, 5 June 2013; interview with Abdelwahab Maalmi, 7 June 2013; Brouksy, 2014: 122–124).

The explicit goal of this rebuff was to draw some red lines and redirect the UN-led negotiation process back to Van Walsum's preference in favour of the autonomy solution (interview with Youssef Amrani in *Al Masaa*, 18 June 2012). Incidentally, another unstated short-term objective might have been to provoke the cancellation of the unprecedented visit to the Western Sahara territory announced by Ross, which was to be the first ever made by a personal envoy of the UN Secretary-General to the very disputed land where the conflict originated (*Lakome*, 30 May 2012) – beyond Rabat, Tindouf and Algiers – and could be expected be greeted with a wave of pro-independence protests. The trip was indeed postponed, although the results yielded by this Moroccan-provoked crisis were far from those intended. Both the UN Secretary-General and the U.S. Administration immediately came out in support of Ross, reaffirming their full confidence in his integrity and impartiality.[28] This firm response soon led the Moroccan foreign ministry to make some more conciliatory statements, clarifying that the refusal to continue working with Ross did not extend to the UN Secretary-General or MINURSO (MAEC, 21 May 2012). Ban Ki-moon had the last word in late June, when he officially renewed the mission of his personal envoy for Western Sahara (*Al Akhbar al Youm*, 26 June 2012).

The *multilateral* crisis with the UN drew to a close when Morocco stepped back and re-accepted Ross after a phone call from the UN Secretary-General to Mohammed VI on the Eid al-Fitr (25 August) – yet not before Ban Ki-moon had ensured that the UN did not intend to modify the terms of its engagement with this conflict. This conversation was to be presented by Moroccan diplomats as a successful outcome, arguing that it led to a 'reframing of UN mediation on the Sahara' (interview with Youssef Amrani in *Le Soir-Échos*, 4 January 2013). Ross eventually travelled to the region in late October and early November 2012, when he was received by the King in Rabat but also fulfilled his desire to visit Moroccan-occupied Western Sahara. In Laayoune he met Sahrawi pro-independence activists along with *unionist* or pro-autonomy actors, local authorities and tribal *sheikhs*. The 'new approach' proposed by him to the Security Council in late November – to start a period of *shuttle diplomacy* with the parties and the neighbouring countries instead of a new round of negotiations (*Lakome*, 21 December 2012) – seemed to be welcomed in principle by the Moroccan foreign ministry.

However, a longer-lasting connected *bilateral* tension was to remain unsolved, i.e. that between Rabat and the Obama Administration. As was acknowledged in a confidential note from the Moroccan foreign ministry, the controversy created around Ross had a 'direct impact' on these bilateral relations, 'as Washington is particularly sensitive to everything related to this U.S. diplomat'. This was also the link between the 2012 episode and the second multilateral crisis between Morocco and the UN one year later: 'The differences between Morocco and the

U.S. on this issue reached their peak within the Security Council in April 2013, with Washington's attempt, narrowly countered by Morocco, to extend MINURSO's mandate to the protection of human rights.'[29]

The 2013 U.S. draft resolution in question – an unforeseen initiative of the U.S. ambassador to the UN which was not consulted with the other members of the Group of Friends of Western Sahara, against the usual practice of consensus – provoked unparalleled panic and 'total mobilisation' among the Rabat authorities, foreign policy decision-makers and media. A crisis meeting was improvised between the main party leaders and advisors of the Royal Cabinet – thus bypassing the government and parliament – whose participants closed ranks in categorically rejecting the U.S. 'partial' and 'unilateral' initiatives to 'distort' MINURSO's mandate (MAP, 15 April 2013; *Lakome*, 15 April 2013, 16 April 2013, 21 April 2013). The African Lion annual joint military exercises with the U.S. army were cancelled by Morocco without explanation (AP, 16 April 2013; *Al Masaa*, 18 April 2013) and a high-level diplomatic delegation was dispatched to 'transmit a message' from Mohammed VI to the permanent members of the Security Council. France was in a particularly awkward position, as it would hardly seem justifiable in this context to exercise its veto, as was expected by its Moroccan ally (*Le Monde*, 17 April 2013; *Alif Post*, 17 April 2013). Therefore, the only hope for Rabat was that the terms of forthcoming resolution 2099 (UNSC, S/RES/2099, 25 April 2013) would be watered down in order to secure a compromise during the discussions of the Group of Friends and the Security Council itself. This is what eventually happened: the U.S. opted to step back from its original proposal due to resistance by France, Russia and Spain – and much to the relief of Morocco (Fernández-Molina, 2013b).

In any case, in this diplomatic 'victory' in extremis, Morocco only won the battle, but not the war. Rabat's tensions with the UN and MINURSO and mistrust of personal envoy Ross were to persist, as was proved by many of the confidential documents from the Moroccan Ministry of Foreign Affairs and Cooperation which were leaked in the autumn of 2014 by a hacker hiding behind the nickname 'Chris Coleman'. Among other things, these communications disclosed the Moroccan strategy aimed at forcing Ross to abandon his mission by 'minimising his trips to Morocco and confining contacts with him to New York' or, 'in case of a visit to Morocco, receiving him at intermediate level (*working level*)', as well as 'disseminating to the unofficial relays (journalists, academics, parliamentarians, etc.), a sceptical message regarding the personal envoy'.[30] As regards U.S. connection, the main revelation was the secret verbal agreement reached between President Obama and Mohammed VI during their first meeting in Washington in November 2013, whereby the U.S. undertook not to ask for an extension of the MINURSO mandate in exchange for three demands placed on Morocco: putting an end to military trials of civilians, allowing the UN High Commissioner for Human Rights to visit Western Sahara and legalising Sahrawi associations such as ASVDH and CODESA (*Orient XXI*, 15 December 2014; *Tel Quel*, 23 December 2014).[31] In the autumn of 2014, Moroccan diplomats considered the possibility of disavowing Ross and predicted 'a second crisis with the Obama Administration', along with 'difficult times both within the UN and with our American partners',[32] although the dialogue was to be resumed in early 2015 with Ross touring the region once again.

In parallel, questions regarding the legality of Morocco's exploitation of the natural resources of Western Sahara (fisheries, phosphate, oil) also became more persistent on international level from 2000 onwards. Regardless of material benefits or losses, this issue had 'inherent symbolic value' (White, 2014) for pro-independence Sahrawis, who could contend that international actors' trading in resources from the territory under Moroccan control represented 'backdoor recognition of the status quo' (Shelley, 2006: 21). A milestone in this regard was the opinion issued by UN legal counsel Hans Corell in 2002 on the legality of contracts signed by Morocco and foreign companies to explore for mineral resources in Western Sahara (Boukhars and Roussellier, 2013: 244–245). His conclusion was that, while these specific contracts (not entailing exploitation) were 'not in themselves illegal',

> if further exploration and exploitation activities were to proceed in disregard of the interests and wishes of the people of Western Sahara, they would be in violation of the international law principles applicable to mineral resource activities in Non-Self-Governing Territories.
> (UNSC, S/2002/161, 12 February 2002)

This was the starting point for growing Sahrawi mobilisation – backed by transnational advocacy networks such as Western Sahara Resource Watch (WSRW) – on the resources issue.

The first target of this new strategy was the EU, a key international actor and economic partner for Morocco which had consistently avoided engaging with the Western Sahara conflict due to intergovernmental divergences (Vaquer, 2004). The Sahrawis capitalised on the increase in the powers of the European Parliament over the EU's external relations following the entry into force of the Lisbon Treaty (2009) in an attempt to hinder EU–Morocco economic cooperation and to give visibility to this neglected conflict in Brussels. In line with the Corell opinion, the legal service of this EU institution resolved in May 2009 that 'compliance with international law requires that economic activities related to the natural resources of a Non-Self-Governing Territory are carried out for the benefits of the people of such Territory, and in accordance with their wishes'. The lack of a convincing demonstration of such benefits was to become a justification for the European Parliament's rejection of the protocol of extension of the 2006 EU–Morocco fisheries agreement in December 2011 (European Parliament, 2011; Smith, 2013), which was interpreted in Rabat as an unprecedented political blow on the *national question*.

All in all, as a result of inter-Sahrawi reconnection and new international/diplomatic strategies as well as Morocco's own problematic *domestic* management of the disputed territory, since 2009 Rabat has faced unprecedented tensions and crises on the Western Sahara issue with such significant international actors as the

UN, the U.S. and the EU – which had traditionally been rather sympathetic (in different ways) to its positions. The role of *spoiler* seemed to have superseded that of *good student* of the international community, as was privately acknowledged by the Moroccan foreign ministry itself: 'Our country is presented by Mr Ross as responsible for the current deadlock in the political process, an idea conveyed in the UN corridors and to the permanent members of the Security Council'.[33]

Moreover, the same tense and defensive Moroccan foreign policy attitude was extended to relations with various international actors, provoking a flurry of impetuous reactions and minor bilateral crises in the event of the slightest inconvenience or disagreement on the Western Sahara conflict. Examples of this include the withdrawal of the Moroccan ambassador from Senegal (MAEC, 19 December 2007), the closure of the representation office in Venezuela (MAEC, 15 January 2009), the severing of relations with Iran (MAEC, 6 March 2009), the abandonment of the celebrations for the fortieth anniversary of the Libyan revolution (*El Imparcial*, 2 September 2009; *Al Sabah*, 4 September 2009) and the expulsion of a Swedish diplomat (*Le Monde*, 19 November 2009). What are regarded under diplomatic practice as extraordinary measures were almost becoming a general rule for Morocco, and were presented within official discourse as gestures of firmness. According to a former diplomat, these were 'deliberate acts' aimed at 'drawing a red line: we will not give way at all on the Sahara issue' (*Tel Quel*, 20–26 November 2009; 28 March 2012).

Overall, this chapter has discussed how the paramount objective of the foreign policy of Morocco, that is the international *legalisation* of its de facto control over Western Sahara, has forced this country to reconcile its role as *territorial champion* with its dependence on external recognition, and to manage this conflict simultaneously at *domestic* and international level. The *inward turn* of the conflict witnessed since the turn of the millennium, as growing international attention was paid to Sahrawi resistance and the human rights situation inside the territory under Rabat's control, has changed the diplomatic game and placed renewed strain on Moroccan foreign policy. This foreign policy has gone through a period of internal and international progress of the idea of autonomy under Moroccan sovereignty, or *third way* (1999–2003), a strategic crisis provoked by Morocco's rejection of the Baker Plan II (2003–2006), a stage of domestic *reconciliation* with the Sahrawi population and international promotion of an Autonomy Plan for the disputed territory (2006–2008) and new setbacks for Moroccan positions at diplomatic level resulting from growing contradictions between the *domestic* and international management of the 'Sahara question' by the Rabat authorities (2009 onwards).

Notes

1 This argument owes much to Aboubakr Jamaï's point made in 2006 that King Mohammed VI's policy on the Western Sahara issue had reduced the importance attached to international relations and increased that of domestic reforms aiming at enabling an autonomy framework (interview with Aboubakr Jamaï, 21 February 2006).

2 Traditional oath of allegiance.
3 For a critique of this distinction between socioeconomic and 'political' demands in the context of Western Sahara's protest sphere, see Veguilla (2010).
4 For a more refined argument along the same lines, with references to the literature on social movements and theories of relative deprivation, see Cherkaoui (2007: 170).
5 A prominent advocate of the *third way* idea was the famous Moroccan Marxist dissident Abraham Serfaty, who returned from exile in September 1999 (*Le Journal Hebdomadaire*, 15–21 March 2003).
6 In a previous meeting held in London in June, Baker had asked Morocco and the Polisario Front whether they would be prepared to consider a 'third way' in view of stalemate in the implementation of the Settlement Plan (Shelley, 2004: 147; Jensen, 2012: 93).
7 See also speech by Mohammed VI, Rabat, 6 November 2000.
8 Another ideational contribution originating within independent press and civil society involved a critical rethink concerning the high economic and financial price paid in order to maintain the Western Sahara conflict, which served as a pragmatic and economistic argument in favour of its resolution (*Tel Quel*, 11–17 April 2009; *Le Journal Hebdomadaire*, 19–25 April 2003; ICG, 2007a: 12–13).
9 www.arso.org/01-f01-15.htm (accessed on 31 January 2015).
10 The PJD's emphasis on the defence of 'territorial integrity' was accentuated after the terrorist attacks in Casablanca in May 2003 as part of a strategy to secure its acceptability within the system (Mohsen-Finan and Zeghal, 2006: 110, 115–117).
11 Many of these 'northerners' were actually ethnic Sahrawis who had been brought into the territory from southern Morocco with a view to distorting the referendum (Willis, 2012: 289).
12 Deeper down, this Moroccan 'apparent lack of self-confidence' (Abraham Serfaty in *Le Journal Hebdomadaire*, 19–25 July 2003) concealed some existential problems concerning the Moroccan regime's own authoritarian nature, the political centrality of the monarchy and the absence of separation of powers (*Le Journal Hebdomadaire*, 31 May–6 June 2003), as well as uncertainty about the future role of the army, which had been excluded from politics since the 1970s in exchange for extraordinary economic privileges granted to its senior officers in Western Sahara (Tobji, 2006).
13 Minutes of Security Council meeting 4801, 31 July 2003. For minister Benaissa's account of Morocco's 'intensive consultations' with the ambassadors of Security Council members in order to avoid the endorsement of the first draft of this resolution in extremis, see MAEC (30 July 2003).
14 For the Moroccan reaction, see MAEC (27 April 2004).
15 According to a cable from the U.S. ambassador in Rabat disseminated by Wikileaks, his Spanish counterpart said in a meeting in March 2006 that Spain was supporting Morocco in the task of drafting a serious autonomy plan (U.S. Embassy in Rabat, cable 06RABAT557, 29 March 2006).
16 The 'marketing' of the Autonomy Plan, in the words of one of CORCAS members (interview, 7 June 2013).
17 The Moroccan proposal of 2003 envisaged a different electoral system for the first elections to the Regional Legislative Assembly and for all subsequent ones.
18 For a detailed analysis of this proposal compared with other European experiences or 'international standards' of state decentralisation and autonomy (from a Moroccan perspective), see El Messaoudi and Bouabid (2008: 12–29). For a critique of its vagueness in such fundamental aspects as the geographical limits of the Sahara Autonomous Region and the modalities of the proposed referendum, see ICG (2007b: 7).
19 U.S. diplomatic cable leaked by Wikileaks.
20 China was to be visited later, in mid-March.
21 The meetings took place on 18–19 June 2007, 10–11 August 2007, 7–9 January 2008 and 11–13 March 2008.

22 These observations were part of a document which Ban Ki-moon finally refused to include in his new report, contrary to the usual practice and thus representing a kind of disavowal.
23 For the Moroccan private reaction, see U.S. Embassy in Rabat (cable 08RABAT832, 5 September 2008).
24 The two houses of the Moroccan parliament also made an appeal to the UN Secretary-General along the same lines (*L'Économiste*, 13 December 2007).
25 See also Lakmahri and Tourabi (2013).
26 MAEC (undated) Pourquoi le 'monitoring' prévu par le texte de la résolution du Conseil de sur le Sahara est dangereux?, leaked document available at www.arso.org/Coleman/Pourquoi_le_monitoring.pdf (accessed on 20 December 2014).
27 These arguments were transmitted to the domestic audience in an interview in *Al Akhbar al Youm* (14 May 2012).
28 The Spanish government reacted with ambiguous and contradictory statements (MAP, 24 May 2012), and only François Hollande's France expressed unconditional support for Moroccan positions (*Jeune Afrique*, 21 June 2012). See MAEC/Embassy in Washington (2012) Entretien avec le Conseiller de l'Ambassade de France à Washington, Washington, 1 June, leaked document available at www.arso.org/Coleman/entretien_avec_le_Conseiller_d.pdf (accessed on 20 December 2014).
29 MAEC/Direction des Affaires Américaines (2014) Note à Monsieur le Ministre, Rabat, 2 October, leaked document available at www.arso.org/Coleman/Fiche_USA_Sahara.pdf (accessed on 20 December 2014).
30 MAEC (2014) Éléments d'une stratégie pour la gestion de l'exercice avril 2014–avril 2015 concernant la question du Sahara marocain, Rabat, 23 April, leaked document available at www.arso.org/Coleman/Note_finale_SG_Sahara23.04.14.pdf (accessed on 20 December 2014).
31 MAEC (2014) Fiche USA-UK/Projet de lettre du MAEC au Roi du Maroc, Rabat, 3 February, leaked document available at www.arso.org/Coleman/Fiche%20usa-uk.pdf (accessed on 20 December 2014).
32 MAEC/Direction des Affaires Américaines (2014) Note à Monsieur le Ministre, Rabat, 2 October.
33 Ibid.

3 The Sisyphean game of Maghrebi integration and normalisation with Algeria

Whilst the Western Sahara conflict is the core issue that dominates the hierarchy of Moroccan foreign policy priorities and is a determining factor for all external behaviour of this state, this interference has always been most apparent and compelling vis-à-vis relations with the Maghreb countries. In general, relations between the states which make up this subregional system have been marked since decolonisation by the paradoxical coexistence of, on the one hand, an ideal of common belonging and regional federation and, on the other hand, the reality of low economic and social interdependence, territorial disputes and clashes between stubborn nationalisms. The tension between the unifying *norm* and the divisive practice of power politics can be considered at this stage as a structural feature. The most advanced project of regional cooperation, the Arab Maghreb Union (AMU), was blocked shortly after its launch in 1989 following setbacks in the implementation of the UN Settlement Plan for Western Sahara and the Algerian political crisis and civil war (Hernando de Larramendi, 2008: 179). In 1994, the closure of the land border between Morocco and Algeria, the two aspiring regional powers, conclusively froze political dialogue at head of state level within the Presidential Council of this organisation, reducing its activity to the discreet operation of its Rabat-based General Secretariat and technical cooperation in areas such as transport, energy and infrastructure (interview with Khalid Naciri, 17 February 2006). The commemoration of the twentieth anniversary of the AMU, in February 2009, was met with widespread indifference (*Jeune Afrique*, 22–28 February 2009).

All of this explains why the subregional system of the Maghreb has tended to be analysed in realist IR terms. Several authors have highlighted how the dynamics of power politics and the balance of power, whilst not leading to open conflict, have historically favoured volatile alliances and alignments among the countries comprising the system. The first special characteristic of this game was that its players were still immersed in their own postcolonial processes of state-building and nation-building (Zoubir, 2000: 44), which made the interaction between foreign policy and domestic politics more complex. Second, regional tensions have remained under control at all times, and have not exceeded the limits of the system's overall balance and stability. For the incumbent regimes and leaders, this has rather appeared as 'a harmless game, as it allows them at the same time to survive domestic crises, strengthen the institutions they defend or embody and, ultimately, maintain a relatively controlled pragmatic balance' (Hami, 2003: 18–19). Third, a different and inevitable kind of interdependence has existed in the field of (external and internal) security, which means that the Maghreb can be described as a 'regional security complex' (Buzan, 1991: 190). Indeed, among other things, the very foundation of the AMU is explained in some analyses as a result of the Maghrebi regimes' perception, in the late 1980s, of a growing threat from Islamist movements and the need to strengthen police and intelligence cooperation to face it – a finding that qualifies the official arguments of the time, which linked increased regional cooperation to the requirements of economic development and trade relations with the European Union (EU), or to the resolution of the Western Sahara conflict (Mezran, 1998).

Anyway, in general it is assumed that a significant characteristic of the Maghrebi regional integration project from the outset was that it was exogenously determined, driven more by external than by internal factors, and was thus rather instrumental in nature. The AMU was largely conceived in order to meet the expectations of the European Economic Community (EEC)/EU and member states such as France and Spain, which were especially concerned about North African stability:

> For the Maghreb countries, the AMU allowed for the possibility of developing privileged relationships with Europe. [...] This objective was fully achieved within the framework of association agreements with the EU. From this viewpoint, the development of regional integration was not the objective.
>
> (Martinez, 2008: 6)

In the late 1990s, the United States also sought to revitalise the AMU and to encourage better relations between Morocco and Algeria with its proposal to establish an economic partnership with the countries of central Maghreb, the so-called Eizenstat Initiative.

This exogenously determined character of the Maghrebi integration project entailed a certain level of duality and role conflict (Cantir and Kaarbo, 2013: 467–468) between different foreign policy roles played by Morocco in its relations with Algeria and the Maghreb. The prevailing domestically defined (*ego*) national role conception (Holsti, 1970) – *champion of national territorial integrity* – led to rather uncooperative behaviour on regional level, whereas external (*alter*) role expectations – the different variations of the role of *good student/ally* of the international community – pushed it in precisely the opposite direction. The desire to single out its relations with the EU and the U.S. forced Morocco to respond at all times in an exemplary way to these actors' demands to fulfil the sub-role of *promoter of horizontal South–South regional integration*. Aside from this, another additional paradox was that Rabat's purely bilateral and selfish approach to relations with Brussels and Washington pushed into the background the project to establish a Maghrebi regional bloc with a minimal level of political and economic homogeneity. An opinion poll conducted in 2008 reflected how embedded this ambivalence was in the Moroccan society. The idea of Maghrebi integration enjoyed quite wide domestic consensus vertically (between leaders and public opinion) (Cantir and Kaarbo, 2012: 11–12): 72 per cent of respondents defined themselves as Maghrebi and 69 per cent claimed that the future of Morocco was linked to regional integration at this level. Yet, at the same time, 64 per cent perceived this as a 'vague' (*flou*) project and only 8 per cent considered it as the top priority for their country (Martinez, 2008: 10–11).

The main research question explored in this chapter is how Moroccan foreign policy under Mohammed VI has combined these two apparently contradictory roles, i.e. *territorial champion* and *promoter of Maghrebi regional integration* in the eyes of the international community. In practice, the fate of Maghrebi regional integration has always been at the mercy of the problematic and fickle bilateral relationship between Morocco and Algeria, the evolution of which appeared to be a Sisyphean labour. References have been repeatedly made to it in emotional language, not without a certain fatalism: 'The relations between the two states are passionate and therefore irrational' (*Le Journal Hebdomadaire*, 29 March–4 April 2008); 'Our relations with the Algerians are passionate because we are too similar' (*Tel Quel*, 21–27 February 2004). Behind this discourse on the 'enemy brothers' lay a very *territorial* vision of the neighbourhood, marked by land and border disputes, plus a compelling collection of mutual perceptions and clichés rooted in selective readings of recent history – the 'underlying psychology which undermines the development of genuine cooperation' (Zoubir, 2000: 69–70; Stora, 2003).

The bilateral territorial dispute over the south-western Algerian Saharan strip which caused the Sands War in 1963 was coupled with the Western Sahara issue during the following decade, which became the bone of contention and has been the key to the struggle for regional hegemony through to the present day. Depending on the time frame chosen, and leaving aside its original decolonisation aspect, this conflict can be seen as a cause or as a consequence of rivalry between Morocco and Algeria. Whereas, in the beginning, this issue became just another ramification of existing bilateral antagonism, over time both states' positions were to solidify and become essentialised, severely limiting their room for manoeuvre and scope for mutual rapprochement in other areas. Other than this, the most glaring incarnation of the inflexibility and the territorial pregnancy that characterised the relationship was the closure of the 1,560-kilometre-long land border between the two countries, which had a deep human, social and economic impact, including the flourishing of smuggling and irregular migration flows (*El País*, 25 May 2008; *L'Économiste*, 29 October 2007, 20 December 2007). A study presented in 2003 by the Chamber of Commerce of Oujda estimated the annual turnover of this 'informal trade' at $550 million (*Jeune Afrique*, 15–21 February 2009).

In any case, according to polls, all of this negative historical burden has coexisted with an equally deep-rooted feeling of affinity or 'brotherhood' between the Moroccan and Algerian societies. In Morocco, despite the construction of Algeria as the enemy figure par excellence in the nationalist discourses, the difficulties in bilateral relations were mainly blamed on the ruling class of both countries: '64 per cent think that the problem between Algeria and Morocco is a problem of leaders who manipulate their conflict for domestic political goals' (Martinez, 2008: 11).

Historicist, economistic, security and social discourses on regional cooperation

Against this background, the development of relations between Morocco and Algeria under Mohammed VI's reign was characterised by overall continuity and the maintenance of the patterns of confrontation and détente that had existed for decades. These ups and downs involved swings between periodic (mainly rhetorical) escalations of tension and phases of easing, which featured more or less emphatic calls for bilateral normalisation. In the meantime, four distinct discourses on the need for greater regional cooperation and integration in the Maghreb were starting to permeate and settle within Moroccan political space, which respectively emphasised historical and cultural affinities, shared pragmatic interests related to economic development, the requirements of security and counterterrorism, and the role of civil society in bringing about 'reconciliation from below' (Martinez, 2008: 5).

First, the historicist discourse based the regional integration project on the idea of a 'common destiny' of the peoples of the Maghreb which would be characterised by shared history, language and religion. This has been part of the discursive arsenal of the Moroccan nationalist movement and the Istiqlal Party (PI) ever since the struggle for independence. Over time, the solidarity and mutual support exhibited by the different North African nationalist movements during the 1940s and 1950s were mythologised and exploited for contemporary political purposes: the 'anticolonial leitmotiv' had become a 'federating discourse' to be ritually invoked at will (Stora, 2002: 15–17, 2003: 16–17), that is, a *norm* in the constructivist sense which constrained the states' behaviour but could equally be manipulated (Barnett, 1998: 11–12). A sign of its persistence was the celebration of the fiftieth anniversary of the Tangiers Conference (1958), in which the nationalist parties of Morocco (PI), Tunisia (Neo Destour) and Algeria (National Liberation Front) met to proclaim the right to independence of the Algerian people, while the latter was still embroiled in its war of liberation, and adopted a resolution on the future 'unification of the Arab Maghreb'. The commemoration organised in the same Moroccan city in April 2008 was attended by these historical parties and some of their heirs, and presented as an event aimed at 'reviving the unionist spirit that held sway over this conference' (interview with Mohamed Larbi Messari in *Aujourd'hui Le Maroc*, 8 April 2008; Habib El Malki in *Jeune Afrique*, 13–19 April 2008).

The second alternative discourse had a more pragmatic and economistic thrust, presenting regional integration as an indispensable step along the road to economic development and social welfare in the Maghreb countries (Martinez, 2008: 5, 7). According to its proponents, the establishment of a viable economic and trading bloc should contribute to growth, investment attraction and job creation in the region, thereby enabling it to overcome the difficulties of its insertion into the global economic system (Martin, 2004: 163). Furthermore, the idea of circumventing seemingly immovable political obstacles by prioritising economic and sectoral cooperation was reminiscent of (neo)functionalist approaches to European integration. The contrast between the historicist and the economistic discourses was raised in a rather black-and-white manner by voices often hailing from the worlds of economics or business. The opposition between the past and the future and the demand for 'concrete objectives' (Elâabadila Chbihna Maaelaynine in *Le Journal Hebdomadaire*, 13–19 December 2003) gave their arguments a certain technocratic flavour: 'The construction of the Maghreb makes no sense unless it is legitimised by a certain economic rationality [...]. The Maghrebi construction should not rely solely on an emotional reading of the past or an outdated historicism' (interview with Abdellatif Chatri in *Jeune Afrique*, 25 February–3 March 2007).

One of the mainstream manifestations of the economistic discourse, which was gradually assimilated by the Rabat institutions (interview with Khalid Naciri, 17 February 2006), was the emphasis on the 'cost of non-Maghreb'. This formula was inspired by that of the 'cost of non-Europe' – based on the 1988 Cechinni Report – and launched by a EU-promoted research project in 1993 (*Jeune Afrique*, 15–21 February 2009). The first official Moroccan document to reproduce it was a 2003 report of the Ministry of Finance and Privatisation which reviewed the economic situation in the region and quantified the potential benefits that would derive from a hypothetical removal of trade barriers between the Maghreb countries. The conclusion was that the total annual growth of their economies as a whole could be as much as $4,600 million. This accordingly resulted in call to action for Maghrebi policymakers, but also a request for institutional and financial support specifically directed at the EU (Ministère des Finances et de la Privatisation, 2003b: 4). This external connection was crucial in what was otherwise presented as an aseptic technical report, omitting any reference to the political obstacles to Maghrebi integration. References to the economic *cost of non-Maghreb* fitted in perfectly with exogenous expectations regarding the development of this region. Not surprisingly, the same subject was to be taken up in the following years by institutions such as the International Monetary Fund (IMF) and the World Bank, which dedicated several reports and international conferences to the issue (*Le Journal Hebdomadaire*, 29 March–4 April 2008; World Bank, 2006).[1] In response, between 2006 and 2008 innumerable events were organised on the *cost of non-Maghreb*, especially in Tunisia and Morocco,[2] and the issue of regional economic integration was officially relaunched by the AMU's Council of Ministers of Trade (Tunis, January 2007).

In October 2008, the Moroccan Ministry of Economy and Finance published a second, more audacious study on the *cost of non-Maghreb*. The vision of the regional construction now went far beyond economics, incorporating also demographic, environmental, energy and security challenges. The diagnosis of the existing situation was less indulgent and highlighted 'persistent political differences'. Moreover, at least on paper, this time priority was given to the advancement of Maghrebi integration over Morocco's bilateral relations with the EU (Ministère de l'Économie et des Finances, 2008: 11–16). In spite of this, differences in approach and scope between the official Moroccan reports of 2003 and 2008 could largely be explained by the new context of relations between Morocco and the EU, which was marked by the launch of the Union for the Mediterranean (UfM) at multilateral level along with negotiations concerning the Advanced Status at bilateral level. At the same time, domestically, this economistic discourse on Maghrebi integration responded to expectations from, and granted a central role to, national private sector actors and organisations such as the General Confederation of Moroccan Entrepreneurs (CGEM). In February 2007, on the anniversary of the creation of the AMU and in the very same city of Marrakesh, employers' organisations of the countries of the region founded the Maghrebi Union of Employers (UME), based on the conviction that, 'if the political Maghreb does not exist, this should not prevent the emergence of an economic Maghreb'. 'It is the economy that is going to break the political wall that currently exists. We want to put pressure on our governments so that they can themselves improve relations', said the vice-chairman of the CGEM (Martinez, 2008: 5).[3]

The third discourse on regional cooperation in vogue over these years has focused on security and counterterrorism requirements. The need to increase cooperation in all matters related to the exchange of information, border control and the surveillance of terrorist – or often simply Islamist – groups, was taken on by Maghrebi authorities as early as the late 1980s and further accentuated during the years of the Algerian civil war (Hernando de Larramendi, 2008: 183). The post-9/11 context could only strengthen this conviction. In the words of the Moroccan foreign minister Taieb Fassi Fihri: 'The Maghreb is a security imperative against terrorism, migration, illegal trafficking and drugs, before which no Maghrebi state will win on its own' (*Aujourd'hui Le Maroc*, 26 May 2008). In practice, due to the absence of mechanisms for security cooperation within the AMU, its member states increasingly resorted to extra-regional frameworks – the Council of Interior Ministers of the Arab League, sectoral meetings within the Euro-Mediterranean Partnership (EMP) or the 5+5 Dialogue – or to pure bilateralism (*L'Économiste*, 23 April 2007). At the same time, the geographic scale of perceived security threats was expanding whist the region was being redrawn at a strategic level to include the bordering area of the Sahel, to which the U.S. paid increasing attention.

The fourth and last discourse on Maghrebi integration emphasised the growing role of civil society, as enabled by the processes of political liberalisation witnessed mainly in Morocco and Algeria, and the possibility for 'reconciliation from below'. This argument was defended in the early 2000s by the French-Algerian historian Benjamin Stora, who was at the time convinced that the two major countries of the region were going through an unprecedented period of 'democratic phase and political pluralism'. This opening up sustained hopes for a bilateral rapprochement not originating in states or governments, but in changing societies and new generations in which the ideological influence of nationalism and/or Arabism was declining, giving rise to new forms of interaction and convergence. The parallel movements pushing for the recovery of historical memory and the questioning of official histories, which had been long used for legitimisation purposes by the respective regimes, were also supposed to contribute to this bottom-up transformation (Stora, 2002: 29–32, 75–84; *Le Journal*, 19–25 February 2000). Voluntaristic as it may seem, this approach was indeed followed by several civil society initiatives which emerged during these years with the purpose of transcending the borders between the Maghreb countries – and acting, in principle, independently from official guidelines. An example of this was the Collectif Sahara-Maghreb, which was founded in 2002 in Morocco with the stated objective of opening up channels of communication and dialogue with individuals and organisations from Algeria and the Polisario Front, and promoting a 'constructive debate' on the construction of a 'Maghreb of the regions' far removed from any chauvinism (*Le Journal Hebdomadaire*, 19–25 April 2003, 19–25 July 2003).

The vicissitudes of bilateral relations with Algeria

Discourses aside, the actual chronology of bilateral relations between Morocco and Algeria between 1999 and 2014 swung like a pendulum from gestures of goodwill and rapprochement to escalating tensions and the hardening of the respective positions, which took both countries back to square one. A key component of this dynamic were the calls for bilateral normalisation and opening of the border which were regularly made by Morocco, with accelerating frequency, through communiqués of the Ministry of Foreign Affairs and Cooperation and statements at international meetings or summits – to which Algiers responded with dilatory arguments. In fact, these appeals and replies, which were always couched in similar terms, featured much political posturing and theatrics in which each party played its own role. In economic terms, it was estimated that Morocco had a greater need for rapprochement and would benefit more than its neighbour from the opening of the border, through trade with bordering areas and the expected influx of Algerian tourists.

In any case, rather than economic interests, Moroccan insistence mainly resulted from foreign policy calculations transcending the Maghrebi space proper, which pertained to relations with the EU and the U.S. and, by extension, to the Western Sahara conflict. The purpose was to demonstrate its goodwill and play the role of *good student/ally*, thus coming across as the more pragmatic and responsible actor – unlike Algeria – in front of the major international powers. A press comment from 2008 revealed domestic awareness of this game:

> By making a good impression on the international community, Morocco would try, in fact, to achieve two objectives. On the one hand, to respond favourably to recent calls by U.S. officials, excited by the idea of closer ties between the two countries. On the other hand, to isolate the Polisario, at a

time when the Manhasset negotiation process is witnessing repeated fiascos, by establishing particularly close relations with the eastern neighbour.
(*Le Journal Hebdomadaire*, 29 March–4 April 2008)

According to Stora: 'Morocco acts as if it was facing a player who does not want to listen to anything, makes Algeria look like an actor that is atypical or outside the norms of international relations' (*Le Journal Hebdomadaire*, 29 March–4 April 2008).

The link between Rabat's appeals to Algiers and relations with the EU was explicit in different statements made by Moroccan officials. 'The Maghreb will only be able to play its role in Euro-Mediterranean cooperation if the borders are open, if passions calm down', said Fassi Fihri after one of the calls for normalisation (*Aujourd'hui Le Maroc*, 26 May 2008). Brussels' expectations were reflected in the EU Declaration on the occasion of the launch of the EU–Morocco Advanced Status, in October 2008: 'In the context of the strengthening of Euro-Mediterranean cooperation, the EU attaches particular importance to subregional cooperation. [...] [The EU] wants Morocco to encourage the AMU to make proposals for strengthening cooperation with the EU in all its dimensions' (EU–Morocco Association Council, 2008b: 2). Another international partner involved was Spain, to the extent that, according to leaked U.S. diplomatic documents, Mohammed VI (unsuccessfully) tried to have President José Luis Rodríguez Zapatero make a statement in favour of reopening the border during his visit to the city of Oujda in July 2008 (U.S. Embassy in Rabat, cable 08RABAT681, 22 July 2008).

For Algeria, by contrast, the issue of borders was not a priority at this point of time and could therefore be addressed with calculated ambiguity. The invariable answer to Moroccan appeals was that this matter could only be resolved through a 'global approach' to bilateral relations. This empty signifier, which became the official Algerian slogan since 1994 and is still used today, indicated a deliberate strategy of issue linkage: a hypothetical negotiation on the reopening of the border should also incorporate other pending bilateral disputes of varying degrees of importance (e.g. the return of lands and other property expropriated by Morocco to the Algerian state and Algerian investors or citizens, social rights of Algerian workers settled in Morocco). In practice, the meaning of this requirement varied over time: Algerian official statements ranged from a strict interpretation of the 'global approach', which necessarily included the Western Sahara conflict, to a more flexible and pragmatic version, which admitted the possibility of isolating this issue for the sake of general progress in relations between the two neighbours. In other words, the dilemma was between addressing and circumventing the most stubborn bilateral obstacle, thus between linking and dissociating it from the rest of the issues. In a context marked by the failure of the Baker Plans and the stagnation of UN-sponsored direct negotiations, the second option seemed more realistic and constructive.

1999

Upon King Mohammed VI's accession to the throne, the main novelty on the Maghrebi regional scene was Algeria's domestic stabilisation and ensuing international rehabilitation – both political and economic. The election of Abdelaziz Bouteflika as President and the enactment of the Civil Concord Law in 1999 represented the beginning of a process of national reconciliation which was welcomed in Europe and the U.S. The revival and renewed international activism of this state (Zoubir, 2004) inevitably aroused suspicion from its Western neighbour, which perceived new threats to its regional leadership, its relative position in the eyes of foreign powers and the latter's support for its positions on the Western Sahara conflict. Morocco was particularly concerned about Algeria's visible rapprochement with the U.S., which during these years significantly increased both investments in and oil imports from this North African country, and also chose it as priority partner in the fight against terrorism following the 9/11 attacks. Notwithstanding this, towards the end of Hassan II's reign there had been a relative thawing in relations within the region, during which ministerial and sectoral dialogue was launched within the AMU (1995–1999) and a first call for bilateral normalisation was made by the *alternance* government of Abderrahmane Youssoufi in September 1998. The Algerian authorities responded with the most flexible version of the 'global approach', that is, expressing a willingness to put the Western Sahara issue aside (Zoubir, 2000: 56). This constructive attitude on both sides was to continue during 1999, also encouraged by the mediation of Saudi Arabia and other Arab countries.

In 1999, new developments started to emerge which foreshadowed better times for bilateral relations.[4] Bouteflika's electoral victory made him the first civilian to hold the presidency of the Algerian republic since 1965. In Morocco, at first, it was believed that his approach to the Western Sahara question, which had played only a minor part in the election campaign, would be less ideological and more pragmatic than that of his predecessors. This led some to expect that he could even come to terms with an autonomy solution under Moroccan sovereignty, or *third way* (*Le Journal*, 17–23 April 1999, 27 March–3 April 1999). Shortly after his inauguration, Bouteflika promised to work to improve relations with Morocco and the construction of the AMU, suggesting that the Western Sahara conflict could be left aside. In June 1999, the fifth conference of interior ministers of the 5+5 Dialogue led to a meeting in Algiers between the new Algerian President and the Moroccan minister Driss Basri, who expressed Rabat's readiness to 'open a new page' in bilateral relations. The Algerian authorities announced that they had changed their view of the 'global approach' and the two parties agreed to a prompt reopening of the border (*Le Journal*, 26 June–2 July 1999). Optimism was to further increase after Hassan II's death and Bouteflika's attendance at his funeral – the first visit to Morocco by an Algerian president since a decade earlier, when he first met Mohammed VI. The holding of a summit between the two new heads of state later this year was almost taken for granted (*Le Journal*, 24–30 July 1999).

However, several border incidents between August and September 1999 prematurely spoiled this budding rapprochement, acting as a precursor for the ups and downs to which Moroccan–Algerian relations were to be subject after the year 2000. First, there was a massacre of civilians in the Algerian border town of Bechar, which was attributed to an armed Islamist group whose leaders were reported to have been arrested in Morocco. The Rabat government flatly denied this assertion, claiming that its borders were secure. The rhetorical escalation went so far that Bouteflika accused Morocco of hosting and funding Islamist terrorists, trafficking arms to his country and acting as an 'international drug dealer'. Subsequently, ten Algerian soldiers entered Moroccan territory and damaged an outpost (*Le Journal*, 16–22 October 1999). In spite of this, this episode did not result in further confrontation. Crises like this marked the 'extreme level of tension possible between the two countries' (Stora, 2002: 32–34) and revealed the interference of respective domestic politics in at least two ways. First, it appeared clear that certain actors in both countries were interested in derailing the bilateral normalisation process – which are commonly known as *spoilers* in theories of negotiation or conflict resolution. Second, both leaders played the card of confrontation with the neighbour according to their own political needs, in order to consolidate their power and legitimacy in front of rival actors inside their respective regimes. This type of analysis became frequent in the Moroccan press at the time, although was always directed exclusively at the Algerian side. With different nuances, 'internal tensions within the Algerian *pouvoir*', i.e. the Algerian military and secret services, became a commonplace (*Le Journal*, 16–22 October 1999, 19–25 February 2000): 'The Algerian President is hostage to the generals' (*Maroc Hebdo International*, 8–14 October 1999).

2000–2002

Regional optimism returned in April 2000, when the heads of state of Morocco, Algeria, Tunisia and Libya met in Cairo on the margins of the first EU–Africa Summit. Despite evident differences over the new Moroccan proposal of a *third way* for Western Sahara, Bouteflika continued to state that this conflict was an issue in the hands of the UN, and thus relations between Algeria and Morocco should not be dependent on it (*El Watan*, 17 June 2000). This time it was the Moroccan King who reintroduced this crippling issue for bilateral rapprochement in an interview during his first visit to the U.S.:

> There is a problem between Morocco and Algeria. There is no problem between Morocco and the Saharan–Arab Democratic Republic [...]. This is Algeria's creation. I refuse to take part in an Arab Maghreb Union meeting should the leaders, me included, enter into a contest on who will speak the loudest. We must deal with real economic and social issues, not with dossiers that will result in a greater division.
> (Interview with Mohammed VI in *Time*, 26 June 2000)

After this succession of give and take, in the Franco-African Conference held in Yaoundé in January 2001, Mohammed VI and Bouteflika agreed to dissociate the question of Western Sahara from other issues of bilateral relations.

Still, contradictory gestures were to remain the norm. In February 2001, Morocco joined the Community of Sahel-Saharan States (CEN-SAD) – which was founded by Libya in 1998 and did not include Algeria – in what seemed to be an attempt to isolate the latter country diplomatically and to favour an alternative regional framework to the problematic AMU.[5] At the same time, the Moroccan Interior Minister Ahmed Midaoui made a visit to Algeria, in which it was decided to convene the Algerian–Moroccan High Joint Commission soon in order to discuss various issues, putting the Western Sahara conflict aside (Zoubir, 2000: 67–68). Over the following months, various contacts and exchanges of delegations occurred which explored possible ways of repairing bilateral relations and relaunching the Maghrebi project. One of the options considered involved the creation of restricted bilateral committees to discuss and seek solutions for the various outstanding issues in a pragmatic spirit (*Le Journal Hebdomadaire*, 12–18 May 2001).

This period of rapprochement attempts came to an end in June 2002, when Mohammed VI chose not to attend the summit of heads of state of the AMU which had been convened in Algiers to revive the battered regional integration project, even though the foreign minister of the host country had travelled to Rabat in May to invite him personally (AFP, 24 May 2002). It was announced that the Moroccan King would be replaced by a government delegation, which would deprive the meeting of the rank of Presidential Council. The event was finally postponed (AFP, 12 June 2002, 17 June 2002). Morocco's snub was interpreted as a gesture of protest against the (alleged) Algerian proposal to divide the Western Sahara territory, which was included as an option in the report of the UN Secretary-General's report of February 2002, following the failure of the Baker Plan I (UNSC, S/2002/178, 19 February 2002), but was considered by Rabat as unacceptable (*Le Journal Hebdomadaire*, 15–21 June 2002; AFP, 18 June 2002). Soon after, during the serious bilateral crisis with Spain caused by the Moroccan occupation of the islet of Perejil in July 2002, Algiers' alignment with Madrid and rejection of 'any policy of fait accompli or violation of international law' – in the words of its minister for Maghreb and African Affairs – only further soured the mood (AFP, 16 July 2002; Planet and Hernando de Larramendi, 2006: 426–427; Dekkar, 2013: 141).

2003

Efforts at rapprochement between Morocco and Algeria did not resume until early 2003. At a meeting of AMU foreign ministers in Algiers, the Moroccan representative, Mohamed Benaissa, asked for a 'new opportunity' for regional construction (MAEC, 2 January 2003). His Algerian counterpart, Abdelaziz Belkhadem, accepted his invitation to visit Rabat with a 'new constructive spirit' and was received in this capital by Mohammed VI himself (MAEC, 6 February

2003). The two ministers agreed to intensify contacts and to carry out an overall assessment of the bilateral issues through joint working groups (MAEC, 7 February 2003). Some analyses associated all of these conciliatory gestures with the appearance on the scene of the Baker Plan II for Western Sahara, which was submitted confidentially to the parties and the neighbouring countries in January this year. Although the different official reactions were not yet known, at this time it was already suspected that the Algerian attitude would be much more welcoming than it was for the Baker Plan I. The coincidence of Belkhadem's visit to Rabat with the release of 100 Moroccan war prisoners by the Polisario Front suggested that Algerian pressure had been exerted on this organisation. Moreover, General Khaled Nezzar, a former strongman of the Algerian regime (1990–1994) who was retired but still influential, said out of the blue that 'Algeria [did] not need a new state on its borders' (*La Gazette du Maroc*, 10–16 March 2003).

Signs of goodwill from Rabat and Algiers were coupled with the interventions by international actors such as France. During his trip to Algeria in March 2003, President Jacques Chirac strongly advocated reconciliation with the Western neighbour. Rumours of a summit between the two heads of state and the subsequent reopening of the border were incessant during these months. In such circumstances, even harbouring serious reservations about the Baker Plan II, Morocco could not help but jump on the bandwagon and participate in the staging of bilateral rapprochement. This was even acknowledged by an official source: 'The most important thing, for now, is to demonstrate diplomatic goodwill so as, if necessary, to bear no responsibility for a failure of the resolution of the Sahara issue' (*Le Journal Hebdomadaire*, 15–21 March 2003). Among domestic developments, the Casablanca attacks of May 2003 revived Morocco's antiterrorist solidarity with Algeria or, at least, reminded this country of the inescapable need for greater regional cooperation in this field. Their impact was noticeable during minister Benaissa's trip to Algiers in mid-June, when he noted that these attacks had constituted 'a shocking test for the Moroccans and a criminal and terrorist act like those which Algeria [had] been unfortunately suffering for years'. 'Now we must cope with them as this country has done' (MAEC, 14 June 2003). On this occasion, moreover, the two countries decided to create three bilateral committees (political, economic and consular), the last two of which became operational in late June and early July (MAEC, 15 June 2003).

The same progression was reinforced by the release of 243 Moroccan prisoners held by the Polisario Front (MAEC, 15 August 2003) and, above all, by the conversations conducted by Mohammed VI and Bouteflika in New York in September 2003, on the margins of the annual session of the UN General Assembly. The two leaders decided to set up a new joint working group which, according to the joint statement, would be charged with 'cooperation against illegal migration and the coordination of efforts by the two countries in the field of public security, including the fight against terrorism and any threats to the security, stability and peace in the two brotherly countries' (MAEC, 26 September 2003). The two subsequently met again at the summit of heads of state and government of the 5+5 Dialogue held in Tunisia in early December (AFP, 1 December 2003; *L'Économiste*, 4 December 2003).

The culmination of these efforts was expected to be, finally, the holding of the long-awaited summit of heads of state or Presidential Council of the AMU. This meeting was scheduled for 23–24 December 2003 in Algiers, and its agenda was to focus on economic issues and the possibility of establishing a regional free trade area – thus dodging controversial political issues as advocated by the economistic discourse on regional integration. Nevertheless, Mohammed VI, who had been officially invited by President Bouteflika, announced at the last moment that he would not attend the meeting and that Morocco would be represented by minister Benaissa (AFP, 16 December 2003, 21 December 2003). After refusing French mediation in an effort to save the meeting, the Council of Foreign Ministers eventually decided to postpone it indefinitely. It was the second time in less than two years, after June 2002, that an AMU high-level summit had been cancelled (AFP, 22 December 2003), and the second time that the Moroccan King had borne personal responsibility. The explanation provided by Benaissa was full of subtexts: 'The Maghreb Union faces, as everyone knows, a set of obstacles. Everyone acknowledges this' (*Aujourd'hui Le Maroc*, 22 December 2003). Many thought of the spectre of the Western Sahara conflict and the give and take around the Baker Plan II, which had been rejected months before by Rabat, but the direct trigger of the Moroccan snub was never clarified.[6]

2004–2005

The bilateral courtship restarted in May 2004. Following a telephone conversation between the two heads of state, minister Benaissa travelled to Algiers to convey a verbal message from Mohammed VI to President Bouteflika and to meet his counterpart. The purpose was to revive the bilateral committees which had been set up the previous year (consular and economic committees) and to schedule their meetings in June in Morocco (MAEC, 29 May 2004). In late July, Benaissa informed the Algerian ambassador in Rabat that visa requirements for Algerians entering Morocco, in force since 1994, had been abolished (MAEC, 30 July 2004). This widely publicised decision was presented as a significant sign of 'Morocco's sincere desire to work for closer relations' and to revitalise the AMU. It also demanded a reciprocal measure from the neighbouring country, if not the reopening of the border straightaway (MAEC, 4 August 2004, 8 August 2004). Now the ball was in the other court and pressure in favour of Moroccan–Algerian normalisation from international actors was concentrated on Algiers. This country's authorities were slow to react (MAEC, 13 August 2004) and did so with delaying statements. In early September, the interior minister demanded that Morocco not only guarantee Algerians' entry into its territory but also free movement within it. The visa requirement for Moroccans was finally removed in April 2005 (MAP, 2 April 2005).

At the same time, a brief escalation of bilateral tension was to begin in September 2004 following what Rabat described as a 'surprising diplomatic campaign' by Algeria, i.e. the positions held by this country on Western Sahara at the UN General Assembly and the recent recognition of the Sahrawi Arab Democratic Republic (SADR) by its ally South Africa. The Moroccan foreign ministry responded by sending to the UN Secretary-General a memorandum on Western Sahara which highlighted Algerian responsibility within the conflict and the reasons for considering this country as an involved party (MAEC, 2004c). According to some media comments at the time, this marked the beginning of 'a stronger and more persuasive mobilisation of Moroccan diplomacy' in relations with Algiers (*La Gazette du Maroc*, 4–10 October 2004). Soon after, the vote on an Algeria-promoted resolution on Western Sahara in the Special Political and Decolonisation Committee of the UN General Assembly led to a Moroccan statement along the same accusatory lines: 'The dispute over the Sahara is absolutely a Moroccan–Algerian dispute and Algeria will remain responsible [...] for any delay in its resolution' (MAEC, 19 October 2004). The visit to Algeria by Prime Minister Driss Jettou and interior minister Mustapha Sahel, announced for the end of the year, did not finally take place.

The next initiative at bilateral rapprochement took place in March 2005, when Mohammed VI personally attended the summit of the Arab League held in Algiers. The Moroccan foreign ministry described as 'historic' what has been, in fact, the only royal visit to the neighbouring country under Mohammed VI's reign (up to 2014) (Maalmi, 2012: 801). The 'fruitful and promising' talks (MAEC, 23 May 2005, 26 April 2005) reportedly conducted by the two heads of state fuelled expectations of a 'thaw' in bilateral relations. However, the episode ended with yet another failure. After responding positively to Colonel Muammar Gaddafi's invitation to the summit of AMU heads of state organised this time in Tripoli, the Moroccan King refused to attend it in protest at several Algerian 'official statements and positions' on the Western Sahara issue – including above all a call for Morocco to accept and implement the Baker Plan II – which, in Rabat's view, 'manifestly [contradicted] the dynamic undertaken in the region' (MAEC, 22 May 2005): 'Boasting on the eve of the Maghreb summit about an unacceptable conditionality for Maghrebi unification, Algeria has assumed responsibility for jeopardising the opportunity to relaunch Maghrebi construction at the highest level' (MAEC, 23 May 2005).

Relations between the two neighbouring countries remained in the doldrums for the next two years, with no new significant attempts to reanimate them. Among other things, in the midst of the crisis caused by collective assaults on the border fences at Ceuta and Melilla by sub-Saharan African migrants – and unlawful expulsions by Morocco – in the autumn of 2005, minister Benaissa accused Algeria and the Polisario Front of 'exploiting' or 'manipulating' a humanitarian issue for anti-Moroccan propaganda purposes (MAEC, 17 October 2005).

2008

Morocco's calls for normalisation did not resume until March 2008, at a crucial moment during negotiations with the EU on the Advanced Status, proving once again that Rabat's moves on these two boards were closely connected and that foreign policy towards the Maghreb often fulfilled an instrumental function in response to expectations from Brussels. One of the main points of the Moroccan official discourse was that this country's coveted privileged relationship with the northern bloc did not contradict its commitment to South–South cooperation and its involvement in the construction of 'an integrated and stable Arab Maghreb' (MAEC, 29 October 2008). In addition, during these months, the U.S. also stated its interest in revitalising the AMU, with a proposal to bring together all member states' foreign ministers on the margins of the annual session of the UN General Assembly States in September (U.S. Embassy in Rabat, cable 08RABAT461, 20 May 2008). In this context, the Moroccan Ministry of Foreign Affairs and Cooperation issued a statement calling for the reopening of the border with renewed energy and arguments:

> 1 – The closing of the border was decided unilaterally by Algeria in 1994 in an international, regional and bilateral context which has now been amply superseded. 2 – The closure of the border between the two brotherly countries constitutes today a unique and exceptional fact in the world, which is contrary to the aspirations of the peoples of the Maghreb, the expectations of their partners and the requirements of regional peace and development. 3 – In this spirit, the Kingdom of Morocco took numerous forward-looking initiatives in 2004 and 2005 in order to promote the normalisation of bilateral relations [...]. 5 – In this context, the Kingdom of Morocco calls with fraternal friendship and total sincerity for the normalisation of bilateral relations and the opening of the border between the two countries. In this way, it will be possible to respond to the manifest aspirations of the two peoples [...], to satisfy the wishes of border populations and particularly the families affected and, finally, to channel flows of goods which are currently the subject of illegal movements and notorious trafficking.
>
> (MAEC, 20 March 2008)

In addition, considerations related to regional security and stability – and, above all, the threat of terrorism – also gained weight in the discourse of Moroccan officials (MAEC, 21 March 2008). The first Algerian reaction, which came from the interior minister, appealed to the conventional formula of the 'global approach': 'The problem of the movement of goods and persons across borders cannot be dissociated from a global approach to what we want to do with our Maghreb' (*Aujourd'hui Le Maroc*, 24 March 2008). The Moroccan foreign ministry preferred not to consider these words as an official answer (MAEC, 3 April 2008), but the Algerian foreign minister, Mourad Medelci, proved to be even more vague and evasive:

> The reopening of the borders is conceivable within the framework of developments wished by both parties which, eventually, will reveal that this or that difficulty has been overcome, which puts us in a better position for opening up in general and the opening of borders in particular.

In any case, the most explicitly mentioned of the 'developments' or conditions to which this decision was subject concerned the Western Sahara issue (*Aujourd'hui Le Maroc*, 9 April 2008).

Since their offer had fallen on deaf ears, Moroccan officials were quick to denounce the 'political blocks and psychological barriers' of the Algerian ruling class (MAEC, 16 April 2008), which in their opinion maintained double standards and linked or disassociated bilateral normalisation and the Western Sahara issue when it suited its interests. Nevertheless, the Rabat authorities persisted in their attempts at normalisation and, in early May, invited Algeria to hold a joint meeting of the foreign and interior ministers (MAEC, 5 May 2008, 7 May 2008). This initiative was a way to reiterate for a second time the appeal made in March and, according to the official press, formed part of a concrete 'action plan' for the relaunch of bilateral relations: 'The Moroccan government takes once more the initiative in this matter [...]. The ball is again on the Algerian court' (*Aujourd'hui Le Maroc*, 7 May 2008). Soon after, Algiers declared its willingness to try to resolve the borders issue putting the Western Sahara conflict aside (*Aujourd'hui Le Maroc*, 30 May 2008).

At the same time, in the field of parallel diplomacy, the commemoration of the fiftieth anniversary of the Tangiers Conference (1958) provided a perfect opportunity for the Moroccan political parties to display their efforts at enhancing regional reconciliation and integration along the official lines. At the meeting in Tangiers organised by the PI and the Socialist Union of Popular Forces (USFP), which was attended by some of their Algerian, Tunisian, Libyan and Mauritanian counterparts, the Moroccan convenors stated that their intention was to 'revive the unionist spirit', arguing that this was a 'demand of all the Maghreb peoples' and likewise 'required by [their] European partners'. Their plans also included 'reiterating the Kingdom's call for a reopening of borders' (*Aujourd'hui Le Maroc*, 8 April 2008, 22 April 2008). In the end, this event resulted in a joint statement stressing the participants' willingness to 'enhance coordination on all matters relating to the Arab Maghreb', though not without an altercation between Moroccan and Algerian politicians (*Aujourd'hui Le Maroc*, 29 April 2008).[7]

In short, the Moroccan diplomatic display in 2008[8] had no effect in bringing about bilateral normalisation with Algeria, but could well have helped this country to meet EU and U.S. expectations, reinforcing its image as a responsible partner and its sub-role as *promoter of horizontal South–South regional integration*, which was derived from the role of *good student/ally* of the international community. Under this surface by contrast, around 2006 Morocco and Algeria had started what the media described as a real arms race. Following the visit to Algeria by Russian President Vladimir Putin in March of that year, during which weapons sales totalling $8,000 million were agreed upon, Morocco decided to sign a contract to acquire fighter jets for which France and the U.S. were to fight hard (*El País*, 24 September 2007). A steady upward progression in military spending was witnessed in the Maghreb (Morocco, Algeria, Tunisia and Libya) throughout the entire decade, with a total increase of 94 per cent between 1999 and 2008 (compared to 45 per cent worldwide) (SIPRI, 2009: 180). In 2007,

Algeria, Morocco and South Africa stood out as the three biggest spenders in the African continent, with their disbursements accounting for no less than 58 per cent of the total (SIPRI, 2008: 191). The factors ensuring buoyancy were the liquidity provided by the boom in oil prices to countries like Algeria and Libya (*Afkar/Idées*, No. 18, Summer 2008), and financial assistance from Saudi Arabia and other Gulf states to Morocco (Saidy, 2009: 126–128).[9]

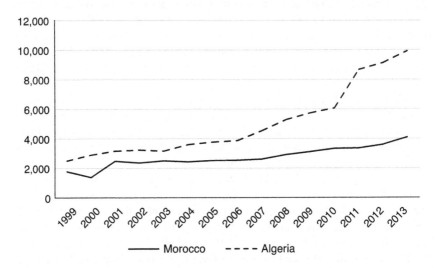

Figure 3.1 Military expenditure in Morocco and Algeria in constant (2011) US$ million, 1999–2013 (source: SIPRI Military Expenditure Database).

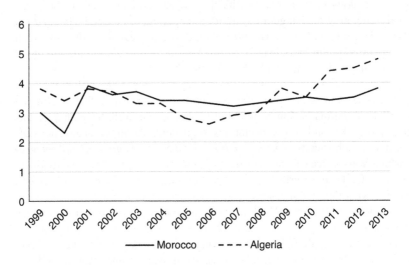

Figure 3.2 Military expenditure in Morocco and Algeria as percentage of GDP, 1999–2013 (source: SIPRI Military Expenditure Database).

Newly dashed expectations after the Arab Spring

A new window of opportunity for bilateral rapprochement between Morocco and Algeria opened up in 2011–2012 in the context of the regional political transformations resulting from the uprisings of the so-called Arab Spring. For some time, both Maghreb countries' authorities likewise confronted domestic protest movements, which they tried to deactivate through reformist measures and socio-economic concessions, as well as the perception of a certain regional isolation following the fall of regimes in neighbouring Tunisia and Libya. Shared threats led them to engage in what was therefore a largely defensive détente. The most visible Moroccan gesture in this regard was the choice of Algiers as the destination for the first trip abroad of foreign minister Saad-Eddine El Othmani in January 2012, after the 2011 legislative elections and the formation of a coalition government led by the Islamist Justice and Development Party (PJD). El Othmani then stated that the revitalisation of relations with Algeria was his 'top priority' and announced the prompt implementation of a concrete action programme engaging both parties (MAEC, 23 January 2012). This was perceived as the PJD's main distinct input or hallmark in foreign policy matters (interview with Abdelwahab Maalmi, 7 June 2013) and coincided with voluntaristic attempts to revive the AMU by the new post-revolutionary Tunisian President, Moncef Marzouki, who intended to host a summit of heads of state of this organisation in Tunis by the end of 2012. The AMU foreign ministers met for this purpose in February and September 2012. Moreover, although they were not primarily exogenously determined as on previous occasions, these moves were also encouraged by the U.S. (Torres, 2013: 14) and the EU. The EU High Representative and the Commission issued a joint communication on 'supporting closer cooperation and regional integration in the Maghreb' (European Commission/HR, 2012).

However, as usual, differences between Morocco and Algeria soon thwarted this regional momentum. The Western Sahara issue reappeared, causing an incident during the funeral of the founding President of the Algerian republic Ahmed Ben Bella, which was abandoned by the Moroccan delegation due to the presence of the Polisario Front and SADR leader, Mohamed Abdelaziz (*Jeune Afrique*, 16 April 2012). Morocco's withdrawal of confidence from the UN Secretary-General's personal envoy for this conflict, Christopher Ross, further increased tensions from May 2012. Two months later, Moroccan Prime Minister Abdelilah Benkirane cast doubt on the holding of the AMU summit, arguing that the conditions were 'not yet ripe': 'As long as the borders between Morocco and Algeria are not reopened, such a meeting will only be purely formal' (*At Tajdid*, 26 July 2012). Algeria rejected this apparent conditionality contending that the border issue was 'exclusively' bilateral and was not linked to the forthcoming Maghrebi summit (AFP, 28 July 2012). In the end, the announced meeting, which had generated many expectations, was indefinitely postponed once again (Hernando de Larramendi, 2012b).

Bilateral relations between Morocco and Algeria were to enter a phase of deep deterioration in 2013 and 2014. In May 2013, the new secretary-general of the PI, Hamid Chabat, made some provocative statements calling for the Moroccan state to officially demand at the UN 'usurped' territory from southern-western Algeria – the so-called 'eastern Sahara' around Bechar and Tindouf (*Lakome*, 2 May 2013) – an old nationalist claim which had lain buried since the early 1970s. Though never officially supported by the government or the palace, this eccentric proposal created much media noise and overshadowed bilateral rows for months (it was repeated by the PI in October).

In late October, six months after the U.S. attempt to extend the mandate of the UN Mission for the Referendum in Western Sahara (MINURSO) to human rights monitoring, President Bouteflika explicitly renewed his backing for this Moroccan-aborted initiative in a message to a solidarity conference in support of the Sahrawi cause held in Abuja, Nigeria. The timing of this public declaration, coming immediately after a visit by Ross to the region which was received with protests in occupied Western Sahara and immediately before Mohammed VI's trip to the U.S. (Roussellier, 2013), made it especially irritating and 'hostile' for Rabat. The Moroccan foreign ministry reacted by recalling the ambassador to Algiers for consultations (MAEC, 30 October 2013) – though only for four days – and organising a meeting at which all national political parties unanimously condemned the Algerian statement (*Tel Quel*, 19 November 2013). On the anniversary of the Green March, the King accusatorily alluded to Algeria denouncing 'money and benefits through which the enemies are trying to buy votes and positions of some organisations which are hostile to our country' (speech by Mohammed VI, Rabat, 6 November 2013). In the meantime, tensions were also stoked by media belligerence from both sides and a sit-in at the Algerian consulate in Casablanca during which an individual removed the Algerian flag (*Alif Post*, 5 November 2013).

Diplomatic skirmishes and border incidents followed in 2014. The Rabat authorities considered that Algeria was seeking to isolate them diplomatically by excluding (or trying to exclude) them from the Global Counterterrorism Forum meeting held in Algiers (MAP, 7 February 2014) and the Fourth EU–Africa Summit in Brussels (MAP, 3 April 2014). The eastern neighbour was also deemed to be behind the African Union's appointment of former Mozambican President Joaquim Chissano as its special envoy for Western Sahara, which was 'entirely rejected' by Rabat as a 'unilateral decision' lacking 'a legal ground' or 'a political base' (MAEC, 1 July 2014). Meanwhile, the Moroccan interior minister announced the ongoing construction of a metal fence along the border with Algeria in order to prevent alleged terrorist threats (EFE, 17 July 2014). This decision had little to do with Rabat's quasi-ritual calls for bilateral normalisation and the opening of the border over the previous decade. Eventually, after a brief détente, the Arab Spring had done nothing but increase the strain between Morocco and Algeria by reinforcing new Sahrawi international strategies, thus reigniting a diplomatic battle which had not been dissociated at any moment from this bilateral relationship. Despite all the ambivalence, Morocco's identity as *territorial champion* seemed to be prevailing within the role conflict over that of *promoter of Maghrebi regional integration*.

Altogether, it can be concluded that the tension and the usual contradictions between those two Moroccan foreign policy roles, which respectively originate from endogenous and exogenous sources, remains unresolved under Mohammed VI's reign. Various historicist, economistic, security and social discourses advocating the need for greater regional cooperation and integration in the Maghreb have become widespread within Moroccan political space, but in practice, Moroccan–Algerian relations have continued to swing like a pendulum from gestures of goodwill and rapprochement to declaratory escalations. Rabat's periodic calls for the 'normalisation' of bilateral relations and the opening of the shared border have often been instrumental in nature, since they resulted from foreign policy calculations transcending the Maghrebi space proper, which pertained to relations with the EU and the U.S.

Notes

1 The European Institute of the Mediterranean (IEMed) and the Spanish Ministry of Foreign Affairs and Cooperation also organised two events entitled 'From the Cost of Non-Maghreb to the North African Tiger' in Madrid (May 2006) and Barcelona (November 2007) (Ghilès, 2010).
2 See also the reference in Comité Directeur du Rapport (2006: 105).
3 See also *L'Économiste* (26 June 2007, 2 July 2007).
4 For an account by a journalist of the Moroccan official news agency, Maghreb Arab Press (MAP), see Dekkar (2013).
5 The founding members of this regional organisation, besides Libya, were Mali, Burkina Faso, Niger, Chad and Sudan. Morocco, Tunisia, Egypt, Nigeria and Somalia joined them at the Khartoum summit held in February 2001.
6 A possible reason could be Algeria's refusal to negotiate a political solution to the Western Sahara conflict directly (bilaterally) with Morocco and outside the UN framework, an alternative that Rabat explored during these months in an attempt to try to overcome the crisis sparked off by its rejection of the Baker Plan II (MAEC, 19 April 2004).
7 Another timely parallel (and public) diplomacy initiative was the first edition of the MEDays forum, which was organised in Tangier in November 2008 by the Amadeus Institute. Its final declaration referred to the need to relaunch the AMU, normalise relations and reopen the border between Algeria and Morocco, and support Morocco's Autonomy Plan for Western Sahara. See Forum MEDays (2008) Déclaration de Tanger, Tangier, 26–28 November.
8 The next call for normalisation and the opening of the border was made by minister Fassi Fihri during the seventh meeting of foreign ministers of the 5+5 Dialogue held in Córdoba, Spain, in April 2009 (MAEC, 21 April 2009).
9 Less alarmist analyses contended that this phase simply involved the renewal of military material (*Tel Quel*, 13–19 December 2008, 20–26 May 2006).

4 A 'model student' in search of a differentiated relationship with the EU

Few analysts doubt that the Western Sahara conflict is the cornerstone around which the puzzle of Morocco's foreign policy has been constructed and structured for decades, and that the first national role conception (Holsti, 1970) underpinning it was, in general, that of *champion of national territorial integrity*. The other role competing for this prevailing and *structuring* place in the country's hierarchy of priorities abroad is that of *model student of the European Union (EU) and Euro-Mediterranean policies*. The ongoing strengthening and preservation of the exclusive nature of the political, economic, social and cultural ties inherited from colonial times has been an unwavering desire of independent Morocco, even at the expense of closer relations with neighbouring Maghreb (White, 1996: 113, 117), Arab or African countries. This 'clear vision', 'strategic political choice' and 'strong political expression of the will to have privileged relations with Europe' at the highest level, from King Mohammed V (1957–1961) to King Mohammed VI, is recognised in Brussels as being 'what makes the difference in the case of Morocco compared to other Arab countries' (interview with Eneko Landaburu, 23 May 2014). In other words, as a role, it brings together an *ego*'s self-definition and *alter*'s role expectations (Aggestam, 2006: 18–20), which influence or *mirror* each other dynamically.

The main research question addressed in this chapter is how Moroccan foreign policy has contributed to achieving and maintaining privileged treatment by the EU, compared to other southern Mediterranean partners, combining regional/multilateral identification and bilateral differentiation under evolving circumstances. The focus will be on factors and dynamics that transcend strictly material and/or rational approaches, thus broadly falling within constructivist International Relations scholarship, and more particularly will draw on the literature on international socialisation in order to explain the relationship between Morocco's role conception and its role performance in relations with the EU.

Due to their disparate sources and normative content, the relationship between Morocco's two prominent roles as *territorial champion* and *model student of the EU* appears to be quite complex. By and large, to date, the two roles have been largely compatible within foreign policy behaviour, since the corresponding targeted objectives have not clashed with each other directly. Building on Raffaella A. Del Sarto's (inverse) argument that a more settled (or less contested) state identity would favour the engagement by countries in region-building in this area (2006: 177), it could even be claimed that the domestic-nationalist consensus built around the Western Sahara issue has been more beneficial than not for Morocco's Euro-Mediterranean commitment and activism. However, since the turn of the millennium there have also been cases of role conflict (Cantir and Kaarbo, 2013: 467–468, 2012: 10–11; Aggestam, 2006: 23). The tension between the nationalist soul – the 'geopolitical constant' (El Houdaïgui, 2003b) – and the pro-European soul remains the ultimate key and dilemma within Moroccan foreign policy.

Morocco's foreign policy role as *model student of the EU* displays five characteristics. First, it enjoys a considerable domestic consensus and low degree of contestation both horizontally (among different political elites) and vertically (between leaders and public opinion) (Cantir and Kaarbo, 2012: 11–12). From a horizontal perspective, it appears that the desire to strengthen Morocco's ties with Europe, as has been emphasised by the official discourse since independence, is supported by the national political elites transversally and practically unanimously. At the very least, there is a 'consensus by default' resulting from the absence of any 'outspoken challengers' to this pro-European orientation (Del Sarto, 2006: 209). In a pioneering survey on the foreign policy perceptions and preferences of the Moroccan elites conducted in 1995, as many as 80 per cent of interviewees supported Morocco's 'accession' to the EU. The EU was also by far the preferred answer to the question concerning the bloc of countries to which the kingdom should become closer (89 per cent), being far ahead of the Maghreb (53 per cent), the United States (40 per cent) and the Middle East (37 per cent) (*Shu'un Magribiya*, February 1996). The arguments on which this widespread *desire for Europe* was based were mainly (71 per cent) economic in nature and suggested the existence of a 'pragmatic Moroccan elite' with 'a largely non-ideological view of the external environment and economic issues shaping their perceptions' (Planet, 1997: 79). At the same time, this orientation was fully aligned with official guidelines. Not by chance, one year earlier the heir to the throne, Prince Mohammed, had completed his PhD thesis on cooperation between the European Economic Community (EEC)/EU and the Arab Maghreb Union (AMU) (Ben El Hassan Alaoui, 1994, 1999).

From a vertical perspective, the extent to which the wider population supports Morocco's pro-European orientation is more difficult to determine in the absence of opinion polls throughout these years. The main data available come from the recent EU Neighbourhood Barometers conducted in 2012, 2013 and 2014, which consistently show that the perception of the EU and Morocco's relations with the EU by Moroccan public opinion is not only overwhelming positive, but also significantly better than the average for the southern Mediterranean countries.[1]

An identity-based explanation for this sizeable consensus is that the role of *model student of the EU* could be easily accommodated with the monarchy's traditional presentation of Morocco's identity as multidimensional and inclusive (Del Sarto, 2006: 182, 206, 218). In other words, 'the monarchy's identity discourse may have succeeded in persuading Moroccans that the country's

Table 4.1 Perception of the EU within Moroccan public opinion (%)

	Spring 2012	Autumn 2012	Spring 2013	Autumn 2013	Spring 2014
Positive	54	69	59	76	77
Neutral	26	20	22	14	15
Negative	8	4	10	3	1
Do not know	12	7	9	7	7

Source: EU Neighbourhood Barometers; data processed by author.

Table 4.2 Perception of Morocco's relations with the EU within Moroccan public opinion (%)

	Spring 2012	Autumn 2012	Spring 2013	Autumn 2013	Spring 2014
Good	82	86	75	87	91
Bad	7	7	16	4	3
Do not know, others	10	6	9	9	6

Source: EU Neighbourhood Barometers; data processed by author.

pro-European and pro-Western orientation "does not infringe on Morocco's sociocultural identity and its personality"' (Del Sarto, 2006: 209; quoting *Maroc Hebdo International*, 25 March 1998).

The second characteristic of Morocco's role as a *model student of the EU* is that it has also settled thanks to the recurring reciprocity and *mirroring* between the Moroccan (*ego*) self-definition and the EU (*alter*) role expectations. Alexander Wendt uses the terms 'reflected appraisals' and 'mirroring' to describe how 'actors come to see themselves as a reflection of how they think Others see or "appraise" them, in the "mirror" of Others' representations of the Self' (1999: 327). Third, this key role lies at the core of a broader role-set (Aggestam, 2006: 21), which encompasses subsidiary sub-roles that have been endorsed in the Moroccan official discourse for decades and featured repeatedly in the speeches of Hassan II with metaphors such as 'stabiliser' or 'balancing pole' of the Euro-Mediterranean region, 'bridge' or 'nexus' (*trait d'union*) between Europe and Africa, and between the 'West' and the Arab and Muslim world, as well as religious 'moderator' (El Houdaïgui, 2003a: 103–146). Their common feature is the implication of mediation or services performed in different parts of the world for the benefit of the EU or the 'West', broadly speaking, as a result of an alleged convergence of interests and approaches.

Fourth, the role of *model student* has been put to strategic use in that it has been consciously handled by the country's decision-makers as a means for achieving particular political goals and, more specifically, privileged treatment by the EU. As has been stressed by Cristian Cantir and Juliet Kaarbo, the strategic use of roles reveals that 'structures do not deterministically impose behaviours but rather become part of the domestic political "game"' (2012: 19). Fifth, in line with the fourth characteristic, this role involves a duality since it fuses together a bilateral and a multilateral component: *model student* of the EU and Euro-Mediterranean policies. In practice, the multilateral dimension seems ultimately to be subordinated to the bilateral one, with Mediterranean identity and engagement being embraced as a means – or as an alternative way – for reinforcing bilateral relations with EU: 'Morocco sees its relations with the EU as a Euro-Moroccan partnership and differentiates this from Morocco's relations with Mediterranean countries' (Pace, 2006: 151).

In practice, as the following sections will show, this national role conception translated into a steady course within Moroccan foreign policy behaviour after 1999. Not only has there been a consistent correlation between role conception and role performance, but this has also borne fruit in terms of the expected results: Morocco has strengthened its economic ties with the EU and its member states, and managed to secure permanent recognition by Brussels of its status as the most advanced southern Mediterranean partner in political terms, despite friction associated at times with agricultural and fisheries relations, control of illegal migration, human rights violations and the Western Sahara conflict.

If only a coincidence, the beginning of the reign of Mohammed VI concurred with a significant turning point in Morocco–EU relations. This King acceded to the throne only a few months before the entry into force, in March 2000, of the new bilateral Association Agreement between Morocco and the EU signed in 1996 in the framework of the Euro-Mediterranean Partnership (EMP) or Barcelona Process (*Le Journal*, 22–28 May 1999). After a long ratification process by the European Parliament and the 15 EU member states, Morocco became the second North African country, after Tunisia (March 1998), to complete this qualitative leap in relations with Brussels. This was precisely the moment chosen by Mohammed VI to put his cards on the table regarding the pro-European aspirations inherent within Morocco's role conception. He seized the opportunity of his awaited visit to Paris to claim that the new legal and institutional framework for bilateral relations with the EU represented only a first step towards the country's desired status, which was:

> A partnership that would be at the same time: more and better than the revised and corrected association in which we have become involved, and perhaps still for some time, a little less than the accession dictated to us however by reason, geography and the everyday realities of economic, social and cultural life in our country.
> (Speech by Mohammed VI, Paris, 20 March 2000)

This royal statement of intent and profession of European faith, which was in keeping with the raising of the stakes made by Hassan II with his formal application for EEC membership in 1987, acted as the leitmotif of the King's official trips to Paris, Rome, Lisbon and Madrid in the spring and autumn of 2000 (Mezran, 2000; Janati-Idrissi, 2000, 2001). The formula 'more than association, less than accession', and its later derivation 'advanced status' (*statut avancé*)[2] – largely empty signifiers – soon became ubiquitous official slogans. The idea was infused into the new institutionalised political dialogue with the EU during the first two meetings of the EU–Morocco Association Council, in October 2000 and October 2001 (Del Sarto, 2006: 201). Eventually, in October 2008, it led to the achievement of the so-called Advanced Status, whereby the EU nominally granted a special relationship to Morocco. The 'roadmap' contained in the Joint Document adopted during the seventh session of the EU–Morocco Association Council (EU–Morocco Association Council, 2008a) is a particularly suggestive object of study from a constructivist perspective, as it represented an unprecedented qualitative leap forward in bilateral relations, mainly due to its *ideational* strength or *symbolic* dimension, regardless of its failure to specify operational measures or clear added value in material or *practical* terms – in relation to the possibilities for convergence and integration already existing within the framework of the European Neighbourhood Policy (ENP). The EU's relatively privileged treatment of Morocco was not affected after 2011 either by the profound regional disruptions caused by the wave of anti-authoritarian protests, revolutionary regime changes and emerging civil conflicts of the Arab Spring, or by the subsequent review of the ENP.

Several factors compete in explaining Morocco's privileged treatment by the EU, but appear to be insufficient. In the first place, from the European perspective, the priority afforded to Morocco does not appear to be justified overall on structural political economy grounds, i.e. by a higher economic (inter)dependence than that existing with other countries in the same region. Morocco's economic dependence on the EU has historically been and still remains very high, in terms of both trade and investment, but essentially operates in a one-way direction;[3] therefore it cannot be said that this imposes any direct constraint on EU foreign policy. Second, a more plausible explanation for the special relationship between the EU and Morocco can be found at the level of EU policymaking. There, it is commonly argued that Morocco enjoys a particular *intergovernmental advantage*, consisting in the persistent ability of France and Spain to impose their preferences on EU policies towards the Maghreb (Colombo and Voltolini, 2014: 53–55), in a clear example of 'geo-clientelism' (Behr and Tiilikainen, 2015: 27–28). Both former colonial powers each have a web of particular interests – economic, social, cultural, 'human' and elite interdependence, which is almost symbiotic for France and more determined by territorial contiguity and security imperatives as far as Spain is concerned – which impels them to preserve at all costs good bilateral understanding with the authorities in Rabat and, additionally, to promote the interests and aspirations of the latter on the EU level. Conversely, since the 1990s Morocco has skilfully exploited differences between member states in order to increase its negotiating power and gather support for its positions vis-à-vis the EU (White, 1996: 113). However, the favourable European intergovernmental setting appears to be a necessary but not a sufficient condition.

Third, it is also necessary to add, as set out below, Morocco's own *agency* and outstanding pro-European activism within the foreign policy sphere, that is, the role performance resulting from the country's role conception as a *model student of the EU*. Ultimately, it can be argued that this foreign policy behaviour has provided a vital contribution in ensuring the continuity of the EU–Morocco special relationship during critical junctures such as in 2011, overshadowing (insufficient) domestic developments and reforms. This causality link has been pointed out by Timo Behr:

> The pattern is clear. Those countries that are willing and able to pursue closer ties with the EU will be rewarded, by obtaining new contractual relations and funding. Unsurprisingly, the countries with the closest and most developed trade and aid relationship with the EU after the Arab Spring are the same as before the Arab Spring. This tendency to equivilate the closeness of a country's ties with the EU as a signal of its reform is worrisome.
>
> (2012: 21)

Fourth, a positive international perception of Morocco's internal political evolution has prevailed over the last two decades. The resulting question is why Morocco has been always the most highly regarded country in the region for the EU and much of the international community in terms of political development, reforms and democratisation. This is associated with the foreign policy behaviour mentioned above, since the international promotion of the 'democratising' image of Morocco, or at least the idea of a 'Moroccan exception' as the lesser evil within a regional context marked by greater political instability and/or authoritarianism, has represented one of the top priorities for this state's foreign policy since the 1990s.

Morocco's superficial but effective socialisation by the EU

Both this exemplary pro-European behaviour and the positive European perception of Morocco can be traced back to phenomena of international socialisation and learning at macro and micro levels – concerning the state or individual policymakers (Checkel, 2006: 4–5, 9). As may be inferred from Morocco's inveterate pro-European foreign policy orientation and its performance of the role of *model student of the EU*, different processes of socialisation have been at work for decades in relations between Morocco and the EU, most notably since the 1990s. However, judging by Morocco's poor record on political reform and democratisation, it appears that Moroccan socialisation by the EU has not, broadly speaking, resulted in any substantial change in interests, values and identity in line with the European political norms but has remained on a more limited and superficial level. The evolution towards a logic of appropriateness has entailed effectively learning what is socially accepted and expected within the context of this asymmetric relationship and adopting new roles accordingly, yet nothing like a genuine internalisation of the community's constitutive political norms and values. This amounts to Jeffrey T. Checkel's type I of internalisation/

socialisation ('conscious role playing') (Checkel, 2006: 6, 9), or what Frank Schimmelfennig describes as the 'adoption of the standard at a superficial level'. The latter is achieved by 'formally subscribing to, but not really acting according to, the social values and norms or by interpreting the values and norms in the way that is most compatible with their interest in political power' (2000: 118). Nonetheless, no matter how superficial Morocco's socialisation eventually turns out to be, the learning process involved seems quite complex. It goes well beyond pure individualistic and rational action, insofar as phenomena such as 'reflected appraisals' and 'mirroring' (Wendt, 1999: 327) play a conspicuous role in interactions between Morocco and the EU.

According to interviews conducted with EU officials in Rabat and Brussels, Morocco's outstanding pro-European foreign policy activism can be understood largely as a product of socialisation.[4] These foreign practitioners point to the relevance of three interrelated long- and medium-term phenomena of socialisation and social learning, which primarily affect the micro level (individual policymakers and officials originating in national elites) but also have an impact, at a later stage, on the macro level (the state administration as a whole) (Checkel, 2006: 4–5, 9). The first factor is the preservation of a French-style elite education model, partly inherited from the colonial period, often including studies in French universities or *grand écoles* (Cebolla, 2004; *Jeune Afrique*, 8 December 2010):

> Since independence, all the Moroccan elites have been educated principally in France. All financial, political, economic and other elites were already fairly steeped in pro-European values. That is very important. We have a political will at the highest level, with Mohammed V and Hassan II favouring rapprochement with Europe, and then an elite which follows, which goes on that way.
> (Interview with Eneko Landaburu, 23 May 2014)

> As far as the education of elites is concerned, firstly, there are those who study in Europe and secondly, the European reference frame is taught, not only the regional one. And that makes a difference, even in the mentality of the country's elite, it is very present.
> (Interview in EU Delegation to Morocco, 6 June 2013)

The second factor is a more specific training and specialisation in EU affairs within certain sectors of the Moroccan state administration: 'In fact, as the country commits itself, the administration is oriented in this [pro-European] direction. There are officials [*cadres*] in the administration who are trained in the idea of maintaining relations with Europe' (interview in EU Delegation to Morocco, 6 June 2013). Third, compared to other southern Mediterranean countries, governmental and administrative knowledge and the understanding of the institutional setting and practices of EU foreign relations ('how to interact with us') is better in Morocco:

[In other southern Mediterranean countries] they do not have the same knowledge, or the same understanding, just a political "feeling" about how the Europeans are. [...] They have no clue about how the European institutions work, the role of each one [...]. But in the Moroccan case, the Mission in Brussels has relays [*relais*] everywhere, in all the institutions. [...] So this makes a difference. The understanding of the functioning of institutions is much better, as also is the knowledge of the agenda of each country, along with cultural and social knowledge.
(Interview in EU Delegation to Morocco, 6 June 2013)

Dorothée Schmid (2003: 26) elaborates on the latter argument:

Since then [1996], Morocco has responded well to European initiatives. The Moroccan bureaucracy has adapted to the necessities of tackling different European regulations better than the administrations of most other Mediterranean partner-countries. The Moroccans have wisely improved their diplomatic abilities in dealing with the Commission over the past five years [...]. Their negotiating skills have produced impressive results in specific issues in the past.

However, this kind of socialisation and social learning has not automatically implied a genuine internalisation of European norms and values by Morocco. It appears to be more akin to an 'adoption of the standard at a superficial level' (Schimmelfennig, 2000: 118):

I do not know to what extent we share *cultural concepts*. We rather share *knowledge*. There are some common values, but this happens also with other countries. And it is difficult to argue that we have common values with Morocco [as a whole]. Morocco is not an entity. The relationship we can have with the administration [might not be extended to the whole society]. There are citizens of Morocco who do not have the same knowledge of Europe, who are distant, who live in a more traditional way and to whom Europe is very alien. [...] At the administrative level, the *knowledge* is very good. [...] I do not think that Morocco is more "European" in its way of thinking or functioning than others. But it is finer when it comes to reflecting strategically on its interests. [...] What is more important is the mutual knowledge and the ability, on the basis of this knowledge, to think about what is interesting for Morocco to replicate.
(Interview in EU Delegation to Morocco, 6 June 2013, emphasis added)

One of the ways in which the Moroccan regime has achieved international legitimacy in the context of its socialisation and asymmetric relations with the EU is by engaging in what Schimmelfennig calls 'rhetorical action', that is, an instrumental use of arguments. The four most common strategies of this kind are 'swotting' (playing the model student of the EU in competition with peer countries), 'shifting the burden' (emphasising the need for more material or political support from the EU in order to comply with its requirements), 'manipulation of European identity' (claiming to share the EU's identity and values on a deep historical level) and 'appeal to community [EU] norms' (urging the EU to respect its own norms when this suits one's own interests) (Schimmelfennig, 2000: 129–131). All of these rhetorical strategies feature distinctively in Moroccan official foreign policy discourse with regard to the EU, with 'swotting' standing out as the most recurrent, in accordance with the role conception of Morocco's national role conception as a *model student of the EU*. Yet again, the implications of playing this role are twofold. On the one hand, as will be shown in the case of the EU–Morocco Advanced Status, there has been a strategic use of the role (Cantir and Kaarbo, 2012: 19), which has even allowed the weaker party to the relationship to impose its own 'definition of the situation' (Wendt, 1999: 329), countering the established power relation.[5] On the other hand, role playing as a socialisation mechanism cannot be conflated with or reduced to mere strategic rational action since it always involves some degree of bounded rationality and 'noncalculative behavioural adaptation' (Checkel, 2006: 11). On a separate note, 'shifting the burden' plays a central role in the Moroccan discourse on the migratory dimension of Morocco–EU relations.

The voiding of the political substance of Morocco's socialisation by the EU has also been facilitated by the depoliticisation or *technocratisation* of the EU's democracy promotion policies, despite the presence of a considerable normative load within rhetoric. According to Milja Kurki, technocratic assumptions prevail in this framework as 'a discursive set of ideals for governance, which emphasise the virtues of depoliticisation, harmonisation, rationalisation and objectification of policymaking and evaluation, and which promotes the role of technical experts in policy-making over substantively "political" or "democratic" public actors' (2011: 216). The pervasive concept of good governance has played a central role in this regard. As part of the global neoliberal reform agenda, it brings to the forefront the values of inclusiveness/pluralism and political accountability, albeit from a managerial efficiency or technical perspective that ultimately emasculates their democratising potential (Zemni and Bogaert, 2010: 97, 100). In the words of a Moroccan political commentator, Omar Saghi, governance as a euphemism represents 'the politeness of benevolent authoritarianism': 'For thirty years, the authoritarian alignment with global standards imposed on developing countries has occurred under this flag' (*Tel Quel*, 7 December 2013).

A telling example of how the fixation with technical expertise and participation that marks the EU governance approach can practically divert or undermine Morocco's prospects for democratisation is provided by the role granted in bilateral relations to certain Moroccan consultative councils made up of civil society and 'experts', which report directly to the palace lacking any organic relationship with representative institutions such as the government or parliament. The most important of these bodies in the context of the negotiations and the resulting document on the Advanced Status was the Consultative Council on Human

Rights (CCDH) – later transformed into National Council on Human Rights (CNDH) in 2011 (Fernández-Molina, 2011a).

An exemplary performance in the Euro-Mediterranean Partnership

Established in the 1995 Barcelona Conference with the stated purpose of transforming the historically unbalanced relations between the EU and the southern Mediterranean countries into a novel partnership among equals to promote (bi)regional integration, shared development and stability, the Euro-Mediterranean Partnership (EMP), or Barcelona Process, has been interpreted in liberal and constructivist IR literature as an original attempt at socialisation and inclusion by the EU in targeting these problematic neighbours. Accordingly, this ambitious initiative sought to project the EU's 'normative power' (Manners, 2002) and practices of cooperative security, region-building and pluralistic integration into the Mediterranean area, encouraging changes in both the domestic structures and the external behaviour of the Mediterranean partner countries. On paper, the three complementary logics of transformation were to be economic (neo)liberal reform (macroeconomic stabilisation, trade liberalisation and opening), political democratisation and multilateral cooperation (Adler *et al.*, 2006: 58–66). By contrast, dissenting realist voices doubted that Euro-Mediterranean relations could easily transcend the historical power imbalance and viewed the EU's behaviour in this area as typically hegemonic – with EU leadership being consented to by *clients* in exchange for certain benefits (Costalli, 2009; Attinà, 2003).

Chief among the EMP's legal and institutional features was its multidimensional character. On the one hand, the traditional hub-and-spoke model of bilateral relations between the EU and individual Mediterranean partner countries was maintained, now manifesting itself in a new generation of association agreements signed from 1995 onwards along with the bilateral institutions created under them (Association Councils, Association Committees). On the other hand, a genuine multilateral dimension was added with the introduction of regular Euro-Mediterranean conferences of foreign ministers and sectoral ministerial meetings attended by all EMP member states, as well as a Euro-Mediterranean Parliamentary Forum/Assembly. Out of all of the southern partners, Morocco's performance within the framework of the EMP was exemplary on both multilateral and bilateral level. Not only did it diligently fulfil its role as a *model student* of the EU, but its officials were also particularly skilful in taking advantage of its dual nature, i.e. 'playing a subtle game between the two main dimensions of the Partnership' (Schmid, 2003: 26). As explained above, precedence was given to the bilateral dimension within Rabat's overall strategy, with the multilateral one dimension taking on a rather instrumental character:

> Given that Morocco has traditionally been seeking closer ties with Europe, it welcomed the EMP as a potential tool to achieve its objectives. [...]

Altogether, Morocco was playing the 'Euro-Mediterranean game' quite well in the time-span under consideration, and it 'used' the EMP to support its developmental strategy and to foster a stronger attachment to the EU.

(Del Sarto, 2006: 201, 203)

Multilateral dimension

At the multilateral level, from the Euro-Mediterranean conferences that followed the inaugural one in Barcelona – Valletta (April 1997), Stuttgart (April 1999), Marseille (November 2000), Valencia (April 2002), Naples (December 2003), Luxembourg (May 2005), Tampere (November 2006) and Lisbon (November 2007) – the first to be held after the accession of King Mohammed VI to the throne and the entry into force of the EU–Morocco Association Agreement was the Marseille Conference. One month before, at the first meeting of the bilateral Association Council, the Presidency announced that an appraisal mission was to be sent to Rabat 'to find out Morocco's views on the difficulties encountered and the prospects of the process [EMP]' (EU–Morocco Association Council, 2000: 4–5). Indeed, the Marseille Conference ended in disappointment, as the awaited Euro-Mediterranean Charter for Peace and Stability was postponed 'owing to the political context' (the escalation of the Israeli–Palestinian conflict with the Second Intifada) (Lannon, 2003: 500–501). With the EMP in the doldrums, the first display of Morocco's Euro-Mediterranean activism occurred in an alternative setting, namely the Mediterranean Forum, an informal mechanism for dialogue and coordination established by southern European and Mediterranean partner countries in 1994 on the margins of the Barcelona Process. Morocco hosted the Mediterranean Forum's eighth regular meeting in Tangier in May 2001 and a special session dedicated to the 9/11 attacks in Agadir in October 2001.

The fifth Euro-Mediterranean conference, which was held in Valencia in April 2002 (Gillespie, 2002), was the moment chosen by Mohammed VI's diplomacy to show its hand and set out its criticisms and expectations vis-à-vis the difficult evolution of the EMP. Morocco presented an official draft or memorandum 'Pour une dynamisation du partenariat euro-méditerranéen' containing proposals for improving the institutional governance of the partnership and certain ongoing policies. In institutional terms, the main complaint was the absence of peer-to-peer structures enabling southern countries to participate in the EMP on an equal footing with their European partners. It was suggested that a co-presidency formula be devised in order to avoid a situation in which the rotating President of the European Council automatically led all EMP institutions, and to alternate meeting locations between the northern and southern shores of the Mediterranean. The proposed remedy against what was described as an 'excessive bureaucratisation' (*surbureaucratisation*) of the Barcelona Process was to improve the flow of information and to second southern Mediterranean officials to the Commission in order to enable them to become familiar with the EU's functioning, rules and practices (MAEC, 2002).

Alongside institutions, this memorandum raised some of Morocco's concerns regarding the EU which remained constant throughout the 2000s: first, the fear that, at a time of growing international attention to security issues – which actually became a priority in the Valencia Action Plan – southern countries were being virtually excluded from political dialogue and the design of the future Mediterranean security architecture; second, the possible negative impact of the then impending Eastern enlargement of the Union on the EMP; third, the insignificant level of horizontal trade between the Mediterranean partner countries and the need to encourage subregional integration within frameworks such as the Agadir Process (launched by Morocco, Tunisia, Egypt and Jordan in 2001) or the still unfulfilled AMU; and fourth, the also insufficient foreign direct investment flowing into these countries, which Morocco suggested be promoted though the creation of a Euro-Mediterranean Bank (offering to host its headquarters) (MAEC, 2002).

Not by chance, the propositional effort made by Rabat in Valencia coincided with the signing of the Association Agreement between the EU and Algeria, which provided evidence of the latter country's return to the international arena under the presidency of Abdelaziz Bouteflika (1999–) after the bloody domestic conflict of the 1990s. Morocco's zero-sum perception of the growing European and U.S. courtship of Algeria, which was considered to undermine its own relative position, enhanced the competitive dimension of 'swotting'. On the other hand, this Euro-Mediterranean conference came at a time of escalating bilateral crisis between Morocco and Spain which also had EU connections, since its first triggering factor was the suspension of EU–Morocco fisheries negotiations in 2001.

In the following years, as the EU's 2004 Eastern enlargement approached, the Maghreb leaders and political actors voiced increasing anxiety over the fate of Euro-Mediterranean cooperation and their countries' place in Brussels' external agenda. Acknowledgement of the potential benefits of an expanded and strengthened Union as a counterweight to U.S. power and a focal point of economic prosperity exported to neighbouring regions did not allay 'the concern at seeing a new "power" Europe emerge north of the Mediterranean, [deploying] its natural arguments of omnipotence [*toute-puissance*] towards its margins and [relegating] them beyond the *limes* instead of bringing them closer' (Youssoufi, 2003a: 48, 2003b). More specifically, there was a fear that the imbalance in the EU's treatment of enlargement and association areas would become more pronounced in key economic aspects such as financial assistance (subsidies to agriculture, structural funds), investment flows, trade or migration policies. Regarding security, the new accessions could bring about a shift in the EU's interest towards its new Eastern borders and even a change in attitude towards U.S. leadership or the Israeli–Palestinian conflict. Finally, not least, Turkey's exclusion from this enlargement process had reopened the thorny debate surrounding relations between Europe and Islam, which also affected Morocco's pro-European aspirations (Ounaïes, 2003).

However, the Moroccan government's discourse on EU enlargement sought to present the glass as half full. In January 2003, in response to an oral question in the House of Representatives, foreign minister Mohamed Benaissa emphasised positive economic expectations such as the opening up of new markets for Moroccan exports (on preferential terms) and the possibility of attracting more investment (i.e. offshoring from Central and Eastern Europe) (MAEC, 29 January 2003, 2 June 2004). He only admitted as a subsidiary matter that

> The expansion of the European space will force Morocco to develop its economy and increase its competitiveness to be in a position of invulnerability in front of the preferential arrangements granted to the ten Central and Eastern European countries that will access the EU space from May 2004.
> (MAEC, 29 January 2003)[6]

Another milestone providing cause for reflection came with the tenth anniversary of the EMP, which was celebrated with a summit of heads of state and government in Barcelona in November 2005. The overall assessments of the first decade of the Barcelona Process reflected a feeling of paralysis and disappointment with what was considered to be a double failure. Expectations had not been met in terms of either economic development or political reforms in the southern Mediterranean countries (Amirah and Youngs, 2005). As for the latter, they criticised in particular the EU institutions' almost exclusive control over the EMP, the insufficient funding allocated to the various programmes (especially in comparison to pre-accession funds for candidate countries) and the excessive bureaucratisation of application procedures, as well as the postponement of critical issues such as agricultural trade and migration management (Soler, 2006: 7).

In spite of this, Moroccan diplomats persisted in their positive appraisal of the results of the EMP and repeatedly defended the 'centrality' of this 'unique, original and coherent regional reference framework', as well as its 'tangible results' in the face of all of the difficulties (MAEC, 30 November 2004). However, a stated concern was the recurring impediment on the development of EMP caused by the Middle East conflict (Youssoufi, 2003a: 52–54). That was one of the justifications for the recovery at the time, within Rabat's official discourse, of the old demand for a multi-speed association or special treatment for the front-running Mediterranean partner countries, as the new ENP envisaged. The deputy minister of Foreign Affairs and Cooperation, Taieb Fassi Fihri, explained in 2005 that the relevance and centrality of the Barcelona Process was not at odds with the implementation of a more country-by-country differentiated approach: 'Internal evolutions depend primarily on the realities of each country, according to their own pace, needs and resources. [...] We have to adapt to the rhythm of each of the partners' (*L'Économiste*, 1 June 2005).

The second argument reiterated by Moroccan officials in this context was the need to restore the balance between the three pillars of the EMP, which was being undermined, in their view, by the growing prominence of security issues:

> Of course, several regional and international developments have strongly raised the issue of security and dialogue between the two shores of the

Mediterranean. On the European side, [there is] a tendency to assimilate these events and try to integrate them into the agenda of the Partnership. This equates ultimately to strengthening the first pillar (political and security cooperation) to the detriment of the second (economic and financial cooperation) and the third (human and cultural cooperation). We the Moroccans want to move forward whilst maintaining a balance between the three pillars, as you cannot walk on only one leg. There is an interaction and all elements are linked with one another.

(Taieb Fassi Fihri in *L'Économiste*, 1 June 2005)

The same message was repeated by Fassi Fihri a year later in the Euro-Mediterranean conference of Tampere (November 2006). However, in practice, Morocco provided valuable contribution in the 2005 Barcelona summit enabling an agreement to be reached concerning the Euro-Mediterranean Code of Conduct on Countering Terrorism along with the implementation of justice and home affairs as the fourth de facto pillar of the EMP (Pardo, 2009: 74).

Morocco exhibited once more its pro-European activism and commitment to the EMP by presenting a flurry of proposals at the Lisbon Conference in November 2007 (MAEC, 5 November 2007). It was announced that in 2008–2009 the country would host Euro-Mediterranean meetings or events at different levels on drug control, the European Security and Defence Policy (ESDP), customs cooperation, tourism, youth, national human development programmes and women (EMP, 2007). This array of initiatives was conspicuously linked up with the gestation of the long-awaited Advanced Status, a political document aimed at singling out the EU–Morocco bilateral relationship which began to be negotiated officially after the sixth session of the Association Council in July 2007. Altogether, on a multilateral level, throughout these years Morocco skilfully enhanced and maintained its reputation as an 'active and engaged' partner of the EMP with an 'open and constructive, consensus-building profile' (Pardo, 2009: 74).

On the margins of the EMP, but closely related to it, another multilateral forum in which Morocco was diligently involved was the 5+5 Dialogue, which was established in 1990 by five Maghreb countries (Morocco, Algeria, Tunisia, Libya and Mauritania) and another five from southern Europe (Portugal, Spain, France, Italy and Malta), and reactivated in 2001–2002 after more than a decade of hibernation to discuss mainly security and migration issues. The attempts to recover and strengthen subregional dialogue and cooperation within loose frameworks such as this were a clear response to the stagnation of the EMP and the growing Western Mediterranean dissatisfaction with the fact that its agenda was permanently hijacked by the Israeli–Palestinian conflict. The experience of the revived 5+5 Dialogue was generally regarded as positive from the outset: this informal and flexible mechanism for exchanging and coordinating positions allowed strategic issues relating to transnational security to be addressed pragmatically and foreign policy divergences between the states involved to be side-stepped (Calleya, 2006: 112–113, 117; Henry, 2006: 19–22). Rabat considered that this framework was particularly appropriate to its own conception of neighbourhood relations, based on the principles of ownership, segmentation and adaptation. The most valued aspects were its 'constructive' working methodology, including the implementation of confidence-building measures, political consultation and decision-making by consensus, as well as its focus on really 'priority issues' (El Houdaïgui, 2012: 93–95; Maalmi, 2012: 804).

Bilateral dimension

The EMP umbrella also covered the bilateral dimension of the relationship between Morocco and the EU, which was regulated legally and institutionally by the Association Agreement signed in February 1996 and in force since March 2000. This legal framework replaced the 1976 Cooperation Agreement and its subsequent adaptation protocols, and was concluded in principle without a defined time limit. Its main features included the establishment of regular political dialogue between the two parties, the gradual creation of a free trade area, sectoral cooperation in a wide range of areas (regional cooperation, education and training, science and technology, environment, industry, promotion and protection of investment, standardisation, approximation of legislation, financial services, agriculture and fisheries, transport, telecommunications and information technology, energy, tourism, customs, money laundering, drug trafficking), cooperation in social and cultural matters, and financial support to accelerate the modernisation of the Moroccan economy and compensate for the negative impact of trade liberalisation (EU/Morocco, 2000).

On an institutional level, the bodies responsible for bilateral cooperation under the Association Agreement were the Association Council, which operated at ministerial level, and the Association Committee, which brought together senior officials. Both were composed of representatives of the Council of the EU, the Commission and the government of Morocco (articles 79 and 82). As a mechanism for political dialogue and the main governing body in the areas covered by this agreement, the Association Council was charged with annually assessing its implementation and the general development of bilateral relations, defining priorities for action and coordinating positions on issues of common interest (including regional matters), with the power to take binding decisions for the parties (article 80) (interview with Alexis Konstantopoulos, 6 June 2014). In practice, most of its responsibilities and decision-making power in the everyday management of the agreement were delegated to the Association Committee (article 81). Alongside this there were also various thematic substructures or sub-bodies in charge of issues such as Customs Cooperation (committee provided for in the Association Agreement); Social Affairs and Migration (working party set up in 2001); Internal Market; Industry, Trade and Services; Transport, Environment and Energy; Research and Innovation; Agriculture and Fisheries; Justice and Security (subcommittees created in February 2003); and Human Rights, Democratisation and Governance (subcommittee created in September 2006).

In fact, contrary to its aspirations to stand out at all times as the regional frontrunner and *model student* in relations with the EU, Morocco was only the third southern Mediterranean country to sign an Association Agreement under the EMP, after Tunisia (July 1995) and Israel (November 1995), and the second to implement it, after Tunisia (March 1998). However, this did not prevent minister Benaissa from presenting Morocco as 'a pioneer in the Euro-Mediterranean region' at the first meeting of the Association Council, in which an EU participant also described EU–Morocco relations as 'pilot relations' and an 'example' (EU–Morocco Association Council, 2000: 5–6).

The area where Rabat really acted as a pioneer following the implementation of the Association Agreement was the launch of a bilateral Reinforced Political Dialogue with the EU in 2003–2004 (the first session was held in June 2004) (IEMed, 2009: 52; Jaidi and Martín, 2010: 39). This was conceived of as a more informal and 'political' mechanism for sharing and coordinating both parties' positions on international issues of mutual interest, complementing the agenda of the Association Council. Another groundbreaking measure in the area of human rights and democracy promotion was the establishment of the Subcommittee on Human Rights, Democratisation and Governance in 2006 (interview with Narjis Benzekri, 23 May 2014). This restricted and in-camera format was supposed to allow more open and frank bilateral dialogue on sensitive domestic issues, and more substantial political demands by the EU, though its actual influence was far from proven (Kausch, 2008: 8).

In any case, the dimension of the Association Agreement that was destined to take the forefront was the economic and commercial one, in accordance with the market logic which has historically dominated Euro-Mediterranean relations and also characterised the EMP. In general, the construction of a Euro-Mediterranean free trade area as envisaged by the 1995 Barcelona Declaration (initially for 2010) implied the parallel conclusion of bilateral hub-and-spoke agreements between the EU and each of its Mediterranean partners (vertical axis) along with bilateral or multilateral agreements among the latter (horizontal axis). This was presented as an experience of *open regionalism* in which the EU would combine the preferential trade treatment granted to certain partners with the multilateral liberalisation commitments agreed with the World Trade Organization (WTO), although the virtual exclusion of agricultural products from the deal called this compatibility into question (Díez Peralta, 2007: 261–262; Al Khouri, 2008: 9–10).

In the case of the EU–Morocco Association Agreement in force since 2000, the novel feature of the free trade area to be implemented over the following 12 years consisted in the replacement of preferential trade treatment based on unilateral and asymmetrical concessions by the EU with a regime of association or *partnership* (among equals) involving reciprocal concessions. The general principles that defined third-generation agreements like this on paper were reciprocity (both the Union and the partner country open their markets), asymmetry (the EU does so to a greater extent) and gradualism (the conditions are negotiated and completed in stages) (Escribano, 2007: 193). In the Moroccan case, however, reciprocity was only to be applied in a 'modulated and asymmetric' way (Díez Peralta, 2007: 262–263). The absence of a significant liberalisation of agricultural trade reduced this deal to a 12-year programme of organised opening of the Moroccan market to European industrial products, with different tariff reduction schedules according to the sensitivity of the goods (Jaidi and Martín, 2010: 40). Otherwise, the Association Agreement included a safeguard clause applicable in the event of 'serious disturbances' in the economy of one of the parties, as well as another article linking its provisions with respect for democratic principles and human rights (article 2) – which has never been invoked though.

The usual protectionist 'agricultural exception' (*Le Journal*, 12–18 October 1998) was reflected in the fact that the Association Agreement did not grant free and unconditional access to the EU Single Market to any of the agricultural products exported by Morocco and maintained the practice of applying tariff quotas and export calendars to most of them (tomatoes, cucumbers, citrus fruits, potatoes). This was critical for a country where agriculture continued to be the primary pillar of the economy, having reduced its weight in terms of GDP to 14 per cent but still employing 43 per cent of the labour force (over four million people including agro-industry), and where more than 70 per cent of agricultural exports went to the EU (Compés *et al.*, 2013: 7). The agreement limited itself to merely stating a generic commitment to move forward gradually and reciprocally on the liberalisation of this sector – a deferral that gave room for the permanent renegotiation and introduction of rules modifying the provisions contained in this chapter (Díez Peralta, 2007: 269–271). In the view of authors such as Carl Dawson, the EU's minimal agricultural concessions definitely made this a 'sub-optimal agreement', or a 'poor deal for Morocco' (2009: 2).

A decade after its entry into force, the commercial balance sheet of the Association Agreement included some positive data – sustained growth in overall bilateral trade of around 9 per cent per annum since 2000 – and some negative ones – the increase in Morocco's trade deficit, as imports grew faster than exports. Moreover, the opening up of the Moroccan market to European industrial goods had mixed effects on local production, which differed depending on the sector concerned and previous levels of competitiveness and internationalisation (Jaidi and Martín, 2010: 40–42, 83). The accompanying measures financed by the MEDA Programme were widely judged to be insufficient in order to improve and upgrade the national productive apparatus, enabling it to be exposed direct to international competition (Escribano, 2007: 193). As regards the increase in foreign direct investment, which was one of the main promised benefits of this agreement and supposedly a vector of modernisation for the local economy, this too fell short of expectations (Khrouz *et al.*, 2004).

The first negotiations relating to agriculture following the EU–Morocco Association Agreement started in 2002 and resulted in a separate four-year agreement, which came into force in January 2004. Based on the principle of asymmetrical reciprocity, it granted preferential treatment to 96 per cent of

Moroccan agricultural exports (against 62 per cent of the EU's), although the benefits for this country were limited as its most important products were not covered. A more ambitious and arduous renegotiation was conducted between 2006 and 2009, passing through ten rounds, based on the principles of the Euro-Mediterranean Roadmap for Agriculture agreed upon at the Luxembourg Conference (May 2005), i.e. progressive and asymmetrical liberalisation of exchanges, the exclusion of a limited number of sensitive products and the adoption of accompanying measures for the southern countries, focusing particularly on rural development. The main change in the negotiations consisted in shifting from a 'positive list' approach to a 'negative list' approach (*L'Économiste*, 9 February 2006). In the end, a deal was reached in December 2009 whereby Rabat succeeded in securing a liberalisation that was gradual, product-differentiated and staggered over transition periods, although it was unable to end the system of export quotas and calendars previously applied. Morocco committed itself to the immediate liberalisation of 45 per cent of agricultural imports from the EU, a figure that would rise to 61 per cent in five years and 70 per cent in ten years. In return, the EU Single Market was to abolish immediately the tariffs on 55 per cent of total imports from Morocco and to increase quotas for the imports of sensitive horticultural products (tomatoes, strawberries, courgettes, cucumbers, garlic, clementines) (Jaidi and Martín, 2010: 45–47). The signature of the agreement was postponed until December 2010, after which the consent procedure at the European Parliament was launched (which was eventually completed in February 2012).

Additionally, alongside its own vertical bilateral agreements with the EU, under the EMP the *model student* Morocco also took on the sub-role of promoter of horizontal South–South regional integration among the EU's Mediterranean partner countries. Morocco's apparent efforts to mitigate the chronic lack of regional integration in this area and strengthen its own trade ties with some of its neighbours resulted in the signature of a bilateral free trade agreement with Turkey in 2004 and the development of the Agadir Process with Tunisia, Egypt and Jordan (launched in 2001 and completed in 2004), which received repeated praise and technical assistance from EU institutions (Calleya, 2006: 121–122). On the other hand, the European attempts to promote the reactivation of the AMU at least at the economic level, overcoming the never-ending political disagreements between Morocco and Algeria, and the inevitable obstacle of the Western Sahara conflict, were rather more unsuccessful.

The payback for Morocco's permanent efforts as a front runner within the EMP, at both multilateral and bilateral level, was the enjoyment of privileged EU treatment in financial terms over the years. Morocco benefited in absolute terms from a volume of EU financial assistance that was noticeably higher than that of its neighbours (Ammor, 2005: 171). Between 1995 and 2006, this country was the largest recipient of funds under the MEDA Programme, i.e. the financial instrument of the EMP, in terms of both commitments and disbursements. It received more than €1,600 million, which were generally intended to accompany the process of trade liberalisation resulting from the Association Agreement and to limit its disruptive effects on the Moroccan economy. This included supporting, as priorities, sectoral reforms required for the economic (neoliberal) transition, modernisation or upgrading (*mise à niveau*) programmes for private companies and projects to improve the socioeconomic balance (Baraka, 2007: 41–42). Even so, the Moroccan authorities repeatedly voiced their dissatisfaction with the slow and intricate administrative procedures of the MEDA Programme, which were highlighted as a major bureaucratic hindrance for bilateral relations (Natorski, 2008: 38–39; Pace, 2006: 151; Del Sarto, 2006: 198).

A self-interested welcome to differentiation within the European Neighbourhood Policy

The other overlapping cooperation framework that has governed relations between Morocco and the EU since 2005 is the ENP. Whereas the ENP was presented to the Mediterranean partner countries as a complement to the EMP that was ultimately aimed at strengthening it, the two policies were actually quite different with regard to their logic and motivation, and the relationship between them seemed unclear from the outset. First, not only was the geographical scope of the ENP much broader, encompassing countries from both the southern shore of the Mediterranean and the new eastern borders of the post-2004 enlarged EU (Belarus, Ukraine, Moldova, Georgia, Armenia and Azerbaijan), but its very conception was inextricably linked to the latest round of accessions and the widespread perception that, at least for the moment, the enlargement of the Union had reached its limits. For this reason, the ENP was described as 'a new institutionalised means of promoting pluralistic integration, without creating expectations of future EU membership' (Adler *et al.*, 2006: 24), or an initiative intended to 'dilute the meaning of its future external border by stretching the four freedoms on which the EU is based (free movement of goods, capital, services, and persons) as far as possible' (Adler *et al.*, 2006: 143). Alternatively, it has been eloquently summed up to be all about 'Europeanisation without Europe' (Escribano, 2006).

Second, the ENP shifted away from the multilateral region-building thrust and the one-size-fits-all approach of the EMP to emphasise differentiated bilateralism, offering countries in the EU's periphery the possibility to upgrade their relations with Brussels individually depending on the progress of each one on agreed political and economic reforms. The main instrument consisted in the bilateral action plans to be negotiated with each of them, based on the principles of joint ownership (objectives defined by both parties) and differentiation (objectives adapted to the needs and capabilities of each country). This was supposed to reinforce and enhance the effectiveness of positive conditionality (Del Sarto and Schumacher, 2005: 21–23). The economic rewards promised by the EU in return for the expected reforms included greater participation in the EU Single Market and financial cooperation. The new European Neighbourhood and Partnership Instrument (ENPI) which was due to become operational with the EU Financial Perspective 2007–2013 would subsume all existing geographical or thematic programmes for neighbouring regions (such as MEDA) with a more country-specific approach.

The responses of southern Mediterranean countries to this new European initiative were quite disparate (Jaidi, 2005). The reactions of scepticism and distrust were the result of the widespread perception of the ENP as: an asymmetric policy (whereby the southern countries were downgraded from the category of 'partners' to that of 'neighbours', which implied a centre-periphery relationship and equal treatment with the eastern post-soviet states); an essentially unilateral and technocratic policy lacking genuine co-ownership (in which, in practice, the Commission predefined the action plans before any consultation); an overly complex and inappropriate policy (especially vis-à-vis project funding mechanisms); an underfunded policy (both in relation to EU demands and compared to the financial support granted to candidate countries); and a policy falling short of the regional cooperation ambitions of the EMP. All in all, again, the inherent contradiction within the ENP's southern dimension lay in the mechanical application of a pre-enlargement logic without offering the incentives and financial means of (pre)accession (Jaidi and Abouyoub, 2008: 18–20). In more practical and simple terms, it was feared that the ENP would aggravate existing imbalances within the EU's treatment of its eastern and southern neighbours (Ammor, 2005: 176–177).

In spite of this, Morocco's official position concerning the ENP was singularly receptive and positive from the outset (interview with Nabil Adghoughi, 13 February 2006). The differentiated or variable-geometry bilateralism that defined the new EU policy fitted in perfectly with Morocco's ongoing wish to distinguish itself as a front-running partner, a *model student*, and to give some exclusiveness to its relations with Brussels. It was, in any case, a more promising starting point than the multilateral uniformity of the Barcelona Process. Moreover, the EU's promise to allow neighbours to participate in 'everything but institutions' (speech by Romano Prodi, Brussels, 6 December 2002) also tallied well with the Moroccan demand for 'more than association, less than accession' expressed by Mohammed VI in 2000. This was the message delivered by the Moroccan minister and deputy minister of Foreign Affairs, Benaissa and Fassi Fihri, to the EU Commissioner for Enlargement, Günter Verheugen, at a meeting held in Rabat in February 2004, when negotiations for the ENP EU–Morocco Action Plan were launched (MAEC, 4 February 2004; *Le Matin*, 5 February 2004).

From this time onwards, and especially in 2004 and 2005, officials from the Moroccan Foreign Ministry officials increased the number of statements emphasising the ENP's 'added value' with regard to the objectives and programmes of the EMP (MAEC, 9 October 2004, 22 November 2005), presenting the new policy as a 'frank and positive response' to the Moroccan demand for a differentiated and privileged relationship with the EU (MAEC, 28 April 2004), which was thus 'in line [*en droite ligne*] with the royal initiative' (MAEC, 5 January 2005). At the same time, these arguments were combined with a defence of the validity of the EMP as a 'unique, original and coherent regional reference framework for partnership in the region' (MAEC, 30 November 2004, 6 May 2005).

In response to an oral question in the House of Representatives, Fassi Fihri warned that the ENP should not 'come at the expense of the Barcelona Process, which remains, despite all obstacles, the global institutional framework for the establishment of Mediterranean relations that are fruitful, balanced and inspired by solidarity' (MAEC, 5 January 2005).

As a result of all of the above, Morocco promptly and enthusiastically signed up to the ENP, though with an essentially self-interested and instrumental approach. The ENP was viewed not as an end in itself, but as a chance, i.e. as 'the long-awaited opportunity to advance its relations with the EU with the prospect of an advanced status for the kingdom' (El Houdaïgui, 2009: 83). In the words of Fassi Fihri himself, 'Morocco sees in the ENP the way towards the Advanced Status and the means for achieving its strategic objective of an "optimum proximity to the EU"' (MAEC, 6 December 2007). Therefore, the fact that Morocco volunteered as one of the first countries to work with the EU in applying the new methodology can be largely understood as being driven by rational choice and strategic calculation.

The ENP procedures were based on the drafting of, in this order, country reports (prepared by the European Commission), national action plans (proposed by the Commission but approved by the corresponding bilateral Association Council) and national indicative framework programmes of the ENPI. The country report on Morocco issued in May 2004 reviewed the state of this country's bilateral relations with the EU, its progress on democracy and the rule of law, human rights and fundamental freedoms, its contribution to regional and global security, its cooperation in the area of justice and home affairs, and its economic and social situation (monetary and fiscal policy, trade deficit, human development, structural reforms and privatisation, trade liberalisation, etc.) (European Commission, 2004). Based on this diagnosis, the Action Plan adopted in July 2005 set as priorities:

- Pursuing legislative reform and applying international human rights provisions;
- enhanced political dialogue on the CFSP [Common Foreign and Security Policy] and ESDP and enhanced cooperation on combating terrorism;
- negotiation of an agreement on liberalising trade in services;
- the development of a climate conducive to foreign direct investment, growth and sustainable development;
- cooperation on social policy with the aim of reducing poverty and vulnerability and creating jobs;
- support for the education and training system, scientific research and information technologies [...];
- effective management of migration flows, including the signing of a readmission agreement with the European Community, and facilitating the movement of persons in accordance with the acquis [...];
- development of the transport sector [...];
- development of the energy sector [...].

(EU–Morocco Association Council, 2005: 3–4)

The Action Plan then listed specific short- and medium-term objectives and actions in the areas of political dialogue and reforms (democracy and the rule of law, human rights and fundamental freedoms, fundamental social rights and core labour standards, cooperation on foreign and security issues, conflict prevention and crisis management, regional cooperation and initiatives); economic and social reform and development (improvement of the macroeconomic framework, structural reform and progress towards a functioning and competitive market economy, agricultural sector reforms, cooperation on employment and social policy, regional and local development, sustainable development); trade, market and regulatory reform (movement of goods, right of establishment and services, capital movements and current payments, movement of persons and workers, taxation, competition policy, state aid, consumer protection, intellectual and industrial property rights...); cooperation in the area of justice and home affairs (migration, border management, fight against organised crime, drug trafficking or money laundering, judicial and police cooperation); transport, energy, information society, environment, science and technology, research and development; and people-to-people contacts (education, training, youth and sport, cultural cooperation, civil society, health) (EU–Morocco Association Council, 2005: 4–33).[7] In order to ensure the implementation of the Action Plan, the Moroccan government established an inter-ministerial body chaired by the prime minister which included four monitoring units (political affairs, productive activities, economic environment and human development) (MAEC, 22 December 2005).

Financial support for these measures came from the ENPI, which became operational under the EU Financial Perspective 2007–2013. After considering the joint policy objectives of the EU and Morocco, the political, economic and social situation of the latter, and existing financial cooperation instruments, the ENPI country strategy paper for the period 2007–2013 established five priorities: the development of social policies (education, health, social protection) and support for the National Human Development Initiative (INDH); economic modernisation (private sector, vocational training, industry, agriculture, fisheries, energy, improvement in the investment and business/innovation climate); institutional support; good governance and human rights; and environmental protection (ENPI, 2007a). The relative financial advantage over its peers enjoyed by Morocco under the EMP and the MEDA Programmes was to be maintained and

Table 4.3 EU financial assistance to Morocco under MEDA Programmes and the ENPI

	Commitments (€ million)	Commitments per year (€ million)	Commitments per year per inhabitant (€)
MEDA I (1995–1999)	660	132.0	4.7
MEDA II (2000–2006)	982	140.3	4.8
ENPI I (2007–2010)	654	163.5	5.4
ENPI II (2011–2013)	580	193.3	6.2

Source: Jaidi and Martín (2010: 84).

accentuated with the implementation of the ENPI, judging by the absolute amounts and the growth rates of this assistance.

Morocco's National Indicative Programme 2007–2010 under the ENPI allotted a total of €654 million to programmes to support social policies (45 per cent), economic modernisation (37 per cent), environmental protection (8 per cent), institutional strengthening (6 per cent) and governance and human rights (4 per cent) (ENPI, 2007b: 44). The sectoral distribution of funds was visibly altered for the €580.5 million in 2011–2013, with institutional support becoming the first priority (40 per cent) and economic modernisation being relegated to last position (10 per cent). Nevertheless, this was justified as a result of the 'complementarity' and 'temporal sequencing' between the two phases, and not by any change in strategic priorities (ENPI, 2011: 36, 10–11).[8]

In any case, irrespective of their volume, these EU financial allocations did not entirely fulfil Moroccan expectations. Their significance became more relative when the population factor was taken into account: the funds assigned to Morocco per annum per inhabitant remained at a modest level from 1995 onwards (around €5), well below those allocated to smaller states such as Tunisia, Lebanon or Jordan. Moreover, the level of assistance received fell far short of that awarded to Central and Eastern European countries during the pre-accession stage or to the new EU's eastern neighbours included in the ENP (Jaidi and Martín, 2010: 69–70; interview with Habib de Fouad, 17 February 2006; Ministère de l'Économie et des Finances, 2007).

Weighing up the costs and benefits of cooperation on migration

One of the areas in which the intricacies of Morocco's socialisation by the EU have been studied in greater depth is the promotion of democracy and human rights. This country already had some experience of how human rights violations could interfere with its relations with the EU, the European Parliament having rejected the fourth financial protocol of the Renovated Mediterranean Policy on

Table 4.4 European Neighbourhood and Partnership Instrument (ENPI) – Commitments in National Indicative Programmes for Morocco, 2007–2010 and 2011–2013

Strategic priority/programme	2007–2010		2011–2013	
	€ million	%	€ million	%
Social policies	296	45.3	116	20
Governance and human rights	28	4.3	87	15
Institutional support	40	6.1	232	40
Economic modernisation	240	36.7	58	10
Environment	50	7.6	87	15
Total 2007–2010	654	100	580	100

Sources: ENPI, 'Morocco. 2007–2010 NIP', 'Morocco. 2011–2013 NIP'.

these grounds in 1992 – although the decision was later reconsidered. Yet in the framework of both the EMP and the ENP, which prioritised bottom-up democracy assistance through the funding of civil society projects over more coercive methods or conditionality (Youngs, 2001: 14–26; Adler *et al.*, 2006: 89), the Rabat authorities managed to play the *model student* while influencing the EU's choices regarding areas of intervention and partners. The latter was made possible by the 'enhanced coordination' within the EMP (Haddadi, 2003: 84–87) and the increased 'co-ownership' proclaimed by the ENP (Gillespie, 2013: 180). The latter for example account for the discrepancies within democracy-related issues between the quite critical diagnosis made by the European Commission in the ENP country report on Morocco (2004) and the subsequent *co-owned* Action Plan (2005), which was much less ambitious and politically meaningful.[9] In short, within a semi-authoritarian regime like this which 'largely adopts the discourse but not the essence of democracy' (Kausch, 2008: 7), the socialisation pursued by EU democracy promotion policies only worked on a superficial level, without achieving a genuine internalisation of values.[10]

Another aspect of Morocco–EU relations in which the subtle interplay between Morocco's socialisation and rational action appears to be most discernible is cooperation on migration issues. In this increasingly prominent dimension of the asymmetric partnership with the northern bloc, the authorities in Rabat have combined the desire to play the *model student* living up to the EU's normative expectations with rational cost-benefit calculating behaviour in pursuit of more selfish interests. On the EU side, the arduous process of harmonisation and communitarisation of immigration and asylum policies which started with the Treaty of Amsterdam (1997) was accompanied by a much swifter development of an 'external dimension' impacting on third countries of origin or the transit of migratory flows, as officialised by the Special European Council on Justice and Home Affairs held in Tampere in 1999 (Lavenex, 2006). Migration cooperation thus became one of the priority target areas of the EU's 'external governance', that is, the expansion of the scope of EU rules beyond EU borders. This implied in practice the outsourcing or offshoring of what had been hitherto purely domestic tasks to neighbouring countries such as those of the Maghreb, which were transformed 'from a springboard space into a buffer space' (Bensaad, 2006: 94). Attempts were also made to make development aid to these countries conditional on cooperation on migration control and the signature of readmission agreements (Alami M'chichi *et al.*, 2005: 20–21).

In parallel, migration issues also gained prominence on the agenda of the EMP. The Barcelona Declaration included them in its third chapter, which was dedicated to cooperation in social, cultural and human affairs, and the ideas of 'co-development' and a 'global' or 'comprehensive' approach to migration – which moved beyond merely combating irregular inflows and controlling borders – made their way into subsequent meetings. Later on, justice and home affairs, including migration, were incorporated into a framework document in the 2002 Valencia Conference and de facto enshrined as the fourth pillar of the EMP within the work programme adopted at the 2005 Barcelona Summit (EMP, 2005).

Migration affairs also required increasing attention on the Moroccan side, with related domestic and foreign policies becoming increasingly intermingled, especially with regard to the EU. Issues such as migration control and security, the integration of migrants within their countries of residence and the development aid received by their areas of origin arose in an interconnected way (Alami M'chichi *et al.*, 2005: 13–15). What is relevant, according to Nora El Qadim (2010), is that far from remaining a passive receiver or executor of European migration policies, Morocco managed to transform these constraints into opportunities and take advantage of the 'geographic rent' resulting from its new status as a transit country for migration flows and an indispensable partner in reducing illegal entries into the EU. Facilitated by the complexity of multi-level negotiations with the EU and some of its member states, along with the European obsession in signing readmission agreements, Morocco's effective counter-strategy allowed the asymmetry of this relationship to be compensated and economic and political benefits to be drawn. This emphasis on southern *agency* and rational action is reminiscent of Gregory White's demonstration of the negotiating power of peripheral states within the context of Morocco–EU economic relations at the beginning of the 1990s, when Morocco exploited divergences between EU member states and EU institutions, turning them into a significant advantage (1996: 113, 116).

As a traditional source of migratory flows which also became a transit country after the turn of the millennium (Khachani, 2006), Morocco began to be used as a test bed for the emerging EU policies in this area in the late 1990s. In December 1998, the new Council-established High-Level Working Group on Asylum and Migration chose Morocco – along with Albania, Somalia, Iraq, Afghanistan and Sri Lanka – as one of six third countries to which the new approach of the Strategy Paper on Immigration and Asylum Policy of the Austrian Presidency would be applied first. According to Abdelkrim Belguendouz (2002: 101), the authorities in Rabat had also in part contributed to the alarmist view of the 'threats from the South' which underlay this kind of document and Driss Basri, the interior minister at the time, had shown a deliberate desire to associate Morocco with the European security-based immigration policy.

In 1999, under Spanish coordination, the same High-Level Working Group drafted an action plan for Morocco which was presented as the product of an innovative approach and dialogue with the Rabat authorities (Council of the EU, 1999). This was not, however, the perception of the Moroccan government, which expressed its disagreement with the plan's content and a desire to participate in its revision (El Qadim, 2010: 97–98). Critical voices noted that most of the proposed measures revolved around the suppression or prevention of illegal immigration: cooperation in the fight against clandestine networks of entry, support for voluntary return, implementation of the existing bilateral readmission agreements between Morocco and some EU member states, and signing of another such agreement on EU level. The financial compensation for these demands was the introduction of a justice and home affairs chapter into MEDA II (2000–2006). As far as Morocco was concerned, this programme allocated a total of €115 million to projects that were directly or indirectly related to migration management (development of the northern provinces, border control and institutional support for the movement of persons) (Belguendouz, 2002: 133–136, 149–153).

From that time, the most frequently recurring issue in the dialogue on migration between the EU and Morocco was Brussels' desire to conclude a readmission agreement that could run smoothly (whereby presumptions or prima facie evidence would be sufficient to enforce a migrant's expulsion) and include citizens of third countries or stateless persons who entered the EU from Morocco (or who held a visa or residence permit issued by this country). Bilateral readmission agreements had been previously signed by Morocco with individual EU states such as France (1983–1993, 2001), Spain (1992), Belgium (1993), the Netherlands (1993), Germany (1998) and Italy (1998), but either they had not entered into force or their implementation was not considered satisfactory (El Qadim, 2010: 102–103);[11] in addition, there was an interest in an EU-wide agreement. This demand, which responded exclusively to European interests, was made explicit from the first session onwards of the EU–Morocco Association Council (October 2000) (EU–Morocco Association Council, 2000: 12, 17). A turning point in Rabat's position occurred at the following year's meeting (October 2001). Shortly after officially requesting EU support for the fight against illegal migration, the Moroccan representatives expressed their 'readiness to engage in a constructive dialogue on readmission with the EU on the basis of mutual interests and respecting the legal and human dimensions of this issue' (EU–Morocco Association Council, 2001). Formal rounds of negotiations with the European Commission started in April 2003. At the same time, this question was consistently raised again at all the subsequent meetings of the Association Council and the working group on Social Affairs and Migration.

The launch of the ENP, with its greater potential for positive conditionality, confirmed the EU's sense of urgency in this area. The 2005 EU–Morocco Action Plan listed among its priorities the 'effective management of migration flows, including the signing of a readmission agreement with the European Community' (EU–Morocco Association Council, 2005: 4).[12] The new financial incentive was the Programme for Financial and Technical Assistance to Third Countries in the Area of Migration and Asylum (AENEAS, 2004–2008), initially amounting to €250 million,[13] one of the main beneficiaries of which was Morocco. Yet three years later, the EU Declaration made on the occasion of the launch of the Advanced Status 'regretted' that the readmission agreement had still not been concluded and 'reiterated the importance' the EU attached to it (EU–Morocco Association Council, 2008b: 5–6).

One legal response by Morocco to the EU's pressures was the adoption, in November 2003, of an Aliens Act[14] which was deemed by national observers to be overly restrictive and focused on sanctions against illegal migration. However, as regards the long-awaited readmission agreement, Rabat remained far from giving in to the demands of Brussels. The Moroccan authorities were not willing to make significant concessions in order to strike a deal which would bring them considerable costs and dubious benefits. Added to the huge logistical effort needed to seal its long borders, there was also the risk that Morocco's relations with some African countries might deteriorate as a result of the imposition of visa requirements on their citizens, which could even affect their position on the Western Sahara conflict (Belguendouz, 2006b; 2002: 135–140, 154–158). Consequently, Morocco first opted for a deliberate strategy of 'issue linkage', i.e. linking migration issues on the table with others such as development aid or access to the EU market. Second, it combined concessions and gestures of goodwill (participation in the SIVE programme,[15] reform of the Aliens Act), which allowed it to maintain its image as a *model student* and its status as a privileged partner of the EU, with an ongoing permanent postponement, or 'opportunistic avoidance', of the signing of the readmission agreement in question (El Qadim, 2010: 109–114; Wallihan, 1998). In the end, the latter negotiations were halted in 2010 after 15 fruitless rounds. This is a telling example of how Rabat handled its socialisation needs vis-à-vis the EU with a considerable degree of rational choice behaviour and strategic calculation.

This behaviour was also accompanied by 'rhetorical action' and, more specifically, by rhetorical strategies such as 'swotting' and 'shifting the burden' (Schimmelfennig, 2000: 129–131). A mainstream diplomatic discourse rejected security-focused analyses of migration and demanded a 'global and integrated approach' (*approche globale et intégrée*), i.e. one that took account of the socio-economic roots of this phenomenon, the 'shared responsibility' of northern and southern countries in the management of human flows, and the integration needs of Moroccan citizens living in Europe (Ammor, 2005: 174). King Mohammed VI himself set this official position – and the corresponding empty signifier – in an audience granted to the European Commissioner for External Relations, Chris Patten, in June 2001. According to the statement made by the Palace spokesman, the EU representative claimed to 'share the Kingdom's approach on migration issues' and the conviction about the need for a 'global approach' (Belguendouz, 2002: 140–141). The arguments repeated by various Moroccan officials pointed to the impossibility of dissociating the 'complex problem' of illegal migration, which was the EU's obsession, from other facets of the same phenomenon, as well as the need for greater Euro-Mediterranean cooperation in this field from a perspective of shared responsibility and reciprocity in international relations. This implied rejecting outright proposals such as the one made by the Spanish government at the European Council in Seville (June 2002) to make development aid to southern countries conditional on controlling irregular migration flows. In addition, typical statements always stressed the need to respect the human rights of migrants and Morocco's particular problems and requirements resulting from its geographical position as a transit country – a way of demanding greater EU political and material assistance (Alami M'chichi *et al.*, 2005: 23–26).

'Swotting' and 'shifting the burden' towards the EU stood out in particular within the discourse of the new Delegate-Ministry for Moroccans Living Abroad, which was placed in 2002 under the control of the Ministry of Foreign

Affairs and Cooperation.[16] Many of the statements made by the holder of this office between 2002 and 2007, Nezha Chekrouni, were aimed at convincing the European authorities that Morocco was 'one of the first countries to defend a shared responsibility in addressing the challenges posed by migration in all its dimensions' (MAEC, 15 September 2006) and 'a credible partner that cannot be ignored' in this field (MAEC, 8 July 2006), that is, legitimising this state as reliable interlocutor, if not a *model student*. The 'shifting the burden' strategy appeared when her discourse emphasised Morocco's inability to cope on its own with the 'strong migratory pressure' (MAEC, 10 November 2005) and the need for greater coordination – even a 'common migration policy' – between states on the two shores of the Mediterranean, which could occur within the framework of the EMP (MAEC, 10 May 2007, 14 December 2005, 24 January 2006). Other than this, Chekrouni's assertions about the need for joint treatment of the problems of legal and illegal migration (MAEC, 15 April 2005), attention to the socioeconomic facets of these phenomena (MAEC, 7 July 2004, 16 March 2006), the implementation of an approach focusing on 'human security' (MAEC, 2 January 2006) and the improvement of integration policies for immigrants in host countries (MAEC, 16 April 2004) were arguably ways of appealing to the EU's own norms and values in order to urge the EU to stick to them.

The crisis triggered in the autumn of 2005 by a wave of collective storming of the border fences at Ceuta and Melilla by sub-Saharan African migrants, which forced the Spanish government to seek assistance from the Moroccan authorities, put the issue of human rights back at the heart of the dialogue on migration between Rabat and Brussels (Hernando de Larramendi and Bravo, 2006). Indeed, migration is one of the areas where interference by Spanish–Moroccan relations in cooperation between the EU and Morocco appears to be more evident (Wunderlich, 2010: 262–263). International condemnation of Rabat's behaviour grew as its security forces were held responsible for the deaths of a dozen illegal migrants during attempts to cross these barriers, the detention of more than 4,000 sub-Saharan Africans in three weeks within its territory, including asylum seekers, and the irregular transfer of some of them to the Algerian border and the Sahara desert (Alami M'chichi *et al.*, 2005: 28). The immediate reaction by the Moroccan authorities was to disavow any responsibility and again to 'shift the burden', asking the EU for a new 'Marshall Plan' to combat immigration from sub-Saharan Africa and 'urgent and substantial assistance' to the transit countries (EFE, 3 October 2005). Deputy minister Fassi Fihri claimed that Morocco was the 'first African victim of this phenomenon' because of the strong concentration of irregular migrants willing to enter the EU through its territory, and that it did not have the capacity to integrate and employ all of these people (MAEC, 12 October 2005).

Shortly after this crisis, a proposal was made to organise a Euro-African Ministerial Conference on Migration and Development in which all the concerned countries could explore new responses to the phenomenon from a 'global approach' (MAEC, 26 April 2006; *L'Économiste*, 10 July 2006). The event, which was jointly convened by Morocco and Spain with the support of France, was eventually held in Rabat on 10–11 July 2006, and brought together delegations from 27 African and 30 European countries, as well as the European Commission. In the final political declaration, the participants agreed to establish a 'partnership between the countries of origin, transit and destination' of migration (Euro-African Partnership for Migration and Development, 2006a). The most significant result of the meeting was agreement on an Action Plan including a long list of measures for the promotion of development and 'co-development'; the joint management of legal migration and the movement of workers and persons; the fight against illegal immigration; and police and judicial cooperation (Euro-African Partnership for Migration and Development, 2006a). Its novel feature lay in its reflection of an 'awareness of the importance of the development dimension of the migration issue "in order to act on the root causes of irregular migration"' (Khachani, 2006: 57), in spite of the lack of specific responsibilities, any schedule, budgetary commitments or financial assistance for its implementation (Sorroza, 2006: 7). This Euro-African dialogue on migration was extended with subsequent conferences in Paris (2008) and Dakar (2011) and became known as the Rabat Process.[17]

Leaving aside the tangible results of the 2006 conference, the actor that achieved the best result in political terms from its organisation was the Moroccan regime. First, this event enshrined the 'Europeanisation' of a crisis which had originally affected only the Spanish–Moroccan border (Sorroza, 2006: 5), helping to dilute responsibilities, 'shift the burden' and dispel international criticism of the abuses committed by Rabat in the management of that episode. The desire for self-justification was evident, for example, in the opening speech made by minister Benaissa:

> I would also like to remind us all that, due to its geographical position, Morocco has registered in recent times a massive and unprecedented influx of migrants coming from the south and bound for an increasingly hermetic Europe. Despite the various problems posed by this influx, Morocco has spared no effort in dealing with this phenomenon, within the limits of its own means.
>
> (Speech by Mohamed Benaissa, Rabat, 10 July 2006: 5–6)

Second, the Moroccan representatives emphasised their own propositional capacity to the point of all but identifying King Mohammed VI as the author of the idea of a 'global approach' to migration, which had become another leitmotif of their official discourse, claiming it had been formally enshrined at this international meeting (MAEC, 16 July 2006): 'His Majesty Mohammed VI has called on several occasions for the adoption of a global approach marked by solidarity within our regional space' (speech by Mohamed Benaissa, Rabat, 10 July 2006: 2). In fact, calls for a 'comprehensive approach' to migration management had been recurrent features within the discourse of the European Parliament and Commission since the 1990s (Lavenex, 2006: 330, 333), and the Council had adopted a so-called Global Approach to Migration in December 2005. Third, the leadership role taken on at this meeting also fitted in perfectly with the proclaimed *new African policy* of Morocco under Mohammed VI, which tried to give a new lease of life to the sub-role of *bridge between Europe and Africa* long held by the kingdom. Morocco's activism in multilateral fora such as this was also a way of making up for its absence from the African Union (AU) due to the Western Sahara conflict. In fact, the only negative feature of this event from a diplomatic perspective was the absence of Algeria (MAEC, 13 July 2006). Although officially justified as a gesture of protest because the EU was meeting only some African countries instead of a regional organisation like the AU, the underlying reason was Algeria's discontent over the prominence given to Morocco at the conference (Sorroza, 2006: 8).

In short, this chapter has shown how consistently Morocco has deployed an outstanding pro-European foreign policy activism, which can be explained as being the result of the high domestic consensus surrounding its role as *model student of the EU* and its superficial but effective international socialisation within the context of this asymmetrical relationship. This role has been put to strategic use, as a means for achieving privileged treatment by the EU compared to other southern Mediterranean partners. To this purpose, the Rabat authorities maintained an exemplary performance within the framework of the EMP at all levels, although precedence was given to the bilateral dimension whilst the multilateral one had a rather instrumental character. The ENP was also welcome, as the variable-geometry bilateralism that characterised it opened a new opportunity for Morocco's strong desire for differentiation. Cooperation with the EU on migration issues has also demonstrated the subtle interplay between socialisation and rational action within Moroccan foreign policy.

Notes

1 See http://euneighbourhood.eu (accessed on 31 October 2014).
2 The first appearance of the expression 'advanced status' as such in a royal address can be found in the speech by Mohammed VI, Rome, 11 April 2000.
3 The relative weight of trade with Morocco for the EU is minimal, never reaching 1 per cent of the EU's total annual trade volume in the 2000s (0.8 per cent in 2013), while the EU was always by far Morocco's first trading partner, with a share of 50–60 per cent of Morocco's total trade (50.3 per cent in 2013) (European Commission, 27 August 2014).
4 For an analysis of the role of socialisation in EU–Tunisia relations, see Powel and Sadiki (2010: 57–67).
5 'Having more power means Ego can induce Alter to change its definition of the situation more in light of Ego's than vice-versa' (Wendt, 1999: 331).
6 For a prospective evaluation of the economic impact of EU's 2004 enlargement on Morocco, see Ministère des Finances et de la Privatisation (2003a). On the hypothetical accession of Turkey, see Ministère des Finances et de la Privatisation (2005).
7 For an assessment by Moroccan civil society, see Réseau Marocain Euromed des ONG (2007).
8 For an overview of the results of the ENPI in Morocco between 2007 and 2013, see ENPI (2014: 28–29).
9 See also EMHRN (2007) and Réseau Marocain Euromed des ONG (2007: 29–46).

10 See also Carbonell (2008) and Khakee (2010).
11 The readmission agreement with Spain was signed in 1992, but its implementation was delayed until 2004.
12 See also Wunderlich (2010: 256).
13 Later renamed Thematic Programme for the Cooperation with non-EU Member Countries in the Areas of Migration and Asylum.
14 Dahir No. 1–03–196 of 16 Ramadan 1424 (11 November 2003) promulgating Law No. 02–03 relating to the Entry and Stay of Foreigners in the Kingdom of Morocco, Irregular Emigration and Immigration, Official Bulletin No. 5162, 20 November 2003.
15 Acronym standing for Sistema Integrado de Vigilancia Exterior (Integrated System for External Surveillance).
16 This department previously operated as a 'delegate-ministry' which was accountable to the head of government (1990–1995) and as an undersecretariat of state reporting to the Ministry of Foreign Affairs (1995–1997). In 2007 it was reclassified as a 'delegate-ministry' of the prime minister.
17 http://processusderabat.net/web (accessed on 31 October 2014).

5 Moments of truth and paybacks
From the Advanced Status to the Arab Spring

This chapter follows up on the previous one by discussing the paybacks obtained by Morocco thanks to its exemplary pro-European foreign policy activism in two moments of truth, namely 2008 and 2011. In 2008 there were two significant novelties in Morocco's relations with the EU affecting respectively their multilateral and bilateral dimensions. In July, the new Union for the Mediterranean (UfM) became operational as a multilateral framework for relations between the EU and its southern Mediterranean partners to replace the EMP. In October an ambitious Joint Document was adopted that set the 'roadmap' for future bilateral relations between the EU and Morocco, which is known as the Advanced Status. According to Moroccan foreign ministry officials, both processes were 'in perfect symbiosis'; they 'converged, complemented and reinforced each other' (MAEC, 30 June 2009, 4 December 2009; GERM, 2010: 25–28).

The year 2011 saw the Arab Spring tsunami and the subsequent review of the ENP, which was presented as the EU's paradigmatic shift in response to these transformations – which, borrowing the terms from Federica Bicchi (2007: 19–25), arguably created 'cognitive uncertainty' and thus a 'policy window' for change in EU foreign policy. A stronger and apparently self-critical emphasis was placed on supporting 'democratic transformation' (European Commission/HR, 2011a) or 'building deep democracy' in the EU's periphery by pursuing greater differentiation and imposing positive ('more for more') and negative ('less for less') conditionality based on each country's progress in terms of democracy and the rule of law (European Commission/HR, 2011c). However, inertia and *business as usual* prevailed in both the underlying conceptual construction of this discourse (Teti, 2012; Teti *et al.*, 2013), financial practices (Bicchi, 2014; Mouhib, 2014) and other settled patterns of behaviour already existing in the EU's relations with different groups of countries. Significantly, the two old *model students* of the EU in the Maghreb, i.e. Morocco and Tunisia, were to remain similarly advantaged, irrespective of the asymmetry between the domestic political changes witnessed in each of them (Biscop *et al.*, 2012: 32). Judging by the political and economic incentives or rewards offered by Brussels, the superficial top-down constitutional reform launched by the Moroccan monarchy with the aim of defusing domestic protests (Maghraoui, 2011; Fernández-Molina, 2011b) was practically equivalent to the promising – however uncertain – revolutionary regime change experienced by Tunisia.

Steering the Union for the Mediterranean towards Morocco's preferences

On the multilateral level, in 2007–2008 discussions and bargaining around Euro-Mediterranean relations concentrated on the gestation of the new UfM, which was for a long time largely a label in search of content. This was a distinctly French initiative which was driven and monopolised by Paris until the European Council adopted it in March 2008, and it was officially launched in July of that year. The original idea was presented by President Nicolas Sarkozy in a speech in Tangier in October 2007 in which he advocated the construction of 'concrete solidarities' among the countries bordering the Mediterranean, that is, an essentially 'pragmatic' and 'variable-geometry' 'union of projects' aiming at remedying the inadequacies of the EMP – yet not necessarily replacing it (speech by Nicolas Sarkozy, Tangier, 23 October 2007). However, this groundbreaking French proposal faced major resistance from the non-Mediterranean EU member states, which were initially excluded from the plan – chief among them Germany – as well as the European Commission. It ended up being redressed and 'Europeanised', with the EU institutions maintaining their role, the EMP acquis being preserved and membership expanded to include all the EU countries (Gillespie, 2011; Soler, 2008: 10–12).

In spite of the attempt to channel Sarkozy's activism towards reinforcing previously existing Euro-Mediterranean policies, in the end the UfM entailed more change than continuity with regard to the EMP. It pointed in a new direction since it involved at the same time: a shift from region building multilateralism to intergovernmentalism in decision-making; a functionalist and economistic thrust as regards policy priorities; and a more ambitious institutional structure aimed at ensuring north-south 'co-ownership' as a distinctive feature (Bicchi and Gillespie, 2012: 1–17; Gillespie, 2011). The coming-out of the UfM occurred at the summit of heads of state and government of European and southern Mediterranean countries held in Paris on 13 July 2008, under the French presidency of the EU. The 43 leaders attending approved a joint statement in line with the spirit of the Barcelona Process, while selecting the six pioneering projects on which the activity of UfM was subsequently to be focused, specifically in the fields of infrastructure (maritime and land highways), higher education (Euro-Mediterranean University), environment (de-pollution of the Mediterranean), energy (solar plan), investments (support for small and medium-sized enterprises) and civil protection. Leaving aside this functional self-limitation, the major novelties in the UfM were institutional, including the regular holding of high-level summits, the establishment of a rotating co-Presidency by a northern and a southern country, and the creation of a permanent 'technical' Secretariat.

After the initial momentum, however, doubts about the UfM resurfaced due to the perceived 'mismatch between the voluntarist rhetoric displayed during the launch of the project and the effective political content which the project-based approach entails' (Jaidi and Abouyoub, 2008: 4). Other criticisms questioned the feasibility – or desirability – of the aim of pragmatically circumventing the most politically pressing problems of the region, such as persisting conflicts and authoritarianism, and the dilution of the EMP's timid democratic conditionality. Indeed, politicisation soon returned through the back door, as the Gaza war of December 2008–January 2009 and the ensuing Arab–Israeli tensions were to paralyse political dialogue within the UfM resulting in the postponement of summits for years.

The southern countries, in general, had not shown much enthusiasm when the French initiative was unveiled (Gillespie, 2012: 6) and did not get involved in what were mainly intra-European negotiations between a few EU member states and the Commission. In order to avoid offending President Sarkozy, most of them opted to wait and see, while trying to influence a still malleable proposal and bring it closer to their own preferences (Soler, 2008: 29). A division emerged between the views of the Arab countries that were most in favour of the UfM (Morocco, Tunisia, Egypt) and those who expressed scepticism (Algeria) or even outright opposition (Libya) (Mohsen-Finan, 2008; Jaidi and Abouyoub, 2008: 30–31). In June 2008, a month before the big event in Paris, Libya sponsored a mini-summit in Tripoli, which was attended by the presidents of Algeria, Tunisia, Mauritania and Syria along with the Moroccan Prime Minister, Abbas El Fassi (*Aujourd'hui Le Maroc*, 12 June 2008). In the Maghreb, where the interest in the UfM was in any case greater than in the Middle East, Rabat and Tunis began to compete with each other with a view to securing greater influence and a leadership role in the new cooperation framework. They both called for the formation of a core including the southern countries that were 'most advanced and motivated' with regard to the UfM project (*Jeune Afrique*, 16–22 March 2008).

Out of the four North African leaders who sent him a message of congratulations on the night of his electoral victory, Mohammed VI was the only one to mention Sarkozy's campaign promises relating to the reshaping of Euro-Mediterranean relations and to express his intention to support him (*Jeune Afrique*, 13–19 May 2007). In October 2007, on the occasion of Sarkozy's first state visit to Morocco and his speech in Tangier on the future UfM, the King solemnly reiterated his commitment to what he described as 'a visionary and bold project' (speech by Mohammed VI, Marrakesh, 23 October 2007). Yet, in fact, the Moroccan authorities did not support the new French project that wholeheartedly; they prioritised, as always, the bilateral component of relations with the EU over any form of multilateralism (*Le Journal Hebdomadaire*, 27 October–2 November 2007). What they were doing was to try to steer the idea towards their own purposes. Rabat's real concern at this time was progress in negotiations on its coveted Advanced Status with the EU, which had precisely been launched at the sixth session of the Association Council in July 2007. This was a crucial turning point for Morocco–EU relations on both the bilateral and the multilateral tracks. At the same time, on the multilateral level, Morocco seemed to be more interested in promoting closer cooperation among the Western Mediterranean countries via the 5+5 Dialogue than in developing yet another all-encompassing framework with which Middle Eastern conflicts would continue to interfere (Bauchard, 2008: 57–58).

Accordingly, Morocco's backing for the UfM arose out of a cost-benefit calculation and resulted in a commitment that was 'reasoned, unreserved, and yet preserved the singularity of the relationship between the two partners' (Jaidi and Abouyoub, 2008: 32). Another non-negligible factor was the purely Franco-Moroccan dimension to this undertaking, i.e. the estimated cost of opposing the French proposal – 'upsetting our friend Sarkozy' (*Le Journal Hebdomadaire*, 27 October–2 November 2007) – during a honeymoon in bilateral relations which had culminated in Sarkozy's visit to Morocco and the announcement of major investments. In line with all of this, the discourse of the Moroccan foreign ministry on the UfM was subsequently articulated around the ideas of 'new regionalism', 'variable geometry' and 'differentiation', as well as the assertion of Morocco's role as a 'pioneer':

> Thanks to the long and rich tradition in its relations with the EU and in favour of the promising dynamic conferred by its 'Advanced Status,' Morocco cannot but be a pioneer in the innovative approach of building the Mediterranean region.
>
> (Fassi Fihri, 2009: 28)

Besides this, a striking point in this discourse was the claim that the UfM should be conceived of as an 'eminently political project' (Fassi Fihri, 2009: 28), whereas much of its novelty in comparison with the EMP lay precisely in its functionalist depoliticisation.

Another unprecedented dynamic fostered by the debate on the UfM in Morocco – also associated with the Advanced Status negotiations – was the mobilisation of a number of young thinktanks dedicated to international and foreign policy issues. The most outstanding case was that of the newly founded Amadeus Institute, which claimed to fall 'directly within this new perspective and Euro-Mediterranean dynamic', and dedicated the first issue of its magazine (in French) to the UfM (*La revue du CAP*, May 2008: 4). Virtually setting itself up as mouthpiece of official Moroccan discourse, this thinktank chaired by Brahim Fassi Fihri, the son of the foreign minister, repeated the view that 'pragmatism, voluntariness, progressiveness and differentiation are the fundamental values that should guide the construction of the UfM' (*La revue du CAP*, May 2008: 44). In July 2008, it convened an international assessment meeting on the Paris summit (*Aujourd'hui Le Maroc*, 25 July 2008). The first edition of the ambitious MEDays forum, which was organised in Tangier in November 2008 and was destined to be repeated annually, also revolved around the same topic. In addition, during the busy months leading up to the Paris summit, the Moroccan Institute for International Relations (IMRI) published a report by a panel of experts on the UfM project (IMRI/KAS, 2008), the Moroccan Interdisciplinary

Centre for Strategic and International Studies (CMIESI) organised a congress in Fes,[1] and Tangier hosted a Euro-Mediterranean forum on the same subject.[2]

This unusual display of civil society and semiofficial initiatives meant that it came as even more of a surprise when Mohammed VI was eventually absent from the grand opening summit of the UfM in Paris. Prince Moulay Rachid was charged at the last minute with representing Morocco. Although officially justified by scheduling problems, the King's non-attendance was widely interpreted as a gesture of protest, either because Morocco had been passed over as host country for the headquarters of the UfM Secretariat, frustrating its aspirations (*L'Économiste*, 20 June 2008), or because its authorities were offended by France's excessive deference to Algeria on the eve of this international event – in which the presence of President Abdelaziz Bouteflika was desired at all costs (*Tel Quel*, 19–25 July 2008; *Rue89*, 13 July 2008; *La Vie Éco*, 25 July 2008). In addition, the absence of the Moroccan head of state from international meetings had become the norm during the new reign (*Le Journal Hebdomadaire*, 19–25 July 2008). Mohammed VI had not participated either in the preparatory mini-summit on the UfM organised by some Arab countries in Tripoli in June that year, which was attended by the presidents of Algeria, Tunisia, Mauritania and Syria.

Morocco's bargaining for a high-profile role in the UfM in any case continued. Since the southern co-Presidency had been assigned in 2008 to Egypt and the Secretariat was eventually opened in 2010 in Barcelona, with a Jordanian diplomat occupying the position of secretary-general, Rabat had to wait until the latter official was replaced. His successors were two prominent Moroccan career diplomats, namely Youssef Amrani (July 2011–February 2012) – who was later appointed as deputy minister of Foreign Affairs – and Fathallah Sijilmassi (March 2012 onwards). These appointments were similarly presented as a 'great victory for the Moroccan diplomacy' (*L'Économiste*, 26 May 2011), or 'a new recognition of the Moroccan diplomacy's input to the Union and an illustration of the relevance of HM King Mohammed VI's vision for an efficient and proactive diplomacy' (MAP, 10 February 2012).

Intergovernmental dynamics and 'rhetorical action' in pursuit of an Advanced Status

From a bilateral perspective, the qualitative leap in Morocco–EU relations came on 13 October 2008, when the Association Council in its seventh session adopted the Joint Document which laid the foundation for the Advanced Status. The raison d'être of this original and exclusive bilateral framework, which was conceived in accordance with the differential spirit of ENP, was to single out a special relationship and foster greater convergence and Morocco's integration into the EU's economic and political structures, to the extent allowed by its non-candidate status. For the moment in any case this was nothing but a political document containing an ambitious and evolving 'roadmap', the measures envisaged under which were to be implemented 'in the short to medium term', without being any more specific. It envisaged the development from 2009 onwards of the new bilateral political framework that would follow the 2005 ENP Action Plan and later, only 'potentially', creating a new legal 'contractual link' (*lien contractuel*) to replace the existing Association Agreement (EU–Morocco Association Council, 2008a: 1).

The very possibility of the Advanced Status was the result of the convergence of, on the one hand, the old Moroccan ambition to set its relationship with the EU apart from those of other southern Mediterranean countries and, on the other hand, the differentiation or asymmetrical bilateralism embraced by the ENP during 2004–2005. On the Moroccan side, the demand for 'more than association, less than accession', as summarised out of King Mohammed VI's famous Paris speech in March 2000 (speech by Mohammed VI, Paris, 20 March 2000), had been present within royal and diplomatic discourse as a leitmotif since the entry into force of the 1996 Association Agreement that month, to the point of becoming one of the main constants of the new reign's foreign policy. The alternative expression 'Advanced Status', which was used as a synonym, appeared for the first time in a royal address in Rome in April of the same year (Maalmi, 2012: 790). Moreover, as explained above, the desire for exclusive or privileged treatment by the EU stemmed from a deep-rooted national role conception as *model student* of the EU/Europe, which had been historically epitomised by King Hassan II's official application for accession to the EEC in 1987. The new Advanced Status idea was essentially an evolution of that symbolic bid, whilst in practical terms implying an acceptance of its futility. By the time preliminary negotiations started (2006–2007), the EU–Morocco Association Agreement had been in force for more than five years and the ENP Action Plan for Morocco, adopted in 2005, had become operational; however, none of these frameworks lived up to the Moroccan ambitions.

In order to understand the peculiar nature and significance of the Advanced Status for Morocco's interests and identity, it must be noted that, according to both observers and practitioners, its *ideational* power or *symbolic* dimension carried far more weight than its *practical* content. Its genuine added value with regard to the possibilities for convergence and integration into EU structures already provided in the ENP Action Plan was unclear from the outset. In the words of an official from the Directorate-General for External Relations of the European Commission who was involved in the negotiations:

> The Moroccans call it Advanced Status, we call it deepening of the bilateral relationship. For us, Advanced Status doesn't mean anything concrete. We don't see it as the end of a process either. We see it as a continuing process of deepening relations.
>
> (Interview quoted in Bremberg, 2012: 130)

Moreover, the lack of concrete commitments reduced the Joint Document to a mere *shopping list* or political agreement on issues that should be negotiated in the future. Therefore, what made a difference for Rabat was the declaratory effect or political labelling resulting from this symbolic upgrading, which reflected the external recognition of the national role conception held for decades:

> For Morocco, as acknowledged in private by its most prominent foreign relations policy makers, in the short term it is mainly a public diplomacy move aimed at maintaining its status as 'role model' for other Arab Mediterranean countries and keeping the pressure on the EU to substantiate this supposedly privileged status in the future.
>
> (Martín, 2009: 242)

Furthermore, and significantly, the idea of the Advanced Status had originated in Rabat (Pardo, 2009: 76; interview with Abdelwahab Maalmi, 7 June 2013; interview with Eneko Landaburu, 23 May 2014) and exceptionally travelled in a South–North direction, which went against the established norm for asymmetric relations between the EU and its periphery. Before anything else, the content of the initiative was the bid itself: the display of Morocco's firm political will, propositional capacity and *desire for Europe*. Yet what appeared at first as nothing more than a Moroccan grandiloquent formula devoid of content – an empty signifier – was later adopted and replicated within EU discourse, and ended up taking on a political life of its own. The weaker party to the relationship achieved a considerable success by managing to impose its own 'definition of the situation' (Wendt, 1999: 329).

All in all, Morocco's determination can be understood as being primarily driven by the search for international legitimacy. The advantages of being singled out as the EU's closest ally or reference partner in the southern Mediterranean were self-evident in terms of international visibility and reputation (Fernández-Molina and Bustos, 2010: 3; Kausch, 2010: 2). Furthermore, international legitimisation could also bring about quite tangible benefits for the state's security and autonomy, material gratifications and a reinforcement of domestic legitimacy and rule. In the case at hand, the Advanced Status could ensure a more positive EU perception of Morocco's strategic interests in vital issues such as the Western Sahara conflict, as well as securing greater influence for its positions on Euro-Mediterranean or African affairs. On the economic level, in addition to boosting reforms in various sectors, this recognition was supposed to enhance the country's credibility and attractiveness to international investors, and to be accompanied by increased financial assistance from the EU (Jaidi and Martín, 2010: 28). From a domestic point of view, the European validation of the political reforms and 'democratisation' discourse of the Rabat authorities arguably contributed to the regime's legitimacy, stability and perpetuation.

From the EU perspective, Rabat's demand was consistent with the offer of 'everything but institutions' and the essential characteristics of the ENP (bilateralism, differentiation, gradual and positive conditionality). Morocco's dynamic and constructive attitude in bilateral relations needed to be rewarded by maximising the opportunities and instruments provided by the ENP. At the same time, this Advanced Status could also serve as a test bed for how to remedy some of the deficiencies or weaknesses identified during the initial years of implementation of this policy. The first was the widespread perception among southern Mediterranean countries that the EU had downgraded them from 'partners' to 'neighbours', devising a largely unilateral policy which lacked real co-ownership (IEMed, 2009: 155). The second was the absence of sufficient incentives to stimulate or reward the huge reform and Europeanisation efforts required from them, since the option of EU accession was not on the table (Kausch, 2010: 3). This meant there was a need for a 'strong political message' from the EU to the southern Mediterranean states and societies (Miguel Ángel Moratinos in IEMed, 2009: 34). In this sense, Morocco's Advanced Status was not conceived of as an exclusive single-country solution, but as an experiment on a model that could be extended in future to other neighbouring countries (IEMed, 2009: 33, 61, 106). The dilemma between exclusivity and proliferation remained intentionally unresolved at this stage, in spite of the risks of sacrificing the coherence of the ENP by multiplying the EU's special relationships with different neighbouring countries (Jaidi, 2009: 163; Mestres and Soler, 2008).[3]

The merits for which the EU decided to reward Morocco within a logic of positive conditionality are listed in the EU Declaration issued at the seventh meeting of the Association Council (October 2008), when the Advanced Status was launched. The document combined a recognition of progress made thus far by this *model student* of EU policies with declarations of trust and recommendations for reforms that were still pending. On the one hand, it highlighted a range of recent evidence of Rabat's 'European vocation' and exemplary behaviour in its relations with the EU: Morocco's rapid implementation of the ENP Action Plan, its commitment to the new UfM, its advantage as the only southern Mediterranean country to have established a permanent Reinforced Political Dialogue with the EU, its interest to associate itself with certain declarations and positions within the framework of the CFSP, its participation in the ALTHEA military operation in Bosnia and Herzegovina within the framework of the ESDP (El Houdaïgui, 2010: 311–312; Bremberg, 2012: 148–149, 158), its valuable cooperation in the fight against terrorism and illegal immigration, and its role in the new European policy towards Africa (EU–Morocco Association Council, 2008b: 1–3). According to authors such as El Qadim, migration control was the real 'keystone' of the EU Declaration (2010: 112).

The complementary side of the coin were the merits relating to Moroccan domestic development and reforms. The EU Declaration stated the EU's desire to support this country's 'courageous process of modernisation and democratisation', without drawing any distinction between the two concepts. In particular, it referred to the reforms launched in the areas of education, human development and poverty reduction, agriculture and justice, the positive evolution of the Moroccan economy in previous years (in terms of economic growth and job creation), the plans for decentralisation and regional development, progress on human rights and fundamental freedoms, and the free and fair development of the legislative elections held in September 2007 (EU–Morocco Association Council, 2008b: 3–4). The Commissioner for External Relations and European

Neighbourhood Policy, Benita Ferrero-Waldner, had similarly praised the 'ambitious process of political, economic and social modernisation' undertaken by Morocco under the leadership of Mohammed VI, highlighting several of these developments (IEMed, 2009: 25–26).

Intergovernmental dynamics and negotiation process

In addition to the EMP's work programme adopted at the 2005 Barcelona summit and the Commission's communication on the strengthening of the ENP (European Commission, 2006), the EU–Morocco Advanced Status was in keeping with the legal provisions of the Treaty of Lisbon – signed in December 2007 – on the EU's 'special relationship with neighbouring countries' (article 8) (EU, 2012). The specific basis for negotiations was the 2005 EU–Morocco Action Plan, the introduction of which expressly mentioned this horizon: 'The deepening of Morocco's relationship with the EU, which will help identify new cooperation measures and strengthen political ties, is a practical response that will allow Morocco to progress towards an advanced status' (EU–Morocco Association Council, 2005: 1). Three reference models could serve as inspiration: first, the European Economic Area established between the EU and three out of four countries from the European Free Trade Association (Iceland, Norway and Liechtenstein), including all four freedoms of circulation (goods, services, capital and persons); second, the preferential conditions granted to candidate countries during the pre-accession phase, such as the customs union agreement with Turkey; and third, the Eastern Partnership at the time in the making with Belarus, Ukraine, Moldova, Georgia, Armenia and Azerbaijan, with strengthened political dialogue, deep and comprehensive free trade areas (DCFTAs), participation in EU agencies and programmes, and increased financial assistance on the table (Jaidi and Martín, 2010: 12–17, 20–22).

However, the very idea that some of these possibilities could be applicable to a southern country such as Morocco would not have been conceivable without the emergence of certain conducive intergovernmental dynamics during these years on the EU policymaking level. More specifically, the close interplay between Morocco's dense bilateral connections with France and Spain, on the one hand, and the relationship with the EU as a whole, on the other, was instrumental throughout the entire Advanced Status negotiation process. From Morocco's standpoint, to a large extent, the ultimate goal of this endeavour was none other than extrapolating onto the wider EU level the privileged historical relationship maintained for decades with France. In the words of a semi-official document: 'What we have been able to build up with France in terms of quality and confidence in bilateral relations can feed our legitimate aspiration to attain it with the EU as a whole and its member states' (Comité Directeur du Rapport, 2006: 107).

In practice, although the idea of a special relationship had been an enduring undertone within EU–Morocco bilateral dialogue since Mohammed VI's Paris speech in March 2000, the gestation of the Advanced Status in its proper sense did not start until late 2005, after the adoption of the ENP Action Plan. In fact, it was the new Franco-Spanish alliance established following the change in government in Madrid in 2004 that proved to be a necessary condition for the success of this project. Significantly enough, in December 2005, a tripartite meeting was held between the deputy minister of Foreign Affairs from Morocco, Taieb Fassi Fihri, the deputy minister for European Affairs from France, Catherine Colonna, and the secretary of state for EU affairs from Spain, Alberto Navarro, in which options were considered for strengthening the mechanisms of political cooperation between Morocco and the EU, and for increasing this country's participation in the ESDP and EU agencies and programmes. Only three months later, in March 2006, Morocco and the Commission exchanged *non papers* on the Advanced Status during a visit to Rabat by Commissioner Ferrero-Waldner (MAEC, 22 March 2006). A group of experts from Spain, France, Portugal and the Commission who met in the same city in July was also receptive to the ideas of the Moroccan representatives (MAEC, 2008: 13–14; IEMed, 2009: 59).

Indeed, these preliminary talks were staged by the actors that were to be most heavily involved in the forthcoming negotiations on the Advanced Status. The most proactive parties were the governments of Spain, France and Portugal, which were united in a common southern European front in the face of relatively unconcerned central and northern countries. The government of José Luis Rodríguez Zapatero was the first to state its public support for the Moroccan project and participated, along with France and Italy, in the reflection group charged with sketching out its fundamental lines before the sixth session of the EU–Morocco Association Council (July 2007). Portugal, which had also previously backed Rabat's demands (MAEC, 19 May 2004), took over this issue as one of the priorities of its presidency of the EU in the second semester of 2007. Finally, the French presidency in the second half of 2008 played a key role in accelerating the negotiation process. It was at this stage that two of the three meetings of the ad hoc working group responsible for defining the content of the Advanced Status were held (18 July and 17 September), and the Joint Document agreed upon at the latter meeting was submitted to the seventh Association Council. Although less visibly, Italy could also be counted among the supporters of this initiative (IEMed, 2009: 7, 21, 33, 59; MAEC, 2008: 24, 28, 31). The intermediary or brokering role of the Commission was also essential throughout these months due to the divergences and dissimilar levels of interest of different EU member states regarding this issue (IEMed, 2009: 163). Ferrero-Waldner took over from Spain and France, and led negotiations after the sixth Association Council meeting, at which it was decided to create the ad hoc group mentioned above.

In the field of parallel diplomacy – that carried on by non-governmental actors but following the guidelines of or coordinated with official foreign policy – the Advanced Status negotiation process was driven forward by two international seminars which brought together senior officials from Morocco, the Commission, the Council's General Secretariat and rotating Presidency, and the foreign ministries of France, Spain, Portugal and Italy. The first one, organised in March 2007 in Barcelona by the European Institute of the Mediterranean (IEMed, 2009; MAEC, 28 February 2007, 2 March 2007),[4] was instrumental in securing a green light from the Commission and the EU Presidency for Rabat's demands and in enabling the next Association Council (July 2007) to set up the ad hoc working group to shape the future Advanced Status (MAEC, 24 July 2007; EU–Morocco Association Council, 2007: 2). The second seminar took place in January 2008 in Rabat, under the sponsorship of the Moroccan foreign ministry, and coinciding with a meeting of the 5 + 5 Dialogue – whose European members were, not by chance, the most interested in Advanced Status negotiations. This time the Moroccan authorities tried to involve also a number of national non-governmental and civil society actors (MAEC, 2008; MAEC, 19 January 2008, 21 January 2008).

'Rhetorical action' and 'mirroring'

The statements and speeches made in these two seminars enable the main elements of the discourse employed by the Moroccan foreign ministry during the negotiations on the Advanced Status to be identified in addition, more specifically, to some of Schimmelfennig's strategies of 'rhetorical action' that were particularly evident within this context. Chief among them was 'swotting', whereby 'state actors depict themselves as industrious students of the community's teaching programme and list all the norms they have already internalised in order to reap the benefits of legitimacy' (2000: 129–130). In the case at hand, first and foremost, Rabat's officials engaged in this behaviour by repeatedly listing all the political and economic reforms implemented by their country domestically, as well as the many achievements in its relations with the EU: successful implementation of the Association Agreement, adoption of the ENP Action Plan, political dialogue, trade flows, absorption of MEDA funds, adoption of the EU acquis, fisheries agreement, negotiations on the liberalisation of agricultural trade and services, negotiations on a readmission agreement, etc.

A second meaningful component of this rhetoric was the emphasis placed on the Moroccan origin of the idea of the Advanced Status and, more generally, on Morocco's performance as a 'force of initiative, a locomotive of bilateral cooperation and also of the Euro-Mediterranean Partnership': 'Long accustomed to this exercise, Morocco remains the country that invites reflection and proposes new perspectives' (Taieb Fassi Fihri in IEMed, 2009: 55, 57). This idea of a Moroccan propositional capacity and role as initiative-taker, which also involved an explicit competitive dimension, was echoed or *mirrored* at different times by various European voices:

> This advanced status is a challenge that Morocco throws down for the EU. [...] The EU is forced to respond to this demand, and this is where [...] the true content of the idea of an advanced status lies: in the definition that we must give to it, in the difficulty of finding, within the Community

> terminology of the different association agreements, the precise meaning of such status.
>
> (Vasconcelos, 2009: 83)

> The Advanced Status has a purely political dimension. That is to say, it is an encouragement [...]. Morocco has always suffered from being part of a group that was not at all homogeneous [...]. They always want to anticipate what will happen in the future, what we could further enhance, what we could develop as a new way of working together. [...] I think this has allowed Morocco at least to have an edge [*avoir une longueur d'avance*], to be a bit like the initiator. Because these ideas did not only come from us, it is a mutual reflection. Morocco wanted to go further and proposed several avenues. And finally, today, this has allowed the partnership between the EU and Morocco to become more dynamic and always be slightly ahead, a kind of model.
>
> (Interview in EU Delegation to Morocco, 6 June 2013)

Even more significantly, Rabat's dynamic and proactive pro-Europeanism took on a normative dimension by being presented as the result of an alleged 'convergence' of values, in what seems to be a clear case of 'manipulation of European identity':

> Relations between Morocco and the EU have always relied on a strong ideological foundation; the two partners share common values of democracy and rule of law. The choices of political pluralism and economic liberalism made by Morocco since the recovery of independence converge with the broad orientations of the European integration project. [...] This ambition establishes its political legitimacy and strategic relevance from the convergence between the society project that Morocco is building under the active leadership of His Majesty the King Mohammed VI and the EU's ambitions to promote the values of openness, progress and prosperity in its Neighbourhood.
>
> (MAEC, 2008: 11–12)

Ultimately, the intended effect of these discursive linkages and normative inference from exemplary foreign policy behaviour was none other than to consolidate the legitimacy of the Moroccan regime both domestically and internationally.

Third, regarding a more procedural aspect, Moroccan official discourse insisted on the 'participatory approach' and the role played by civil society in these negotiations, reflecting fashionable EU approaches and discourses on democratisation in an obvious effort to live up to EU expectations. Moreover, the usual argument established continuity between foreign policy and domestic politics:

> Like all strategic and fundamental issues for the Moroccan nation, the issue of the advanced status with the EU follows the same internal dynamics and

the same democratic methodology desired by His Majesty the King. That of an open and constructive discussion, that of a necessary involvement of all the national actors concerned in the conception, gestation and development of a project of this magnitude, that of the ownership of the project by all, parliamentary institution, local bodies, representatives of the business community, academia, the arts, the media and NGOs [...]. Thus, the Government of His Majesty the King will not be able to launch credible comprehensive negotiations [...] within the framework of the ad hoc working group which has been officially established without previously ensuring a participatory process [*démarche participative*] associating everyone with the desired partnership project.

(Taieb Fassi Fihri in MAEC, 2008: 18)[5]

This idea of a 'participatory approach' was strongly emphasised during the parallel diplomacy seminar held in Rabat in January 2008 (MAEC, 21 January 2008; *L'Économiste*, 22 January 2008), in which the Moroccan authorities claimed that they were counting on 'the active participation of many associative networks, elected representatives, business communities, decentralised communities, universities, research centres and the media' (MAEC, 19 January 2008). Such arguments were echoed in both the final conclusions for the event and the address by Commissioner Ferrero-Waldner, who called for a 'real participatory approach' (MAEC, 2008: 58–59, 68–69, 20). Accordingly, the draft document presented by Morocco as its initial negotiating position at the first meeting of the ad hoc working group was appropriately described as the result of a nationwide consultation process:

The Government of His Majesty the King has launched national consultations which have involved all public, territorial, private and associative actors. This participatory process [*démarche participative*] has enabled the expectations and aspirations of all these actors and participants concerning the future path of our partnership with the EU to be taken into consideration.

(EU–Morocco Working Group on the Advanced Status, 2008)

Out of the plethora of stakeholders allegedly involved, it was the role of Moroccan civil society that featured most prominently in official discourse, despite criticisms regarding the 'total lack of consultation' voiced by the European Economic and Social Committee and the Euro-Mediterranean Human Rights Network (Jaidi and Martín, 2010: 74):[6]

Our partnership with the EU stands out due to the increasing involvement of NGOs and non-state actors, which highlights the growing role of the Moroccan associative fabric and its contribution [*accompagnement*] to strengthening the democratic project which Morocco has committed itself to building, under the leadership of His Majesty the King Mohammed VI. The inclusion of the associative sector gives a huge boost to the neighbourhood dynamics and the Morocco–EU partnership, and strengthens the Moroccan civil society.

(MAEC, 2008: 53)

In all these cases, Morocco's own 'rhetorical action' was effectively complemented by 'mirroring' (Wendt, 1999: 327) in interactions with the EU, as is clear from the multiple reflections and echoes between discourses, preferences and also taboos (silences) apparent within bilateral dialogue at this stage.

The drafting and content of the Joint Document

Public statements aside, quite substantial reflections were also visible within the drafting process for the text on the Advanced Status between the content of the initial Moroccan proposal and the Joint Document ultimately adopted. The ad hoc working group established by the Association Council in July 2007 included representatives from Morocco, the EU member states, the Commission and the General Secretariat of the Council, and met three times in 2008: on 16 May, 18 July and 17 September. The delegation from Rabat included senior officials from different ministries and was headed by the then director-general for Bilateral Relations at the Ministry of Foreign Affairs, Youssef Amrani. It was the Moroccans who at the first meeting presented the first draft document which would serve as basis for the negotiations – allegedly the result of extensive domestic consultations[7] – to which the EU was to respond later with its amendments (Bremberg, 2012: 125, 130; MAEC, 17 July 2008; *Aujourd'hui Le Maroc*, 19 September 2008). The fact that it was left to the Moroccan party to formulate the first version allowed it to set the fundamental parameters and arguably created some kind of textual path-dependence. In the end, the structure of the Joint Document reproduced almost point by point that of the first Moroccan draft.

The Moroccan draft document contained provisions addressing the political, economic-financial and human dimensions of EU–Morocco relations, as well as Morocco's participation in EU agencies and programmes. The areas in which it was most ambitious and innovative in relation to the ENP Action Plan were political and strategic dialogue – with proposals such as institutionalising regular bilateral summits – and financial support – with a groundbreaking demand to make Morocco eligible for EU regional policy funds:

> On a financial level, the Advanced Status must provide clear added value and mark a break from existing mechanisms [...]. Based on the experience of EU enlargements [...], the Advanced Status should [...] make the Morocco–EU financial cooperation move towards the logic of structural and cohesion funds [...]. Such evolution requires substantial financial resources to be made available to Morocco, involving figures and terms of implementation similar to those granted to the candidate countries for EU accession.
>
> (EU–Morocco Working Group on the Advanced Status, 2008: 13)

From the Advanced Status to the Arab Spring 141

Boldly requesting a qualitative change such as the *extraterritorial* extension (to outside the EU) of EU Structural Funds and the Cohesion Fund, and making the success of the Advanced Status conditional upon this financial upgrading can also be understood as forming part of a rhetorical strategy of 'shifting the burden' to the EU.

The Joint Document submitted to the Association Council and adopted in its seventh session in October 2008 followed the structure and retained most of the measures contained in the Moroccan proposal, although considerably reined in the latter's funding ambitions. The political dimension and, within it, political and strategic dialogue was the area which brought most potential novelties compared to existing frameworks. Several mechanisms were envisaged for the ensuring coordination between the two parties on bilateral or international issues, such as the holding of bilateral summits, meetings at the United Nations (UN) between the Moroccan foreign minister and the EU high representative for Foreign Affairs and Security Policy, informal meetings of various sectoral ministers with their European counterparts, Reinforced Political Dialogue, harmonisation of positions in multilateral fora, meetings of senior officials from Morocco and the Political and Security Committee (COPS), and the participation of a Moroccan ambassador or senior official in the meetings of certain Council committees or groups. In any case, all of these meetings were only agreed upon in principle and were expected to take place only on an ad hoc basis, while the initial Moroccan aim was for at least the first two to be regular. The only case in which there was talk of 'ensuring a regular frequency' was that of Reinforced Political Dialogue. Other measures included in this section were increased dialogue within the framework of the ESDP, Moroccan support for certain CFSP declarations, the development of a 'partnership for peace and security in Africa', and the institutionalisation of cooperation on civil protection. This was followed by measures aimed at strengthening relations on parliamentary level (joint parliamentary committee, exchanges between parties and political groups) and the already existing cooperation on security and judicial affairs (EU–Morocco Association Council, 2008a: 2–3).

In the economic field, the general objective set out in the Joint Document was 'the establishment of a common economic space between the EU and Morocco, characterised by the Moroccan economy's increased integration into that of the EU, and inspired by the norms that govern the European Economic Area' (EU–Morocco Association Council, 2008a: 4). To this end, it was agreed that action would be taken in four complementary areas: the rapprochement of Morocco's legal framework to the EU acquis; the conclusion of a DCFTA; economic and social cooperation in various areas (investment, employers' organisations, industry, support for small and medium-sized enterprises, technical standardisation and regulation, intellectual property, employment and social affairs); and Morocco's connection to trans-European networks (transport and energy) and sectoral cooperation (information and communication technologies, agriculture, fishing, mining, environment, water) (EU–Morocco Association Council, 2008a: 4–11).

142   From the Advanced Status to the Arab Spring

Regulatory convergence appeared to constitute the practical touchstone for the economic dimension to the Advanced Status, specifically amounting to an indispensable prerequisite for the free access of Moroccan industrial products to the EU market. In fact, in this area, the Joint Document did not go beyond what had already been provided for in the ENP Action Plan (Martín, 2009: 240). The EU had been providing specialised technical assistance in this area for years and in 2004, in the framework of the Support to the Association Agreement Programme, had launched a plan of institutional twinning including 20 projects in various sectors (MAEC, 30 November 2005). The new step now envisaged was to establish a joint mechanism to draw up an inventory of all legislative and regulatory devices existing in Morocco and the EU in order to ensure further progress on the more systematic adoption of the EU acquis. Later on, the establishment of an inter-ministerial coordination authority for regulatory convergence was proposed, along with the development of a national programme for this purpose. Financial services, public markets and quality and industrial safety standards were the areas prioritised in 2009 (Jaidi and Martín, 2010: 58–60).

The DCFTA envisaged would have the novel feature of including agriculture and services in addition to industrial products, and would be based on the four freedoms of the European Economic Area, albeit subject to explicit reservations on the movement of persons. The Joint Document proposed 'the free movement of goods [...], services, capital and the temporary presence of natural persons for professional purposes' (EU–Morocco Association Council, 2008a: 5). As initial practical steps in this direction, it referred to the conclusion of the bilateral negotiations already in progress concerning the liberalisation of, on the one hand, trade in services and the right of establishment (2007–) (*L'Économiste*, 11 June 2007, 27 June 2007) and, on the other hand, trade in agricultural, processed agricultural and fishery products (2006–). Thus, in practice, the European Commission rendered the launch of new DCFTA negotiations conditional on the signing of preliminary agreements on these two complex issues (Jaidi and Martín, 2010: 44). In addition, the future trade agreement was supposed to be based on the principles of special treatment for certain sensitive sectors, asymmetry of commitments and progressive implementation (EU–Morocco Association Council, 2008a: 5). There was no mention of the possibility of a customs union, which would be a necessary condition for the establishment of a genuine common market.

The measures contained in the Joint Document relating to the human dimension were intended to encourage exchanges and consultations between civil society actors from both shores of the Mediterranean, relations between territorial (regional and local) bodies, the rapprochement of Morocco's university and vocational education systems to their European equivalents, the joint implementation of a 'global approach' to migration – again the same slogan adopted by Morocco – and the training of Moroccan diplomats and officials on EU issues (EU–Morocco Association Council, 2008a: 11–13). Significantly, the proposed enhanced dialogue on human rights between the EU and the CCDH – an official non-elected and non-representative institution reporting directly to the King – was included in this chapter and not in the political dimension to the Advanced Status.

As far as cooperation on migration was concerned, it was enunciated in a sparing and undefined manner, without offering any concrete commitment, although did however appear to be the only aspect of the entire 'roadmap' that was subject to a clear prerequisite or conditionality, i.e. the conclusion of a readmission agreement. The EU Declaration was more explicit in this regard:

> The EU regrets that the negotiations on a readmission agreement have not been completed since the last session of the Association Council. The EU reiterates the importance it attaches to the prompt conclusion of this agreement, which will open new opportunities for the development of cooperation with Morocco.
> (EU–Morocco Association Council, 2008b: 5–6)

The widespread perception within the Moroccan civil society that this was the true bargaining chip in the new deal with the EU forced foreign minister Fassi Fihri to declare that 'Morocco [was] not going to be the gendarme of Europe in exchange for an Advanced Status' (*Al Masaa*, 30 October 2008). On a different note, as noted by Larabi Jaidi and Iván Martín (2010: 74), there was

> A flagrant contradiction between, on the one hand, the absence of any reference to or consultation with civil society during the Advanced Status drafting process and, on the other hand, the role which is supposed to be assigned to civil society within such a framework.

A final section of the Joint Document envisaged the participation of Morocco (without additional funding) in EU agencies such as the European Aviation Safety Agency (first pillar), the European Monitoring Centre for Drugs and Drug Addiction, Eurojust and the Institute for Security Studies (third pillar); as well as in programmes such as the one on Competitiveness and Innovation, Customs 2013, SESAR (air traffic control) or Marco Polo (transport) (EU–Morocco Association Council, 2008a: 13–14). In fact, this list was much smaller than the general one published by the European Commission in October 2007 including all the EU agencies and programmes that were potentially open to participation by ENP partners. Negotiations on this matter had been launched in June 2007 with a group of pioneer third countries including Morocco, and hence the Advanced Status did not provide any added value on this score (Jaidi and Martín, 2010: 64; Martín, 2009: 241).

Similarly, no qualitative leap was envisaged in EU financial commitments either. As Morocco had been the first recipient of both MEDA funds (€1,600 million in 1995–2006) and the ENPI I (€654 million in 2007–2010), and given that the EU Financial Perspective 2007–2013 had been closed, the Joint Document acknowledged that there was very limited room for manoeuvre at the time in order to increase these figures. No substantial changes would arrive in this respect until at least 2014. With a view to that new stage, there was a call to launch a joint reflection on how to improve 'the access to appropriate EU financial resources to accompany Morocco within the logic of the EU's regional and cohesion policy, and the adoption of new application procedures' (EU–Morocco Association Council, 2008a: 14). It was the first time that a bilateral document mentioned, albeit only tentatively, the possibility of Morocco someday benefiting from EU Structural Funds, or similar funds, as this country had been demanding. This would mean moving from a logic of cooperation to one of integration as far as financial support is concerned (Jaidi and Martín, 2010: 70–73).

International legitimacy for domestic consumption

Leaving aside this hypothetical financial upgrading and the immediate political declaratory effect, observers expressed from the outset doubts about the substantial added value of the Advanced Status in relation to the existing bilateral frameworks for Morocco–EU relations (mainly the ENP Action Plan). In view of the intangible nature of its benefits, it could be concluded that the main rationale for the Moroccan authorities – and the area in which they actually made a greater step forward – was the search for international legitimacy from a powerful 'socialisation agency' like the EU. The political effects of this legitimisation included the reinforcement of domestic legitimacy and rule, as the political reforms and 'democratisation' discourse of the Rabat authorities were externally validated even without any substantial (structural) political transformations. On the occasion of the seventh Association Council (October 2008), the EU globally commended Morocco's 'courageous process of modernisation and democratisation' (EU–Morocco Association Council, 2008b: 3), while Commissioner Ferrero-Waldner opted to use only the former term ('ambitious process of political, economic and social modernisation') (IEMed, 2009: 25–26). In any case, during the whole Advanced Status negotiation process no added pressure was placed on the Moroccan regime to undertake substantial political reforms in exchange for the special treatment expected from the EU. Similarly, the Joint Document did not include any concrete commitments, deadlines, benchmarks or assessment criteria. Therefore, there was arguably no serious hint of democratic conditionality in either the process or the outcome.

The EU Declaration contented itself with mentioning Morocco's need to strengthen public institutions and good governance, along with some evident shortcomings in the human rights sphere (freedom of expression and association, abuses committed by the security forces and the death penalty), but only as a counterpoint to an overall rosy picture of the situation. It further stated that the September 2007 parliamentary elections had represented 'new progress in the democratisation process' (EU–Morocco Association Council, 2008b: 4), leaving aside a historically low voter turnout (37 per cent) which severely questioned the representativeness of the new parliament and government. This is just one example of the EU's use of liberal democracy-related vocabulary in a formalistic way, without touching on essential political issues associated with the inner distribution of power and the willingness to engage in structural change within non-democratic partner countries – in other words, the depoliticisation or *technocratisation* of the EU approach to democratisation. For her part, Ferrero-Waldner underscored Morocco's willingness to establish a Reinforced Political Dialogue (2004) and a Subcommittee on Human Rights, Democratisation and Governance within the Association Council (2006), as well as the positive evaluation of the first year of implementation of the ENP Action Plan (IEMed, 2009: 25–26), all of which amounted to progress in Morocco's foreign policy behaviour and relations with the EU rather than purely domestic political reforms.

As a consequence, the Advanced Status could be portrayed within Moroccan official discourse as 'a mark of trust by the EU in the Moroccan model and the reforms undertaken by the Kingdom', which were allegedly viewed as an example for other countries (MAEC, 14 October 2008, 15 October 2008):

> The royal call for an 'advanced status' gained real strength thanks to the successful and bold advances made along the path of institutional modernisation, the momentum of the democratic process, the building of the rule of law, good governance, the modernisation [*mise à niveau*] of the national economy, the provision of infrastructure and the improvement in the living conditions of citizens by fighting poverty and social exclusion.
> (MAEC, 28 October 2008)

On the other side of the scale, the positive implications of the Advanced Status for domestic political reform in Morocco included some modest steps taken by the Rabat authorities during the negotiation process, which were possibly related to it. The main example was the National Action Plan on Human Rights and Democracy drafted from April 2008 onwards, which applied the recommendations of the Vienna Declaration (1993) whilst also receiving financial support (€2 million) from the EU (AFP, 25 April 2008; *Aujourd'hui Le Maroc*, 12 December 2008). Other than this, the Western Sahara conflict was notably absent from the Advanced Status negotiations, and was not referred to at all in the Joint Document. Such striking silence, which was already present in the 2005 ENP Action Plan, amounted to a reflection or replication of taboos within Moroccan official discourse. This can be regarded as an unintended consequence of the ENP's mild introduction of co-ownership, which in practice allowed neighbouring countries to exclude any topic they wished from bilateral dialogue or negotiations with the EU (Gillespie, 2013: 180). After all, aside this convenient omission which suited the Moroccan interests, Fassi Fihri was confident that the new privileged relationship with the EU would be a valuable asset for Morocco in order to 'defend its superior interests and demonstrate the legitimacy of its position on the issue of the Sahara' (MAEC, 29 October 2008).

In the year following the achievement of the Advanced Status, there was an increase in the intensity of bilateral political dialogue, sectoral negotiations and the transposition of the EU acquis, whilst little substantial progress in key areas for Morocco such as trade liberalisation, financial assistance or mobility (Jaidi and Martín, 2010: 28–31). The most significant development was the conclusion in December 2009 of the arduous EU–Morocco negotiations on trade in agricultural and fishery products, although ratification of this agricultural agreement by the Council and the European Parliament was delayed until the second half of 2010. The eighth session of the Association Council held in December 2009 gave a positive assessment of the implementation of the new bilateral framework (MAP, 7 December 2009). The only noticeable nuance in the corresponding EU Declaration was the greater urgency with which Morocco was asked to advance justice reform, insisting on the need for an 'independent and transparent judicial system' (EU–Morocco Association Council, 2009: 4). Indeed, the lack of tangible progress led the Delegation of the Commission in Rabat to suspend financial support in this area for 2010. In any case, the Advanced Status was to bring the bilateral political dialogue to its highest point and enshrine Morocco's privileged treatment by the EU in March 2010, when the first EU–Morocco summit was held in Granada under the Spanish presidency. This was the EU's first high-level bilateral meeting with a southern Mediterranean country and the second with an African state, after South Africa (Martín, 2010; El Yaakoubi, 2010).

'Business as usual' after (and despite) the Arab Spring

The greatest test for the continuity of Morocco's privileged relations with the EU came in 2011, with the Arab Spring's transnational wave of anti-authoritarian uprisings and the self-critical paradigm shift with which the EU initially intended – or at least claimed – to react to them, promising to acquiesce less in the lack of democracy in this region in future. While it did not reach the same magnitude and attract the same international attention as the revolutionary regime changes in Tunisia, Egypt or Libya, Morocco's unprecedented pro-democracy protests led by the 20 February Movement and the subsequent reformist response from the regime were also carefully monitored from Brussels and other European capitals. The main concern for the authorities in Rabat was to handle and defuse the protest movement by prioritising the *carrot* – socioeconomic concessions and negotiations with all the national political actors – over the *stick* – overt state repression and violence – so as to give credibility to the revamped discourse on the 'Moroccan exception' both domestically and internationally.

Indeed, not only was King Mohammed VI quick to announce in early March a much-advertised top-down constitutional reform, which was supposed to reinforce the rule of law and the separation of powers, but also the constitution drafting process was accompanied by an intense diplomatic campaign to 'sell' its results in advance to Morocco's main international partners (Fernández-Molina, 2011b: 440). Under the coordination of the Ministry of Foreign Affairs, delegations of Moroccan ministers and representatives from the main political parties were sent to New York (UN), Washington, Paris, London, Madrid and Brussels

(European Parliament). These journeys included talks at prestigious thinktanks such as Chatham House and the Institut Français des Relations Internationales (IFRI), and were supplemented by international media interviews and articles in European newspapers penned by minister Fassi Fihri (*Le Monde*, 31 March 2011) or his then secretary-general Amrani (*El País*, 28 April 2011).

Some of the fruits of this charm offensive were seen in the prudence evident within EU public declarations on the situation in Morocco during this turbulent 2011. The first joint statement by the EU High Representative Catherine Ashton and Commissioner Štefan Füle did not address the protests taking place in this country but the King's announcement of a constitutional reform, which was immediately described as a 'qualitative leap' and a 'commitment to further democratisation' 'in line with the ambitions of the Advanced Status' (European Commission/HR, 2011b). In May, following some episodes involving an intensified crackdown on demonstrators, the spokesperson of Commissioner Füle expressed the EU's 'concern' about the 'violence used' by the security forces (AFP, 30 May 2011; *Al Masaa*, 1 June 2011; *Al Quds al Arabi*, 1 June 2011). However, this moderate EU criticism, which was extremely appreciated by the youth of the 20 February Movement, soon gave way to repeated praise for the new constitutional text when the accelerated drafting process was concluded (European Commission/HR, 2011d) and when it was approved by referendum on 1 July with 98.5 percent voting in favour:

> We welcome the positive outcome of the referendum on the new Constitution in Morocco and commend the peaceful and democratic spirit surrounding the vote. The reforms proposed in it constitute a significant response to the legitimate aspirations of the Moroccan people [...]. Now we encourage the swift and effective implementation of this reform agenda.
> (European Commission/HR, 2011e)

The newly appointed EU Special Representative for the Southern Mediterranean, Bernardino León, further claimed that Morocco was 'a good example that fundamental reforms can be made maintaining stability', 'as an evolution, not revolution' (*El País*, 7 August 2011; *Al Ittihad al Ishtiraki*, 22 July 2011), and thus a 'reference' or a 'leader' in terms of political development for the whole region (*Morocco Tomorrow*, 18 September 2011, 20 November 2011). The pattern in 2011 has been summarised as follows:

> The EU chose a double strategy to respond to the 'Arab Spring'. Democratic movements were welcome if the country faced an overhaul of the system such as Egypt, Tunisia or Libya and the regimes supported if the country remained relatively stable like Morocco or Jordan.
> (Maggi, 2013: 22)

According to observers sympathetic to the Moroccan opposition, the EU representatives' tilt towards clear-cut support for the incumbent regime and its announced reforms contributed to weakening the 20 February Movement. Around June–July 2011, the young activists' initial expectations of international recognition or backing were dashed, replaced by the perception that the EU had 'let them down' (*les a laissés tomber*) (interview with Mohammed Madani, 5 June 2013). Officials at the EU Delegation in Rabat claimed in their defence that, first, no member of the 20 February Movement as such ever sought them out 'in an articulated way'. This lack of a 'structured approach' or 'institutionalised dynamics' prevented them from accessing financial resources. NGOs to which some of these activists were affiliated in parallel could have applied for EU project funding but, 'as an institution, we do not have the tools to finance a youth group that is disgruntled and hits the streets'. Second, regarding the denunciation of repression:

> We did say that it is not normal to crack down on demonstrations. We say that in all the political dialogue with Morocco, in public reports such as the annual ENP follow-up report. I do not think we have engaged in double talk [*langue de bois*].

Third, and more generally:

> We are not here to choose sides or support a revolution. [...] It is better to encourage a gradual change in regime that is not perfect but might be going in the right direction. [...] We do accompany political change in Morocco, but with means that can provoke frustration for people operating within a revolutionary dynamic. Yet we are not eager for Morocco to become like Tunisia or Egypt.
> (Interview in EU Delegation to Morocco, 6 June 2013)

As a result of the external validation of Morocco's 2011 constitutional reform and positive comparison with its increasingly destabilised neighbours, various actors and observers consider this state – or its regime – to have emerged internationally reinforced after the Arab Spring (interview with Brahim Fassi Fihri, 6 June 2013). As far as the EU is concerned, Morocco continued to be considered 'top of the class' (Colombo and Voltolini, 2014: 48). The only snag was the renewed competition with post-revolutionary Tunisia for this role of *model student* (interview with Eneko Landaburu, 23 May 2014).

The first evidence of the EU's 'confidence in the Kingdom's commitment to a process of democratisation and reforms', in the words of EU Ambassador Rupert Joy (*EU Neighbourhood Info Centre*, 9 July 2013), concerned money – one of the famous 'three Ms' which the Partnership for Democracy and Shared Prosperity with the Southern Mediterranean offered as the EU's support in response to the Arab Spring (money, market and mobility) (speech by Rupert Joy, Rabat, 10 February 2014). Morocco was included from the outset in the new Support to Partnership, Reforms and Inclusive Growth (SPRING) programme, along with Tunisia, Egypt and Jordan.[8] This distinct financial programme was launched in

September 2011 as part of the ENPI with the aim of responding to the pressing socioeconomic needs of southern Mediterranean countries and helping them in their 'transition to democracy' (European Commission, 2011b). The allocation of funds was supposedly based 'on an assessment of progress in building and consolidating deep and sustainable democracy and on needs' (European Commission, 2011a). Of the €350 million budgeted for the first phase (2011–2012), Morocco received 80 million, which were chiefly allocated to the newly created CNDH and Inter-Ministerial Delegation for Human Rights (*EU Neighbourhood Info Centre*, 9 July 2013). In the second phase (2013) it was granted 48 million (out of a total of 150 million), with a flagship project to support the House of Representatives 'in improving standards and procedures to tackle new responsibilities as a result of constitutional reform' (*EU Neighbourhood Info Centre*, 20 May 2014).

Later on, in the EU Financial Framework 2014–2020, the SPRING programme as such ceased to exist and became fully integrated into the European Neighbourhood Instrument (ENI) in the form of multi-country umbrella programmes with the same incentive-based approach (to which 10 per cent of the global financial envelope of the ENI was to be reserved) (ENI Regulation, article 7.6). The decision to remove the SPRING acronym was attributed by Moroccan diplomats to growing discomfort with the reference to the Arab Spring: 'Does the EU see now the Arab Spring the same way [as in 2011]? And maybe there are countries that have not witnessed the Arab Spring proper, that is revolution, and do not agree with the terminology' (interviews with Mounir Belayachi and Faiçal Akkor, 23 May 2014).[9]

Second, regarding market access, Morocco was the first southern Mediterranean country to start negotiating a DCFTA with the EU. The objective was to broaden and upgrade the existing Association Agreement by, on the one hand, incorporating formerly uncovered areas such as trade in services, public procurement, investment protection, competition and intellectual property rights, and on the other hand, reducing non-tariff barriers posed by industrial standards, technical regulations or sanitary and phytosanitary measures in order to favour Morocco's gradual integration into the EU Single Market (European Commission, 22 April 2013). In fact, some of these issues had already been long under discussion, such as trade in services since 2008, but were incorporated into the budding DCFTA. After informal preparatory talks in 2012, the first round of negotiations took place in April 2013 and was followed by others in June 2013, January 2014 and April 2014, reportedly involving the private sector and civil society (employers' organisations, corporative associations) (*EU Neighbourhood Info Centre*, 7 April 2014). Yet in July 2014 the fifth round was postponed (MAP, 9 July 2014), pending the completion by the Moroccan government of studies on some economic sectors of special sensitivity, such as the craft industry, which were deemed to require more detailed examination. The overall goal for Rabat was to reach an agreement that was 'balanced, asymmetric, progressive and accompanied' by financial and technical support (interview with Khalid Lahsaini, 23 May 2014).

Third, on the matter of mobility, Morocco was also a pioneer within the region in concluding a Mobility Partnership with the EU. Created as an instrument in the framework of the EU's Global Approach to Migration (2005), mobility partnerships were non-binding agreements between a third country, the European Commission and some interested EU member states. Official negotiations on the Mobility Partnership with Morocco started in October 2012 and involved nine individual countries besides the Union (France, Spain, Portugal, Italy, Belgium, Netherlands, Germany, United Kingdom and Sweden). The joint political declaration signed by all participating actors in June 2013 was conceived as 'a long-term cooperation framework', i.e. a roadmap including broad objectives or lines of action in four areas: mobility, legal immigration and integration; preventing and combating illegal immigration, people-smuggling, border management; migration and development; and international protection (of refugees and asylum-seekers). An annexed action plan listed 103 concrete initiatives or projects that either the EU or a member state committed itself to launching in order to achieve the previous goals (EU/Morocco, 2013).

In practice, again, the cornerstone of this long catalogue of measures was the EU's calls for Morocco to resume negotiations concerning a readmission agreement (article 13). The novelty of the Mobility Partnership was to offer more attractive compensation in return for this concession, including not only EU financial and technical support but also, and chiefly, visa facilitation for certain groups of people such as business professionals, students and researchers (articles 3 and 7). The readmission agreement and visa facilitation were conditional upon each other and had to be discussed in parallel thereafter. In any case, the 2013 joint declaration marked nothing but the start of a long, complex and open-ended negotiation process (*Lakome*, 9 June 2013; EMHRN, 2014; interview in EU Delegation to Morocco, 6 June 2013; interview with Nabil Abderrazaq, 23 May 2014).[10] Besides visa facilitation and financial and technical support, the main Moroccan demands made in exchange for a readmission agreement were that the EU compel sub-Saharan countries to implement the article 13 of the Cotonou Agreement, under which they would commit themselves to accept the repatriation of their citizens unlawfully present in Europe; that the EU launch negotiations to conclude similar readmission agreements with Morocco's neighbouring countries (such as Algeria); and that the existing bilateral agreements with individual EU member states be abrogated (interview with Mounir Belayachi, 23 May 2014).

An associated domestic development highly welcomed by the EU authorities was the decision to reform Morocco's own migration policy, which was taken by the King Mohammed VI himself – bypassing the government – after growing international criticism and an unprecedented report by the CNDH admitting serious human rights abuses against sub-Saharan African migrants passing through or settled in this country (CNDH, 2013; EU Delegation to Morocco, 26 September 2013). Following the recommendations of this consultative council, an exceptional regularisation process for irregular migrants was launched in early 2014 (*Jadaliyya*, 24 February 2014, 3 March 2014; HRW, 2014: 49).

Fourth, straddling the gap between the EU proper and other institutions, Morocco was chosen, along with Tunisia, as a priority target for the new three-year regional programme entitled Strengthening Democratic Reform in the Southern Neighbourhood, which was launched in January 2012 in strategic partnership by the EU (funding) and the Council of Europe (implementation) (European Commission, 22 December 2011). Before that, in June 2011, the Moroccan parliament had been the first to obtain the new status of Partner for Democracy granted by the Parliamentary Assembly of the Council of Europe (PACE), which implied embracing the values of pluralist democracy, the rule of law and respect for human rights and fundamental freedoms (CoE, 21 June 2011; *Al Ittihad al Ishtiraki*, 2 June 2011, 15 July 2011).

At the same time, leaving aside these new (or recycled) initiatives in response to the Arab Spring, Morocco's relations with the EU largely continued along a *business as usual* track. The most relevant bilateral negotiations under way before the outbreak of the uprisings were those concerning a new five-year ENP Action Plan to replace the one from 2005, which was due to expire in 2010 but was extended. The new negotiation process lasted from December 2010 until November 2012 and resulted in the Action Plan in the Framework of the Advanced Status (*Plan d'Action pour la Mise en Œuvre du Statut Avancé*, PASA), which was adopted by the Association Council at its eleventh session in December 2013 (*EU Neighbourhood Info Centre*, 17 December 2013).

This document was a synthesis of the 2005 Action Plan and the Joint Document on the Advanced Status, and claimed to place the latter's 'roadmap' on an operational footing, based on the principles of differentiation and co-ownership (*appropriation*). Its content was structured differently, distinguishing between measures to advance 'towards a space of shared values' (political and strategic dialogue; democracy, the rule of law and governance; cooperation in justice and security; rapprochement between peoples) and 'towards a common economic space' (economic and social reform; trade, market and regulatory reform; transport, energy, environment, information society, research and development; education, training and health), as well as Morocco's participation in EU programmes and agencies. Rather than in this long catalogue of provisions, it was in some statements contained in the introduction that the Arab Spring's imprint was evident:

> The intensity of EU support will be tailored to the ambitions and progress of reforms pursued by Morocco as well as the country's needs and capabilities. The EU and Morocco will continue to work in this direction, which corresponds with the new Moroccan Constitution adopted on 1 July 2011 and the new EU strategy developed under the Partnership for Democracy and Shared Prosperity with the Southern Mediterranean.
> (EU–Morocco Association Council, 2013: 1)

When comparing the action plans from 2005 and 2013, Moroccan diplomats stressed three key differences. First, according to them, both plans had 'nothing to do' with each other because the former had the objective of giving body and soul to the Association Agreement, whereas the latter was about implementing the content of the Advanced Status. Second, the 2005 Action Plan was primarily based on the principle of differentiation, while the 2013 Action Plan added that of co-ownership (*appropriation*):

> That is to say, we no longer accept that the EU can dictate to us the projects or the sectors in which it wants to accompany us. Now, it is we who ask if the EU is willing to accompany or not *our* reforms or *our* priorities in Morocco.

At the same time, an additional component 'imposed' by the EU within the framework of the revised ENP was the 'more for more' principle (interview with Mounir Belayachi, 23 May 2014). Third, in keeping with the emphasis on permanent progress and improvement in the relations with the EU, the 2013 Action Plan was presented as a crucial step towards the next horizon desired by the Moroccan authorities, that is, a new bilateral legal framework or 'contractual link' (*lien contractuel*) to replace the Association Agreement two decades after it was signed (interview with Youssef Amrani in *Le Soir-Échos*, 4 January 2013).

This tendency of the Moroccan authorities to constantly raise the bar of ambitions vis-à-vis the EU could also become problematic when exaggerated and lacking precise content. For example, in 2012 the EU Delegation in Rabat was forced to curb demands for an 'Advanced Status Plus' (*Statut Avancé Plus*) expressed by some members of the new Moroccan government:

> Our message was: be careful, it is necessary to keep credibility. [...] You are going to look like a country that only does public relations [*un pays qui ne fait que de la communication*]. [...] We have to be careful not to invent too many new slogans, but to put in some substance. [...] Because otherwise, we have models that are devoid of meaning. The risk exists. And we manage this risk.
> (Interview in EU Delegation to Morocco, 6 June 2013)

Rabat's rhetorical zeal paradoxically coexisted with a somewhat widespread perception that the rhythm of Morocco–EU relations was slowing down. Supporting arguments were quite disparate depending on the point of view. According to the Moroccan foreign minister, Saad-Eddine El Othmani (2013: 297):

> There is no doubt that interesting developments have been unfolding in recent years in the context of the Barcelona Process/UfM process and the adoption of the Morocco–EU Joint Document on the Advanced Status. However the 'Arab' spring that swept through North Africa has slowed down if not delayed this encouraging momentum.

His deputy Amrani reckoned that there had simply been some 'deceleration in the intensity of discourse', as the EU devoted more public statements to revolutionary Tunisia, Egypt or Libya (interview in *Le Soir-Échos*, 4 January 2013). National observers pointed first to the economic crisis affecting the EU and, more particularly, its southern member states with closer ties with the Maghreb (interview with Hassan Bouqentar, 5 June 2013). Yet some of them also acknowledged the lack of experience of the 2012 Moroccan government in Euro-Mediterranean issues and certain difficulties in the implementation of the Advanced Status, concluding that, altogether, 'one can say that this is a transition stage' (interview with Abdelwahab Maalmi, 7 June 2013).

On the EU side, statements by different officials from the Delegation in Rabat (*Lakome*, 5 February 2013, 21 February 2013), the Commission (*Lakome*, 21 March 2013) and the European External Action Service (EEAS) (*Libération*, 19 September 2013) coincided in the regret expressed for the 'slowness' or insufficient ambition of the Moroccan reforms compared to their expectations, most notably in politically crucial areas like the development of new organic laws to implement the 2011 constitution and the reform of the judiciary. More significantly, these criticisms were reflected in the annual country progress reports on the implementation of the ENP in 2012 and 2013, which Moroccan diplomats considered to be biased and based solely on the views of the press and 'certain associations that are intentionally not involved in the reforms of sectors like justice for ideological reasons, lack of trust or bad faith'. According to their grievances, these kind of documents were drafted 'without listening to all the parties' and 'without any consultation' (*sans concertation*) with the Moroccan authorities, thus violating the ENP's 'spirit of co-ownership' (interview with Mounir Belayachi, 23 May 2014).

Other relative hurdles to Morocco's relations with the EU emerged following the entry into force of the Lisbon Treaty in December 2009, as a result of the increased powers granted to the European Parliament in the EU's external relations. The fact that parliamentary consent (yes/no vote) became mandatory for all international agreements covering fields to which the ordinary legislative procedure applies, such as agriculture or fisheries, created an unprecedented opportunity for pro-Sahrawi organisations to raise the profile of the Western Sahara conflict in Brussels and stand in the way of EU–Morocco economic cooperation. The most serious setback for Morocco was the European Parliament's rejection of the protocol of extension of the 2006 fisheries agreement in December 2011, on the legal grounds that it included the waters of the non-self-governing territory of Western Sahara whilst its direct benefits for the local Sahrawi population had not been demonstrated as required – along with other economic, environmental and developmental arguments (European Parliament, 2011; Smith, 2013). This no vote came as a surprise, provoking frustration and alarm in Morocco, the Commission and the EU member states involved (most notably Spain). Moroccan officials saw their country as a scapegoat for the EU's post-Lisbon inter-institutional tensions:

> In the EU there is conflict among the different institutions and sometimes Morocco bears the cost [*fait les frais*]. While we have good relations with

the Commission, sometimes we do not have good relations with other institutions. [...] We negotiated and completed the fisheries protocol with the European Commission, and then it was rejected by the European Parliament.... But tell us what you want!

(Interview with Mounir Belayachi, 23 May 2014)

In any case, this impediment was qualified by the fact that negotiations on a new protocol were launched immediately afterwards. The latter was signed after six rounds in July 2013 and this time approved by the Parliament in December, amid intense campaigning both for and against it (Reuters, 10 December 2013; MAEC, 10 December 2013). Faced with similar lobby mobilisation and legal uncertainty due to the non-exclusion of Western Sahara, plus fierce opposition on the part of southern European farmers, the EU–Morocco agricultural agreement signed in December 2010 also eventually received the Parliament's consent in February 2012 (Compés et al., 2013: 7–8). Morocco's growing attention to this EU institution's activities in connection with bilateral economic agreements, human rights and the Western Sahara issue[11] was confirmed by the creation of an informal EU–Morocco parliamentary friendship group in mid-2011,[12] in addition to the official Joint Parliamentary Committee set up as part of the Advanced Status' innovations a year earlier (interview with Menouar Alem in *Le Matin*, 1 December 2013; interview with Abderrahman Fyad, 23 May 2014).

All in all, Morocco emerged from the test posed by the Arab Spring as the same *model student* with a privileged relationship with the EU it had been for decades, regardless of the absence of structural pro-democratic political changes in the domestic sphere. It was put on an equal footing with post-revolutionary Tunisia in receiving new EU incentives in the form of money (SPRING programme), markets (negotiations of DCFTA) and mobility (Mobility Partnership), while negotiations concerning the 2013 Action Plan moved forward with *business as usual*, enabling a new bilateral legal framework to be envisaged whilst maintaining an illusion of permanent change.

However, in some respects the *model student* appeared to be increasingly disgruntled and moaning. Having been forced to compete with Tunisia for this advantaged position and struggling to adapt to the complexities of the post-Lisbon EU institutional setting, the Rabat authorities complained that they were being treated unfairly in ENP progress reports and they got 'less for more' from the EU in comparison to neighbouring countries:

The message is that more is given to countries like Tunisia, Libya or Egypt which have had a revolution; that amounts to saying: make the revolution and we will give you more, instead of engaging in peaceful and calm evolution. [...] Morocco does its utmost and does the best in the whole eastern and southern Neighbourhood, but in return, it is pointed out with the finger [*pointé du doigt*] and put on an equal footing with countries like Algeria. [...] For us this is unacceptable, unfair.

(Interview with Mounir Belayachi, 23 May 2014)

Maybe to reassure the Moroccans of the EU's continuing recognition of their 'pioneering spirit', the new EU Commissioner for ENP and Enlargement Negotiations Johannes Hahn chose this country for his first visit in the southern Mediterranean in December 2014 and claimed there that 'Morocco is an indispensable strategic neighbour of Europe' (European Commission, 11 December 2014).

In short, the main paybacks for Morocco's exemplary pro-European foreign policy came in 2008 and 2011. At multilateral level, Rabat's support for the French initiative of the UfM largely resulted from a cost-benefit calculation in which the primary stakes concerned bilateral relations with the EU and France. At bilateral level, the signing of the EU–Morocco Advanced Status represented the enshrinement of Rabat's persistent determination to single out a special relationship and had a strong *symbolic* significance in spite of the limited *practical* added value of this political document with regard to the ENP Action Plan. This Moroccan achievement was facilitated by conducive intergovernmental dynamics on the EU policymaking level – chiefly the Franco-Spanish alliance established from 2004 onwards – and by Rabat's 'rhetorical action' throughout the entire negotiation process. The benefits reaped by the Rabat authorities in terms of external legitimation or validation also helped them to overcome the test posed by the Arab Spring, after which Morocco continued to enjoy privileged EU treatment without engaging in structural domestic transformation.

Notes

1 Congrès International sur l'Union pour la Méditerranée: Quelles conditions pour quelles perspectives?, Fez, 4–6 June 2008. See www.cmiesi.ma (accessed on 31 October 2014). Subsequent meetings of this forum were held in 2009 and 2010.
2 Forum Euro-méditerranéen de Tanger: Penser la Méditerranée, Tangier, 4–7 June 2008.
3 Jordan, Tunisia and Egypt soon requested from the EU a new bilateral framework similar to that of Morocco. Negotiations concerning the *upgrading* of EU–Israel relations also progressed in the same direction, until they were frozen in December 2008.
4 The IEMed also commissioned several expert studies on the Advanced Status at different stages of the negotiations: Lannon *et al.* (2007), Jaidi and Martín (2010). See also Afkar/Idées, No. 14, Summer 2007.
5 The same arguments can be found in MAEC (2008: 9–10); MAEC (21 January 2008).
6 The Moroccan parliament did not play any relevant role regarding the Advanced Status either, since this was not an international legal agreement requiring ratification by it (interview with Abdelwahab Maalmi, 7 June 2013).
7 In the EU Delegation in Rabat, however, there was the perception that the Advanced Status was being pushed basically by the Moroccan foreign ministry, while other ministries such as Finance and Interior showed greater caution (Bremberg, 2012: 131).
8 The programme was extended to other southern Mediterranean countries in 2012.
9 Overall, the ENI's Single Support Framework for Morocco for 2014–2017 foresaw an indicative allocation of between €728 and €890 million to be distributed among equitable access to basic social services (30 per cent), support to democratic governance, the rule of law and mobility (25 per cent), jobs, sustainable and inclusive growth (25 per cent) and complementary support for capacity development and civil society (20 per cent) (ENI, 2014; MAP, 25 July 2014).

10 The Commission asked the Council for a mandate to launch discussions on visa facilitation in October 2013 (*EU Neighbourhood Info Centre*, 4 October 2013).
11 In December 2012, the Parliament expressed 'its concern at the deterioration of human rights in Western Sahara' and appointed a *rapporteur* to follow the issue (European Parliament, 2012).
12 http://groupedamitieuemaroc.wordpress.com (accessed on 31 January 2015).

6 The unbalanced postcolonial triangle with France and Spain

This chapter will complement the two previous ones by disentangling the contents of the *intergovernmental advantage*, which remains one of the key factors – and indeed a necessary condition – for Morocco's privileged treatment by the EU (Colombo and Voltolini, 2014: 53–55). It will consider Morocco's bilateral relations with France and Spain, i.e. the two European countries with which Morocco maintains a denser network of connections on all levels, which has largely been inherited from their shared colonial protectorate over the kingdom (1912–1956), and the two EU member states which have exercised the most influence over EU policymaking towards the Maghreb, in a clear example of 'geo-clientelism' (Behr and Tiilikainen, 2015: 27–28). Since independence, Morocco has formed an unbalanced postcolonial triangle with France and Spain in which Paris has played the role of the main ally and Madrid has occupied a secondary place, and Franco-Spanish relations have swung back and forth between competition and cooperation – as may be seen from the first decade of Mohammed VI's reign. In addition, albeit at different times, the two former colonial powers have Europeanised their foreign policies towards the Maghreb in a bottom-up manner, raising their priorities and concerns at the EU level (Barbé *et al.*, 2007: 36). As a result, their respective relations with Morocco have been played out simultaneously on two levels, namely the bilateral level and the European level, albeit with multiple intertwinement and interference.

The research questions examined here concern the manner in which Moroccan foreign policy has approached the relations with France and Spain in the 2000s, reacting to changing attitudes and policies from Paris and Madrid, and how the behaviour and discourses observed relate to the Morocco's different national role conceptions (Holsti, 1970). With regard to France, a country with which high socioeconomic interdependence and interpenetration of elites have ensured an extraordinary intensity and stability within the bilateral alliance, the only Moroccan role that can be identified appears to be a variation of that of the *model student of the EU*, yet one that is weighed down by a distinct postcolonial – or neocolonial – load. The latter is often conveyed by dressing up the deep-rooted power asymmetry with affective and family language, but lacks a distinct and explicit verbalisation in the Moroccan foreign policy discourse. Critical French observers have not hesitated to describe bilateral relations as 'a family affair' (Tuquoi, 2006), and Morocco as 'a sort of favourite son', 'noble, alluring and fragile' (Rapport Avicenne, 2007: 24), or France's 'pampered country' (Khadija Mohsen-Finan quoted in *El País*, 28 July 2007), all of which would somewhat suggest a role of *good son*. In any case, whilst recurring in the media and informal comments, these paternalistic terms would never be acceptable in the official discourse of either of the parties and belong to the category of *non-dit*. This means that *good son* cannot fully constitute a national role conception in the sense of Kalevi J. Holsti (based on the policymakers' own definitions) and that the extent to which Moroccan (*ego*) self-definition and the French (*alter*) role expectations actually match up remains difficult to determine.

As far as Spain is concerned, bilateral relations have always been far more complex as they have featured a permanent duality of cooperation and conflict, as well as a more limited historical power asymmetry (compared to that existing with France). Whilst the interdependence promoted in a top-down fashion by the authorities in Madrid and Rabat since the 1990s has increased substantially, especially in economic terms, it has never been sufficient to defuse bilateral chronic tensions ultimately linked to territorial issues, such as the unresolved decolonisation of Western Sahara and the Moroccan claim to the cities of Ceuta and Melilla. Therefore, Moroccan foreign policy towards Spain has persistently revealed role conflict (Cantir and Kaarbo, 2013: 467–468, 2012: 10–11; Aggestam, 2006: 23) between the role of *model student* – the most accurate variation of which within this geography-driven and less unequal relationship would be that of *good neighbour* – and the role of *champion of national territorial integrity*. The 'geopolitical constant' (El Houdaïgui, 2003b) has jeopardised the compatibility of the two roles, especially in times of crisis. The strain has been twofold since, in addition to the discrepancy between two different Moroccan (*ego*) national role conceptions, there has often been tension between a domestically defined (*ego*) national role conception (*territorial champion*) and an externally set (*alter*) role expectation (*good neighbour*). The latter has come not only from Spain but also, and more critically, from the EU as a whole – in the eyes of which Morocco has tirelessly pursued a 'swotting' (Schimmelfennig, 2000: 130) behaviour – and even the U.S.

An exceptional socioeconomic and elite interdependence with France

The unique nature of the bilateral relationship between Morocco and France on both sides is such that it might be described as one of symbiosis rather than mere interdependence. These relations occupy a disproportionate place in French foreign policy according to most *objective* parameters and compared to those maintained with other former colonies. Conversely, the links also extend beyond economic and political dependence, and involve a social identity component – in the sense of identifying with each other and even an identity of interests on the level of elites. The 'Paris-Rabat axis' has often been claimed to have a special status by leaders of both states. Otherwise, whilst relations with France are not usually mentioned as a top priority in Moroccan official foreign policy discourse, this is simply because their relevance is taken for granted and goes without saying.

Fifty years after the end of the protectorate, evidence of the persistence of the colonial umbilical cord can be found in almost all areas, from the economy to social and 'human' connections, and not least in politics. In economic terms, France has for decades been – and still remains – Morocco's main trading partner, largest foreign investor, first public creditor and first bilateral donor of development aid. In this deeply unbalanced relationship, while France is a vital partner for Morocco, Morocco only carries secondary weight for the French economy: it occupies around the twentieth position in the rankings of French export customers, suppliers and destination countries for foreign direct investment (FDI). On the trade front, between 1999 and 2012, France absorbed on average 28.6 per cent of Moroccan exports whilst providing 18.2 per cent of Moroccan imports.[1] Despite the decline in its relative position since 2000, France maintained its status as Morocco's first client (with a market share of 21.4 per cent in 2013) and only ceded its position as Morocco's first supplier to Spain in 2012 and 2013 (12.9 per cent market share in 2013) (Ministère des Affaires Étrangères-France, 2014). The balance of bilateral trade has almost always been negative for Morocco – except for the period 2002–2004 – although the rate of reabsorption of the structural deficit accelerated between 2009 and 2013 (Ministère Délégué chargé du Commerce Extérieur, 2014a: 4).

France also retained its leadership position in Morocco in the field of foreign direct investment, despite greater short-term fluctuations and the Gulf countries' arrival in the Maghreb from the around 2005 onwards. French investments over the period 2001–2011 amounted on average to almost €1,200 million per year and accounted overall for 46.5 per cent of total foreign direct investment

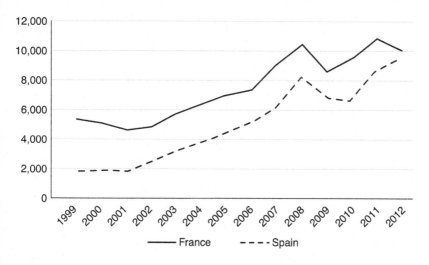

Figure 6.1 Total value of Moroccan trade with France and Spain, 1999–2012 (US$ million) (source: World Bank/World Integrated Trade Solution – WITS).

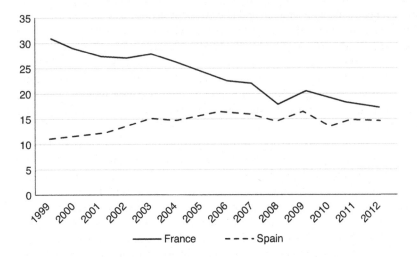

Figure 6.2 Share of France and Spain in Morocco's total trade, 1999–2012 (%) (source: World Bank/World Integrated Trade Solution – WITS).

Morocco, focusing on sectors such as banking, telecommunications, real estate and tourism. The number of subsidiaries of French companies established in Morocco was estimated to be 750 in 2009, including most of the largest national business groups as well as many small and medium-sized enterprises. In addition, a large number of Moroccan companies were run by French businessmen and/or capital (Ministère des Affaires Étrangères-France, 2014).

As a result, wide sections of the Moroccan economy were under the direct or indirect control of the former colonial power: from large infrastructure projects (Bouygues), water and electrical supply (Suez, Veolia) and the hotel industry (Accor) to telecommunications (Vivendi, Orange), the car industry (Renault-Nissan) and the financial sector (Caisse de Dépôts et de Consignations, BNP Paribas, Société Générale, Crédit Agricole). Among other things, this influx of investment was made possible by the wave of (full or partial) privatisations of state-owned companies and the substantial contracts awarded to French groups by public tender in the late 1990s and into the early reign of Mohammed VI (Beau and Graciet, 2007: 134–150). However, from 2003 onwards, tensions emerged between some major French groups and members of the King's entourage – including his influential personal secretary Mounir Majidi – who launched a campaign denouncing a supposed French 'plot' to take control of the Moroccan economy and the royal-owned ONA group. Whilst this short-lived Moroccan nationalist fever apparently responded to particular interests, it resulted in some notorious business disputes and complaints to the French Embassy and President in 2005–2006: 'With great naivety certainly, the French business world considered Morocco as a definitively conquered market' (Graciet and Laurent, 2012: 85).

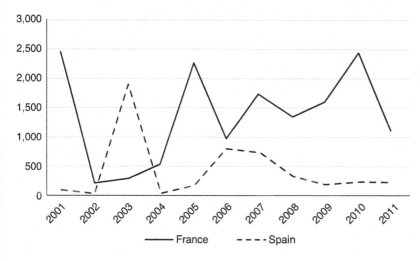

Figure 6.3 FDI flows in Morocco originating from France and Spain, 2001–2011 (US$ million) (source: UNCTAD FDI/TNC database, based on data from the Office des Changes, Morocco).

French prominence was also conspicuous in the third leg of bilateral economic relations, i.e. financial assistance and development cooperation. In the years after 2000, France continued to be Morocco's first bilateral donor; in 2009 alone it contributed more than a quarter of total bilateral public aid from the states included in the Development Assistance Committee (DAC) of the Organisation for Economic Cooperation and Development (OECD). Conversely, Morocco was the primary beneficiary of funds from the French Development Agency (AFD), with commitments of around €100 million per year in the first half of the decade, which subsequently increased steadily (460 million for 2007–2009, 600 million for 2010–2012) (*L'Économiste*, 11 December 2006; AFD, 8 April 2008; April 2014). A more special case was that of French cultural, educational and linguistic cooperation, which was separated from development cooperation from 1999 onwards. Based on the activities of 15 cultural centres (Institut Français, Alliance Française) and the extensive network of primary and secondary schools owned by the French state in Morocco (28), this historically rooted policy of influence continued to exert a decisive impact on the socialisation of the Moroccan elites, even though it faced increasing criticism due to its anachronistic and elitist nature, which even reached the French parliament.[2]

Economic ties were thus complemented by close 'human' interdependence at different levels. Chief amongst these were the connections between the elites of both countries, which were deeply intertwined as a result of linguistic affinity, education and socialisation. Traditionally, most members of the Moroccan ruling class were educated in local French schools before moving to French universities or its exclusive *grandes écoles* – which were preferred even ahead those in the U.S. and the United Kingdom. For decades, the children of the royal family themselves attended a Royal College that was generously funded by the French state (Cebolla, 2004; *Jeune Afrique*, 8 December 2010). All of this explains the strong attraction towards France, the French media and the *francophonie* of the Moroccan political, economic and social elites, who have made Paris their second capital and home base in Europe. The Moroccan state's foreign policy and lobbying in France have also been facilitated by the possibility to 'line up an army of young diplomats, engineers and senior officials perfectly integrated into the French culture' when it was necessary to defend any official position or argument (Amar, 2009: 182).

In parallel, for years the Moroccan regime cultivated a lavish policy of hospitality towards French politicians from the major parties, who were frequently invited on luxury holidays, thereby blurring the lines between private leisure and diplomacy (*Le Journal Hebdomadaire*, 11–17 October 2003; *Le Monde*, 9 February 2011). A privileged transnational network was also maintained by the thousands of French citizens who settled in the city of Marrakesh, including influential businessmen, intellectuals and politicians (Tuquoi and Amar, 2012). Conversely, a rather unstructured but pervasive 'Moroccan lobby' operated in France based on certain civil society organisations dating back to the 1990s (Cercle d'Amitié Franco-Marocaine, Alliance France-Maroc), parliamentary friendship groups including politicians of all leanings and high-society personalities, businessmen, intellectuals, academics, journalists and artists who portrayed themselves as 'friends of Morocco' (Tuquoi, 2006: 51, 123–139, 240–243; Amar, 2009: 314–317; Brouksy, 2014: 206–213).

On the level of popular classes, the human foundation for Moroccan–French interdependence consisted in the large community of Moroccan migrants settled in France, which is first host country of Moroccans living abroad, having between 1.1 and 1.3 million inhabitants of Moroccan origin – many of whom however belong to the second generation and/or have dual citizenship (Fondation Hassan II, 2003: 209–267). Rabat always paid great political attention and tried to preserve ties with this diaspora, which was seen as a useful link to the host country as well as a source of substantial flows of capital in the form of remittances. These amounted to €1,500 million in 2013 (38.3 per cent of the total received by Morocco) (Ministère des Affaires Étrangères-France, 2014).

From paternalism to a pragmatic and economistic turn

All of these varied ingredients have rendered unique the relationship between Morocco and France, representing almost a guarantee of the intensity and stability of bilateral ties. This has also been reflected in political and diplomatic practices such as the continuous exchange of official visits. The resulting constant features of French behaviour have been threefold: support for the status quo and low interest in democracy promotion in Morocco (Daguzan, 2002); defence of Morocco's interests and aspirations in the context of the EU; and backing for its positions on the Western Sahara conflict – and its role as *territorial champion* – in the international arena. Since Rabat's performance has always been more reactive, the most salient criterion when breaking down chronologically the period between 1999 and 2014 is that of alternation in the French presidency: 'Everything goes back to the two palaces' (*Orient XXI*, 22 January 2015). Indeed, the markedly personalistic, almost familial bond between heads of state that characterised the presidency of Jacques Chirac (1995–2007) contrasted with the pragmatic and economistic approach that Nicolas Sarkozy (2007–2012) tried to impose on Moroccan–French relations and, not least, the greater French restraint and judicial turmoil of François Hollande's first years in office (2012 onwards).

President Chirac's policy towards Morocco has often been presented as an example of the impact of the 'human factor' in international relations. Even though the exceptional status of the Moroccan–French relationship and the direct connection between the Alawite throne and the French presidency date back a long time, it was this neo-Gaullist conservative leader who took them to their height. Although some degree of idealism might have underpinned this endeavour, its most obvious source was Chirac's personal friendship and the favours owed over decades to King Hassan II, who had unfailingly supported his political career from the late 1970s, initiated him into the political 'complexities' of the Arab and Muslim world and put him in contact with the Gulf royal families. Feeling indebted when he came to power, Chirac became a stubborn advocate of the interests of the Moroccan monarchy in all areas. France's relations with this favourite country came under immediate presidential control, with the foreign ministry often being sidelined.

The French President's personal loyalty to Hassan II turned virtually into paternalism upon Mohammed VI's accession to the throne in 1999. Shortly before, the previous King, near to death, had asked him to take care of his country, his family and the heir. 'Your Majesty, I owe much to your father and, if you so wish, I will do everything possible to return you all that he has given to me', Chirac promised to Mohammed VI at the funeral. In the following months, he redoubled public efforts to defend the aptitude of the new and inexperienced Moroccan head of state, showing an unparalleled proximity to the royal family (Tuquoi, 2006: 61–73, 143–144, 29–46; interview with Mohammed VI in *Le Figaro*, 4 September 2001). However, King Mohammed VI, who belonged to another generation and was relatively less francophile than his father,[3] was to establish a much more impersonal and pragmatic relationship with Chirac, trying to 'get rid of the invasive paternalism of the French President' (Beau and Graciet, 2007: 175).

In any case, the change in tone did not lessen the firmness of the French-Moroccan alliance or prevent France from acting as an advocate for the Moroccan interests within the EU institutions. This role was played on various levels: from the 'discreet but effective lobbying in favour of Morocco' in the European Parliament (Graciet and Laurent, 2012: 184) to the controversial performance of the French ambassador Michel de Bonnecorse at some meetings of EU member states' representatives in Rabat (Tuquoi, 2006: 107–108). At the same time, the apparent affinity – almost identity – of interests between Paris and Rabat could not fail to provoke suspicion in other EU countries that perceived themselves as potential victims, including specifically Spain. Indeed, the interference of Chirac's France in Moroccan–Spanish relations was noticeable during the bilateral crisis which affected the latter between 2001 and 2003, when competition prevailed between the two European vertices of this triangle. The first episode in which this manifested itself was the failure of negotiations on the renewal of the EU–Morocco fisheries agreement conducted in 2000–2001, in which the EU member state that was most affected and harmed was Spain. According to the conservative Spanish President of the Government José María Aznar, Chirac not only avoided contributing to the success of the conversations, but straightforwardly 'advised Morocco not to conclude any fishing agreement' (Cembrero, 2006: 50).

Second, the occupation of the islet of Perejil by Moroccan gendarmes in July 2002 further revealed France's scant solidarity with an EU partner like Spain when relations with its southern neighbour were at stake. Chirac publicly provided unfailing backing to Rabat and mobilised his diplomacy to act along the same lines. After Aznar personally sought support from the 15 heads of state and government of the EU plus the U.S., the French President was the only one to dissociate himself from the unanimous response of solidarity. However, most important was the impact of French resistance on EU common positions including the Common Foreign and Security Policy (CFSP). While in a first reaction to the incident the Commission spokesperson condemned it as a 'violation of Spanish territory' and the Danish presidency called upon Morocco to withdraw 'immediately' (*The Guardian*, 13 July 2002, 15 July 2002), a few days later the same EU institutions were trying to reduce the whole episode to a bilateral dispute between Madrid and Rabat (European Commission, 16 July 2002, 17 July 2002). The shift was mainly due to pressure from France (Cembrero, 2006: 50–58; Tuquoi, 2006: 79–91; Planet and Hernando de Larramendi, 2006: 425–426). As a source in the French Ministry of Foreign Affairs admitted later, Chirac '[prioritised] the alliance with Rabat and the defence of Mohammed VI's throne over European solidarity' (Tuquoi, 2006: 85).

Moreover, it came to light years later that, within the same turbulent context, the French President sent the Moroccan King recommendations to 'oppose the Spanish penetration in Morocco' in the economic field, according to a confidential note issued in late 2002 by the French Directorate-General for External Security (DGSE) (*El País*, 30 November 2006). The Morocco–France–Spain triangle did not return to a cooperative dynamic until Socialist José Luis Rodríguez Zapatero came to power in Madrid in April 2004 and adopted a more accommodating policy towards Rabat. The regained Franco-Spanish harmony was displayed in the tripartite meeting of deputy foreign ministers held in Rabat in December 2005, which represented the starting point for the gestation of the EU–Morocco Advanced Status.

More significantly for role as territorial champion, the mutual understanding between Morocco and Chirac's France was also apparent on the Western Sahara issue. The support of French diplomacy became more valuable than ever under

Mohammed VI's reign, when Morocco tacitly abandoned the path of the self-determination referendum to resolve the conflict and a new exploratory stage started in which the idea of a *third way* (autonomy under Moroccan sovereignty) made progress on the domestic and international scene. Following the launch of the Baker Plan I (2001), which was warmly welcomed by Rabat, France intervened within the Group of Friends of the Western Sahara at the United Nations (UN) in an attempt to overcome Russian and Spanish resistance – due to the previous rejection by the Polisario Front and Algeria – and to help to ensure that the proposal made it to the Security Council. Accounts from the Spanish government of the time indicate that it was his conviction that French lobbying would be successful that prompted Mohammed VI to state with unfounded optimism that he had 'settled the Sahara issue' (interview with Mohammed VI in *Le Figaro*, 4 September 2001). In actual fact, however, this plan had stalled and never received the seal of approval of the Security Council.

Two years later, Paris' backing proved to be vital once again during the difficult period for Rabat following the rejection of the Baker Plan II (2003), which was 'supported' unanimously by the Security Council in late July. First, France voted in favour of Resolution 1495 in order to avoid becoming isolated within this body, but only after securing watered-down terms, which reduced the status of this decision to a non-binding political endorsement. Second, over the following months, when Morocco had to face considerable international pressure to revise or relax its position, Chirac came out in defence of his ally by adamantly ruling out any coercive solution. 'Needless to say [*il va de soi*] no formula can be imposed and any solution must count on the agreement of the parties', said the President during the state visit to Morocco in October that year (*Le Journal Hebdomadaire*, 11–17 October 2003). He also advocated 'a realistic and lasting political solution that *respects the sovereignty of Morocco* and the aspirations of the people' (speech by Jacques Chirac, Fes, 9 October 2003, emphasis added), and assured Moroccan parliamentarians that France would vote again in favour of their country in the Security Council (Cembrero, 2006: 51–52, 64; Tuquoi, 2006: 97–100). Once this critical period had passed, France was to be one of the allied countries that most encouraged the Moroccan authorities to draft a 'serious and credible' autonomy proposal for Western Sahara (along with the U.S. and Spain).

All in all, Moroccan–French relations developed with remarkable calmness throughout Chirac's years in power. 'The political differences between the two countries are nonexistent', stressed a French presidential spokesperson (*Le Journal Hebdomadaire*, 11–17 October 2003).[4] The only public bilateral dispute in the early 2000s came with the start of negotiations on the Free Trade Agreement between Morocco and the U.S., which was to be signed in 2004. French displeasure was expressed by the deputy minister of Foreign Trade, François Loos, who said in Rabat that an agreement of this kind with Washington 'would be incompatible with the strengthening of economic relations between Morocco and the EU' (*Le Journal Hebdomadaire*, 18–24 January 2003).

Other tensions emerged during the final part of Chirac's presidency. These were primarily economic in the first place, due to the campaign (mentioned above) waged by members of the King's entourage against French companies investing in Morocco, which turned into a diplomatic issue in 2005–2006. Second, the legal case concerning the kidnapping and murder of the Moroccan opposition leader Mehdi Ben Barka in Paris in 1965, which had never been resolved, returned to the forefront. In 2005, the French judge in charge of the investigation, Patrick Ramaël, travelled to Morocco and issued a number of international letters rogatory seeking to question some of the few Moroccan officials linked to the case who were still alive, although received scant cooperation from the Rabat authorities.

The next chapter in Moroccan–French relations started with the French presidential elections of April–May 2007, which were followed in Morocco almost as a domestic event and preceded by speculation of an imminent reversal of France's policy towards the Maghreb and the Arab world. The debate was partly fuelled by criticisms of French diplomats and experts in the region who asked to 'proceed without delay to a reassessment' of this policy in the so-called 'Rapport Avicenne' (2007: 3–4). However, there were strong indications from conservative candidate Sarkozy which ruled out a radical shift in the approach to relations with Morocco. His private and professional journeys to this country and his dealings with its authorities dated back many years. In his years at the head of the Ministry of the Interior (2002–2004, 2005–2007), he had maintained close relations with top security officials from the Rabat regime and praised Morocco's 'strong democracy' on several occasions, as well as the 'exemplary nature' of the link between Paris and Rabat (Tuquoi, 2006: 248; Beau and Graciet, 2007: 222–223; Amar, 2009: 310–314). He was only slightly more cautious with regard to the Western Sahara conflict, on which he avoided taking a stance during the electoral campaign (*Jeune Afrique*, 7 October 2007).

On the very night of Sarkozy's election, Mohammed VI sent him a message of congratulations in which he explicitly supported the idea of a 'Mediterranean Union', which had been launched by the French candidate during the campaign and was later to result in the UfM. Yet, despite being the first North African leader to participate in this budding project (*Le Journal Hebdomadaire*, 7–13 July 2007; *Jeune Afrique*, 13–19 May 2007), the King's gesture was not rewarded with the privileged treatment Rabat was accustomed to. The new President decided that his first contact with the Maghreb would be a short and calculated trip to Algeria, Tunisia and Morocco in July. He was scheduled to stop for just a few hours in the Moroccan border town of Oujda (where he would meet Mohammed VI), after visiting the capitals of the two neighbouring countries. In keeping with the attempt at balance that guided the organisation of this tour, the aim was to convey the message of a 'quiet break' with Chirac's vision and practices in French–Maghrebi relations, including the precedence granted to Morocco (*El País*, 28 July 2007). The need to ensure the stability of energy supplies also made it advisable to seek a rapprochement with Algiers (*L'Économiste*, 10 July 2007, 11 July 2007).

What Paris did not expect was that the Moroccan authorities would cancel the appointment in Oujda at the last minute. Although the decision was officially taken for 'agenda reasons', it was clear that the Moroccan authorities had not appreciated the fact that they were put on an equal footing with their Maghrebi counterparts. Morocco wanted to have its own state visit, which should be more exclusive and relaxed, as was appropriate given the proclaimed uniqueness and 'excellence' of its bilateral relations with France. The initial French wish to 'handle the sensibilities of Moroccans and Algerians' was thwarted once again (*Le Journal Hebdomadaire*, 7–13 July 2007; *L'Économiste*, 9 July 2007).

Sarkozy's state visit to Morocco was eventually scheduled for three months later, after Moroccan legislative elections had been held (September 2007) and the new parliament and government had been formed in Rabat. Its purpose was predominantly economic. The French President was accompanied by several ministers (Foreign Affairs, Economy, Finance and Industry, Justice, Ecology) and a delegation of 70 business owners. In his speech to the Moroccan parliament, he highlighted the 'democratic vigour' and 'pluralism' of Moroccan politics and the 'total transparency' of the previous elections. 'Sarkozy's visit closes the electoral chapter, giving it the international sanction that our leaders so much expected', noted the Moroccan independent press (*Le Journal Hebdomadaire*, 27 October–2 November 2007). Reportedly, some members of the French government had even received the order not mention human rights issues (Amar, 2009: 319). On the issue of Western Sahara, the French President dispelled earlier doubts by explicitly siding with Rabat. He described the Moroccan Autonomy Plan that had been presented in the spring of 2007 as 'serious and credible', 'a new propositional element after years of deadlock' that could serve as 'basis for negotiation in the search for a reasonable settlement' (*El País*, 23 October 2007; *Le Journal Hebdomadaire*, 27 October–2 November 2007; U.S. Embassy in Rabat, cable 07RABAT1657, 29 October 2007).

The only politically disturbing element of this cordial state visit was the calculated media resurgence of the Ben Barka case. Right at this moment, a scoop revealed that Judge Ramaël had issued an international arrest warrant against General Housni Benslimane, a close collaborator of Mohammed VI. The newly sworn-in Moroccan minister of Foreign Affairs, Taieb Fassi Fihri, accused the judge himself of being responsible for the leak. The action taken by the French courts actions against a man standing at the pinnacle of the Moroccan regime and the timing of the announcement brought both countries to the brink of a diplomatic incident. The entourages of the two heads of state had to do their utmost behind the scenes to prevent this issue capturing the media's interest. As in previous and subsequent *judicial crises* between Morocco and France, Sarkozy could do nothing but publicly state that 'the French justice is independent' (Amar, 2009: 297–306; *L'Économiste*, 22 October 2007).

In any case, as noted above, the agenda of this trip was essentially economic, and encouragement of French investment in Morocco was the main goal. Sarkozy succeeded in signing some 15 civil and commercial contracts, with a total value of €3,000 million (*L'Économiste*, 24 October 2007, 24 October 2007). In fact however, the starting point had been a resounding failure, that is, the aborted sale of 18 Rafale fighter jets from the French company Dassault to the Moroccan army for some €2,300 million. Negotiations had started in 2006, amid a sudden arms race between Rabat and Algiers, and had been subject to numerous political vicissitudes. In the end, Rabat decided to purchase aircraft from the American Lockheed Martin, which had made a counteroffer of 24 brand new F-16 for $2,000 million (€1,500 million). Besides the lower price, the latter bid had the advantage of possible joint funding by a Saudi loan and *development assistance* from the Millennium Challenge Account (MCA). In short, Morocco was able to take advantage of the intense competition unleashed between the companies and lobbies of its two major international partners. The Lockheed Martin order was announced during Sarkozy's visit (*Jeune Afrique*, 7 October 2007; Amar, 2009: 322–324), which made it impossible for its political dimension to pass unnoticed (*L'Économiste*, 1 October 2007).

Thus, in order to make up for this snub, the Rabat authorities granted major French companies – without public tender – most construction contracts for the first section of the first high-speed rail line in the country between Tangier and Casablanca, which was valued in total at about €2,000 million. This ambitious project was highly controversial from the outset due to its exorbitant cost, its financing difficulties and its disconnect from Morocco's most pressing development needs. Critical voices even described it as 'economic extortion' and an 'aberration' (*Larbi.org*, 27 September 2011; *Demain Online*, 7 October 2011; Amar, 2009: 325–326; Brouksy, 2014: 217–221).

Thereafter, during the five years of Sarkozy's presidency, in spite of talk of a break with the past, relations between Morocco and France continued to be largely characterised by the patronising and protective tone that had been familiar for decades, which affected the relations with the EU, the Western Sahara conflict and Morocco's own domestic politics. The first political priority, in 2007–2008, was the culmination of negotiations for the EU–Morocco Advanced Status. Whilst the process had started with the tripartite Moroccan–French–Spanish meeting of deputy foreign ministers that was held in Rabat in December 2005, the French presidency of the EU was vital for the acceleration and completion of talks in the second half of 2008. Second, on the Sahara issue, France unfailingly helped to block attempts to extend the mandate of the UN Mission for the Referendum in Western Sahara (MINURSO) to human rights monitoring since 2009 at the UN Security Council (Bouqentar, 2010: 336).[5]

Third, French protection was to be requested again, and with greater urgency, in early 2011 with the outbreak of the Arab Spring uprisings. Two days after the first demonstrations by the 20 February Movement in Morocco, Mohammed VI travelled personally to Paris to meet President Sarkozy, who assured him of his support for the 'stability' of the Moroccan monarchy while urging him to 'at least announce' some political reforms (Brouksy, 2014: 15, 71). French diplomats in Rabat also overtly tried to influence and moderate the young Moroccan protesters, in what witnesses such as the political scientist Youssef Belal consider 'one of those moments of renewal of the neocolonial pact that binds the monarchy and the French' (Brouksy, 2014: 213–215). Altogether, Sarkozy's term in office started with an attempt at normalisation of the rather abnormal – and indeed excessive – bilateral relations between France and Morocco, upon which the President tried to impress a more pragmatic and economistic focus: 'After Chirac's frank friendship, now it is the turn of Sarkozy's realpolitik' (*Le Journal Hebdomadaire*, 27 October–2 November 2007). But afterwards, contrary to intentions, inertia prevailed and the promised change or *dechiraquisation* was nothing but relative, at most amounting to a change of style within continuity.

Like that of Sarkozy, the presidency of Socialist Hollande also began with competition between Morocco and Algeria for his first visit to the Maghreb. Hollande's official trip to Algiers in December 2012 had to be coupled with an almost simultaneous visit by Prime Minister Jean-Marc Ayrault to Rabat in order to avoid offending Morocco's sensibilities (*Jeune Afrique*, 12 December 2012, 18 December 2012). The presidential state visit to the latter country only occurred in April 2013. Less than one year later, a new judicial issue related to human rights violations in Morocco was to develop into the most serious bilateral crisis between this country and France since the early 1990s.

In February 2014, a French NGO filed two lawsuits for 'complicity in torture' of four French citizens (of Moroccan/Sahrawi origin) against Abdellatif Hammouchi, the head of the Moroccan domestic intelligence agency Directorate-General for Territorial Surveillance (DGST), which coincided with a trip by this senior security official to Paris. French police officers went to the very residence of the Moroccan ambassador in this city to serve the court summons on Hammouchi, without previously alerting Moroccan diplomats. The Moroccan foreign ministry immediately summoned the French ambassador to 'vigorously' protest a 'rare and unprecedented incident' (MAEC, 22 February 2014) and the French ministry then promised to 'shed all the light' on 'this unfortunate incident' (*Yabiladi*, 23 February 2014) – prompting criticism of interference in judicial affairs (*Demain Online*, 23 February 2014). Moreover, President Hollande himself phoned Mohammed VI to ensure him of the 'constant friendship between France and Morocco' (*Alif Post*, 23 February 2014, 24 February 2014; *Le Monde*, 25 February 2014). However, the diplomatic escalation continued and the Moroccan authorities suspended implementation of all judicial cooperation agreements with France (AFP, 27 February 2014). In addition, a demonstration was organised in front of the French embassy in Rabat and several political parties raised their nationalist rhetoric (MAP, 1 March 2014). The Moroccan Ministry of the Interior brought its own counter lawsuit for defamation in Paris against the three individual authors of the lawsuit against Hammouchi (*Yabiladi*, 26 March 2014; *Alif Post*, 26 March 2014).

Although Mohammed VI travelled to Paris when Morocco needed France's support during the renewal of the MINURSO's mandate at the UN (*Alif Post*, 22 April 2014), the overcoming of the bilateral crisis continued to be impeded by new incidents which were perceived in Rabat as 'unacceptable acts' or 'humiliations', such as the search to which the Moroccan foreign minister Salaheddine Mezouar was subjected at a Paris airport (*Yabiladi*, 28 March 2014; *Alif Post*, 28 March 2014) and the so-called 'moral aggression' suffered by General

Abdelaziz Bennani while hospitalised also in the French capital (an opponent of the regime, the former captain Mustapha Adib, left a virulent accusatory letter against him in his hospital room) (MAP, 19 June 2014; Brouksy, 2014: 28).

By and large, human rights-based *judicial crises* like this – a paradoxical consequence of tight social and 'human' interdependence – proved to be virtually the only indirect way in which the extraordinary stability of the French-Moroccan alliance could be disrupted. Their most relevant long-term consequence was the potential undermining of Morocco's (implicit) postcolonial role as *good son* of France. The nationalist rhetorical outburst that accompanied this episode, which was very unusual in relation to France, even involved a temporary reconsideration of longstanding national role conceptions and patterns of alliance and hostility: 'Paradoxically, this France that Rabat's official media and diplomacy were describing until last February as the strategic ally has suddenly turned into a formidable enemy of the Kingdom!' (*Alif Post*, 23 June 2014). 'Our feeling is that our French partner does not have real political will to obstruct anti-Moroccan manipulations emanating from sectors that are well-known for their hostility against us.' 'The time of tutelage is over', warned minister Mezouar resorting to anticolonial rhetoric (*Jeune Afrique*, 11–17 January 2015).[6] In the end, Mohammed VI and Hollande met and officially made peace in February 2015, after which bilateral judicial cooperation was restored.

The duality of increased cooperation and territorial obstacles with Spain

Morocco's relations with Spain, in comparison, have always been more complex as they have combined elements of both cooperation and conflict and involved, on the part of Morocco, role conflict between the roles of *good neighbour* and *champion of national territorial integrity*. The reason for this twofold soul is that the bilateral interdependence which the authorities of both countries have tried to instil in a top-down fashion since the 1990s has had to coexist with recurring tensions of – direct or indirect – territorial origin. These frictions date back a long way, as Spain is the only European country to have maintained a territorial presence in North Africa after Algerian independence (1962). At the turn of the millennium they persisted on two main points, i.e. the Moroccan claim to the cities of Ceuta and Melilla – along with the *peñones* (rocks) of Alhucemas and Vélez de la Gomera and the Chafarinas Islands – and the unresolved decolonisation of Western Sahara.

On the one hand, from the official perspective of Madrid, sovereignty over the two Spanish autonomous cities in North Africa had never been an issue for bilateral relations with Rabat. However, the taboo concerning the existence of a dispute did not prevent this *non-issue* par excellence from resurfacing periodically in the Moroccan debate and interfering with bilateral relations with varying intensity, depending upon tactical considerations (Planet, 1998). On the other hand, as regards the Western Sahara issue, the Spanish state officially claimed that all of its obligations as a colonial power had ended with the Madrid Accords

(1975), whereby it transferred the administration of this territory – whilst not its sovereignty – to Morocco and Mauritania. In any case, the stance of 'active neutrality' invariably proclaimed by governments in Madrid, which translated into support for the UN's efforts at conflict resolution from the 1990s, could hardly disguise the constant and ambiguous balancing act which Spain was fated to perform in this area. Expectations and pressure from both parties to the conflict were heightened by the idea of Spanish historical responsibility for the fate of the Sahrawi people and the influence of Madrid's positions on this issue within part of the international community – including on occasion the U.S. For Morocco, the particular stance adopted in relation to Western Sahara has always been the touchstone for determining the vitality of any relationship with any international actor, which contrasts with Spain's desire to separate this conflict from other bilateral issues (Iglesias, 2010: 302).

The antidote to these territorial obstacles within Moroccan–Spanish relations devised in the 1990s, following democratic Spain's international normalisation and accession to the European Economic Community (EEC), was to attempt to move the bilateral game from the classical realist/geopolitical chessboard – balance of power – to a logic of complex interdependence. This was the novel approach which Spanish diplomatic discourse of the time dubbed as *colchón de intereses* (buffer of interests), that is the creation of a dense network of shared interests on the basis of institutionalised political dialogue and cooperation in various fields, in order to cushion against cyclical tensions associated with long-standing disputes between the two neighbouring countries. In practice, the new strategy involved an expansion of the bilateral agenda to include issues and actors that had been hitherto absent or neglected, at a time when the boundaries between high and low politics were increasingly blurred. In addition to governmental action, it was envisaged that interaction between a wide range of actors and the proliferation of all kinds of economic, technological, communicational and human transnational flows would encourage the cooperative interaction and reduce the likelihood of any conflict spilling over into the military arena. All these ideas distinctly resonated with liberal interdependence theory in International Relations (Gillespie, 2006: 120–121; Keohane and Nye, 1977).

Furthermore, the change of approach was coupled and reinforced by a parallel process of Europeanisation of Spanish–Moroccan relations, whereby Spain *uploaded* to Brussels in a bottom-up fashion not only its overall vision of and preferences relating to Euro-Mediterranean relations (Gillespie, 2000: 134), but also some quite thorny aspects of its own bilateral economic relations with Morocco, such as agriculture and fisheries (Vaquer, 2003). In addition to expanding the thematic agenda and the range of actors involved (Hernando de Larramendi and Mañé, 2009), this new European and multi-level dimension also contributed to 'broadening the repertoire of practices' in Moroccan–Spanish relations, creating a 'larger cooperative framework which [drew] on practices that constitute security communities, namely consultation, reciprocity and self-restraint', and even bringing about possible 'socialisation effects' of both counties' diplomats and officials (Bremberg, 2012: 139).

In any case, from this time onwards, the new interdependence approach did not result in the sudden disappearance of the *structural* bilateral disputes of territorial origin, but simply in their coexistence with increasingly diversified practices of cooperation. That is to say, relations between Morocco and Spain were to simultaneously follow two divergent logics. This duality involves a coexistence or overlapping of international orders that are antagonistic in theory, such as balance of power and security communities (Bremberg, 2012: 49–54): 'While analytically and normatively distinct, radically different orders, and in particular, the security systems of governance on which they are based (such as balance of power and security community), often coexist or overlap in political discourse and practice' (Adler and Greve, 2009: 60).

Economic indicators stand out as proof of the actual increase in interdependence between Morocco and Spain since the 1990s. In this respect, the starting position of Spain was much less advantageous than that of France. Spain's limited economic colonisation of the northern part of the protectorate, which was Morocco's most disadvantaged region, had hardly left any strong ties of this kind between the two neighbours. Yet notwithstanding this, their economic relations visibly intensified since the late 1980s in all respects and, in the middle of the next decade, Spain became Morocco's second largest trading partner, investor and source of tourists. The total volume of bilateral trade continued to grow steadily in the 2000s. Between 1999 and 2012 it multiplied almost by five, following an upward trend that was only broken in 2009 and 2010. Over the same period, on average, Spain absorbed 17.2 per cent of Moroccan exports and provided 11.3 per cent of Moroccan imports.[7] It remained as Morocco's second client and surprisingly overtook France, becoming its primary supplier in 2012 and 2013 (Oficina Económica y Comercial, 2014: 37) – conversely, Morocco was only Spain's nineteenth supplier and tenth client. Besides the uneven importance of these exchanges for each of the two countries, the trade balance was always negative for Morocco and, in contrast to the trend with France, Morocco's deficit increased further over the 2009–2013 period (Ministère Délégué chargé du Commerce Extérieur, 2014b: 4).[8]

Spanish foreign direct investment in Morocco was somewhat more variable. It reached outstanding peaks in years of major privatisations, such as the one that resulted in the acquisition of 80 per cent of the capital of the state tobacco company Régie des Tabacs by the French-Spanish firm Altadis in 2003. In any case, the overall trend was upwards. In 2004–2012 Spain was Morocco's third largest investor in terms of accumulated investment stock, after France and the United Arab Emirates, and the second largest in terms of number of companies, being present in sectors such as industry, real estate, banking, commerce, tourism, energy and mining (Oficina Económica y Comercial, 2014: 42). Spain also played a not insignificant role during these years in the area of development cooperation with Morocco. The subsequent Spanish cooperation plans (2001–2004, 2005–2008, 2009–2012) invariably included the southern neighbour within the group of priority states receiving a larger volume of resources. Besides being the first recipient of Spanish aid in the Maghreb, Morocco benefited from a more than three-fold increase in gross bilateral official development assistance between 2005 (€43.2 million) and 2009 (€158 million),[9] before the financial crisis hit the Spanish public budget.

Spain's engagement in cultural and educational cooperation was also prominent as a result of the legacy of the protectorate and the unique cultural policy towards the Arab world pursued by Francisco Franco's dictatorship. Morocco hosted almost half of the primary and secondary schools run by the Spanish state abroad (ten) as well as a high number of Instituto Cervantes centres (six). Also significant in terms of 'human' interdependence was the fast expansion since the 1990s of the community of Moroccan migrants settled in Spain, which originated in a much more recent flow than that of France but reached 700,000–800,000 people in 2008 – the most important group of foreigners in terms of citizenship living in this country (López Sala, 2012: 2; Fondation Hassan II, 2003: 141–207). On a legal level, the growing number of bilateral treaties and agreements signed by Morocco and Spain on the basis of the 1991 Treaty of Friendship, Good Neighbourliness and Cooperation reflected the gradual diversification of areas of cooperation and the introduction of new issues onto the agenda (Del Valle and El Houdaïgui, 2006: 163–202).[10]

In short, several indicators demonstrate that the increase in Moroccan–Spanish interdependence in various areas over the past two decades has been tangible and significant, and not simply a matter of good intentions. This evidence supports the claims repeatedly asserted within the discourse of the Spanish foreign ministry: 'Spain and Morocco have a relationship of global strategic partnership that is characterised by its maturity and dense content' (Miguel Ángel Moratinos in *Ecoestrecho.com*, February 2010). Yet it is equally true that this has not had all of the preventive or soothing effects promised by the *colchón de intereses* approach, since bilateral crises associated with territorial issues have continued to reappear at regular intervals. The spiral of misunderstandings during the 2001–2003 period and the Moroccan occupation of the islet of Perejil in July 2002 made this clear: interdependence, which had been advocated as a beneficial alternative to the realist game of balance of power in which relations between these two countries were historically embedded, has proven not to be a panacea either; it is subject to its own limitations and insufficiencies. For Richard Gillespie, the mistake lay in having built this particular interdependence, in practice, 'upon too narrow an agenda, primarily economic, which failed to address "difficult" aspects of the relationship, such as regime differences and historically based cultural tensions' (2006: 110). For instance, the elite socialisation factor that could almost be taken for granted in Morocco's relations with France remained limited for Spain.

The acknowledgement of the limits of both realism and the interdependence approach when trying to explain Moroccan–Spanish relations leads into a consideration of the role played by the factors that are privileged by constructivism, i.e. identity-based and socially constructed views, *norms* and discourses prevailing on both sides of the Strait of Gibraltar. Arguably, the two previous theoretical approaches are essentially rationalistic, while the complex neighbourhood relations at hand are characterised, according to many observers, by a varying dose of 'irrationality' (interview with Mohamed Larbi Messari, 24 October 2007):[11] 'Spain is one of the limits of realism within Moroccan foreign policy' (confidential interview). The title of the compilation of articles by Bernabé López García (2007), *Morocco and Spain: A History against All Logic*, also speaks volumes. A primarily economic buffer of interests that was still underdeveloped in terms of contacts between civil societies, mutual knowledge and perceptions of public opinion (Affaya and Guerraoui, 2005) could hardly be fully effective in the face of these intangible yet powerful obstacles. In addition, there were also differences between the political regimes in the two countries. As explained by Laura Feliu:

> The absence of democracy in Morocco introduces an element of unpredictability in bilateral relations, which cannot be overcome by simply reinforcing the latter. The complications witnessed due to bilateral disputes are partly related to this lack (pressure and fait accompli policy on the Moroccan side, lack of control and opacity of this foreign policy, manipulation of public opinion, corruption at borders, accumulation of wealth by certain sectors [...]).
>
> (Feliu, 2004b: 2)

From the 2001–2003 conflict spiral to the repairing of bilateral relations

Against this backdrop, the evolution of Moroccan foreign policy towards Spain and the combination of roles of *good neighbour* and *champion of national territorial integrity* during the period 1999–2014 were exogenously determined by the alternation in power in Madrid between the governments of the Conservative José María Aznar (1996–2004), the Socialist José Luis Rodríguez Zapatero (2004–2011) and the Conservative Mariano Rajoy (2011 onwards). To be sure, this chronological breakdown is not meant to over-emphasise the partisan and personal dimension to Spanish foreign policy, as the political and media discourse of both sides did for years to the bounds of caricature, ignoring significant elements of continuity and other nuances.[12] The main cross-party constant feature of Spanish behaviour was, similarly to France, the stability-centred approach and low profile given to democracy promotion in Morocco (López García and Hernando de Larramendi, 2002). This was a telling example of the 'foreign policy paradox' whereby 'the closer the relations between two countries, the more possibilities of influencing the practice of the other state, but at the same time the more reticence in applying the instruments available, owing to the interests at stake' (Feliu, 2003: 92).

However, the timeline based on changes in the Spanish government remains relevant insofar as it reflects how relations with Spain were interpreted and framed by the Moroccan policymakers. In Rabat, the coming to power of the Spanish People's Party (PP) in 1996 was regarded with some reservations although, in fact, Aznar's first foreign policy programme and discourse were essentially continuity-oriented, respecting the existing 'consensuses', pragmatic and 'realistic'. In bilateral relations with Morocco, this meant, first, the maintenance of the previous *colchón de intereses* approach and, second, strong support for King Mohammed VI at the time of his accession to the throne. The only disturbing novelty at that point was Madrid's conspicuous rapprochement with Algiers, which was made possible by falling levels of violence in that country and guided primarily by economic and energy interests (Feliu, 2005: 6, 17). A year later, during his first state visit to Spain, Mohammed VI did not avoid mentioning the well-known Moroccan–Spanish difficulties, 'limits that are naturally imposed on our partnership in the fields of agriculture, fisheries and movement of people, goods and services', although did present them in a positive light, as a challenge or incentive to 'revise and correct' the framework of bilateral relations (speech by Mohammed VI, Madrid, 18 September 2000). The role of the *good neighbour* was still prevailing.

Yet in spite of this, the looming bilateral crisis finally broke out in late October 2001 with the unexpected recall of the Moroccan ambassador to Madrid, Abdeslam Baraka. This diplomatic move 'of indefinite duration' was decided by the King himself at a time when Prime Minister Abderrahmane Youssoufi was abroad (Planet and Hernando de Larramendi, 2006: 415). The Moroccan foreign ministry justified it as a response to 'a number of Spanish attitudes and positions with regard to Morocco', without providing any further explanation. The *note verbale* sent to the Spanish ministry did not give more clues. The ambassador in question denounced in the press the 'demonisation of Morocco in Spain': 'Hence I think it is time to reflect and clarify our relationship' (*El País*, 29 October 2001; *Le Journal Hebdomadaire*, 3–9 November 2001). Reference was made not so much to a specific event as rather an accumulation of grievances that had been perceived in Rabat over the previous months (MAEC, 11 December 2001). As Mohammed VI himself explained three years later:

> Our bilateral relations with Spain deteriorated sharply between April and October 2001. We then witnessed statements, attitudes and positions in various fora that were frankly hostile to Morocco's politics, economy and security. This succession of events prompted me to recall the ambassador to Madrid for consultations in order to draw the attention of the Spanish government to its negative attitude.
> (Interview with Mohammed VI in *El País*, 16 January 2005)

In short, this bilateral crisis was characterised by its multiple and catalytic nature, as it 'synthesised the broad range of contentious issues accumulated since 1956' (Iglesias, 2010: 226) and developed as a 'spiral of negative interdependences' (Hernando de Larramendi, 2004: 3).

The first ingredient was the failure of negotiations concerning the renewal of the EU–Morocco fisheries agreement, which had been ongoing since September 2000 and ended without any results in late April 2001. The background to this complex negotiation process, as analysed by Jordi Vaquer, was the bottom-up Europeanisation or 'transfer to a higher level' of the problematic Spanish–Moroccan fisheries relations in the second half of the 1980s (2009: 50–51). During the 2000–2001 talks, Morocco maintained a defensive attitude due to the widespread perception that the previous agreement (1995) had proved to be detrimental to national economic interests.[13] Accordingly, this time the Moroccan representatives remained inflexible in their demands (as to the level of financial compensation, length of the agreement, technical conditions and volume of fishing allowed), even though these conditions were considered to be unacceptable from the outset by Spain, the member state that was visibly defining the EU positions. It was only when the Commission threatened to break off negotiations that Rabat offered a partial agreement allowing the traditional small-scale Andalusian and Portuguese coastal fleets to fish temporarily in Moroccan waters. However, this option was dismissed at the request of the Madrid government, which stuck to its defence of the interests of its fishing industry as an indivisible whole (Vaquer, 2003: 71–73). Nevertheless, the Spanish authorities unreservedly blamed Morocco alone for the failure of the negotiations. The reaction that most upset Rabat was a statement by Aznar warning of the 'consequences' of this fiasco for Spanish–Moroccan and EU–Moroccan relations, which was interpreted as a threat (Obiols and Solanilla, 2002: 296).

Second, Spanish accusations escalated to cover the alleged 'laxity' of Morocco in controlling illegal migration from its territory, during a summer in which the influx of illegal boats to the coasts of Andalusia and the Canary Islands increased sharply. The Spanish interior minister blamed the authorities of the neighbouring country, with a member of his department airing the suspicion that 'the Rabat government opens and closes the valve when it suits it'. The foreign minister summoned the Moroccan ambassador in late August to demand 'more effort' in combating this phenomenon. Madrid was also irritated by the delay and irregularity in the implementation of the bilateral readmission agreement signed in 1992 (Delmote, 2002; Khachani, 2003). But the outrage was no less intense on the other side, as was reflected in the counterattack by Mohammed VI: 'Also in Spain there are mafias [of illegal migration], and they are richer than in Morocco. [...] Let us say that the responsibility is shared. But on Morocco's side, it is largely due to a lack of resources' (interview with Mohammed VI in *Le Figaro*, 4 September 2001). Amid mutual recriminations, in November, the Aznar government unilaterally suspended the bilateral agreement on labour mobility that had been signed in July of the same year (Marrero, 2005: 430; El Qadim, 2010: 107; Belguendouz, 2002: 15). In addition, at the European Council held in Seville in June 2002, Madrid also tabled a proposal to cut EU aid to southern partners that did not make demonstrable efforts to curb irregular migratory flows.

Third, another source of controversy in December 2001 was the authorisation granted by the Spanish government to Repsol YPF to explore for oil along the median line boundary separating the Canary Islands and the Moroccan and Western Saharan coast, including waters where the border was not legally demarcated. The Rabat government reacted with a statement reminding Spain of 'the need to respect the international law and custom that prescribe the non-unilateral maritime delimitation'. The foreign ministry also protested against 'this unilateral, debatable and unfriendly Spanish act' (statements quoted in Belguendouz, 2002: 18–19; MAEC, 22 May 2002).

Forth, the 'straw that broke the camel's back' for Rabat (*L'Économiste*, 30 October 2001) was definitely the Spanish attitude to the Western Sahara conflict at the time the Baker Plan I was launched. In June 2001, Madrid decisively contributed to blocking this Moroccan-supported proposal – which was rejected by the Polisario Front and Algeria – within the Group of Friends of Western Sahara at the UN, acting against the positions of the U.S., the United Kingdom and France (Cembrero, 2006: 90–91). The Rabat authorities therefore blamed their northern neighbour directly for the failure of the one UN initiative in history that was most suited to their interests. Still, what most exasperated them was a symbolic protest action originating within civil society, and thus outside the control of the Madrid government, which involved the holding of a mock referendum on Western Sahara by an Andalusian pro-Sahrawi civic platform in mid-October. The Moroccan embassy inquired about this in a *note verbale* sent to the Spanish Ministry of Foreign Affairs, which simply replied that it was a 'private initiative' (*El País*, 29 October 2001; Obiols and Solanilla, 2002: 297). Last but not least, this series of bilateral offences and clashes was amplified by the media's virulence in both countries and domestic political confrontation in Madrid between the Aznar government and the opposition Spanish Socialist Workers' Party (PSOE), which was accused at times of disloyalty (*Le Journal Hebdomadaire*, 22–28 December 2001; Cembrero, 2006: 112–119).

The climax of the Moroccan–Spanish crisis – and the most strained bilateral episode since the 1975 Green March – came on 11 July 2002 with the occupation of the islet of Perejil by Moroccan gendarmes (*mokhazni*), which was considered by the Madrid government as an invasion of Spanish territory (despite the unclear legal status of this particular islet). In a way, what Morocco achieved with this action was to reintroduce the most primal territorial element into a dispute that had previously been developing in other related issue areas (fisheries, migration, oil exploration, the delineation of maritime boundaries and the Western Sahara conflict). Prior to that time, compared to his father, Mohammed VI had appeared to be rather pragmatic on the question of Ceuta and Melilla, including the rocks and islets. He had not made reference to the historical Moroccan claim over them in any of his speeches and some of his closest advisors had even admitted to the press that this issue was not a priority (Cembrero, 2006: 222–223; González and Pérez, 2008: 6). In retrospect, it can be said that the occupation of Perejil allowed Rabat to transform the ongoing bilateral crisis with Spain into a 'conflict' with high symbolic value, reviving old anticolonial approaches and Morocco's national role conception as a *territorial champion*. This southern country was also proving that it was able to 'reopen the framework of bilateral relations with Spain, putting itself on an equal footing in order to negotiate with its Iberian neighbour' (Iglesias, 2010: 328).

In any case, the official explanation given by the Moroccan authorities was that the Perejil manoeuvre occurred within the context of the fight against illegal migration, drug trafficking and international terrorism in the Strait of Gibraltar: 'We were being accused of not doing enough to stop illegal migration' (interview with Mohammed VI in *El País*, 16 January 2005). The origin of the decision was a matter of much speculation. It was clear that it was not made by the Youssoufi government, which was only informed after the fact, causing unease for some of its members (López García, 2002; Dalle, 2004: 742–743; Planet and Hernando de Larramendi, 2006: 420; Abouddahab, 2006: 63; Tuquoi, 2006: 80). Some time later, it became known that the order had been issued during a meeting between the King and his closest companions and advisors – Fouad Ali El Himma, secretary of state of the Interior, Taieb Fassi Fihri, secretary of state for Foreign Affairs, and General Housni Benslimane. The occasional cause was Spanish naval manoeuvres around the coast of Al Hoceima over the previous few days, which had been interpreted by this Moroccan clique as an unfriendly or arrogant display of force (Cembrero, 2006: 48–49; Sehimi, 2003: 105).

The reaction of the Spanish government was to demand firmly an immediate Moroccan withdrawal from Perejil and a return to the previous situation, while trying to gather support from its EU partners and the U.S., and maintaining phone conversations with the Rabat authorities against the clock. Yet five days later, when a negotiated agreement seemed to be on the cards, this government recalled its ambassador to Rabat (16 July) and ordered an intervention by a group of special forces from the Spanish army in order to evacuate the islet (17 July). This turn of events not only violated the terms of the bilateral Treaty of Friendship concerning the non-use of force and the peaceful settlement of disputes, but was also perceived in Morocco as an unnecessary humiliation. According to the communiqué by the Moroccan foreign ministry:

> This is a use of force contrary to the rules of international law and unjustifiable in a time when discussions were being held since Morocco and Spain had agreed to resolve the crisis through diplomatic channels, as is evident from the Spanish official statements yesterday.
>
> (MAEC, 17 July 2002)

The King described this episode in highly subjective and emotional terms:

> Before the Spanish troops invaded the islet there were talks at all levels. Spanish diplomats assured us then [...] that a solution would be reached without resorting to force. Morocco felt *slapped in the face* when it saw, soon afterwards, how it had been treated. Morocco felt *insulted*.
>
> (Interview with Mohammed VI in *El País*, 16 January 2005, emphasis added)[14]

In order to defuse the crisis, it was necessary for U.S. Secretary of State Colin Powell to intervene, who personally mediated between these two U.S. allies in order to arrange the future of what he later described as a 'stupid little island' (*GQ*, 5 May 2004). As a result of his efforts, at a meeting in Rabat of the foreign ministers Mohamed Benaissa and Ana Palacio, Morocco and Spain agreed to restore the *status quo ante* on the islet (no presence of military or security forces of either country, without discussing its sovereignty) and to launch a process of dialogue with the aim of repairing bilateral relations after a three-month truce.

Nevertheless, the echoes of this episode remained visible within the official Moroccan discourse still for some time. It was particularly remarkable that the king's speech for the next Throne Day mentioned the claim to Ceuta and Melilla for the first time in his reign, reasserting Morocco's role as *territorial champion*:

> Certainly, the ultimate goal of our diplomacy is to make Morocco a country with full territorial integrity [...]. The first of these rights is that of safeguarding the national sovereignty and territorial integrity of the Kingdom in its rightful boundaries, within the framework of respect for international law. [...] In this regard, Morocco since independence has never ceased to demand the end of the Spanish occupation of Ceuta, Melilla and the surrounding islands, despoiled from the north of the Kingdom [...]. It preferred to take for this purpose the path of lucid reason and a peaceful and civilised strategy [...]. But much to Our regret, so far We have not found a receptive ear on the part of Spain.
>
> (Speech by Mohammed VI, Tangier, 30 July 2002)

In any case, beyond the authorities, political parties and media, the attitude of the Moroccan population throughout this crisis was one of relative indifference (Fibla, 2005: 51). The Moroccan–Spanish bilateral relationship gradually restabilised over the next year (interview with Mohamed Larbi Messari, 24 October 2007). In January 2003, the two foreign ministers met and five joint working groups were established to deal with five further points of contention (migration, Western Sahara, maritime boundaries, economic relations, mutual perceptions and civil society) (Fibla, 2005: 45–51, 195–207). In February, ambassadors were once again exchanged. In December, a high-level meeting put the détente on an official footing – coupled with a financial aid package to Morocco of €390 million (*Le Journal Hebdomadaire*, 13–19 December 2003). An intervening factor in this rapprochement was the discrete influence of the Spanish Confederation of Employers' Organisations (CEOE), which maintained good relations with its counterpart the General Confederation of Moroccan Entrepreneurs (CGEM), as well as with the new technocratic Moroccan Prime Minister Driss Jettou (*Le Journal Hebdomadaire*, 2–8 November 2002, 8–14 March 2003). As argued by Héctor Cebolla (2004), 'the technocrats on the rise within the Moroccan ruling class are not in favour of overly tense bilateral relations with Spain [...]. The Moroccan technocrats want Spanish investments.' This was compounded by the perception, in the wake of the terrorist attacks in Casablanca (May 2003) and Madrid (March 2004), of a new shared security threat against which it was essential for the two neighbouring states to collaborate.

A third factor of reconciliation was the performance of Spanish diplomacy in relation to the Baker Plan II for Western Sahara, rejected by Morocco, which was submitted to the UN Security Council at a time when Spain was a non-permanent member and occupied the rotating presidency (July 2003). Foreign minister Palacio and her ambassador to the UN worked hard to secure the unanimous adoption of Resolution 1495. Thus, in order to prevent a French veto, they convinced the U.S. representative of the need to tone down the first draft resolution, ultimately depriving it of binding or coercive character, which suited Moroccan interests (Cembrero, 2006: 95–98).

In any case, the definitive repairing of bilateral relations could only occur following the return to power in Madrid of the PSOE, a political party with a background of good understanding with the Rabat authorities and which had been quite critical of the 'mistakes' allegedly made by the Aznar government in this area. Hostility towards Aznar in Morocco had reached such a point that the satisfaction with the electoral victory of his opponent was almost unanimous. The change in course promised by Zapatero was understood and framed on the other side in essentially emotional terms: 'I will summarise it in one word: trust. [...] Now, between us, mutual respect has been restored' (interview with Mohammed VI in *El País*, 16 January 2005). 'We are [...] determined to open a new page' (speech by Mohammed VI, Rabat, 30 July 2004). The staging of reconciliation reached its high point with the state visit by the King of Spain to Morocco in January 2005, which proved the enduring relevance of the 'diplomacy of kings' established decades before by Hassan II and Juan Carlos I. Mohammed VI reiterated his willingness to work for 'a real strategic, multidimensional partnership, based on a *contract of trust*' (speech by Mohammed VI, Marrakesh, 17 January 2005, emphasis added).

This emphatic Spanish–Moroccan rapprochement had triangular implications for relations with their respective neighbouring countries. On the European side, it was associated with the Spanish Socialist government's express wish to closely coordinate its Maghrebi policy with France, drawing a line under previous differences of opinion – a new alliance which, as argued above, also furthered EU–Morocco relations and the prospects for the Advanced Status. On the Maghrebi side, the new Madrid authorities endeavoured from the outset to prevent their reconciliation with Morocco from damaging bilateral relations with Algeria. That is to say, a pledge was made to avoid falling back into the old infamous Spanish 'balancing policy' towards the Maghreb (addressing the rivalry between Rabat and Algiers as a zero-sum game), which was supposed to be replaced by 'global policy' (encouraging regional integration as a win-win solution). The new Spanish approach involved fostering the revitalisation of the Arab Maghreb Union (AMU), highlighting the 'cost of non-Maghreb' to the governments and civil societies of the region, supporting any rapprochement between Morocco and Algeria and, especially, becoming more actively involved in the resolution of the Western Sahara conflict (Feliu, 2004b).

The willingness to play a more proactive mediating role in the Western Sahara conflict was one of the most controversial foreign policy issues in Spain under this government. It was surrounded by considerable discursive ambiguity and referred to with the empty signifier of 'active neutrality'. Yet aside some initial intensive contacts with all parties (Fibla, 2005: 190–191), in the context of the failure of the Baker Plan II (2003), the resignation of its author, UN Secretary-General's personal envoy James Baker (2004), and the launch of the Moroccan Autonomy Plan for the territory (2007), the Zapatero government ended up essentially siding with Rabat. Significantly enough, the King of Morocco himself referred to this realignment with a similar euphemism:

> I wish Spain [...] helps us constructively, pursuing a policy of *positive neutrality* as do other friendly countries [...]. I have urged them to be our partner in finding a solution to the problem of the Sahara, bearing in mind though that the territory is Moroccan.
> (Interview with Mohammed VI in *El País*, 16 January 2005, emphasis added)

For instance, despite the trouble caused by the Sahrawi protests in the Moroccan-occupied territory in mid-2005 (Vaquer, 2007: 137), in 2006 the Spanish government and diplomats gave discrete and cautious backing to the work of the Royal Consultative Council for Saharan Affairs (CORCAS), which had been charged by Mohammed VI with drafting a formal Autonomy Plan (interview with the Spanish ambassador Luis Planas in *L'Économiste*, 31 May 2006; U.S. Embassy in Rabat, cable 06RABAT557, 29 March 2006). The resulting proposal was praised by the Spanish foreign minister as a 'novel element of undoubted interest' which 'could generate a new dynamic of dialogue' (*El País*, 13 March 2007; Vaquer, 2007: 138).

A second area in which the convergence of positions between Morocco and Spain was visible after 2004 was migration management and border control. The first and most striking novelty was Rabat's acceptance to finally implementing the 1992 bilateral readmission agreement, including in relation to citizens of third countries. This set a precedent and was also vital in mitigating the impact of the crisis caused by the collective assaults on the border fences of Ceuta and Melilla by sub-Saharan African migrants in the autumn of 2005 – even though the treatment of many of these migrants by the Moroccan security forces was heavily criticised by international NGOs (Hernando De Larramendi and Bravo, 2006: 167–168). Second, the growing centrality of migration issues within the bilateral agenda was reflected in the development, in just a few years, of a dense framework of political and legal agreements, as well as joint action to monitor transit migration (López Sala, 2012). Third, at the diplomatic level, Spain was at this time one of the most receptive countries to the Moroccan discourse on a 'global approach' to migration, which manifested itself in the joint Moroccan–Spanish organisation of the Euro-African Ministerial Conference on Migration and Development in Rabat in July 2006. This initiative suited the two countries' shared interest in Europeanising what was originally a bilateral migration crisis (Sorroza, 2006: 5) and 'shifting the burden' to the EU (Schimmelfennig, 2000: 130) in order to demand more financial support:

We have always asked Spain, and the EU as a whole, to provide us with the means to combat this plague [illegal migration]. Now we lack them. I have proof that Spain is currently a good advocate of our cause in Europe.

(Interview with Mohammed VI in *El País*, 16 January 2005)

Western Sahara and migration aside, Moroccan–Spanish cooperation also gained unparalleled momentum in these years in the field of justice and home affairs, as was required by the perception of a shared terrorist threat following the attacks in Casablanca and Madrid. Another landmark decision, this time regarding international security, was the deployment of a Spanish–Moroccan joint military-police unit in Haiti as part of the United Nations Stabilisation Mission in Haiti (MINUSTAH) from August 2004 onwards.

On the economic front, the honeymoon with Spain was equally crucial for the relaunch of negotiations for the renewal of the EU–Morocco fisheries agreement, previously abandoned in 2001, after more than five years of inactivity of European vessels in waters falling under Moroccan sovereignty or jurisdiction. In contrast with previous Moroccan resistance, the 2005 deal was reached in only three months after the European Commission received the mandate to start negotiations from the Council (*L'Économiste*, 24 May 2005). The official Moroccan justification for this sharp change in attitude was that the new agreement reflected a novel EU willingness to preserve the country's fishery resources from a sustainable development perspective; this resulted in exclusions for crustacean and cephalopods fishery and the exploitation of the Mediterranean coast, as well as a lower number of licensed vessels (MAEC, 28 July 2005). However, despite the Moroccan–Spanish convergence, this time ratification of the agreement was delayed on EU level. The European Parliament raised the question as to whether, under international law, it was legal to include the waters of Western Sahara, whose final status was not yet resolved.[15] The agreement was not approved until May 2006 (*L'Économiste*, 24 March 2006, 17 May 2006; *Aujourd'hui Le Maroc*, 4 May 2006). In April 2007, it entered into force and fishing activity resumed.

In another vein, all of the progress made in bilateral cooperation and trust-building between Rabat and Madrid was to clash once again with the tenacious 'limits of voluntarism' (Gillespie, 2007) posed by territorial issues and Morocco's role as a *territorial champion*. A new full-blown diplomatic crisis was caused by the visit of the King and Queen of Spain to Ceuta and Melilla on 5–6 November 2007, which was unprecedented in the history of democratic Spain and ill-advisedly coincided with the anniversary of the Green March (interview with Mohamed Larbi Messari, 5 December 2007). The first Moroccan response was to recall the ambassador to Madrid, Omar Azziman, 'for an indefinite period' (MAEC, 2 November 2007). The Rabat government spokesman insisted that the Spaniards should not cross 'red lines on the territorial integrity of Morocco' and that 'colonialist approaches [had] finally expired'. After a vigorous speech by Prime Minister Abbas El Fassi at an extraordinary session of the House of Representatives, all parliamentary groups agreed to describe the

Spanish royal visit as a 'provocation' and to stress the 'need to recover the two cities' (EFE, 6 November 2007; *L'Économiste*, 7 November 2007). This angry institutional reaction was joined by some civil society associations, apparently acting independently, such as the Committee for the Liberation of Ceuta and Melilla and the Coordination Committee of Civil Society in Northern Morocco (EP, 6 November 2007).

In view of the nationalist escalation, Mohammed VI was forced to issue a special statement through his advisor Mohammed Moatassim in which he expressed his 'strong condemnation and [...] vigorous rejection of this unprecedented visit', which was described as 'nostalgic act, belonging to a dark old time that we have left behind'. This time he could not avoid putting Morocco's old territorial claim on the table along with the proposal to engage in negotiations with Spain on Ceuta and Melilla: 'The best way to solve and manage this territorial conflict requires respecting the virtues of a sincere dialogue that is frank and open to the future' (Rojo, 2008: 81–82). On the other hand, despite the rhetorical outcry, relations with Spain began to return to normality only ten days after the royal trip (*El País*, 15 November 2007). The episode was finally settled with a letter from President Zapatero to Mohammed VI on 2 January 2008, after which the Moroccan ambassador Azziman returned to his post.

In the end, this turned out to be a rather brief and low-intensity crisis which, unlike the Perejil episode, did not contaminate bilateral relations as a whole, lead to the use of force or have any strategic impact whatsoever. The main variable to account for these differences was its careful handling by senior authorities and diplomats in both countries. In Morocco, it was first and foremost the King who tried to control, restrain and channel the nationalist reaction of the political parties and other actors with a public performance containing a lot of 'mandatory dramatisation' (Iglesias, 2010: 332). The perception of an official double discourse was widely shared, from the Moroccan press to the U.S. embassy. 'Despite the public flash of anger, we doubt the incident will do sustained damage to the relationship. [...] Heated complaints from the Moroccan side were followed by assurances that bilateral cooperation would continue as usual', reported a U.S. diplomat (U.S. Embassy in Rabat, cable 07RABAT1695, 2 November 2007; U.S. Embassy in Rabat, cable 07RABAT1706, 7 November 2007). 'Does Morocco really want that the two usurped cities return to the national territory?' asked *Al Masaa* (7 November 2007). In other words, even though Moroccan foreign policy towards Spain continued to be constrained by nationalist *norms*, in this episode the role of *good neighbour* eventually prevailed over that of *territorial champion*.

Once this hurdle had been passed, from 2008 onwards Morocco's relations with Spain were to remain cordial and harmonious for several years. Mohammed VI received Zapatero in Oujda in July 2008, after the latter's re-election for a second term in government (U.S. Embassy in Rabat, cable 08RABAT681, 22 July 2008), and the ninth bilateral high-level meeting was held in Madrid in December the same year. Later on, at the time of the Arab Spring, Spanish diplomacy was largely absent from the regional picture due to the inward-looking turn that the deep economic crisis in this country had entailed, yet the reformist response of the Moroccan regime was consistently supported.

Continuity also prevailed, against all odds, in the new political cycle that started almost in parallel in both countries in November–December 2011, with the electoral victories and rises to government of the conservative PP in Madrid and the Islamist Justice and Development Party (PJD) in Rabat (the latter only in coalition). Possibly due to the precedent set by the crisis under the Aznar government in 2001–2003, the two new prime ministers, Abdelilah Benkirane and Mariano Rajoy, were particularly cautious and made outstanding efforts to stress a good bilateral understanding from the outset. This kind of preventive activism could be detected in the flurry of official visits in both directions during 2012. These included a somewhat more anomalous first trip to Spain by Benkirane in May, which was originally organised as a 'private visit' to Barcelona to meet members of his party and the Moroccan community in Catalonia, and was only made official ex post by adding a stopover and scheduling an appointment with Rajoy in Madrid (Fernández-Molina and Soler, 2013).

Within Moroccan official discourse, emphasis was placed on the convergence of both countries' interests in the economic sphere and the King's commitment to, 'in the current difficult economic situation, [...] fostering the emergence of new economic conditions favourable to the creation of shared wealth, thus giving concrete content to the deep bonds of active solidarity uniting our two countries' (speech by Mohammed VI, Rabat, 30 July 2012). This was not mere rhetoric, since part of the struggling Spanish productive sector had actually found in the Moroccan market a lifeline to compensate for the decline in domestic consumption. The rapid growth of these exports – which increased by 21 per cent from 2011 to 2012[16] – turned Spain into Morocco's primary source of imports, ahead of France, as of 2012. The Moroccan and Spanish positions also converged on the fisheries issue, as both countries saw themselves as victims of the European Parliament's unexpected rejection of the protocol of extension of the 2006 EU–Morocco fisheries agreement in December 2011 (European Parliament, 2011) and pushed for a new protocol to be negotiated immediately – which was signed in July 2013 and swiftly approved this time by the Parliament. The only sector characterised by outright bilateral divergence and clashing interests was agriculture. Significant tensions arose in February 2012 on the eve of parliamentary approval for the EU–Morocco agricultural agreement, which provided for a reduction of 70 per cent of tariffs for Moroccan exports and aroused the unanimous opposition of Spanish farmers and political parties. However, both governments made equally noteworthy diplomatic efforts to prevent this disagreement from spilling over the confines of its sectoral domain (MAP, 24 February 2012).

The same self-restraint was exercised in relation to incidents of territorial and border origin, as well as some linked to historical memory, which reappeared in the summer of 2012. These included certain nostalgic gestures made by the Rajoy government regarding the Rif War between colonial Spain and northern Moroccan rebels in the 1910s and 1920s, which were perceived in Rabat as a 'glorification of colonisation' (*Hespress*, 13 July 2012). The Moroccan contribution to this historicist escalation was foreign minister Saad-Eddine El Othmani's proposal to launch a bilateral dialogue in order to clarify the use of chemical weapons by the Spanish army during the Rif War (EFE, 16 July 2012). El Othmani also placed the Moroccan claim to Ceuta and Melilla on the table once again, stressing that there had been 'no change' in the official position of his country and expressing a desire to 'engage in dialogue' concerning the status of the two cities (EP, 20 June 2012). On the Spanish side, it was announced that a permanent detachment of the Guardia Civil would be dispatched to the Chafarinas Islands in order to improve the fight against drug trafficking and illegal immigration. However, after El Othmani summoned the Spanish ambassador to Rabat to express his 'disapproval', this measure was postponed indefinitely.

In addition, another migration crisis was caused by new mass storming of the border fences of Ceuta and Melilla, plus new arrivals of boats in Spanish territory through the islets of Alborán and Chafarinas. Moroccan security forces responded to the Spanish demand for cooperation with massive and violent arrests of hundreds of sub-Saharan African migrants in the northern provinces of the country. A few ultranationalist activists of the Committee for the Liberation of Ceuta and Melilla also took the opportunity to raid and briefly plant Moroccan flags on the rock of Vélez de la Gomera.

Yet the most significant aspect of all of these bilateral tensions was how quickly they were defused as a result of the political will on the part of decision-makers in both Rabat and Madrid. Mohammed VI's words on the convergence of the economic interests of both countries defined the pragmatic and economistic spirit of the tenth high-level meeting held in Rabat in October 2012, which resulted in the signing of eight bilateral agreements or programmes. As Benkirane said: 'We have talked about what Morocco and Spain want to do together. [...] For the rest, we already know what each other's positions are' (*El Mundo*, 3 October 2012). The following summer, King Juan Carlos I visited Morocco accompanied by an exceptionally large business delegation in order to highlight again the economic benefits of good bilateral relations (*Hespress*, 12 July 2013, 15 July 2013; *Lakome*, 15 July 2013). The pardoning by Mohammed VI immediately afterwards of 48 Spanish convicts jailed in Morocco, as a diplomatic gesture to please the northern neighbour, resulted in a huge political scandal when it became known that the prisoners released had accidentally included a paedophile and serial child-rapist. However, eventually, in spite of the bilateral implications of the so-called 'Danielgate', popular outrage and blame were focused on the Moroccan authorities, and hence the crisis was contained to the domestic sphere (*Lakome*, 8 August 2013; *Al Monitor*, 16 August 2013; Brouksy, 2014: 116–120).

Overall, Morocco's role as a *good neighbour* continuously came to the forefront. This also confirms Niklas Bremberg's (2012: 140) argument that 'the notion that things can always "go wrong"' has led to

An embryonic version of the practice of self-restraint, [...] a disposition among Spanish and Moroccan diplomats to try and prevent situations where things get out of hand, and to find a *modus operandi* to prevent the escalation of what appear to be almost cyclical crises.

The main reward for Rabat was the Rajoy government's discreet but consistent support in the Western Sahara conflict, most notably in the critical periods caused by Morocco's withdrawal of confidence from the UN envoy Christopher Ross in May 2012 and the U.S. attempt to extend the mandate of MINURSO to human rights monitoring in April 2013. Accordingly, Spain's election as a non-permanent member of the UN Security Council for 2015–2016 was seen as a 'gain' by Morocco (*Yabiladi*, 17 October 2014), not least in view of the ongoing bilateral crisis with France at the time (*Alif Post*, 25 June 2014, 20 October 2014).

In sum, Morocco's bilateral relations with its two main European partners, i.e. France and Spain, display contrasting features. High socioeconomic interdependence and elite symbiosis have ensured an extraordinarily intense and stable postcolonial alliance with France, a country that has consistently backed the Moroccan regime and its positions in the EU and international arena. The relationship has evolved from President Chirac's paternalism to Sarkozy's pragmatic and economistic focus, and even a serious bilateral crisis under Hollande, but remains far from being normalised. Moroccan foreign policy towards Spain has been more complex since it involves a duality of cooperation and conflict, and tension between the roles of *good neighbour* and *territorial champion*. Whilst bilateral interdependence has increased substantially since the 1990s, especially in economic terms, it has coexisted with chronic tensions linked to different territorial issues, such as Western Sahara and Ceuta and Melilla. After a deep multi-faceted crisis in 2001–2003, the repairing of bilateral relations has led both neighbouring countries to prioritise convergent interests and positions on the Western Sahara conflict, migration, security and economic cooperation.

Notes

1 Author's calculation based on data from the World Bank/World Integrated Trade Solution (WITS) database, http://wits.worldbank.org.
2 Sénat-France (2000) Rapport d'information fait au nom de la commission des Finances, du contrôle budgétaire et des comptes économiques de la Nation sur les crédits d'aide publique au développement affectés aux pays du Maghreb, 16 November, p. 109.
3 While still a prince, Mohammed VI completed his PhD at the University of Nice (1993) but continued to reside in Morocco.
4 A situation which more critical observers viewed in a less positive light: 'What I am concerned about, on the part of France, is that there is no distance any longer with Moroccan affairs. Moreover, Morocco expects France to support it against all the odds' (interview with Rémy Leveau in *Le Journal Hebdomadaire*, 11–17 October 2003).
5 On Moroccan lobbying and the careful handling of the issue of Western Sahara in French politics, see *Bakchich* (1 September 2008) and Amar (2009: 317–318).

6 Mezouar even refused to participate in the demonstration of world leaders that followed the terrorist attacks in Paris in January 2015, on the pretext that 'blasphemous' cartoons of Prophet Mohammed would be displayed (MAEC, 11 January 2015).
7 Author's calculation based on data from the World Bank/World Integrated Trade Solution (WITS) database, http://wits.worldbank.org.
8 These figures do not take into account smuggling or 'atypical trade' from Ceuta and Melilla to Morocco.
9 Data from the follow-up reports on the Annual International Cooperation Plans, Agencia Española de Cooperación Internacional para el Desarrollo (AECID).
10 See also Base de Datos sobre Política Exterior (BDPEX), www.bdpexonline.org (accessed on 31 January 2015).
11 See Messari (2009).
12 Two books which reflect more extensively the Moroccan vision on bilateral relations over these years are Bennis (2008) and Dahbi (2011).
13 On the negotiations and the fisheries agreement of 1995, see Damis (1998); White (1997); El Houdaïgui (2001) and El Houdaïgui (2003a: 244–256).
14 For a more critical Moroccan perspective on the actions of the Rabat authorities, see *Le Journal Hebdomadaire* (20–26 July 2002, 27 July–2 August 2002).
15 The response of the parliamentary legal services was positive, but was conditional upon the requirement that the EU's financial compensation contribute to the development and welfare of the territory's population.
16 Author's calculation based on data from the World Bank/World Integrated Trade Solution (WITS) database, http://wits.worldbank.org.

7 An uneasy loyalty

Remaining a 'good ally' of the United States in times of Middle East turmoil

After the *national question* of Western Sahara and Morocco's privileged partnership with the European Union (EU) and some of its member states, the third priority that has determined Moroccan foreign policy since independence is the country's relationship with the United States. Indeed, Morocco has played the role of *good ally* and has been recognised as occupying a unique position as Washington's oldest and most loyal partner in the Maghreb in a remarkably consistent way across different historical stages. This was the case during the Cold War and in the 1990s, when the U.S. took no more than a limited and circumstantial interest in this region, accepting it to be under primarily European influence, and remained so after the turn of the millennium. Not only has Morocco been overall the second highest Arab recipient of U.S. assistance (after Egypt) since it gained independence, but it also obtained military and logistical support from Washington which was vital in tipping the scales in its favour during the first years of the Western Sahara conflict, despite U.S. formal neutrality.

The main research question that this chapter tries to answer is how Moroccan foreign policy has attempted to reap the benefits of maintaining a close alliance with the U.S. while avoiding the increasing costs this entailed in terms of domestic legitimacy, especially between 2001 and 2009. This balancing act between foreign policy and domestic politics involved both rational choice and identity elements, which to a large extent corresponded to foreseeable benefits and costs, respectively. It bears some of the features of Robert D. Putnam's (1988) 'two-level games', yet with the qualification that it transcends the strictly rationalistic focus of this approach given the importance of the identity constraints on Moroccan foreign policy.

Indeed, the most outstanding characteristic of Morocco's longstanding role as *good U.S. ally* – and the key feature distinguishing it from those of *champion of national territorial integrity* and *model student of the EU* – is the lack of domestic consensus about it at both horizontal level (among different political elites) and vertical level (between leaders and public opinion) (Cantir and Kaarbo, 2012: 11–12). Such domestic contestation reached one of its highest peaks in 2003–2004, when according to some surveys, no less than 68 per cent of Moroccans had a negative view of the U.S. (Pew Research Center, 2004).

In general, arguably, this has been the result of the widespread consideration that the role taken on by the Rabat authorities vis-à-vis Washington clashes in a quite overt way with Morocco's deep-rooted Arab-Muslim identity and the self-assigned foreign policy role as *pan-Islamic leader* which has been invoked in parallel. The identity-based 'norms of Arabism' identified by Michael N. Barnett (1998: 11–18), which have historically constrained the states' external behaviour across this region – even when they were cynically manipulated – and took on a more Islamic/Islamist tone since the 1970s, prescribe a certain distancing from the 'West'. Whilst the Moroccan monarchy has a long experience in qualifying and turning this *norm* upside-down, having managed to largely dissociate it from relations with Europe, its influence remains still weighty from a societal viewpoint, especially concerning the U.S.

Second, as in the case of other foreign policy roles, Morocco's (*ego*) self-definition of its role as *good U.S. ally* has been regularly recognised and validated by the concerned other party or *alter*. Third, a larger role-set (Aggestam, 2006: 21) depends on this core role, including sub-roles such as 'bridge' between the 'West' and the Arab and Muslim world, 'moderator' within the Arab regional system and 'moderator' also in religious affairs – willing to promote, among other things, interreligious and intercultural dialogue – many of which are equally significant for relations with the EU. Finally, this role has also been used strategically within the context of rational-choice foreign policy behaviour.

In terms of rational costs and benefits, since Morocco is not economically or commercially dependent on the U.S. – unlike the EU – the main objective of its foreign policy towards Washington since the 1970s has been to obtain and maintain diplomatic and military support for the dispute over Western Sahara. The diplomatic backing became vital when the UN intervened in the matter in the later 1980s, owing to the U.S. veto power as a permanent member of the Security Council. Another strategic component of this relationship are the recurring 'triangular games' whereby Moroccan foreign policy has traditionally tried to maintain some equidistance and capitalise on transatlantic rivalry – especially between the U.S. and France – to reap greater benefits from its European partners (Berramdane, 1987: 412; Willis and Messari, 2003: 165). For example, in the U.S.–Morocco Free Trade Agreement signed in 2004, many observers detected a Moroccan strategy to 'play the American card to induce the EU to meet its expectations', particularly with regard to negotiations on agricultural trade (Baghzouz, 2007: 601). Conversely, the corresponding cost or price that Morocco has had to pay for its friendship with the U.S. has included committing itself to an unwavering pro-Western alignment during the Cold War – entailing Morocco's intervention as a proxy, both regular and irregular, in various African conflicts – taking on the role of 'moderator' in the Arab regional system, being willing to normalise relations with Israel and participating in the informal U.S.-led coalition waging War on Terror after the 9/11 terrorist attacks.

However, the merits which qualified Morocco for the role of *good U.S. ally* were presented within Rabat's official discourse in a quite different light, as stemming chiefly from convergence of values:

190 *An uneasy loyalty with the United States*

> Enjoying exceptional political stability and a longstanding tradition of moderation and openness, the Kingdom of Morocco offers exemplary evidence that it can be at the same time a state of law, a multi-party democracy open to government alternation, a competitive liberal economy fostering the private sector, enterprising spirit and direct foreign investment, and also a land of tolerance where all citizens coexist in dignity and in racial and religious harmony.
>
> (Speech by Mohammed VI, Washington, 20 June 2000)

The strategic importance of this alliance for Rabat was confirmed when Mohammed VI made an official visit to Washington in June 2000 just months after succeeding to the throne. In his welcoming remarks, Democratic President Bill Clinton (1993–2001) described Morocco as a 'sterling example of Islamic tolerance' (*The Washington File*, 20 June 2000). The trip took place against the backdrop of the brand-new Eizenstat Initiative, a partnership project launched in 1998 between the U.S. and the three central Maghreb countries (Morocco, Algeria and Tunisia) in order to lift trade and investment barriers. At this point in time, the paths down which this thriving bilateral relationship was expected to develop were primarily economic. According to the speech delivered by the King, a new cooperation framework in keeping with the new geopolitical, technological and economic realities would 'raise our economic relations to the level of our political dialogue'. He stressed that his country was doing its homework in order to meet U.S. requirements with regard to attracting investment, including trade liberalisation, reforming the investment code, reorganising the financial system, privatising public companies and preserving macroeconomic balance (speeches by Mohammed VI, Washington, 20 June 2000).

However, this was not long before the focus of U.S.–Moroccan relations turned from the economic and trade chessboard back to high politics and security. The inevitable turning point was the 9/11 terrorist attacks and the subsequent change in the foreign policy priorities of the new Republican administration of George W. Bush (2001–2009) (Grimaud, 2003: 46; *Le Journal Hebdomadaire*, 22–28 September 2001). From that moment onwards, within the context of a destabilised region subject to new and acute tensions, three basic lines would come to define the relationship between Rabat and Washington: support for the war in Afghanistan, collaboration on security matters – two aspects of the recently declared War on Terror – and a willingness to act as a role model in the region in fulfilment of U.S. expectations, building upon the diplomacy of interreligious dialogue and the adaptation of Morocco's political discourse and practices to international democratic standards.

In subsequent years, this early commitment was to result in a notable strengthening of Morocco–U.S. bilateral ties, seen in, for example, the choice of Rabat to host the first edition of the Forum for the Future, in the framework of the G-8's Broader Middle East and North Africa (BMENA) initiative, the declaration of Morocco as a major non-NATO U.S. ally and the signing of a bilateral Free Trade Agreement which was pioneering (second only to Jordan's) among

Washington's Arab partners. Morocco tried to capitalise on this honeymoon in the diplomatic battle over Western Sahara but did not see its aspirations completely fulfilled. While Rabat secured valuable declarations of support for its 2007 Autonomy Plan for the disputed territory from the Bush administration, the U.S. were unwilling to alter the formal neutrality that had always characterised their position.

Morocco's multifaceted participation in the War on Terror after 9/11

For the foreign policies of most of the Arab states, the main consequence of the 9/11 attacks – and of the subsequent unilateral and militaristic shift in U.S. foreign policy – was an intensification of the identity-based dilemmas and two-level games which maintaining ties with the U.S. has recurrently involved. In these critical circumstances, attempts to harmonise foreign policy and domestic politics came up against growing public disaffection towards the U.S. and, especially, negative perceptions of the latter's actions in the Middle East. In particular, it was the leaders of the countries willing to play the role as *good U.S. allies* which were most trapped between international and domestic pressures, and forced to reconcile contradictory needs, i.e. the Bush administration's desire to incorporate them into its informal War on Terror coalition and rampant anti-Americanism among their population (Addi, 2001; Zoubir and Aït-Hamadouche, 2006). The U.S. interest in strengthening ties with countries like Morocco could be explained by reasons of political legitimacy and operational effectiveness. Washington, on the one hand, needed to shatter the image of isolation resulting from its unilateral shift in foreign policy and the fact that it was increasingly perceived as an enemy of Arab people or countries and, on the other, wanted to take advantage of the knowledge and accumulated experience of these regimes' security services in the fight against Islamist terrorism.

In turn, being problematic in terms of domestic legitimacy, Morocco's decision to participate in the War on Terror in its different facets – supporting the war in Afghanistan and cooperating with security and intelligence – seemed to stem from rational choice related primarily to the Western Sahara issue. The immediate alignment with the U.S. was attributed to the recently crowned monarch's cost-benefit calculation 'that any other move would harm Morocco's interest in the Western Sahara'. 'He took the risk, confirming that the highest priority of the Moroccan state is the Western Sahara issue' (Willis and Messari, 2003: 169). A second motivating factor for Rabat was its permanent competition with Algiers over both regional leadership and recognition of its role as the preferred interlocutor for Washington in the Maghreb. This was particularly true at a time when Algeria's bilateral relations with the U.S. were advancing as much or more than Morocco's. Added to the 2001–2003 bilateral crisis with Spain, this reinforced the perception of geopolitical fragility which is constant among the Moroccan elite. Finally and more immediately, Morocco could expect a significant increase in aid for its armed forces and security services (information, technical assistance, training, materials, weapons, etc.) from the U.S. in addition to financial and development aid.

The immediate Moroccan official reaction to the 9/11 attacks came in the form of statements of condemnation issued by the King and government, and the organisation of an ecumenical ceremony in memory of the victims at the cathedral of Rabat attended by senior government officials, which, considering the circumstances, was above all a foreign policy decision (Belhaj, 2009: 86, 255; Régragui, 2013: 31–34). Domestically, the disapproval of terrorist violence united the main Moroccan political forces, including the Islamists from the Justice and Development Party (PJD), who attended the ecumenical ceremony, and those from Al Adl wal Ihsan, who presented their condolences to the U.S. embassy. The only dissenting voice came from 16 non-official 'ulema' who issued a *fatwa* denouncing the religious ceremony as ungodly, criticising the contents of the official Friday sermon on the attacks and decrying the decision made by the Moroccan regime to join the anti-terrorist alliance announced by Washington. Publication of this *fatwa* resulted in an immediate call for order and the arrest of some of the 'ulema'. In December, several members of the government participated in a second ceremony at the U.S. embassy. They came with instructions from the King to convey to the American people 'the condolences and sympathy of the Moroccan people and government' (Chaarani, 2004: 14).

Morocco's joining of the informal U.S.-led coalition for War on Terror was formalised by some symbolic visits and measures. Between 2002 and 2006, a number of U.S. officials travelled to Rabat, including Secretary of State Colin Powell (April 2002, December 2003 and December 2004), Adjunct Secretary of State for Near Eastern Affairs William J. Burns (December 2001, December 2002, October 2003 and October 2004), Secretary of Defence Donald Rumsfeld (February 2006) and the director of the Central Intelligence Agency (CIA) George Tenet (February 2002). Emblematic measures included Morocco's ratification of the International Convention for the Suppression of the Financing of Terrorism (adopted by the General Assembly of the UN in 1999) in July 2002 and the passage of anti-terrorist legislation in May 2003 which toughened criminal sanctions and lowered limitations on police activity, working from an imprecise definition of the phenomenon in question.

In practical terms, the first manifestation of Morocco's participation in the War on Terror concerned support for the war in Afghanistan, which was already underway. This war was launched by the U.S. a mere month after the 9/11 attacks with backing from the UN Security Council, invoking the right to legitimate self-defence and the goal of toppling the Taliban regime and removing any possible refuge for the Al Qaeda terrorist network. The position taken by Morocco regarding the invasion of this Muslim country was implicit support without military participation. The condition for Moroccan consent, according to the Ministry of Foreign Affairs and Cooperation, was that the U.S. operation be prudent and restrained, and not affect the civilian population. Foreign minister Mohamed Benaissa insisted that 'innocent lives [should] not be endangered' (quoted in Chaarani, 2004: 15).[1] Mohammed VI himself said that: 'There is no such thing as zero risk in a war. But we cannot ignore the fact that these images, these civilians dying every day, are aggravating the frustrations that feed extremisms' (interview with Mohammed VI in *Paris Match*, 31 October 2001).[2] In December – after the UN conference in Bonn that established the Afghan Interim Authority and paved the way for the election of a new government in Kabul – Morocco officially became involved in this country's 'reconstruction' programme (MAP, 24 December 2001). The Rabat authorities offered support in the form of technical cooperation for agriculture, the food industry and water management (Chaarani, 2004: 16; interview with Jaafar Alj Hakim, 17 February 2006).

The Moroccan authorities' objective was to avoid giving the impression that the country was meekly submitting to U.S. demands. The sensitivity of public opinion and domestic pressure against this alignment were intensifying. A survey published in October 2001 by the newspaper *Al Ahdath Al Maghribia* revealed that a broad swathe of the Moroccan population simultaneously condemned the 9/11 attacks and opposed Moroccan support for the U.S. war in Afghanistan – which was rejected by more than 90 per cent (*Le Journal Hebdomadaire*, 3–9 November 2001). Accordingly, the political parties in the ruling coalition opted to keep quiet, leaving the most critical arguments in the hands of the non-governmental left and Islamist groups. Meanwhile, the tone of the declarations made by the most representative Islamist organisations was generally moderate and circumspect, and they were rarely accompanied by protests against the official position. The most important initiative of this nature – a demonstration convened by the Moroccan section of the Islamic Nationalist Congress[3] in Rabat in late October to support the Afghan people and oppose the 'savage and growing' U.S. aggression – was banned by the authorities in the end (*L'Économiste*, 24 October 2001).

The second consequence of 9/11 for U.S.–Morocco relations – as for other countries in the region – was intensified cooperation between the respective security and intelligence services in all matters relating to counter-terrorism. Ties between the CIA and the Moroccan secret services (technical assistance, training and liaisons) date back to the 1960s (*Le Journal Hebdomadaire*, 11–17 January 2003) and had not been diminished by the end of the Cold War or the succession of the new King. However, the War on Terror marked a qualitative leap forward as the functions of the Moroccan services under U.S. orders were extended, often in disregard of international law (Amar, 2009: 246–254). For example, various enquiries and evidence from later years have revealed that, in December 2001, some Moroccan agents travelled to Pakistan to capture a group of alleged terrorists from their country, who were later transferred to the U.S. offshore detention centre at Guantánamo, Cuba. Beginning in early 2002, other members of the Directorate for Territorial Surveillance (DST), the Moroccan domestic intelligence agency, participated in interrogations and analysed information obtained from supposed members of Al Qaeda imprisoned in this centre.

From that moment onwards, bilateral contacts at different levels and trips by U.S. investigators to Morocco multiplied. In June, the public prosecutor in

Casablanca announced with great fanfare that three Saudis had been arrested under the accusation of planning a suicide attack against ships from the U.S. Sixth Fleet in the Strait of Gibraltar – an operation that various observers would later label pure 'security marketing' (Chaarani, 2004: 20–22, 66–69, 72–73). Additionally, the DST headquarters in Temara became part of the vast network of secret detention and torture centres for supposed terrorists set up by the CIA during these years in order to outsource practices that flagrantly violated international and U.S. law to third countries with few scruples about human rights (*New York Times*, 17 January 2015). Morocco was a common stopover in the programme of extrajudicial transfer and abductions known as 'extraordinary rendition', which was uncovered by the *Washington Post* (17 November 2005) and Human Rights Watch (HRW) in late 2005 (*Le Journal Hebdomadaire*, December 2005; *Maroc Hebdo International*, 20–26 January 2006). Still, the Rabat authorities categorically denied at all times the existence of any secret detention centres under the authority of foreign countries in Morocco (AFP, 21 January 2006).

This extensive and diligent anti-terrorist intelligence collaboration, via both irregular and regular channels, was recognised with various gestures of appreciation by the U.S. administration ranging from a telephone conversation between President Bush and the King in July 2002 to declarations made by Colin Powell in December 2003 affirming that Morocco occupied a very high position in U.S. foreign policy (Chaarani, 2004: 81–82, 67, 21; MAEC, 3 December 2003). On the domestic side, some Moroccan intelligence service top officials – most notably General Hamidou Laanigri, the head of the DST since September 1999 – took advantage of these circumstances to strengthen their own positions as U.S. interlocutors and secure their political futures (Brouksy, 2014: 156–158). In his 'ostentatious willingness' (Amar, 2009: 253) to collaborate with his U.S. counterparts, Laanigri even personally travelled to Guantánamo to interrogate Moroccan prisoners (Chaarani, 2004: 53; Amar, 2009: 201).

Third, beyond supporting the war in Afghanistan and cooperating with counter-terrorism efforts, Morocco's adaptation to the post-9/11 international context also involved a socialisation component, that is, intensifying this state's performance as a role model for the Arab and Muslim world in line with U.S. expectations. This role-playing included two elements, i.e. what Abdessamad Belhaj (2009) has termed the 'diplomacy of interfaith dialogue' – sometimes also intercultural dialogue – and the adaptation of Moroccan domestic political practices and discourse to international democratic standards. Regarding the former, there was nothing new about proclamations regarding the need for a 'rich dialogue between cultures and civilisations' (speech by Mohammed VI, Washington, 22 June 2000) in the monarchy's discourse aimed at the outside world. Rather, this was a ramification of the Moroccan king's status as *Amir al-Muminin* (Commander of the Faithful), which had previously allowed Hassan II to set himself up at will as representative of the entire Muslim *umma*, serving as the standard bearer for values like moderation, tolerance and openness. From the moment he accessed the throne, Mohammed VI wholeheartedly emulated the discourse of his father in this regard (speech by Mohammed VI, Rabat, 30 July 1999). Yet it was one year later, in the aftermath of the 9/11 attacks, when the Rabat authorities most championed this image of a moderate and pluralist Muslim country open to dialogue. Ismaïl Régragui (2013) has studied this 'religious branding' as the result of a deliberate strategy of public diplomacy whereby the Moroccan monarchy has mobilised its symbolic capital at the service of foreign policy objectives. The payback for these efforts was reflected in different panegyrics, such as Donald Rumsfeld's words expressing 'admiration for the initiatives of His Majesty aiming at encouraging religious dialogue and tolerance' during his visit to Morocco in February 2006 (*Le Matin*, 12 February 2006).

As regards the reforms made by the Moroccan authorities to adapt to international democratic standards after Mohammed VI's succession, these ranged from human rights reforms (symbolically ending impunity for the human rights violations committed during the so-called *years of lead*, recognition of Amazigh identity, reform of the family code and promotion of women's rights) to holding more regular and transparent elections (regardless of their real impact on the distribution of power) to the institutional integration of part of the Islamist movement, which was regarded as a yardstick by U.S. analysts advocating for the normalisation of 'moderate' Islamist parties (Zoubir and Dris-Aït-Hamadouche, 2006: 259–260). The dissemination of these advances abroad was boosted by parallel and public diplomacy efforts entrusted to, among others, consultative councils dependent on the King such as the Consultative Council on Human Rights (CCDH). Al Akhawayn University in Ifrane (AUI) also played a role, organising a conference on Morocco–U.S. relations in collaboration with the foreign ministry in January 2002, a crucial moment for the future development of these relations (Ouaouicha *et al.*, 2003).

The BMENA initiative and the hosting of the Forum for the Future

Morocco's role as *good ally* and regional model in accordance with the U.S. administration's expectations was to become even more valuable after the initiation of the 2003 Iraq War and the U.S. decision to launch the Greater Middle East Initiative, which was reshaped and adopted by the G-8 in June 2004 as the Broader Middle East and North Africa (BMENA) initiative. The months of diplomatic frenzy that preceded the March 2003 U.S.-led attack on Iraq, which had been accused of non-compliance with UN resolutions and possessing weapons of mass destruction, showed the extent to which Morocco was incapable of maintaining an autonomous position independent of Washington on a burning international issue (Sehimi, 2003: 110). The statements made by Mohammed VI and the foreign ministry never exceeded the limits of a cautious and innocuous discourse, based on appeals to international law and the search for a peaceful solution, similar to that of most Arab leaders. By contrast, the Moroccan independent press echoed a heated debate about the kingdom's subordination to the U.S. and reduced room of manoeuvre in foreign policy in critical circumstances like these (*Le Journal Hebdomadaire*, 11–17 January 2003).

The degree to which Rabat supported or collaborated with the Iraq War in practice was never made public. The authorities avoided disclosing this information in view of the strong opposition to the war from a large segment of the population. The first document that officially mentioned Morocco as a member of the U.S.-led international coalition involved in the conflict was a list drawn up in late 2003 by the Department of Defence establishing the top priority countries for contracts to rebuild post-war Iraq (*Le Journal Hebdomadaire*, 13–19 January 2003). On a number of occasions in mid-2004, the foreign minister was forced to deny that Morocco was considering sending troops to that country, even though the post-war phase was officially underway (MAEC, 17 June 2004). One of the implications of this conflict for U.S.–Morocco relations was a resurgence of anti-Americanism among Moroccans. A survey on global attitudes conducted by the Pew Research Center and published in March 2004 found that 68 per cent of the Moroccans polled had a somewhat unfavourable (22 per cent) or very unfavourable (46 per cent) view of the U.S. A broad majority believed that the war in Iraq had negatively impacted the fight against terrorism (67 per cent) and had even less confidence than before the war in the U.S. desire to promote democracy in the region (66 per cent). The interviewees believed that the U.S. underlying objectives were to control Middle East oil, achieve world domination, support Israel and threaten enemy Muslim groups and governments (Pew Research Center, 2004; *Le Journal Hebdomadaire*, 27 March–2 April 2004).

The goal of the 2004 BMENA initiative was, indeed, to provide diplomatic coverage and legitimation by the G-8 for the U.S. interventionist plans for Iraq and the rest of the region. With the democratisation of Iraq transformed into the ex post justification for the occupation of that country, the debate on the pending political reform in the Middle East and North Africa, by extension, gained unusual momentum. However, the U.S. continued to face a serious legitimacy problem, as evidenced by the decision taken by some Arab countries to present an alternative reform plan at the Arab League's Tunis summit initially scheduled for early April 2004. Moroccan diplomats, working hand in hand with the host country, played an essential role in aborting that Arab project and postponing the meeting (*Le Journal Hebdomadaire*, 23–29 April 2004; Fernández-Molina, 2014: 11). Against this backdrop, one of the European proposals to overcome the Arab reluctance and gain support for the BMENA initiative was to organise what would come to be called the Forum for the Future, an non-institutionalised venue for representatives of the G-8 countries to meet with political, business and civil society leaders from this region, and to discuss consensual objectives and reform projects on an annual basis.

The choice of Rabat to host the first meeting of this international forum on 11 December 2004 was a new gesture that ratified the 'brand' of Morocco as a 'model country' in the Arab world (Belhaj, 2009: 263). Ministers of foreign affairs, economy and finance from 21 countries in the region – almost all of the

Arab states, plus Turkey, Pakistan and Afghanistan – and their counterparts from the G-8 met in what was presented as a 'setting for an informal, flexible, open and inclusive dialogue' (MAEC, 11 December 2004), co-chaired by Colin Powell and Mohamed Benaissa. Representatives from international organisations like the Arab League, the Arab Maghreb Union (AMU), the Gulf Cooperation Council (CCG) and the EU also attended. The absence of Israel was the necessary condition for the participation of so many countries. The order of the day was essentially economic and 'pragmatic', as can be seen from the topics of most of the initiatives presented (migrant remittances, tourism, microfinance, creation of a funding network and foreign investment) (Forum for the Future, 2004). This tallied well with the economistic discourse in vogue in the foreign policy of Morocco, a country that expressed interest in the creation of a training centre for entrepreneurs at AUI (MAEC, 28 December 2004).

Of course, the Moroccan authorities could not ignore the domestic political cost of their decision to host and co-organise this meeting, which triggered intense criticism and demonstrations from a large number of political and social organisations in the country. Political parties like the PJD and even the Party of Progress and Socialism (PPS) – which was part of the government coalition – openly opposed the event, which they saw as a veiled way of legitimising the U.S. occupation of Iraq and this country's economic control and political interference in the region, beyond the rhetoric about democratisation and all of the development projects. In the sphere of civil society, a Moroccan Cell against the Forum for the Future (CEMACOFA) was formed and a large demonstration was organised for 28 November which combined criticism of this international meeting with solidarity for the victims of the conflicts in Palestine and Iraq,[4] but which ultimately became a demonstration of the strength of the powerful Islamist association Al Adl wal Ihsan (*Maroc Hebdo International*, 3–9 November 2004; *Tel Quel*, 4–10 December 2004; *Al Tajdid*, 29 November 2004; interview with Abderrazak Drissi, 11 June 2009). At the same time, the associations that were most conciliatory and inclined to collaborate with the political leaders meeting in Rabat organised a parallel civil society forum and communicated their recommendations to the governmental one (*Tel Quel*, 11–17 December 2004; Desrues, 2006: 267).

The deputy minister of Foreign Affairs and coordinator of the Moroccan team, Taieb Fassi Fihri, explained the dilemma being faced by the authorities in his country:

> The choice we had to make from the outset was between two extremes: doing nothing because of Iraq and Palestine, and thus having an excuse for our inaction, or shutting up and accepting without complaint everything proposed by the North under the leadership of the G-8. [...] We decided that there was another option: to participate and be involved in the organisation of this Forum for the Future. [...] Morocco decided to run the risk and that was the right thing to do.
>
> (*Maroc Hebdo International*, 17–23 December 2004)

In return, the main expectation of the Moroccan regime was to increase its international political visibility (Mustapha Sehimi in *Maroc Hebdo International*, 10–16 December 2004) and ultimately capitalise on its leading role with regard to Western Sahara.

In response to the critics condemning Rabat's unconditional alignment with Washington, the Moroccan foreign ministry adopted a self-justifying discourse modelled on the language used by the U.S. and G-8 which emphasised the spirit of 'shared responsibility and mutual respect' that motivated the proponents of the Forum for the Future, their objectives of contributing to economic development in the region and promoting home-grown reforms adapted to the particular needs of each country, and the complementarity with cooperation with the EU in the framework of the Euro-Mediterranean Partnership (EMP) (speech by Mohamed Benaissa, Rabat, 11 December 2004). According to Fassi Fihri, the goal of the meeting was 'neither more nor less than to obtain the resources that [would] allow the group of the eight most industrialised countries to contribute to the development of the Middle East and North Africa and to the introduction of necessary reforms', always provided that 'reforms [originated] in the region' (MAEC, 4 December 2004).

The choice of Morocco to host the first meeting of the Forum for the Future was presented as the result of the kingdom's 'significant advances' on the path to political openness and human rights, as well as its 'very clear positions' on the conflicts in the Middle East and Iraq (MAEC, 9 December 2004): 'Morocco is certainly not the only country in the region to have embarked upon a process of far-reaching reforms, but it is probably one of the pioneering countries in this respect' (speech by Mohamed Benaissa, Rabat, 11 December 2004). Even the demonstrations held in Rabat opposing this international meeting were turned into an example of the freedom of expression existing in the country and the open and participatory nature of the Forum, arguing, in the words of Fassi Fihri, that it is 'very healthy that people express their positions and points of view' (MAEC, 9 December 2004). In later parliamentary appearances, minister Benaissa said that he was satisfied with the results of the meeting, because 'Morocco reaffirmed its active and positive presence on the international stage' and 'the final declaration reflected the hopes and concerns of the peoples in the region' (MAEC, 15 December 2004, 28 December 2004).[5]

Strengthening economic ties through highly 'political' aid and trade

The economic implications of the strengthening of Morocco–U.S. ties in this context involved both aid and trade: Morocco became eligible for funds from the new Millennium Challenge Account (MCA) launched in January 2004 and signed off a pioneering bilateral Free Trade Agreement (FTA) with the U.S. that same year, the second of its kind in the region only after the one with Jordan. In any case, the rationale of these two measures transcended by far the strictly economic sphere and was regarded by many as highly 'political'. The stated novelty of the MCA's approach lied in linking development cooperation to ideas about governance in vogue at the time: candidate countries were required to meet minimum requirements related to 'ruling justly' (political rights, civil liberties, control of corruption, government effectiveness, rule of law and accountability), 'economic freedom' and social investment (Hewko, 2010: 2). At the same time, its political justification was consistent with the spirit of the BMENA initiative and the War on Terror: 'A part of the rationale is to demonstrate that greater development improves people's lives and may hinder the rise of violent forms of Islamist activity' (ICG, 2005: 29). Morocco was included among the recipients of the MCA within the category of low-income countries, despite the fact that it did not meet all the eligibility criteria concerning 'ruling justly'.[6] The agreement with the Millennium Challenge Corporation was made official in August 2007 and went into force in September 2008, granting a compact of $697.5 million for the following five years. The bulk was earmarked for improving agricultural productivity, modernising artisanal fisheries, developing artisanal crafts, strengthening financial services and supporting enterprises.[7] The programme in Morocco was administered by the new Agency of Partnership for Progress (APP), presided over by the prime minister (*L'Économiste*, 16 November 2007, 13 February 2008; MAP, 15 September 2008; Abouddahab, 2010b: 402).

In the case of the 2004 U.S.–Morocco FTA there was a precedent, i.e. the U.S.–North Africa Economic Partnership, known as the Eizenstat Initiative after its author. Launched in mid-1998, this programme sought to establish a stable economic partnership between the U.S. and the three central Maghreb countries (Morocco, Algeria and Tunisia) (AFP, 16 June 1998).[8] Three years before the 9/11 terrorist attacks, Washington's priority in this region was to increase economic cooperation – which had always lagged behind political and security issues – and thus make headway in terms of trade and investment into an area heretofore virtually monopolised by European interests. Competition with the EU, whose incipient EMP provided for the creation of a free trade zone, seemed inevitable at this stage (*Le Journal*, 27 November–3 December 1999). In what was most likely an attempt to emulate the EMP, one of the distinctive characteristics of the Eizenstat Initiative was its regional or 'bi-multilateral' approach. The Clinton administration wanted to treat the Maghreb as a single unit and ensure an integrated market for U.S. products. Accordingly, it was urging for the lifeless AMU to be resuscitated, the border between Morocco and Algeria to be reopened and even a free trade zone to be establish between these countries (Chigueur, 2001: 85–87; Zoubir and Benabdallah-Gambier, 2005: 182; *Le Journal Hebdomadaire*, 22–28 September 2001).

In 2001, the Bush administration put aside the Eizenstat Initiative and began contemplating the possibility of a bilateral FTA with Morocco shortly thereafter (Grimaud, 2003: 48–50; White, 2005: 602). However, it was not until the aftermath of 9/11 that Washington launched an unprecedented free trade negotiation programme with Arab countries, now with visible links to security and strategic considerations. Within this context, not only was it argued that global trade liberalisation was an essential piece of the U.S. fight against terrorism, but a connection was also established between free trade and democracy promotion (Al Khouri, 2008: 1–3). The Arab states given priority status in this context were Jordan, Morocco and Egypt, i.e. countries that, on the one hand, lacked oil reserves and, on the other, had a close relationship with the U.S. and generally aligned themselves with U.S. foreign policy positions – including most notably a conciliatory attitude towards Israel (Benmoussa, 2003: 15). In economic terms strictly speaking, the bilateral approach chosen for these negotiations can be explained by U.S. dissatisfaction with existing multilateral trade agreements and a desire to bypass the rules and requirements of the World Trade Association (WTO). This bilateralism did not only allow the U.S. to set the terms for every agreement according to the particular circumstances of each country, but also to 'deploy its hegemonic bargaining power' (Al Khouri, 2008: 5–6; Crombois, 2005: 219–220).

Meanwhile, Morocco had embarked during these years upon a real race to sign preferential trade agreements. In 2004 alone, the kingdom signed deals of this nature with Turkey in April, the U.S. in June and Tunisia, Egypt and Jordan – the so-called Agadir Agreement – in February. Historically, due to geographical remoteness and the lack of complementarity in respective exports, Morocco's trade relations with the U.S. had always been marginal, especially in comparison to the EU's hegemonic position. Exchanges with the EU Single Market represented 65 per cent of this country's total trade, whereas the U.S. only took in 3.4 per cent of its exports and provided 6.5 per cent of its imports (Jaidi, 2008: 182; White, 2005: 601). Initially and from an economic standpoint, the potential advantages of concluding a trade agreement with the U.S. were due to the latter's more ambitious and liberalising horizons when compared to European protectionism: from the outset negotiations covered all goods and services without exception – including, most importantly for an economy like Morocco's, agriculture – and only limited negative lists of products subject to exceptional treatment were admitted (Escribano, 2007: 191).

The idea of a bilateral agreement with Morocco was presented at a meeting in Rabat on 10 April 2002 by Catherine Novelli, the Assistant Trade Representative for Europe, the Middle East and North Africa under U.S. Trade Representative Robert B. Zoellick. It especially gathered momentum following Mohammed VI's official visit to Washington at the end of that month, after which President Bush authorised the beginning of conversations (AFP, 23 April 2002; *Maroc Hebdo International*, 26 April–2 May 2002; *Le Journal Hebdomadaire*, 18–24 May 2002). In early July, the King appointed Taieb Fassi Fihri to coordinate and handle the dossier, acting as sole Moroccan interlocutor with the U.S. authorities throughout the process (Benmoussa, 2003: 27–28), which officially began in January 2003. The final text (U.S./Morocco, 2004) was agreed upon in March 2004 after 13 months and seven rounds of talks, an unusually short negotiation period in the eyes of many observers. The agreement was signed in mid-June and, after congressional ratification in both states, entered into force in January 2006.

The FTA did not include any explicit mention of non-economic issues. However, there was more than enough evidence to conclude that the driving force behind its gestation was highly 'political' and strategic in nature. The choice of a royal visit for the starting signal, the speed of the negotiations and the timing of the successive announcements all gave an idea of the 'two countries' strategic interest in solidifying strong bonds of "friendship" as soon as possible' (*Le Journal Hebdomadaire*, 11–17 January 2003). Washington needed to stage its alliance and reward a model student in the Arab world to demonstrate its good will and legitimise its much maligned policies toward this region, especially in the post-Iraq War context (*Tel Quel*, 13–19 March 2004; *Le Journal Hebdomadaire*, 23–29 April 2004). Zoellick himself made this connection explicit when he said that 'open trade is a strong tool to help reformers' and that 'the policies that foster economic freedom open the door for political freedom' (speech by Robert B. Zoellick, Washington, D.C., 15 June 2004).[9]

Morocco's rational-choice political interest, on the other hand, lay in singling out its close relations with the U.S. and redressing the balance of power in the region in its favour at a time of visible rapprochement between Washington and Algiers. In particular, Rabat expected that reinforcement of the existing alliance could lead the U.S. to abandon its formal neutrality on the Western Sahara issue and provide vital support for Morocco after the latter's controversial rejection of the Baker Plan II, which the UN Security Council had 'supported' the year before as a way to resolve the conflict (*Le Journal Hebdomadaire*, 6–12 March 2004; Desrues, 2006: 251–252; White, 2005: 609). Notwithstanding all this, however, the Moroccan foreign ministry insisted that the agreement was 'exclusively economic and commercial' in nature. The anticipated benefits cited in the official discourse were essentially related to creating new opportunities for exporting Moroccan products to the U.S. market, attracting U.S. foreign direct investment, transforming Morocco into a platform for U.S. companies seeking better access to Europe, Western Africa and the Arab world, and pushing for the necessary restructuring and modernisation (*mise à niveau*) of the national economy (MAEC, 2004a).

To the domestic audience, the negotiating mandate for the agreement was presented as being 'the outcome of a nationwide process of consultation and dialogue between different government and private actors' – that is, according to Rachid el Houdaïgui's classification (2003a: 205–206), a relatively complex decision-making process, characterised by the involvement of various domestic political and economic stakeholders. Before the first round started, an interministerial negotiation team was set up and consultations were conducted with different ministries and the private sector.[10] According to the official discourse, the methodology chosen to define the Moroccan positions was based on the work of 13 thematic groups made up of representatives from some 30 different ministries and departments, all under the general coordination of the foreign ministry. This was coupled with 'consultation with parliament' – several sessions devoted to the FTA within the Committee on Foreign Affairs, National Defence and Islamic Affairs, in addition to oral questions for the government from both parliamentary houses – and 'consultation with the private sector' – meetings with representatives from different business federations and associations like the

National Foreign Trade Council (CNCE), plus coordination of each thematic group with its corresponding part of the private sector (MAEC, 2004a). However in practice, beyond all this complex appearance, it was Mohammed VI's right-hand man, Fassi Fihri, who was ultimately responsible for the inter-ministerial negotiation team. He reported directly to the King, bypassing both his theoretical superior, minister Benaissa, and the head of government, Driss Jettou, in yet another evidence of the palace's persistent control over foreign policy (*Le Journal Hebdomadaire*, 6–12 March 2004; Crombois, 2005: 221).

Seven rounds of negotiations took place between January 2003 and March 2004,[11] all carried out with discretion because of the delicate international situation at the time. The beginning of the Iraq War did not interrupt the process, but did warrant moving the second round in March 2003 to the Swiss city of Geneva – Fassi Fihri's non-attendance of this meeting being the only sign of condemnation of the U.S. invasion of the Arab country (*Le Journal Hebdomadaire*, 29 March–4 April 2003; White, 2005: 603). From the statements and speeches issued by the foreign ministry, it appears that from the outset, the overwhelming concern of the Moroccan team was to make their U.S. counterparts understand the need for the fledgling agreement to adapt to their country's 'particular features, constraints and socioeconomic realities' (MAEC, 2004a, 27 January 2004, 4 March 2004). Defending Morocco's economic interests was considered to require the establishment of transitory phases for tariff dismantling, accompanying measures to mitigate the negative effects of opening the national market and, above all, special treatment for the agricultural sector. The latter necessitated an 'approach of global development that [would not be] limited to commercial logic' (MAEC, 6 May 2003), taking account of the characteristics of the production and marketing of Moroccan agricultural products as well as living conditions in the rural world (MAEC, 10 June 2003).

Behind these Moroccan concerns lay the problem of the FTA's mixed objectives: it was difficult to successfully negotiate the specific conditions of a trade agreement which was essentially political in origin but would certainly have critical long-term consequences for this country's economy (White, 2005: 598–599). This was, at least, the assessment of independent newspapers like *Le Journal Hebdomadaire*: 'The strong desire to conclude the agreement as quickly as possible could prejudice [*biaiser*] the quality of the negotiations as economic issues are made to conform to political ones' (*Le Journal Hebdomadaire*, 11–17 January 2003). This led to a general acknowledgement of the need to listen to the specific demands of Moroccan entrepreneurs. Officially, the involvement of the private sector in the negotiation process through 'institutionalised and general' dialogue (MAEC, 2004a) on 'a regular basis and at various levels' was essential, since only thus could the 'country's genuine interests and concerns' be identified and taken into consideration (MAEC, 2004b).

In its final assessment of the FTA, the General Confederation of Moroccan Entrepreneurs (CGEM) highlighted its own contribution during three phases, i.e. prior consultations to define the Moroccan proposals, the subsequent negotiation rounds and the stage of implementation and establishment of accompanying measures. However, the CGEM leaders recognised that their influence had been substantially greater during the preliminary stage, when the confederation had a representative in each thematic working group (interview with Soundouss Fikry, 16 October 2007), than in the negotiating process proper, where it was only involved in the discussions about the textile sector (*CGEM Infos*, 12 March 2004).[12] Ex post evaluations from some of the CGEM's former leaders were more critical. Most were convinced that the FTA was largely based on a 'political' decision and that their organisation had only been included in the negotiations late in the process in order to 'limit the damage' (interview with Mouhcine Ayouche, 29 October 2007). This viewpoint coincided with that of the independent press, which maintained that the Moroccan representatives hardly ever took the positions of the private sector into account until late 2003, when there was an about-turn in the negotiating strategy due to the 'increasingly persistent discontent among Moroccan economic operators' (*Le Journal Hebdomadaire*, 6–12 December 2003).

In addition to business organisations, a fair number of Moroccan political and social actors did somehow take part in the domestic negotiation process that accompanied the development of the FTA – yet mainly in order to oppose it. Various civil society associations, spearheaded by the Moroccan Association for the Fight Against AIDS (ALCS), warned about the FTA's possible negative consequences for access to generic drugs. Some artist groups highlighted the threat to Moroccan 'identity' and 'cultural pluralism' from an avalanche of U.S. audio-visual products. Finally, Islamist and leftist groups criticised the alignment with the Bush administration's international policies implicit in signing the FTA.[13] These miscellaneous social mobilisations contrasted with the lukewarm way in which the Moroccan political parties participated in the debates on the FTA, which was attributed by some observers to their usual tendency, 'including the Islamist party (PJD), to bandwagon foreign policy decisions seen as very much the reserved area of the *Makhzen*' (Crombois, 2005: 221–222).

The outcome of the whole process was an agreement that lifted barriers for more than 95 per cent of the trade between the two countries, yet in an asymmetrical way. The opening of the Moroccan agricultural market to U.S. products – particularly grain – would take place gradually in order to safeguard a very sensitive part of the national economy. Imports were to be subject to a complex system of quotas which would be progressively expanded such that tariffs would not be fully dismantled until after a 15-year transition period. Exports to the U.S., in turn, were liberalised but subject to sanitary and phytosanitary standards (non-tariff barriers) which were not always easy to comply with. In the textile sector, export quotas for Morocco were to increase over ten years until tariffs were completely dismantled, but remained subject to strict rules of origin. As far as the service sector was concerned, the agreement eased conditions to operate in Morocco for U.S. companies related to banking, insurance, telecommunications and tourism (U.S./Morocco, 2004; Benmoussa, 2003: 42–68; Khader, 2008; MAEC, 21 April 2004). In practice, between 2006 and 2007, the first year of the FTA, total bilateral trade was to grow by more than 44 per cent, although the bulk of the increase was due to imported U.S. products (+67 per cent) and not Moroccan exports (+17 per cent). U.S. investment in Morocco, in turn, increased by 184 per cent between 2005 and 2006 (*Le Matin*, 31 March 2007; *L'Économiste*, 1 February 2008).[14]

The Moroccan negotiators declared they were satisfied with the results achieved with the FTA with regard to some of the more controversial issues on the table, which had aroused protests by civil society groups, i.e. the protection of the national agricultural sector (MAEC, 4 March 2004), the consequences of the FTA's provisions regarding intellectual property on marketing of generic drugs (MAEC, 27 January 2004, 4 March 2004) and the maintenance of subsidies and protection of national cultural industries ('cultural exception') (MAEC, 27 January 2004, 4 March 2004). Another recurring point in the foreign ministry's discourse during and after the negotiations was the absence of any incompatibility or contradiction with the Association Agreement between Morocco and the EU (MAEC, 6 May 2003, 5 June 2003). This was a response to some declarations made by EU Commissioner for Trade Pascal Lamy and French deputy minister for Foreign Trade François Loos, which revealed European suspicions about U.S. penetration into what they saw as their terrain (*Le Journal Hebdomadaire*, 18–24 January 2003).

Finally, the Moroccan authorities did not squander the opportunity to capitalise on the agreement politically. They presented it as unequivocal proof of international validation of the regime and the political and economic reforms undertaken during Mohammed VI's reign and, at the same time, a sign of the exclusive and special treatment granted to a model student by a big international power. According to Fassi Fihri: 'Officially, Morocco is seen as a reference point for other Maghreb countries in the area of economic reform and a locomotive for market economy and democratic reform in the Arab world' (MAEC, 10 July 2003). However, Morocco did not score any political points as far as the Western Sahara conflict was concerned since, unlike various legal and political EU documents, the FTA with the U.S. was not to be applied to the disputed territory under Moroccan control. This was made clear in a letter from Robert B. Zoellick, the U.S. chief negotiator, to Congressman Joseph Pitts: 'The FTA will cover trade and investment in the territory of Morocco as recognised internationally, and will not include Western Sahara'.[15]

Security cooperation in a reshaped Maghreb-Sahel region

In addition to intelligence cooperation, the BMENA initiative and the FTA, the international context following 9/11 could not fail to affect U.S.–Morocco relations in strategic and military affairs. One of the repercussions of the War on Terror was the development, for the first time, of specific U.S. security and military policies for the Maghreb region, which was regarded as increasingly connected with the neighbouring area of the Sahel (Pham, 2010). The perception of threat was particularly exacerbated by the January 2007 announcement of the creation of Al Qaeda in the Islamic Maghreb (AQIM), a local group – the result of the rebranding and name change of the Algerian Salafist Group for Preaching and Combat (GSPC) – which swore allegiance to Osama Bin Laden's organisation and was formally recognised as its branch or franchise in the area (Steinberg and Werenfels, 2007; Filiu, 2009; ICG, 2005). The multilateral response to the emergence of AQIM was a considerable increase in attention on the part of NATO to a strategically redrawn Maghreb-Sahel region (Zoubir, 2009) as well as the Strait of Gibraltar. Organising military manoeuvres and strengthening local information services in the area required intensified cooperation with the governments. This led to significant gestures like the meeting of NATO's highest authority, the North Atlantic Council, in Rabat, the capital of a non-member country, in April 2006. In 2010, NATO's Public Diplomacy Division co-organised a conference in the same city with the Moroccan foreign ministry on 'The Cooperation between Morocco and NATO at the Service of Peace and Stability in the Mediterranean' (NATO, 25 January 2010), at which representatives from Rabat called for horizontal enlargement of the Atlantic Alliance to include Sahel and Sahara countries (*World Tribune*, 4 February 2010; *Al Ousboue*, 12 February 2010).

Morocco also played the role of *good ally* within the U.S. individual military policy towards the region, which was characterised during these years by the launch of the Pan-Sahel Initiative (2002) and the Trans-Sahara Counter-Terrorism Initiative (2005) – the latter including Morocco, Algeria and Tunisia. After boosting bilateral military assistance in the framework of programmes like Anti-Terrorism Assistance (ATA) and the Terrorist Interdiction Program (TIP) (Zoubir, 2009: 993; *Maghreb Confidentiel*, 30 October 2003), in July 2004 the U.S. designated Morocco a major non-NATO ally, a category that brought advantages in financial terms and regarding weapons supplies. In the words of a senior official in the Bush administration, 'the President took this step in recognition of the close U.S.–Morocco relationship, our appreciation for Morocco's steadfast support in the global War on Terror, and for King Mohammed's role as a visionary leader in the Arab world' (*BBC News*, 4 June 2004). For the Moroccan foreign affairs minister,

> This White House initiative is also an expression of the U.S. acknowledgement of Morocco's role as a nucleus of peace and security in the region, [...] a reaffirmation of Morocco's achievements in terms of stability, serenity and calm [*quiétude*] under the leadership of HM the King.
> (MAEC, 4 June 2004)

This privileged status boosted sales of U.S. arms to Morocco, which became in 2008 the second largest recipient of U.S. weapons in the world (*Tel Quel*, 12–18 September 2009). At the end of 2007, Morocco concluded a much-discussed purchase of two fleets (24) of U.S. F-16 fighter aircrafts for $2,000 million, which was financed jointly by Saudi credit and the MCA (*Le Journal Hebdomadaire*, 22–28 September 2007, 6–12 October 2007). At the same time, domestic opposition to this military alliance became apparent during protests like the one that greeted U.S. Secretary of Defence Donald Rumsfeld on his visit to Rabat in 2006 (*Aujourd'hui Le Maroc*, 13 February 2006). The Moroccan Association for Human Rights (AMDH) organised a demonstration against a man they considered to be one of the main culprits behind the 'crimes against humanity, war crimes, mass extermination and aggression committed by American imperialism', and against 'the integration of Morocco – in the name of the fight against terrorism – into the American military and security strategy, with consequences for the security of our people and the independence of our country' (AMDH, 11 February 2006; AFP, 12 February 2006).

The moment of truth that exacerbated the dilemmas arising from Morocco's closer military alliance with the U.S. occurred in February 2007 when President Bush ordered the creation of the U.S. African Command (AFRICOM), which was aimed at covering all the countries on the continent except Egypt. Despite the careful discourse used during the presentation of the mission – described as an experiment in civil-military cooperation designed to help African countries build professional militaries and also promote development (Pham, 2008: 257) – the various African governments reacted with widespread suspicion (*Jeune Afrique*, 30 September–6 October 2007). Indeed, the U.S. army's repeated attempts to find a location for the AFRICOM headquarters on the continent were met so coolly, even in the Maghreb (*Washington Post*, 24 June 2007), that the base was maintained in Stuttgart in the end.

In the case of Morocco, the country that had been pointed out by the U.S. Congress as the most plausible choice to host AFRICOM (Congressional Research Service, 16 May 2007), calculations about the desirability of complying with U.S. aspirations involved an additional element: the U.S. sounding out coincided with the Moroccan diplomatic campaign to promote the Autonomy Plan for Western Sahara presented to the UN in April 2007. This proposal was defended in Washington as an 'appropriate response to the many security challenges being faced by the regions of North and West Africa' (MAEC, 13 February 2007). Thus, the link between the persistence of the Western Sahara conflict and the terrorist threat in the Maghreb-Sahel, which had formed part of Moroccan propaganda for several years, was reinforced within official discourse. Not surprisingly, then, different rumours during these months claimed that Morocco was bidding for the AFRICOM headquarters (*World Tribune*, 9 February 2007; *Middle East Newsline*, 9 February 2007). However, in June 2007, Morocco emphatically rejected this possibility following the examples of Algeria and Libya. The official denial arrived after the publication of a statement from the PJD parliamentary group which took for granted that the Moroccan government had made an offer to Washington in this regard: 'The Ministry of Foreign Affairs and Cooperation wishes to categorically deny this information, which is devoid of any basis. In doing so, the ministry also questions the true intentions and real motivations behind the publication of this statement' (MAEC, 16 June 2007).

Rumours and speculation abounded once again in early 2008 when the recently appointed AFRICOM commander visited Morocco in what many saw as a new 'seduction operation' aimed at the kingdom's authorities (*Le Journal Hebdomadaire*, 23–29 February 2008). Several media reports at the time maintained that an agreement was about to be signed with the U.S. to establish a shared base that would hold the AFRICOM general headquarters near the city of Tan-Tan (*Aujourd'hui Le Maroc*, 31 January 2008). In the end, once again there was no agreement. U.S. diplomats summarised the Moroccan authorities' 'caution' regarding AFRICOM this way:

> Previous interactions with [government of Morocco] officials indicate that military leaders are opposed to AFRICOM basing a headquarters element in Morocco. However, Morocco has offered to send a military liaison officer to the AFRICOM headquarters in Germany and has offered to assist U.S.-led efforts engaging with African countries.
> (U.S. Embassy in Rabat, cable 08RABAT727, 4 August 2008)

The final refusal of the Rabat authorities can be explained by the identity-based two-level game posed by the hypothetical hosting of AFRICOM headquarters in a time of rising anti-Americanism, when domestic reactions were doomed to be negative and detrimental to the regime itself. In particular, this discontent could be capitalised on by jihadist groups operating in Moroccan territory or Islamist political parties integrated into the system such as the PJD, for which some polls predicted an unprecedented electoral victory in the legislative elections of September 2007.

Lobbying in Washington over the Western Sahara issue

The rational-choice backdrop to all Moroccan foreign policy towards the U.S. was, invariably, the Western Sahara issue and Rabat's desire to obtain explicit support for its position from Washington. While the facts indicate that the U.S. stance regarding this conflict had been 'unambiguously pro-Moroccan' since 1975 (Mundy, 2006: 300), at no time had Washington formally recognised Moroccan sovereignty over the territory under its de facto control (Ouaouicha *et al.*, 2003: 83–85). In the late 1990s, growing doubts about the viability of the UN Settlement Plan led the U.S. to support UN attempts to find a political solution directly negotiated between the parties, which materialised in the Baker Plans I (2001) and II (2003) (Zoubir and Benabdallah-Gambier, 2005: 186–187). Therefore, Morocco's rejection of the Baker Plan II, which had been unexpectedly accepted by the Polisario Front and unanimously 'supported' by the Security Council (Resolution 1495), put to a test the loyalty to Rabat of the Bush administration, which was forced to qualify its position ex post. Despite initial incomprehension of Rabat's decision, U.S. Assistant Secretary of State for Near Eastern Affairs William J. Burns assured Morocco during a visit in October 2003 that his country would 'not impose a solution on Morocco or any other party' (AFP, 28 October 2003). However, not even the ostensible rapprochement between Morocco and the U.S. seen in 2004 put an end to Washington's formal neutrality and wariness on this issue, as reflected by the fact that Western Sahara territory was excluded from the FTA signed in 2004. On the other hand, the

Bush administration chose to conspicuously support the Autonomy Plan for Western Sahara presented by Rabat in 2007. The Department of State immediately described it as a 'serious and credible proposal' (AP, 11 April 2007) and a year later, the White House reaffirmed that 'autonomy under Moroccan sovereignty [was] the only viable solution for the dispute in Western Sahara' (MAP, 24 June 2008).

Morocco's permanent state of dissatisfaction with the ambiguous backing it was receiving from the U.S. regarding this quintessential *national question* explains the country's lobbying efforts in Washington and more particularly vis-à-vis the U.S. Congress, which became a crucial battlefield in the diplomatic war over Western Sahara. Despite the fact that Morocco had begun to hire the services of lobbyists and public relations professionals in the late 1970s (Kalpakian, 2006: 59–60), two decades later, the independent weekly *Le Journal* nonetheless criticised the Moroccan ambassador at the time (and later foreign minister) Mohamed Benaissa for neglecting this powerful legislative body (*Le Journal*, 30 October–5 November 1999). Similarly, under Mohammed VI, the paper argued that 'the Moroccans' weak point in Washington [continued] to be the Congress' (*Le Journal Hebdomadaire*, 7–13 December 2002).

To remedy this relatively disadvantageous situation and respond to the Polisario Front's offensives on Capitol Hill, Morocco hired Cassidy and Associates, one of the most renowned lobbying firms in Washington (*Maghreb Confidentiel*, 1 April 1999), between 1998 and 1999. The country also drew on the support of experts and political representatives with ties to the American Israel Public Affairs Committee (AIPAC), a powerful pro-Israeli pressure group, in a move that generated criticism from some national media outlets (interview with Aboubakr Jamaï, 21 February 2006). The fruit of these efforts would not be seen until after the promotional campaign for the Autonomy Plan in April 2007, when some 170 members of Congress urged President Bush to support the Moroccan initiative in a letter that underscored the risk to regional security represented by the perpetuation of the Western Sahara conflict (Solà-Martín, 2007: 404). Not surprisingly, Morocco invested nearly $3.4 million between 2007 and 2008 in lobbying firms that specialise in influencing Congress, making it the sixth largest foreign spender in this type of activity (*ProPublica*, 18 August 2009). Beyond the legislative sphere, but connected to Western Sahara, the Livingston Group organised several meetings with Moroccan leaders and U.S. lobbyists. Campaigns were also launched to denounce the supposed recruitment of young Sahrawis from Tindouf by the Cuban regime and to demand the liberation of Moroccan prisoners of war who remained in the hands of the Polisario. The latter offensive was the work of the Moroccan American Center of Policy (MACP), a platform created in 2005 under the patronage of Mohammed VI (Amar, 2009: 255–262; *Le Journal Hebdomadaire*, 21–27 May 2005, 8–14 April 2006).[16]

In late 2008 and early 2009, the network of lobbyists and 'friends' of Morocco in Washington was fully mobilised after Barack Obama won the presidential election, reflecting the general uncertainty about the new Democratic administration's position on the Western Sahara conflict (*Jeune Afrique*, 5–11 April 2009; *Al Ousboue Assahafi*, 11 December 2008). Within this context, seven members of Congress, 41 NGO representatives and sundry other U.S. public figures sent two letters to the newly arrived President urging him to support a self-determination referendum for the Sahrawi people and to extend the powers of the UN Mission for the Referendum in Western Sahara (MINURSO) to include human rights monitoring (*Al Ayam*, 13 April 2009). At the same time, by contrast, a report was published by the Potomac Institute for Policy Studies (2009), endorsed by prominent figures like former Secretary of State Madeleine Albright and Ambassador Stuart E. Eizenstat, which openly advocated for the Moroccan Autonomy Plan for Western Sahara. A mere month after this report was disseminated, 220 members of Congress signed a letter to President Obama in support of the Moroccan position (*ProPublica*, 18 August 2009).

Indeed, a relative shift was to occur in the U.S. policy towards the Western Sahara issue, but the main turning point came only four years later, with the coming into office of the second Obama administration in early 2013 (interview with Abdelwahab Maalmi, 7 June 2013). The appointment of John Kerry as secretary of state replacing Hillary Clinton, who was considered to be rather pro-Moroccan, took place shortly after Morocco's crisis with the UN provoked by its withdrawal of confidence from the Secretary-General's personal envoy Christopher Ross, which was negatively perceived in Washington. The bilateral distancing was also reinforced by the growing influence in U.S. Democratic circles of the Robert F. Kennedy Center for Justice and Human Rights, which lobbied in favour of pro-Saharawi positions. All these developments resulted in the deep crisis caused by the circulation of an unexpected U.S. draft resolution envisaging the extension of MINURSO's mandate by the Security Council to human rights monitoring. Not having been previously agreed with the other members of the Group of Friends of Western Sahara at the UN, the U.S. initiative encountered Moroccan outcry and accusations of unilateralism until it was eventually withdrawn (Fernández-Molina, 2013b). However, in order to avoid facing a similar U.S. attempt the following year, Mohammed VI had to accept unprecedented U.S. conditionality regarding human rights in Western Sahara. During his first meeting with President Obama in Washington in November 2013, he secretly committed himself to putting an end to military trials of civilians, allowing the UN High Commissioner for Human Rights to visit Western Sahara and legalising pro-independence Sahrawi associations.[17] All in all, it can be said that never before had Morocco's foreign policy role as *good U.S. ally* clashed so overtly with that of *territorial champion* – according to the perception of the Rabat authorities.

Western Sahara aside, Morocco's role as *good U.S. ally* in its more classical version continued to be recognised and cultivated by Washington, and was ratified by the launch of a U.S.–Morocco Strategic Dialogue in September 2012.[18] In practical terms, it returned to the fore in 2012–2013, when Morocco occupied a seat as a non-permanent member at the UN Security Council and became the diplomatic driving belt between Western and Arab League/Gulf governments regarding the civil conflict in Syria (Fernández-Molina, 2014: 4), and even more so since August 2014, when the U.S. started to form a coalition of allied countries to fight the compelling transnational terrorist threat posed by the self-proclaimed Islamic State of Iraq and Syria (ISIS/Daish). As late as three weeks after the U.S. official announcement that Morocco would participate in this anti-ISIS coalition, this country's foreign ministry simply informed that military and intelligence 'active support' was to be provided to the United Arab Emirates 'in their fight against terrorism and for the preservation of regional and international peace and stability' (MAEC, 28 October 2014). Just like a decade earlier during the 2003 Iraq War, the Rabat authorities opted for ambiguity as to their commitment to the emerging international alliance for fear of the domestic legitimacy – and security – costs of openly supporting another U.S.-led intervention in the Middle East. Anyway, at the end of this year U.S. appreciation of Morocco's role as *good ally* in regional security affairs seemed to be prevailing again over concerns about human rights in Western Sahara, as suggested by the fact that, in their meeting in November 2014, U.S. Vice-President Joe Biden and King Mohammed VI 'discussed more terrorism and less Sahara' (*Yabiladi*, 20 November 2014; White House, 19 November 2014).

All in all, this chapter has analysed Morocco's role as *good U.S. ally* as the only prominent foreign policy role taken on by this country that does not enjoy domestic consensus. The identity-based dilemmas it entails were multiplied in the aftermath of the 9/11 attacks and the U.S. declaration of War on Terror. Morocco's early commitment to the latter resulted in a manifest strengthening of its bilateral relations with the U.S. In 2004, Rabat was chosen to host the first edition of the Forum for the Future, in the framework of the G-8's BMENA initiative, Morocco was designated major non-NATO U.S. ally and a highly 'political' bilateral Free Trade Agreement was signed between the two countries. The domestic costs that this rapprochement brought about were accepted by the Rabat authorities as part of a rational-choice calculation which prioritised potential benefits regarding U.S. support in the Western Sahara conflict, although the latter has never been fully achieved to the extent expected.

Notes

1 See also *Le Journal Hebdomadaire* (13–19 October 2001).
2 The same arguments were repeated in another speech by Mohammed VI (Tangier, 30 July 2002).
3 A branch of the Arab Nationalist Congress, which is a non-governmental pan-Arab forum for political parties and associations headquartered in Beirut.
4 The demonstration was organised by the CEMACOFA in conjunction with the National Action Committee in Support of Iraq and Palestine.
5 Morocco hosted the Forum for the Future again in November 2009 in Marrakesh (U.S. Embassy in Rabat, cable 09RABAT952, 4 December 2009).
6 See http://carnegieendowment.org/files/mccfactsheet1.pdf (accessed on 31 January 2015).
7 See www.mcc.gov/pages/countries/program/morocco-compact (accessed on 31 May 2012).

8 In another vein, Morocco and the U.S. had also signed a Trade and Investment Framework Agreement (TIFA) in 1995, which was seen as a stepping stone to the FTA.
9 See also Zoellick's article in *The New York Times* (12 June 2004).
10 In addition, Morocco's lobbying efforts resulted in a letter of support for the FTA signed by 55 U.S. members of Congress, as well as the creation of the U.S.–Morocco FTA Business Coalition.
11 Rounds were held in Washington (January 2003), Geneva (March), Rabat (June), Washington (July), Rabat (October), Washington (January 2004) and Washington (February–March).
12 The CGEM President at the time, Hassan Chami (2000–2006), said that he was extremely satisfied because 'never before [had] business actors been so closely involved in an agreement process'. 'We were partners in our own right' (*Tel Quel*, 13–19 March 2004).
13 The *Bilaterals.org* webpage (www.bilaterals.org, accessed on 31 May 2012) on Morocco contains a large number of documents related to these debates and protests.
14 For an assessment of the economic consequences of the FTA during the first years of its implementation, see Hufbauer and Brunel (2009). For more long-term data concerning the period 2006–2014, see *Hespress* (25 February 2015).
15 Available at www.bilaterals.org/IMG/pdf/0407191-ustr-moroccoFTA.pdf (accessed on 31 January 2015).
16 The network of pro-Moroccan organisations established in the U.S. also included the American Moroccan Institute, Friends of Morocco, Washington Moroccan Club, Moroccan American Cultural Center and the Moroccan American Community Center (*Maghreb Confidentiel*, 23 July 2009).
17 MAEC (2014) Fiche USA-UK/Projet de lettre du MAEC au Roi du Maroc, Rabat, 3 February, leaked document available at www.arso.org/Coleman/Fiche%20usa-uk.pdf (accessed on 20 December 2014).
18 According to the memorandum of understanding signed by both countries, the U.S.–Morocco Strategic Dialogue would involve regular meetings of four bilateral working groups on political, economic, security and educational and cultural issues, as well as annual high-level summits to be held alternately in Rabat and Washington D.C. (U.S./Morocco, 2012).

Conclusions

Underneath its placid and clear surface, its everlasting commonplaces and the constant feeling of déjà vu, the foreign policy of Morocco is reluctant to reveal its secrets. Whilst this poses problems for the very accumulation of raw data and the reconstruction of factual accounts, it makes it even harder to develop a theoretically informed study, drawing on some of the approaches to Foreign Policy Analysis (FPA). Nevertheless, assuming some imbalances between the initial theoretical ambitions and the harsh reality of the empirical research process, this book has shed some light on the overall construction of Morocco's place in the world and proverbial 'extraversion' (Bayart, 2000) since the accession of King Mohammed VI to the throne and the turn of the millennium, placing the emphasis on the *agency* of the Rabat authorities and questioning the extent to which their active international performance has been successful in terms of their stated top objectives as well as the legitimation of the incumbent regime.

Mohammed VI received from Hassan II a decidedly rich heritage in the realm of foreign policy, which included a certain disproportion between the modest size of the country and the activism deployed in order to assert itself as a 'relational power', as well as a duality in the hierarchy of objectives due to the unresolved dichotomy between realist/geopolitical/territorial and liberal/pragmatic/economistic approaches to 'national interest'. On this basis, the main discernible and stable historical outlines of Moroccan foreign policy crystallised over time in the stated or unstated roles of *champion of national territorial integrity*, *model student of the European Union (EU)*, *good son* of France, *good neighbour* of Spain and *good ally* of the United States and the 'West', as the same time as *pan-Islamic leader*. In the first two decades of the twenty-first century, this composite identity-based and normative heritage had to face new constraints and particularly intricate and challenging circumstances on regional and international level. The dynamics of change originating from the 1990s – the end of the Cold War and the accelerated processes of economic and communicational globalisation – were now coupled by the earthquake caused by the 9/11 attacks, and the subsequent U.S. declaration of War on Terror. The Arab regional system entered a new phase following the destabilisation caused by the 2003 Iraq war, the (theoretical) increase in international pressures for the reform and democratisation of its political regimes, the advance of economic globalisation and the emergence of 'new media' such as the internet and pan-Arab satellite television. A second period of regional turbulence was unleashed in 2011 by the so-called Arab Spring, which catalysed many of the tensions created by the previous developments, jeopardising authoritarian resilience across various Arab countries, but also bringing about new pressing security threats (civil conflicts, terrorism), instability and counterrevolutionary dynamics.

Overall, discontinuity in Moroccan foreign policy over the 1999–2014 period was much greater as far as regional and international constraints were concerned than within this country's domestic sphere – and, until 2011, the Maghrebi subregional environment. At home, there were no structural changes in a political system marked by the hegemony of a historically stable monarchy and a relative liberalisation of its authoritarianism from the 1990s onwards, although the Rabat authorities showed at all times a remarkable ductility and capacity for adaptation to internal and external circumstances and expectations. Weighing up all of its determinants, it can be concluded that the driving forces behind the changes in the foreign policy of this state over these years have generally been more exogenous than endogenous.

Upon his accession to the throne, Mohammed VI announced some changes in the priorities and implementation of Moroccan foreign policy, which were publicised in two key royal speeches delivered in April 2000 and August 2002. More specifically, the two major declared innovations of the new reign were the paying of greater attention to the economic dimension of foreign policy and reform of the foreign ministry and service. The interest in the so-called *economic diplomacy* fitted in perfectly with the rising technocratic leanings of the new Moroccan political elite. Externally, this resulted in an apparently depoliticised, pragmatic and economistic foreign policy discourse, which was applied in varying forms to the kingdom's relations with the EU, the Maghreb, the Middle East and Gulf Arab countries, as well as the proclaimed *new African policy*. Meanwhile, plans for the reform and modernisation (*mise à niveau*) of Moroccan 'diplomacy' launched in August 2002, in apparent response to mounting dissatisfaction with the implementation of this foreign policy, resulted in several initiatives to improve the training of foreign ministry officials and a quite extensive renewal of the ambassador corps, although they did not prevent arbitrariness and patronage from continuing to determine access to the diplomatic career.

The overview offered in this book of Moroccan foreign policy between 1999 and 2014 confirms one of the intuitions posed at the beginning of the research process: the prevalence of almost absolute continuity with the final years of Hassan II's reign and, more broadly, the historical guidelines established after the country gained independence. Continuity can be detected in both the decision-making processes and the resulting foreign policy output of behaviour. As far as decision-making is concerned, as in the Moroccan political system overall, there have been movements at sub-systemic level, or regime changes without democratisation (Albrecht and Schlumberger, 2004), of mainly three types: elite change – a renewal of the formal and informal circles of the King's advisors, the promotion to these and other influential positions of a new generation of technocrats; co-optation – the incorporation into the diplomatic corps of figures from the political parties of the historical opposition, academia and civil society, as well as unionist Sahrawis; and institution building – the creation and upgrading of consultative councils endowed with significant functions of parallel and public diplomacy. However, before all of this, and irrespective of the personality of each king, a high degree of centralisation, opacity, royal supremacy and neopatrimonial practices have continued to characterise decision-making.

Among the subordinate institutional actors placed outside the direct control of the palace, the successive Moroccan governments of these years have displayed fewer aspirations for autonomy and less willingness to assert their powers in the realm of foreign policy, which never ceased to be regarded as part of the *reserved domain* of the monarchy. Evidence of this was the anomalous hierarchical duality or duumvirate at the head of the Ministry of Foreign Affairs and Cooperation in 1999–2007 and 2012–2013. On a more peripheral level, there were no substantial changes in the contribution of Moroccan political parties to foreign policymaking, which contrasted with the greater involvement of politically significant civil society actors such as the employers' organisation CGEM, certain human rights associations and the less institutionalised fraction of the Islamist movement. In any case, illustrative episodes such as the international campaign to promote the Autonomy Plan for Western Sahara (2007), the Perejil crisis with Spain (2002) and the negotiations concerning the Free Trade Agreement with the U.S. (2004) provide ample evidence of the real *who is who* of Moroccan foreign policy, behind the institutional façade, demonstrating the disproportionate influence of the king's closest associates, the atypical diplomatic facet of the external intelligence agency DGED, the impotence or marginalisation of the government in moments of crisis and the duumvirate within the foreign ministry.

As regards foreign policy behaviour, continuity can be explained in structuralist terms, as an inevitable consequence of the narrow room for manoeuvre left to this dependent state by constraints from the international and regional environment. However, confining the analysis to this basic acknowledgment would amount to some kind of determinism and undermine Morocco's own *agency*. In fact, this continuity has also been a deliberate and endogenous choice of the Rabat authorities, resulting from rational and strategic calculation, from adherence to previously existing identity-related *norms* for reasons of 'self-image' and 'self-preservation' (Barnett, 1998: 11–12), or most often from a mix of both. First, continuity is apparent in the persistence of the two competing realist and liberal approaches upon which Morocco's 'national interest' has been dichotomously constructed for decades, that is, the tension between this country's nationalist soul and pro-European soul – but also in the deep-rooted perception of geopolitical fragility (El Houdaïgui, 2003b) which, where objectives clash, often tips the balance in favour of territory-related goals. Second, continuity has prevailed in the foreign policy roles that Mohammed VI's Morocco has opted to play on the international scene – *territorial champion, model student of the EU, good ally of the U.S.*, etc. – all of which actually dated from the previous reign. Third, there has been continuity as well, in relation to the 1990s, in the three overriding objectives pursued, i.e. the international recognition and *legalisation* of Morocco's control over Western Sahara, the continuous strengthening and preservation of privileged bilateral relations with the EU, and the international promotion of the 'democratising' image of this country.

From a liberal/pluralistic perspective which places the focus on the political games and input of domestic actors, the main conclusion that can be drawn, besides the hierarchical structure of decision-making, is that the internal use of foreign policy is not attributable solely to the monarchy. From the centre to the periphery of the decision-making system, and regardless of their uneven capacity for influence, all players resort to this self-interested behaviour on occasion with various objectives. The possible goals include improving or restoring the position of the actor concerned within the national political scene; publicly displaying political strength and mobilisation capacity; increasing this capacity for mobilisation and recruitment; and opposing or criticising the Moroccan regime – by highlighting the contradictions between its foreign policy behaviour and the *norms* which it itself invokes. While the first objective is more easily achieved by capitalising on consensual and legitimation-prone issues such as the Western Sahara question, the latter three largely correspond to areas that bring about domestic dissent and sometimes public protest, such as relations with the U.S. and the Middle East. The domestic actors that tend to engage in this open criticism of official foreign policy stances are actually the same as those which constitute the genuine opposition to the regime – and not only to the government – and demand an authentic democratic constitutional reform, i.e. small critical leftist parties and related trade unions, AMDH, Al Adl wal Ihsan and independent press. Therefore, to some extent it can be argued that movements of solidarity with Arab/Islamic causes such as Palestine and Iraq worked for years as a breeding ground for opposition networking and coalition-building among actors of different ideological leanings (critical secular left and Islamists), which were to become the main supporters of the protests led by the 20 February Movement in 2011 (Fernández-Molina, 2011b: 436).

From the viewpoint of 'domesticated' constructivism, the book's most relevant finding concerns the production and circulation of foreign policy discourses from the centre to the periphery of the Moroccan decision-making system. The arguments and slogans – often empty signifiers – which originate from or are promoted by the core, e.g. 'economic diplomacy', 'advanced status', 'more than association, less than accession' and 'new African policy', are parroted uncritically by most domestic actors, some of whom at times even claim authorship. The only relevant examples of ideas to have made headway in the opposite direction, from the periphery to the centre, are those of the *third way* for Western Sahara, which was intensely promoted in the late 1990s by pro-democracy critical sectors and the independent press, and the 'cost of non-Maghreb', which was previously discussed in academia. Still, despite the repetitive tenor, it is possible to classify the Moroccan foreign policy discourses that complement or stray somehow from the mainstream official discourse formulated by the monarchy and the foreign ministry.

The first of them is the technocratic semiofficial discourse, which has been on the rise since Mohammed VI's accession to the throne and become virtually assimilated into the monarchy's official discourse. Its main features are the (neoliberal) economistic and pragmatic thrust, the emphasis on *economic diplomacy* and the priority granted to Morocco's privileged relations with the EU, which are presented in their most depoliticised version. This discourse is also applied with functionalist reminiscences to lowly integrated regional spaces such as the Maghreb – with the idea of the *cost of non-Maghreb* – and the Arab world, where economic cooperation is presented as a promising way of overcoming entrenched ideological constraints and political tensions, as well as areas with which Morocco is trying to diversify its economic relations, such as sub-Saharan Africa and Latin America. Another hallmark is a relatively more conciliatory and cooperative stance on relations with neighbouring Spain. The voices that disseminate these arguments are located in a large part of the state administration and the foreign ministry, relevant sectors of the major political parties and, from civil society, the CGEM, which was during these years formally associated with the making and implementation of Moroccan foreign economic policy.

Second, the nationalistic semiofficial discourse is voiced by actors integrated into the institutional political game who continue to greatly cherish the nationalistic ideological *norms* which constrain foreign policy behaviour, such as territorial integrity and the 'Moroccanity' of Western Sahara, up to the point of occasionally decrying the Moroccan authorities for breaching them – for instance, during the official endorsement of the *third way* for Western Sahara in 2000. Its main proponents are parties from the historical opposition such as the Istiqlal Party (PI). The influence of these *norms* does not seem residual in any sense. Foreign policy serves as the last bastion against the tendency towards the 'exhaustion of political nationalisms created for independences' (Stora, 2002: 113). Furthermore, nationalism provides the main locus for intersection between the foreign policy discourses of most of the Moroccan political forces and is a necessary condition for the full inclusion and participation in the national political system – as the experience of the Islamist PJD as a newcomer demonstrates.

Third, the Islamist semiofficial discourse corresponds precisely to the mainstream and 'moderate' Islamists of the PJD, a party which joined the electoral and parliamentary game in the late 1990s and whose priority at this stage was to gain ground and consolidate its own political normalisation, both inside and outside Morocco's borders. Therefore, this party chose not to deviate one inch from the nationalistic consensus on the Western Sahara issue and relations with Algeria while, at the same time, making continuous professions of pro-European faith. The only significant difference with regard to the official foreign policy guidelines, almost as an ideological imperative, concerned stances on Middle East conflicts. By contrast, positions on bilateral relations with the U.S. – especially the Free Trade Agreement – have been characterised by openness and pragmatism, enabling party representatives to maintain smooth relations with U.S. diplomats.

Fourth, a leftist critical discourse has been maintained during this period by small critical socialist and Marxist parties, the AMDH and a part of the dwindling independent press, that is, the secular component of the genuine opposition to the regime. This discourse highlights the dysfunctional aspects of Moroccan foreign policy, its design and implementation, linking them to the democratic deficit in decision-making and the Moroccan political system as a whole. Whilst being critical of U.S. action in the region and bilateral relations with Rabat, it stands out more for decrying the reinforcement of the status quo and the scant contribution to Morocco's democratic transformation made by the EU and EU member states such as France and Spain. With regard to Algeria and the Maghreb, this discourse supports convergence efforts by civil society and democratic actors, and the possibility for 'reconciliation from below'. However, these domestic actors' relationships with *norms* related to territorial nationalism and positions on the Western Sahara conflict have continued to be problematic and generated deep internal divisions.

Fifth, the Islamist critical discourse, mainly represented by Al Adl wal Ihsan, is the furthest from official discourse and the consensus prevailing in the national political scene, although it generally maintains rather pragmatic positions. This non-institutionalised Islamist organisation coincides with the PJD in combining the centrality of 'Muslim issues' with an interest in asserting itself as a partner for the EU and the U.S. At the same time, it shares with secular leftist critics the denunciation of the undemocratic nature of the Moroccan regime and its foreign policy, as well as the influence of anti-imperialist or anti-globalisation approaches. The issue of Western Sahara is maintained in the background, with Al Adl decrying official 'chauvinism' whilst not commenting on the substance of the conflict.

As regards the interaction between foreign policy and domestic politics, Morocco appears to be placed in an intermediate position along the continuum of foreign policy 'decision regimes' imagined by Charles W. Kegley. It is one of those

> States that embrace multiple objectives, many of which are incompatible and none of which so overrides the others that any single set gains dominance. Nonetheless, this situation does not preclude the possibility that consensus about norms may emerge with respect to particular policy sectors or selected issues.
>
> (Hermann *et al.*, 1987: 257)

The empirical findings in this book to some extent play down the initial hypothetical distinction between consensual and legitimising foreign policy areas (territory-related issues, neighbourhood relationships and relations with the EU) on the one hand and dissent-prone foreign policy areas (relations with the U.S. and the Middle East) on the other. At the very least, the divide between these two categories does not seem to be either absolute or static in practice. The boundaries of national consensus(es) vary, as they can be enlarged or reduced depending on the domestic, regional and international political circumstances.

Returning to the initial hypotheses on the *functionality* of Moroccan foreign policy in terms of the legitimation of the regime, it has been confirmed that the exploitation of nationalist *norms* and discourses prevailing within national political culture still favours consensus among various political actors, and that the Western Sahara issue continues to be a necessary condition for domestic political stability. That said, it seems highly doubtful that this *national question* is still a sufficient condition for the preservation of the regime's legitimacy and that it can enable the Rabat authorities to achieve widespread and effective 'national' mobilisation. As argued by Ahmed Benchemsi, from a domestic viewpoint, the major lesson of the 'Chris Coleman' affair in late 2014 was to highlight 'the extent to which the Moroccans are losing interest in the Sahara issue' (*Le Monde*, 2 January 2015). Meanwhile, Morocco's pro-European orientation and role as *model student of the EU* appears to be enjoying a broad domestic consensus and a low degree of contestation horizontally (among different political elites) and even – although this is more difficult to determine – vertically (between leaders and public opinion). The absence of significant challengers is certainly favoured by the technocratic and depoliticised discourse which surrounds Morocco–EU relations, enabling internal dissent to be avoided and a low-risk strategy of 'accommodation' (Hagan, 1995: 128–132) to be followed.

On the other hand however, with regard to the dissent-prone foreign policy areas, the tensions between the demands of Morocco's 'pro-Western' alignment and concessions to pro-democracy and Islamist sensibilities do not seem to have been as compelling and difficult to manage as was hypothesised at the beginning. The domestic dysfunctionality and legitimacy costs of foreign policy towards the U.S. or the Middle East are to be found primarily in episodes of crisis and intense politicisation, which ultimately do not involve a lasting threat to the regime. Nevertheless, the widely perceived Moroccan 'withdrawal' from the Arab scene and mediation in the Middle East conflict under Mohammed VI, in comparison with the Hassan II era, may have arisen due to an increase in domestic constraints and the costs of any controversial action or stance, coupled with the dwindling room of manoeuvre resulting from Rabat's unconditional alignment with U.S. policies, especially during the administration of George W. Bush (Fernández-Molina, 2014: 4–6). The areas of Moroccan foreign policy that have not been addressed in this book, i.e. relations with the Middle East and sub-Sahara Africa, were not certainly among the kingdom's top strategic priorities over the period 1999–2014, even though they occupied a significant position in the discursive sphere due to powerful identity-based *norms* that multiplied their domestic impact – in the former case – and the official promotion of a so-called *new African policy*.

One final reflection concerns the assessment of recent Moroccan foreign policy in terms of success of failure. The answer is mitigated as far as Rabat's stated top three objectives are concerned. Success has been noteworthy in relations with the EU and the international promotion of the 'democratising' image of this country. As a result of Morocco's superficial but effective international socialisation, the former relationship has been reinforced and recognised as being differentiated and special at the bilateral level, as was enshrined by the Advanced Status in 2008. The latter policy has enabled the Rabat authorities to adapt effectively to European and U.S. expectations in the post-Arab Spring context, and even to emerge internationally reinforced – externally validated – from this crucial test. Other additional indications of the success of Moroccan foreign policy were the election of this country as a non-permanent member of the UN Security Council for 2012–2013 and, in another vein, the large international indifference and silence regarding the 'Chris Coleman' scandal in 2014:

> Morocco has proved to be weak because its system of government communication and the emails of its secret agents have been massively hacked for months, perhaps years. Morocco is strong because it has managed to prevent anybody from talking about this, whilst embassies and foreign ministries which deal with Rabat are on the alert for what Chris Coleman posts at any time.
> (Ignacio Cembrero in *Orilla Sur*, 17 November 2014; *Tel Quel*, 1 December 2014)

By contrast, Moroccan foreign policy has failed to achieve full international recognition and *legalisation* of this county's control over Western Sahara, which is precisely the foreign policy area that arises from the most powerful *norm*, that is *territorial integrity*, and which is more inextricably linked to the regime's domestic legitimacy. It could even be claimed that it is the very compelling force of this *norm* that prevents the Rabat authorities from straying from the established path, sorting out their own contradictions and adopting a more flexible and pragmatic behaviour in order to find a solution to the conflict: 'The "national cause" remains more than ever the main determinant of our diplomacy, at the risk of becoming its Achilles heel' (*Tel Quel*, 23 January 2015).

References

Books, articles, reports and working papers

Abouddahab, Z. (2006) La politique étrangère du Maroc. Diagnostic actuel et scénarios d'avenir, in: S. Zerhouni (ed.) *L'avenir se discute: Débats sur les scénarios du Maroc à l'horizon 2025* (Rabat: FES), pp. 57–78.

Abouddahab, R. (2010a) L'immigration à l'aune du dialogue des civilisations et des cultures. Une lecture marocaine, in: CEI (ed.) *Une décennie de réformes au Maroc (1999–2009)* (Paris: Karthala), pp. 365–390.

Abouddahab, Z. (2010b) Le redéploiement de la politique commerciale du Maroc. Multilatéralisme et régionalisme, in: CEI (ed.) *Une décennie de réformes au Maroc (1999–2009)* (Paris: Karthala), pp. 391–406.

Addi, L. (2001) La perception des attentats du 11 septembre dans le monde arabe et musulman, *Confluences Méditerranées*, 40, pp. 165–169.

Adler, E. (2002) Constructivism and International Relations, in: W. Carlsnaes, T. Risse and B.A. Simmons (eds) *Handbook of International Relations* (London: Sage), pp. 95–118.

Adler, E. and P. Greve (2009) When Security Community Meets Balance of Power: Overlapping Regional Mechanisms of Security Governance, *Review of International Studies*, 35(1), pp. 59–84.

Adler, E., F. Bicchi, B. Crawford and R.A. del Sarto (eds) (2006) *The Convergence of Civilizations: Constructing a Mediterranean Region* (Toronto: University of Toronto Press).

Affaya, N. and D. Guerraoui (2005) *La imagen de España en Marruecos* (Barcelona: CIDOB).

Aggestam, L. (2006) Role Theory and European Foreign Policy: A Framework for Analysis, in: O. Elgström and M. Smith (eds) *The European Union's Roles in International Politics: Concepts and Analysis* (Abingdon, UK and New York: Routledge), pp. 11–29.

Al Khouri, R. (2008) *EU and U.S. Free Trade Agreements in the Middle East and North Africa* (Washington, DC: Carnegie Endowment for International Peace).

Al-Alkim, H.H. (2011) *Dynamics of Arab Foreign Policy-Making in the Twenty-First Century: Domestic Constraints and External Challenges* (London: Saqi).

Alami M'chichi, H., B. Hamdouch and M. Lahlou (2005) *Le Maroc et les migrations* (Rabat: FES).

Albrecht, H. and O. Schlumberger (2004) 'Waiting for Godot': Regime Change without Democratization in the Middle East, *International Political Science Review*, 25(4), pp. 371–392.

Amar, A. (2009) *Mohammed VI. Le grand malentendu* (Paris: Calmann-Lévy).
Amirah, H. and R. Youngs (eds) (2005) *The Euro-Mediterranean Partnership: Assessing the First Decade* (Madrid: Real Instituto Elcano/FRIDE).
Ammor, F.M. (2005) Morocco's Perspectives towards the EMP, in: H. Amirah and R. Youngs (eds) *The Euro-Mediterranean Partnership: Assessing the First Decade* (Madrid: Real Instituto Elcano/FRIDE), pp. 149–156.
Assouguem, D. (2001) *Migrations et droits de l'homme dans les relations euro-marocaines*, PhD thesis, Université Hassan II Casablanca.
Attinà, F. (2003) The Euro-Mediterranean Partnership Assessed: The Realist and Liberal Views, *European Foreign Affairs Review*, 8(2), pp. 181–199.
Baghzouz, A. (2007) La compétition transatlantique face à l'enjeu maghrébin, in: *L'Année du Maghreb 2005–2006* (Paris: CNRS), pp. 585–607.
Baraka, N. (2007) El apoyo europeo a las reformas. Clave del éxito de la transición en Marruecos, in: A. Fernández-Ardavín and M. Goded (eds) *Europa y Marruecos. Diez años del Proceso de Barcelona* (Madrid: Biblioteca Nueva/IDEE), pp. 21–44.
Barany, Z. (2013) Unrest and State Response in Arab Monarchies, *Mediterranean Quarterly*, 24(2), pp. 5–38.
Barari, H.A. (2015) The Persistence of Autocracy: Jordan, Morocco and the Gulf, *Middle East Critique*, 24(1), pp. 99–111.
Barbé, E. and A. Herranz-Surrallés (eds) (2012) *The Challenge of Differentiation in Euro-Mediterranean Relations* (Abingdon, UK and New York: Routledge).
Barbé, E., L. Mestres and E. Soler (2007) La política mediterránea de España. Entre el Proceso de Barcelona y la Política Europea de Vecindad, *Revista CIDOB d'Afers Internacionals*, 79–80, pp. 35–51.
Barnett, M.N. (1998) *Dialogues in Arab Politics: Negotiations in Regional Order* (New York: Columbia University Press).
Barre, A. (1988) *Les relations maroco-africaines 1972–1987. Enjeux politiques et coopération*, thesis, Université Mohammed V Rabat.
Barreñada, I. (2012) Asociacionismo y cuestión nacional en el Sáhara Occidental, *Revista de Estudios Internacionales Mediterráneos*, 13.
Bauchard, D. (2008) L'Union pour la Méditerranée. Un défi européen, *Politique étrangère*, 73(1), pp. 51–64.
Bayart, J.-F. (1985) L'énonciation du politique, *Revue Française de Science Politique*, 35(3), pp. 343–373.
Bayart, J.-F. (2000) Africa in the World: A History of Extraversion, *African Affairs*, 99, pp. 217–267.
Beau, N. and C. Graciet (2007) *Quand le Maroc sera islamiste* (2nd edn) (Paris: La Découverte).
Behr, T. (2012) After the Revolution: The EU and the Arab Transition (Paris: Notre Europe).
Behr, T. and T. Tiilikainen (eds) (2015) *Northern Europe and the Making of the EU's Mediterranean and Middle East Policies* (Farnham and Burlington: Ashgate).
Belalami, M. (2006) *Contribution à l'étude de la diplomatie économique du Maroc*, thesis, Université Hassan II Casablanca.
Belgourch, A. (2001) *Les politiques étrangères maghrébines: 1962–1992. Spécificités des trajectoires nationales et divergences des pratiques*, thesis, Université Cadi Ayyad Marrakesh.
Belguendouz, A. (2002) *L'ahrig du Maroc, l'Espagne et l'UE. Plus d'Europe ... sécuritaire* (Kenitra: Boukili).

Belguendouz, A. (2006a) Le traitement institutionnel de la relation entre les Marocains résidant à l'étranger et le Maroc (Florence: EUI/RSCAS).
Belguendouz, A. (2006b) UE-Maroc. L'obsession de la réadmission, *Afkar/Idées*, 9, pp. 62–65.
Belguendouz, A. (2009) Le Conseil de la communauté marocaine à l'étranger. Une nouvelle institution en débat (Florence: EUI/RSCAS).
Belhaj, A. (2009) *La dimension islamique dans la politique étrangère du Maroc. Déterminants, acteurs, orientations* (Louvain: Presses Universitaires de Louvain).
Ben El Hassan Alaoui, M. (1994) *La coopération entre l'Union européenne et les pays du Maghreb* (Paris: Nathan).
Ben El Hassan Alaoui, M. (1999) Le Maroc et l'Union européenne à l'aube du XXIe siècle, *Panoramiques*, 41, pp. 208–215.
Ben El Hassan Alaoui, M. and M.R. Chraïbi (1985) *Al-Ittihad al-'Arabi al-Afriqi wa stratiyiya at-ta'amul ad-dawli li-l-Mamlaka al-Magribiya* (Rabat: Imprimerie Royale).
Benali, A. (1999) Bye bye le français? Demain, l'anglo-américain? *Panoramiques*, 41, pp. 175–181.
Benaomari, M. (1995) *Essai sur quelques déterminants de la politique étrangère marocaine*, thesis, Université Mohammed V Rabat.
Benchemsi, A. (2012) Morocco: Outfoxing the Opposition, *Journal of Democracy*, 23(1), pp. 57–69.
Bencherif, Y. (2003) The Impact of Foreign Media on Moroccan Foreign Relations: The Case of 'The Gilles Perrault Affair' (Ilfrane: Al Akhawayn University).
Bendourou, O., R. El Mossadeq and M. Madani (eds) (2014) *La nouvelle Constitution marocaine à l'épreuve de la pratique* (Casablanca: FES/La Croisée des Chemins).
Benjelloun, M.O. (2002) *Projet national et identité au Maroc. Essai d'anthropologie politique* (Casablanca/Paris: Eddif/L'Harmattan).
Benjelloun, T. (1991) *Visages de la diplomatie marocaine depuis 1844* (Casablanca: Eddif).
Benmoussa, B. (2003) *Accord de libre échange entre les États-Unis d'Amérique et le Royaume du Maroc*, thesis, Université Hassan II Casablanca.
Bennafla, K. (2013) Illusion cartographique au Nord, barrière de sable à l'Est. Les frontières mouvantes du Sahara occidental, *L'Espace Politique*, 20, https://espacepolitique.revues.org/2644.
Bennani-Chraïbi, M. (2008) Les conflits du Moyen-Orient au miroir des 'communautés imaginées'. La 'rue arabe' existe-t-elle? Le cas du Maroc, *A contrario*, 5(2), pp. 147–156.
Bennani-Chraïbi, M. (2010) Quand négocier l'ouverture du terrain c'est déjà enquêter, *Revue internationale de politique comparée*, 17(4), pp. 93–108.
Bennis, S. (2008) *Les relations politiques, économiques et culturelles entre le Maroc et l'Espagne (1956–2005)* (Rabat: Confluence).
Bensaad, A. (2006) De l'espace euro-maghrébin à l'espace euroafricain. Le Sahara comme nouvelle jonction intercontinentale, in: *L'Année du Maghreb 2004* (Paris: CNRS), pp. 83–100.
Berramdane, A. (1987) *Le Maroc et l'Occident (1800–1974)* (Paris: Karthala).
Berramdane, A. (1992) *Le Sahara occidental, enjeu maghrébin* (Paris: Karthala).
Bicchi, F. (2007) *European Foreign Policy Making toward the Mediterranean* (New York: Palgrave).
Bicchi, F. (2014) The Politics of Foreign Aid and the European Neighbourhood Policy Post-Arab Spring: 'More for More' or Less of the Same?, *Mediterranean Politics*, 19(3), pp. 318–332.

Bicchi, F. and R. Gillespie (eds) (2012) *The Union for the Mediterranean* (Abingdon, UK and New York: Routledge).
Biscop, S., R. Balfour and M. Emerson (2012) *An Arab Springboard for EU Foreign Policy?* (Brussels and Ghent: Egmont/Academia Press).
Boukhars, A. (2012) *Simmering Discontent in the Western Sahara* (Washington, DC: Carnegie Endowment for International Peace).
Boukhars, A. and J. Roussellier (eds) (2013) *Perspectives on Western Sahara: Myths, Nationalisms, and Geopolitics* (Lanham: Rowman & Littlefield).
Bouqentar, H. (2002) *Al-siyasa al-kharijiya al-magribiya. Al-fa'alun wa-l-tafa'alat* (Rabat: Babel).
Bouqentar, H. (2010) La politique étrangère marocaine. Un changement dans la continuité, in: CEI (ed.) *Une décennie de réformes au Maroc (1999–2009)* (Paris: Karthala), pp. 325–342.
Bouqentar, H. (2014) *Al-siyasa al-kharijiya al-magribiya 2000–2013* (Rabat: REMALD).
Boussaid, M. (1990) *Les relations entre le Maroc et l'Espagne de l'indépendance à 1990*, thesis, Université Mohammed V Rabat.
Braveboy-Wagner, J.A. (ed.) (2003) *The Foreign Policies of the Global South: Rethinking Conceptual Frameworks* (Boulder and London: Lynne Rienner).
Bremberg, N. (2007) Between a Rock and a Hard Place: Euro-Mediterranean Security Revisited, *Mediterranean Politics*, 12(1), pp. 1–16.
Bremberg, N. (2012) *Exploring the Dynamics of Security Community-Building in the Post-Cold War Era: Spain, Morocco and the European Union* (Stockholm: Stockholm University).
Brouksy, O. (2008) Redefining the Sahrawi Political Identity, in: *Mediterranean Yearbook 2007* (Barcelona: IEMed/CIDOB), pp. 161–164.
Brouksy, O. (2014) *Mohammed VI derrière les masques. Le fils de 'notre ami'* (Paris: Nouveau Monde).
Brown, L.C. (ed.) (2001) *Diplomacy in the Middle East: The International Relations of Regional and Outside Powers* (London and New York: I.B. Tauris).
Budde, D. and M. Großklaus (2014) Talking Power: The EU's Soft Steering Modes in the Neighbourhood Policy, paper presented at the 4th EUIA Conference, Brussels.
Buzan, B. (1991) *People, States and Fear: An Agenda for International Security Studies in the Post-Cold War Era* (2nd edn) (Hemel Hempstead: Harvester Wheatsheaf).
Bynander, F. and S. Guzzini (eds) (2013) *Rethinking Foreign Policy* (Abingdon, UK and New York: Routledge).
Calleya, S.C. (2006) The Euro-Mediterranean Partnership and Sub-Regionalism: A Case of Region-Building? In: E. Adler, F. Bicchi, B. Crawford and R.A. del Sarto (eds) *The Convergence of Civilizations: Constructing a Mediterranean Region* (Toronto: University of Toronto Press), pp. 109–133.
Callies de Salies, B. (2003) Sahara occidental. L'enlisement du plan de paix, *Confluences Méditerranée*, 45, pp. 165–170.
Cammett, M. (2007) Business–Government Relations and Industrial Change: The Politics of Upgrading in Morocco and Tunisia, *World Development*, 35(11), pp. 1889–1903.
Cantir, C. and J. Kaarbo (2012) Contested Roles and Domestic Politics: Reflections on Role Theory in Foreign Policy Analysis and IR Theory, *Foreign Policy Analysis*, 8(1), pp. 5–24.
Cantir, C. and J. Kaarbo (2013) Role Conflict in Recent Wars: Danish and Dutch Debates over Iraq and Afghanistan, *Cooperation and Conflict*, 48(4), pp. 465–483.

224 References

Capella, R. (2011) Human Rights: An Obstacle to Peace in the Western Sahara? (Madrid: Real Instituto Elcano).

Carbonell, L. (2008) Las agendas de la Unión Europea y Marruecos en democracia y derechos humanos: ¿Una convergencia recurrente? (Barcelona: CIDOB).

Castaño García, I. (1993) *La democratización de la política exterior y la Constitución española*, PhD thesis, Universidad Complutense de Madrid.

Castaño García, I. (2004) La política mediterránea de la Unión Europea, *Revista Española de Desarrollo y Cooperación*, 14, pp. 9–27.

Catusse, M. (1999) *L'entrée en politique des entrepreneurs au Maroc. Libéralisation économique et réforme de l'ordre politique*, PhD thesis, Institut d'Études Politiques d'Aix-en-Provence.

Catusse, M. and F. Vairel (2003) 'Ni tout à fait le même ni tout à fait un autre'. Métamorphoses et continuité du régime marocain, *Maghreb-Machrek*, 175, pp. 73–91.

Cavatorta, F. (2005) The International Context of Morocco's Stalled Democratization, *Democratization*, 12(4), pp. 548–566.

Cebolla, H. (2004) Las decisiones en Marruecos se toman en el Sur. Sobre el equilibrio entre francófilos e hispanófilos (Madrid: FRIDE).

Cembrero, I. (2006) *Vecinos alejados. Los secretos de la crisis entre España y Marruecos* (Madrid: Galaxia Gutenberg/Círculo de Lectores).

Centre d'Études Internationales (ed.) (2010) *Une décennie de réformes au Maroc (1999–2009)* (Paris: Karthala).

Centre d'Études Internationales (ed.) (2011) *Maroc-Algérie. Analyses croisées d'un voisinage hostile* (Paris: Karthala).

Chaarani, A. (2004) *La mouvance islamiste au Maroc. Du 11 septembre 2001 aux attentats de Casablanca du 16 mai 2003* (Paris: Karthala).

Chambre des Représentants (1990) *Pour l'entente entre les peuples. La Chambre des Représentants au service de la diplomatie marocaine* (Rabat: Mithaq-Almaghrib).

Charillon, F. (2002) Maroc, Jordanie, Syrie. Les héritiers, *Études*, 397(6), pp. 587–597.

Charillon, F. (2006) Les pays arabes à l'épreuve de la privatisation de la politique étrangère (Brussels: European Parliament).

Checkel, J.T. (ed.) (2006) *International Institutions and Socialization in Europe* (Cambridge: Cambridge University Press).

Cheikh, A. (1987) *La politique étrangère des partis politiques marocains. Cas du PPS, de l'Istiqlal et de l'USFP*, thesis, Université Mohammed V Rabat.

Cherkaoui, M. (2007) *Morocco and the Sahara: Social Bonds and Geopolitical Issues* (Oxford: The Bardwell Press).

Chigueur, M. (2001) L'opportunité de la proposition américaine pour le partenariat entre les États-Unis et le Maghreb, *Revue marocaine d'études internationales*, 6, pp. 84–97.

Chneguir, A. (2004) *La politique extérieure de la Tunisie 1956–1987* (Paris: L'Harmattan).

CNDH (Conseil National des Droits de l'Homme) (2013) Étrangers et droits de l'homme au Maroc. Pour une politique d'asile et d'immigration radicalement nouvelle (Rabat).

Collectif Sahara-Maghreb (2003) Contribution en faveur de la résolution du conflit du Sahara dans une optique de construction maghrébine.

Colombo, S. and B. Voltolini (2014) 'Business as Usual' in EU Democracy Promotion towards Morocco? Assessing the Limits of the EU's Approach towards the Mediterranean after the Arab Uprisings, *L'Europe en Formation*, 371, pp. 41–57.

Comité Directeur du Rapport (2006) *50 ans de développement humain. Perspectives 2025* (Rabat: CDR).

Compés, R., J.M. García and T. García (2013) *EU–Mediterranean Relations in the Field of Agriculture: The Example of Morocco and Turkey* (Paris: Notre Europe).
Costalli, S. (2009) Power over the Sea: The Relevance of Neoclassical Realism to Euro-Mediterranean Relations, *Mediterranean Politics*, 14(3), pp. 323–342.
Crombois, J.F. (2005) The US–Morocco Free Trade Agreement, *Mediterranean Politics*, 10(2), pp. 219–223.
Daadaoui, M. (2008) The Western Sahara Conflict: Towards a Constructivist Approach to Self-Determination, *Journal of North African Studies*, 13(2), pp. 143–156.
Dafir, A. (2014) Le Maroc face à la crise internationale. Contribution de la diplomatie économique, *Revue Internationale de Management et de Stratégie*, 5(1), www.revue-rms.fr/Le-Maroc-face-a-la-crise-internationale-contribution-de-la-diplomatie-economique_a23.html.
Dafir, A. and K. Haoudi (2014) La diplomatie économique et l'insertion internationale de l'économie marocaine, *International Journal of Innovation and Applied Studies*, 6(4), pp. 850–859.
Daguzan, J.-F. (2002) France, Democratization and North Africa, *Democratization*, 9(1), pp. 135–147.
Dahbi, O. (2011) *Maroc-Espagne. La guerre des ombres (2000–2010)* (Casablanca: ALM).
Dalle, I. (2001) Le Maroc attend le grand changement, *Le Monde Diplomatique*, June.
Dalle, I. (2004) *Les trois Rois. La monarchie marocaine, de l'indépendance à nos jours* (Paris: Fayard).
Damis, J. (1998) Morocco's 1995 Fisheries Agreement with the European Union: A Crisis Resolved, *Mediterranean Politics*, 3(2), pp. 61–73.
Dann, N. (2014) Nonviolent Resistance in the Western Sahara, *Peace Review*, 26(1), pp. 46–53.
Daoud, Z. (2007) *Les années Lamalif: 1958–1988. Trente ans de journalisme au Maroc* (Casablanca and Mohamedia: Tarik/Senso Unico).
Darbouche, H. and Y.H. Zoubir (2008) Conflicting International Policies and the Western Sahara Stalemate, *The International Spectator*, 43(1), pp. 91–105.
David, S.R. (1991) Explaining Third World Alignment, *World Politics*, 43(2), pp. 233–256.
Dawisha, A. (ed.) (1983) *Islam in Foreign Policy* (Cambridge: Cambridge University Press).
Dawson, C. (2009) *EU Integration with North Africa: Trade Negotiations and Democracy Deficits in Morocco* (London and New York: I.B. Tauris).
Deeb, M.-J. (1989) Inter-Maghribi Relations since 1969: A Study of the Modalities of Unions and Mergers, *Middle East Journal*, 43(1), pp. 20–33.
Deeb, M.-J. (1993) The Arab Maghribi Union and the Prospects for North African Unity, in: I.W. Zartman and W.M. Habeeb (eds) *Polity and Society in Contemporary North Africa* (Boulder: Westview), pp. 189–203.
Dekkar, T. (2013) *Maroc-Algérie. La méfiance réciproque* (Paris: L'Harmattan).
Del Sarto, R.A. (2006) *Contested State Identities and Regional Security in the Euro-Mediterranean Area* (New York: Palgrave).
Del Sarto, R.A. and T. Schumacher (2005) From EMP to ENP: What's at Stake with the European Neighbourhood Policy towards the Southern Mediterranean? *European Foreign Affairs Review*, 10(1), pp. 17–38.
Del Valle, A. and R. el Houdaïgui (eds) (2006) *Las dimensiones internacionales del Estrecho de Gibraltar* (Madrid: Dykinson).

Delmote, G. (2002) L'Espagne face au laxisme marocain, *Confluences Méditerranée*, 42, pp. 123–131.

Denoeux, G.P. and H.R. Desfosses (2007) Rethinking the Moroccan Parliament: The Kingdom's Legislative Development Imperative, *Journal of North African Studies*, 12(1), pp. 79–108.

Desrues, T. (2006) De la monarchie exécutive ou les apories de la gestion de la rente géostratégique, in: *L'Année du Maghreb 2004* (Paris: CNRS), pp. 243–271.

Desrues, T. (2007) Entre État de droit et droit de l'État. La difficile émergence de l'espace public au Maroc, in: *L'Année du Maghreb 2005–2006* (Paris: CNRS), pp. 263–292.

Desrues, T. (2013) Mobilizations in a Hybrid Regime: The 20th February Movement and the Moroccan Regime, *Current Sociology*, 61(4), pp. 409–423.

Desrues, T. (2014) La fronde de l'Istiqlal et la formation du gouvernement Benkirane II. Une aubaine pour la Monarchie? in: *L'Année du Maghreb 2013* (Paris: CNRS), pp. 253–272.

Desrues, T. and M. Hernando De Larramendi (eds) (2011) *Mohamed VI. Política y cambio social en Marruecos* (Córdoba: Almuzara).

Díez Peralta, Eva (2007) Balance y perspectivas de la zona de libre comercio euromediterránea. El caso de Marruecos, in: A. Fernández-Ardavín and M. Goded (eds) *Europa y Marruecos: Diez años del Proceso de Barcelona* (Madrid: Biblioteca Nueva/IDEE), pp. 257–276.

Droz-Vincent, P. (2003) Les dilemmes des régimes arabes après l'intervention américaine en Irak, *Politique étrangère*, 68(3–4), pp. 553–566.

Droz-Vincent, P. (2004) Quel avenir pour l'autoritarisme dans le monde arabe? *Revue française de science politique*, 54(6), pp. 945–979.

El Alaoui, M.H. (2014) *Journal d'un prince banni. Demain, le Maroc* (Paris: Grasset).

El Hassane, H. (1984) *La politique marocaine de non alignement de 1961 à 1979. Analyse des déterminants*, thesis, Université Hassan II Casablanca.

El Houdaïgui, R. (2001) La crise de la pêche maroco-européenne (1994–1995). Un nouvel enjeu de sécurité au Sud de Gibraltar, *Revue marocaine d'études internationales*, 6, pp. 40–62.

El Houdaïgui, R. (2003a) *La politique étrangère sous le règne de Hassan II. Acteurs, enjeux et processus décisionnels* (Paris: L'Harmattan).

El Houdaïgui, R. (2003b) La politique étrangère du Maroc entre la constante géopolitique et les contraintes de la mondialisation, *Revue marocaine d'études internationales*, 11, pp. 29–48.

El Houdaïgui, R. (2006) *Les politiques étrangères dans le monde arabe. Une approche sociologique de l'élaboration de la décision* (Brussels: European Parliament).

El Houdaïgui, R. (2009) Le Maroc et la politique européenne de voisinage, in: A. Morillas and I. Blázquez (eds) *La cooperación territorial en el Mediterráneo. La Política Europea de Vecindad* (Sevilla: UNIA), pp. 78–87.

El Houdaïgui, R. (2010) La politique étrangère de Mohammed VI ou la renaissance d'une 'puissance relationnelle', in: CEI (ed.) *Une décennie de réformes au Maroc (1999–2009)* (Paris: Karthala), pp. 295–324.

El Houdaïgui, R. (2012) La perception marocaine du Dialogue 5+5, in: J.-F. Coustillière (ed.) *Le 5+5 face aux défis du réveil arabe* (Paris: L'Harmattan), pp. 93–98.

El Maslouhi, A. (1999) Le domaine réservé en politique étrangère à la lumière de l'histoire et du droit marocains, *Revue juridique, politique et économique du Maroc*, 31–32, pp. 67–81.

El Messaoudi, A. and A. Bouabid (2007) *Technocratie versus démocratie?* (Fondation Abderrahim Bouabid/FES).

El Messaoudi, A. and A. Bouabid (2008) *Autonomie et régionalisation* (Fondation Abderrahim Bouabid/FES).
El Mossadeq, R. (1995) *Consensus ou jeu du consensus? Pour le réajustement de la pratique politique au Maroc* (Casablanca: Najah El Jadida).
El Othmani, S.-E. (2013) Morocco's Advanced Status with the EU: A Locomotive and a Model for Reforms in the Region, *European Foreign Affairs Review*, 18(3), pp. 297–302.
El Ouali, A. (2007) *Autonomie au Sahara. Prélude au Maghreb des régions* (London: Stacey International).
El Ouali, A. (2010) *Autonomie et régionalisation. Perspective marocaine* (Casablanca: Les Éditions Maghrébines).
El Qadim, N. (2010) La politique migratoire européenne vue du Maroc. Contraintes et opportunités, *Politique européenne*, 31, pp. 91–118.
El Yaakoubi, A. (2010) Vers un statut… avancé?, *Afkar/Idées*, 26, pp. 50–51.
EMHRN (Euro-Mediterranean Human Rights Network) (2007) *Les droits de l'homme dans le Plan d'Action Maroc-UE dans le cadre de la Politique Européenne de Voisinage* (Tunis).
EMHRN (Euro-Mediterranean Human Rights Network) (2014) *Document d'analyse du Partenariat de Mobilité signé entre le Royaume du Maroc, l'Union Européenne et neuf États membres le 7 juin 2013* (Tunis).
Escribano, G. (2006) *Europeanisation without Europe? The Mediterranean and the Neighbourhood Policy* (Florence: EUI/RSCAS).
Escribano, G. (2007) Marruecos y la Unión Europea. 10 años después de la Conferencia de Barcelona, in: A. Fernández-Ardavín and M. Goded (eds) *Europa y Marruecos: Diez años del Proceso de Barcelona* (Madrid: Biblioteca Nueva/IDEE), pp. 187–208.
Et-Tajani, M. (1984) *Le 'regain d'intérêt' dans les relations maroco-américaines (1975–1982)*, thesis, Université Hassan II Casablanca.
Evans, P.B., D. Rueschemeyer and T. Skocpol (eds) (1983) *Bringing the State Back In* (Cambridge: Cambridge University Press).
Fassi Fihri, T. (2009) The Union for the Mediterranean: An Active Commitment for Ambitious Accomplishments, in: *Mediterranean Yearbook 2009* (Barcelona: IEMed/CIDOB), pp. 27–29.
Fawcett, L. (ed.) (2013) *International Relations of the Middle East* (3rd edn) (Oxford: Oxford University Press).
Feliu, L. (2001) La situation du Maghreb sur la scène internationale actuelle, in: IEEE (ed.) *Magreb. Perception espagnole de la estabilité en Méditerranée, prospective en vue de l'année 2010* (Madrid: Ministerio de Defensa), pp. 17–64.
Feliu, L. (2003) A Two-Level Game: Spain and the Promotion of Democracy and Human Rights in Morocco, *Mediterranean Politics*, 8(2–3), pp. 90–111.
Feliu, L. (2004a) *El jardín secreto. Los defensores de los derechos humanos en Marruecos* (Madrid: Los Libros de la Catarata).
Feliu, L. (2004b) *Hacia la normalización de las relaciones entre España y Marruecos* (Madrid: FRIDE).
Feliu, L. (2005) *España y el Magreb durante el segundo mandato del Partido Popular. Un periodo excepcional* (Madrid: FRIDE).
Feliu, L. and M.A. Parejo (2013) Morocco: The Reinvention of an Authoritarian System, in: F. Izquierdo (ed.) *Political Regimes in the Arab World: Society and the Exercise of Power* (Abingdon, UK and New York: Routledge), pp. 70–99.

228 References

Ferabolli, S. (2014) *Arab Regionalism: A Post-Structural Perspective* (Abingdon, UK and New York: Routledge).

Fernández-Molina, I. (2007) *Le PJD et la politique étrangère du Maroc. Entre l'idéologie et le pragmatisme* (Barcelona: CIDOB).

Fernández-Molina, I. (2011a) Los consejos consultivos. Gobierno sin representación y diplomacia paralela, in: T. Desrues and M. Hernando de Larramendi (eds) *Mohamed VI. Política y cambio social en Marruecos* (Córdoba: Almuzara), pp. 139–175.

Fernández-Molina, I. (2011b) Between the 20 February Movement and Monarchic Reformism: Who Holds the Reins of Political Change in Morocco? *Mediterranean Politics*, 16(3), pp. 435–441.

Fernández-Molina, I. (2013a) *La política exterior de Marruecos en el reinado de Mohamed VI (1999–2008). Actores, discursos y proyecciones internas*, PhD thesis, Universidad Complutense de Madrid.

Fernández-Molina, I. (2013b) *Breaking the Deadlock in the Western Sahara* (Washington, DC: Carnegie Endowment for International Peace).

Fernández-Molina, I. (2014) *Morocco and the Middle East under Mohammed VI*, Al-Sabah Publication Series, Durham University.

Fernández-Molina, I. (2015) Protests under Occupation: The Spring inside Western Sahara, *Mediterranean Politics*, 20(2), pp. 235–254.

Fernández-Molina, I. and R. Bustos (2010) *El Estatuto Avanzado UE-Marruecos y la Presidencia española de la UE* (Madrid: Fundación Alternativas/OPEX).

Fernández-Molina, I. and E. Soler (2013) España-Marruecos. Una continuidad inesperada, in: *Anuario Internacional CIDOB 2013* (Barcelona: CIDOB).

Fernández-Molina, I., S. Kirhlani and R. Ojeda (2011) Las elecciones municipales de 2009 y el nuevo 'partido del rey'. Mutaciones del escenario político marroquí dentro y fuera de las urnas, *Revista de Estudios Políticos*, 153, pp. 181–211.

Fibla, C. (2005) *España-Marruecos desde la orilla sur* (Barcelona: Icaria).

Filali, A. (2008) *Le Maroc et le monde arabe* (Paris: Scali).

Filali Meknassi, R. and F. Abdelmoumni (2006) Droits de l'Homme, substitut aux idéologies? (Fondation Abderrahim Bouabid/FES).

Filiu, J.-P. (2009) Al-Qaeda in the Islamic Maghreb: Algerian Challenge or Global Threat? (Washington, DC: Carnegie Endowment for International Peace).

Fondation Hassan II (2003) *Marocains de l'extérieur* (Rabat: Fondation Hassan II pour les Marocains Résidant à l'Etranger/OIM).

Garçon, J. (2000) Maroc. Mohammed VI seul en scène, *Politique internationale*, 89, pp. 421–436.

Gause, F.G., III (2013) Kings for All Seasons: How the Middle East's Monarchies Survived the Arab Spring (Brookings Doha Center).

GERM (Groupement d'Études et de Recherches sur la Méditerranée) (2010) *L'annuaire de la Méditerranée 2009. Le Statut avancé à l'épreuve de l'Union pour la Méditerranée* (Rabat: GERM/FES).

Ghilès, F. (2010) Le 'non-Maghreb' coûte cher au Maghreb, *Le Monde Diplomatique*, January.

Gillespie, R. (2000) *Spain and the Mediterranean: Developing a European Policy towards the South* (Basingstoke: Macmillan).

Gillespie, R. (2002) The Valencia Conference: Reinvigorating the Barcelona Process? *Mediterranean Politics*, 7(2), pp. 105–114.

Gillespie, R. (2006) 'This Stupid Little Island': A Neighbourhood Confrontation in the Western Mediterranean, *International Politics*, 43(1), pp. 110–132.

Gillespie, R. (2007) Les limites du volontarisme espagnol au Maghreb, *Afkar/Idées*, 13, pp. 48–50.

Gillespie, R. (2011) The Union for the Mediterranean: An Intergovernmentalist Challenge for the European Union? *Journal of Common Market Studies*, 49(6), pp. 1205–1225.

Gillespie, R. (2013) The Challenge of Co-ownership in the Euro-Mediterranean Space, *Geopolitics*, 18(1), pp. 178–197.

Gillespie, R. and R. Youngs (eds) (2002) *The European Union and Democracy Promotion: The Case of North Africa* (London: Frank Cass).

Gimeno, S. (2013) Situación de los derechos civiles y políticos en el Sáhara Occidental: de 1999 a la actualidad (Seminario de Investigación para la Paz).

Gómez Martín, C. (2012) Sahara Occidental. Quel scénario après Gdeim Izik? in: *L'Année du Maghreb 2011* (Paris: CNRS), pp. 259–276.

González, C. and Á. Pérez (2008) *Ceuta y Melilla. Nuevos elementos en el escenario*, (Madrid: Real Instituto Elcano).

Gourevitch, P. (1978) The Second Image Reversed: The International Sources of Domestic Politics, *International Organization*, 32(4), pp. 881–912.

Graciet, C. and É. Laurent (2012) *Le Roi prédateur* (Paris: Éditions du Seuil).

Grimaud, N. (1984) *La politique extérieure de l'Algérie (1962–1978)* (Paris: Karthala).

Grimaud, N. (1995) *La Tunisie à la recherche de sa sécurité* (Paris: PUF).

Grimaud, N. (2003) Les États-Unis et le Maghreb depuis le 11 septembre, *Études internationales*, 6, pp. 46–54.

Groom, A.J.R. and M. Light (eds) (1994) *Contemporary International Relations: A Guide to Theory* (London: Pinter).

Guessous, M. (1983) *Les commissions mixtes de coopération maroco-étrangères. Essai sur le 'système' marocain de coopération bilatérale*, thesis, École Nationale d'Administration Publique de Rabat.

Guillaume, X. (2010) *International Relations and Identity: A Dialogical Approach* (Abingdon, UK and New York: Routledge).

Haddadi, S. (2003) The EMP and Morocco: Diverging Political Agendas? *Mediterranean Politics*, 8(2–3), pp. 73–89.

Hagan, J.D. (1987) Regimes, Political Oppositions, and the Comparative Analysis of Foreign Policy, in: C.F. Hermann, C.W. Kegley and J.N. Rosenau (eds) *New Directions in the Study of Foreign Policy* (Boston: Allen and Unwin), pp. 339–365.

Hagan, J.D. (1995) Domestic Political Explanations in the Analysis of Foreign Policy, in: L. Neack, J.A.K. Hey and P.J. Haney (eds) *Foreign Policy Analysis: Continuity and Change in its Second Generation* (Englewood Cliffs: Prentice Hall), pp. 117–143.

Halliday, F. (1994) *Rethinking International Relations* (Basingstoke: Palgrave Macmillan).

Hami, H. (1984) *Les relations maroco-sénégalaises. Analyse des aspects culturel et stratégique*, thesis, Université Hassan II Casablanca.

Hami, H. (2003) *L'ambivalence salutaire. Essai sur la logique du conflit et de la coopération au Maghreb* (Rabat: REMALD).

Hami, H. (2005) *La dimension spirituelle des relations transnationales. Le Maroc et l'Afrique subsaharienne* (Rabat: Bouregreg).

Harnisch, S. (2012) Conceptualizing in the Minefield: Role Theory and Foreign Policy Learning, *Foreign Policy Analysis*, 8(1), pp. 47–69.

Hasenclever, A., P. Mayer and V. Rittberger (1997) *Theories of International Regimes* (Cambridge: Cambridge University Press).

Henry, J.-R. (2006) La Méditerranée occidentale en quête d'un 'destin commun', in: *L'Année du Maghreb 2004* (Paris: CNRS), pp. 7–26.

Hermann, C.F., C.W. Kegley and J.N. Rosenau (eds) (1987) *New Directions in the Study of Foreign Policy* (Boston: Allen and Unwin).
Hernando de Larramendi, M. (1997) *La política exterior de Marruecos* (Madrid: Mapfre).
Hernando de Larramendi, M. (2004) *Las relaciones con Marruecos tras los atentados del 11 de marzo* (Madrid: Real Instituto Elcano).
Hernando de Larramendi, M. (2005) *Al-siyasa al-kharijiya li-l-Magrib* (Rabat: Azzaman).
Hernando de Larramendi, M. (2008) Intra-Maghrebi Relations: Unitary Myth and National Interests, in: Y.H. Zoubir and H. Amirah (eds) *North Africa: Politics, Region, and the Limits of Transformation* (Abingdon, UK and New York: Routledge), pp. 179–201.
Hernando de Larramendi, M. (2010) La cuestión del Sáhara Occidental como factor de impulso del proceso de descentralización marroquí, *Revista de Estudios Internacionales Mediterráneos*, 9, pp. 132–141.
Hernando de Larramendi, M. (2012a) La política exterior, in: A. Remiro Brotóns and C. Martínez Capdevila (eds) *Unión Europea-Marruecos: Una vecindad privilegiada?* (Madrid: Academia Europea de Ciencias y Artes).
Hernando de Larramendi, M. (2012b) Construction maghrébine après le 'Printemps arabe', *Afkar/Idées*, 36, pp. 22–24.
Hernando de Larramendi, M. and F. Bravo (2006) La frontière hispano-marocaine à l'épreuve de l'immigration subsaharienne, in: *L'Année du Maghreb 2004* (Paris: CNRS), pp. 153–171.
Hernando de Larramendi, M. and I. Fernández-Molina (2015) The Evolving Foreign Policies of North African States (2011–2014): New Trends in Constraints, Political Processes and Behavior, in: Y.H. Zoubir and G. White (eds) *North African Politics: Change and Continuity* (Abingdon, UK and New York: Routledge).
Hernando de Larramendi, M. and A. Mañé (eds) (2009) *La política exterior española hacia el Magreb. Actores e intereses* (Barcelona: Ariel).
Hewko, J. (2010) *Millenium Challenge Corporation: Can the Experiment Survive?* (Washington, DC: Carnegie Endowment for International Peace).
Hill, C. (2003) *The Changing Politics of Foreign Policy* (New York: Palgrave Macmillan).
Hinnebusch, R. (2005) Explaining International Politics in the Middle East: The Struggle of Regional Identity and Systemic Structure, in: G. Nonneman (ed.) *Analyzing Middle East Foreign Policies and the Relationship with Europe* (Abingdon, UK and New York: Routledge), pp. 243–256.
Hinnebusch, R. and A. Ehteshami (eds) (2002) *The Foreign Policies of Middle East States* (London: Lynne Rienner).
Hodges, T. (1983) *Western Sahara: The Roots of a Desert War* (Westport: Lawrence Hill).
Hoffmann, A. and C. König (2013) Scratching the Democratic Façade: Framing Strategies of the 20 February Movement, *Mediterranean Politics*, 18(1), pp. 1–22.
Holsti, K.J. (1970) National Role Conceptions in the Study of Foreign Policy, *International Studies Quarterly*, 14(3), pp. 233–309.
Holsti, K.J. (1996) *The State, War, and the State of War* (Cambridge: Cambridge University Press).
Horst, J., A. Jünemann and D. Rothe (eds) (2013) *Euro-Mediterranean Relations after the Arab Spring: Persistence in Times of Change* (Farnham and Burlington: Ashgate).
HRW (Human Rights Watch) (2014) *Abused and Expelled. Ill-Treatment of Sub-Saharan African Migrants in Morocco* (New York).

Hudson, V.M. (2005) Foreign Policy Analysis: Actor-Specific Theory and the Ground of International Relations, *Foreign Policy Analysis*, 1(1), pp. 1–30.

Hudson, V.M. (2007) *Foreign Policy Analysis: Classic and Contemporary Theory* (Maryland: Rowman & Littlefield).

Hudson, V.M. and C.S. Vore (1995) Foreign Policy Analysis Yesterday, Today, and Tomorrow, *Mershon International Studies Review*, 39(2), pp. 209–238.

Hufbauer, G.C. and C. Brunel (eds) (2009) *Capitalizing on the Morocco–US Free Trade Agreement: A Road Map for Success* (Washington, DC: Peterson Institute for International Economics).

ICG (International Crisis Group) (2005) Islamic Terrorism in the Sahel: Fact of Fiction? (Brussels).

ICG (International Crisis Group) (2007a) Western Sahara: The Cost of the Conflict (Brussels).

ICG (International Crisis Group) (2007b) Western Sahara: Out of the Impasse (Brussels).

IEMed (Institut Europeu de la Mediterrània) (2009) *Le Maroc et l'Union européenne. Vers un statut avancé dans l'Association euro-méditerranéenne* (Barcelona: IEMed).

Iglesias, M. (2010) *Conflicto y cooperación entre España y Marruecos (1956–2008)* (Sevilla: Centro de Estudios Andaluces).

Ihraï, S. (1986) *Pouvoir et influence. État, partis et politique étrangère au Maroc* (Rabat: Edino).

Ihraï, S. and A. Aouchar (1991) *Les relations internationales du Maroc du XVIe siècle au début du XXe*, thesis, Université Hassan II Casablanca.

IMRI (Institut Marocain des Relations Internationales)/KAS (Konrad Adenauer Stiftung) (2008) Rapport du groupe d'experts réuni au sein de l'IMRI sur le projet d'Union pour la Méditerranée (IMRI/KAS).

Ismael, T.Y. and G.E. Perry (eds) (2014) *The International Relations of the Contemporary Middle East: Subordination and Beyond* (Abingdon, UK and New York: Routledge).

Izquierdo, F. (ed.) (2013) *Political Regimes in the Arab World: Society and the Exercise of Power* (Abingdon, UK and New York: Routledge).

Jaidi, L. (ed.) (2005) *La politique de bon voisinage. Quelle lecture des pays maghrébins?* (Rabat: FES).

Jaidi, L. (2008) Gestion des réformes économiques et transition démocratique au Maroc, in: P. Gandolfi (ed.) *Le Maroc aujourd'hui* (Bologna: Il Ponte), pp. 175–205.

Jaidi, L. (2009) The Morocco/EU Advanced Status: What Value Does it Add to the European Neighbourhood Policy? in: *Mediterranean Yearbook 2009* (Barcelona: IEMed/CIDOB), pp. 149–154.

Jaidi, L. and H. Abouyoub (2008) Le Maroc entre le statut avancé et l'Union pour la méditerranée (Fondation Abderrahim Bouabid/FES).

Jaidi, L. and I. Martín (2010) Comment faire avancer le Statut Avancé UE-Maroc? (Barcelona: IEMed).

Janati-Idrissi, A. (1998) Le ministère des Affaires étrangères et la coordination des relations extérieures du Maroc, *Revue marocaine d'études internationales*, 1, pp. 55–73.

Janati-Idrissi, A. (1999) La politique étrangère du Maroc d'après la déclaration de politique générale du premier gouvernement d'alternance, *Revue marocaine d'études internationales*, 2, pp. 110–131.

Janati-Idrissi, A. (2000) Chronique des relations diplomatiques du Maroc (1er semestre 2000), *Revue marocaine d'études internationales*, 5, pp. 101–121.

Janati-Idrissi, A. (2001) Chronique des relations diplomatiques du Maroc (2ème semestre 2000), *Revue marocaine d'études internationales*, 6, pp. 122–144.

232 References

Jensen, E. (2012) *Western Sahara: Anatomy of a Stalemate?* (2nd edn) (Boulder and London: Lynne Rienner).
Julien, C.-A. (1978) *Le Maroc face aux impérialismes 1415–1956* (Paris: Jeune Afrique).
Kalpakian, J. (2006) Managing Morocco's Image in United States Domestic Politics, *Journal of North African Studies*, 11(1), pp. 55–69.
Kasbaoui, N. (1978) *Les relations internationales maghrébines et le conflit du Sahara occidental*, thesis, Université Hassan II Casablanca.
Katzenstein, P.J. (1976) International Relations and Domestic Structures: Foreign Economic Policies of Advanced Industrial States, *International Organization*, 30(1), pp. 1–45.
Kausch, K. (2008) How Serious is the EU about Supporting Democracy and Human Rights in Morocco (London and Madrid: ECFR/FRIDE).
Kausch, K. (2009) The European Union and Political Reform in Morocco, *Mediterranean Politics*, 14(2), pp. 165–179.
Kausch, K. (2010) *Morocco's 'Advanced Status': Model or Muddle?* (Madrid: FRIDE).
Keohane, R.O. and J.S. Nye (1977) *Power and Interdependence: World Politics in Transition* (Boston: Little, Brown).
Kerdoudi, J. (2003) *Le Maghreb face au défi européen* (Casablanca: Publishing Maroc).
Khachani, M. (2003) La question migratoire dans les relations entre le Maroc et l'Espagne, *Paix et sécurité internationales*, 1, pp. 57–77.
Khachani, M. (2006) *La emigración subsahariana: Marruecos como espacio de tránsito* (Barcelona: CIDOB).
Khader, B. (2008): A Controversial Agreement between Morocco and the United States Comes into Effect, in: *Mediterranean Yearbook 2007* (Barcelona: IEMed/CIDOB), pp. 211–216.
Khakee, A. (2010) Assessing Democracy Assistance: Morocco (FRIDE).
Khakee, A. (2014) The MINURSO Mandate, Human Rights and the Autonomy Solution for Western Sahara, *Mediterranean Politics*, 19(3), pp. 456–462.
Khrouz, D., M. El Ayadi, A. Boulahcen, A. Amallah and K. Meslouhi (2004) *Barcelona Monitoring. Suivi de l'accord de libre-échange. Politique, économie, entreprise, éducation* (Rabat: FES).
Knopf, J.W. (2003) The Importance of International Learning, *Review of International Studies*, 29(2), pp. 185–207.
Korany, B. (1983) Review: The Take-Off of Third World Studies? The Case of Foreign Policy, *World Politics*, 35(3), pp. 465–487.
Korany, B. and A.E.H. Dessouki (eds) (1991) *The Foreign Policies of Arab States: The Challenge of Change* (2nd edn) (Boulder: Westview Press).
Korany, B. and A.E.H. Dessouki (eds) (2009) *The Foreign Policies of Arab States: The Challenge of Globalization* (3rd edn) (Cairo: AUC Press).
Kubálková, V. (ed.) (2001) *Foreign Policy in a Constructed World* (New York: Sharpe).
Kurki, M. (2011) Democracy through Technocracy? Reflections on Technocratic Assumptions in EU Democracy Promotion Discourse, *Journal of Intervention and Statebuilding*, 5(2), pp. 211–234.
Lakmahri, S. and A. Tourabi (2013) Le Maroc a-t-il échoué au Sahara? *Zamane*, 28, pp. 34–41.
Lannon, E. (2003) La mutation progressive des relations entre le Maghreb et l'Union européenne au sein de l'espace pan-euro-méditerranéen, in: *Annuaire de l'Afrique du Nord 2000–2001* (Paris: CNRS), pp. 499–514.
Lannon, E., J. Braga de Macedo and Á. de Vasconcelos (2007) *Maroc-UE. Vers un statut avancé dans le cadre du PEM et de la PEV* (Barcelona: IEMed).

Larsen, H. (1997) *Foreign Policy and Discourse Analysis: France, Britain and Europe* (Abingdon, UK and New York: Routledge).

Lavenex, S. (2006) Shifting Up and Out: The Foreign Policy of European Immigration Control, *West European Politics*, 29(2), pp. 329–350.

Leveau, R. (2000) The Moroccan Monarchy: A Political System in Quest of a New Equilibrium, in: J. Kostiner (ed.) *Middle East Monarchies: The Challenge of Modernity* (Boulder and London: Lynne Rienner), pp. 117–130.

López García, B. (2000) *Marruecos en trance: Nuevo rey. Nuevo siglo. Nuevo régimen?* (Madrid: Política Exterior/Biblioteca Nueva).

López García, B. (2002) Una crisis, dos perspectivas (Real Instituto Elcano).

López García, B. (2007) *Marruecos y España. Una historia contra toda lógica* (Sevilla: RD/Fundación Tres Culturas).

López García, B. (2011) Sahara-Marruecos. El miedo a la autonomía, *Política Exterior*, 139, pp. 38–46.

López García, B. and M. Hernando de Larramendi (2002) Spain and North Africa: Towards a 'Dynamic Stability', *Democratization*, 9(1), pp. 170–191.

López Sala, A.M. (2012) Donde el Sur confluye con el Norte: Movimientos migratorios, dinámica económica y seguridad en las relaciones bilaterales entre España y Marruecos (CIDOB).

Maalmi, A. (ed.) (2012) *Droit et mutations sociales et politiques au Maroc et au Maghreb* (Paris: Publisud).

Madani, M. (2006) *Le paysage politique marocain* (Rabat: Dar al Qalam).

Madani, M., D. Maghraoui and S. Zerhouni (2012) *The 2011 Moroccan Constitution: A Critical Analysis* (Stockholm: International IDEA).

Maddy-Weitzman, B. (2003) Islamism, Moroccan-Style: The Ideas of Sheikh Yassine, *Middle East Quarterly*, 10(1), pp. 43–51.

Maggi, E.-M. (2013) Change to Stay the Same: The European Union and the Logics of Institutional Reform in Morocco, in: J. Horst, A. Jünemann and D. Rothe (eds) *Euro-Mediterranean Relations after the Arab Spring: Persistence in Times of Change* (Farnham and Burlington: Ashgate), pp. 21–38.

Maghraoui, A. (2003) Ambiguities of Sovereignty: Morocco, The Hague and the Western Sahara Dispute, *Mediterranean Politics*, 8(1), pp. 113–126.

Maghraoui, D. (2011) Constitutional Reforms in Morocco: Between Consensus and Subaltern Politics, *Journal of North African Studies*, 16(4), pp. 679–699.

Manners, I. (2002) Normative Power Europe: A Contradiction in Terms? *Journal of Common Market Studies*, 40(2), pp. 235–258.

Marrero, I. (2005) The Implications of Spanish–Moroccan Governmental Relations for Moroccan Immigrants in Spain, *European Journal of Migration and Law*, 7(4), pp. 413–434.

Martín, I. (2004) The Labyrinth of Subregional Integration in the South Mediterranean, in: *Mediterranean Yearbook 2003* (Barcelona: IEMed/CIDOB), pp. 163–167.

Martín, I. (2009) EU–Morocco Relations: How Advanced is the 'Advanced Status'? *Mediterranean Politics*, 14(2), pp. 239–245.

Martín, I. (2010) Sommet bilatéral UE-Maroc: quelles avancées? *Afkar/Idées*, 26, pp. 47–49.

Martinez, L. (ed.) (2008) *Le Maroc, l'Union du Maghreb Arabe et l'intégration régionale* (Barcelona: Euromesco).

Mastanduno, M., D.A. Lake and G.J. Ikenberry (1989) Towards a Realist Theory of State Action, *International Studies Quarterly*, 33(4), pp. 457–474.

234 References

Mesa, R. (1982) *Aproximación al Cercano Oriente* (Madrid: Akal).
Mesa, R. (1988) *Democracia y política exterior en España* (Madrid: EUDEMA).
Mesa, R. (1986) *La reinvención de la política exterior española* (Madrid: Centro de Estudios Constitucionales).
Messari, M.L. (2009) *Las relaciones difíciles. Marruecos y España* (Córdoba: Almuzara).
Messari, N. (2001a) Identity and Foreign Policy: The Case of Islam in U.S. Foreign Policy, in: V. Kubálková (ed.) *Foreign Policy in a Constructed World* (New York: Sharpe), pp. 227–246.
Messari, N. (2001b) National Security, the Political Space, and Citizenship: The Case of Morocco and the Western Sahara, *Journal of North African Studies*, 6(4), pp. 47–63.
Mestres, L. and E. Soler (2008) *El estatuto avanzado de Marruecos. No perdamos la oportunidad* (CIDOB).
Mezran, K. (1998) Maghribi Foreign Policies and the Internal Security Dimension, *Journal of North African Studies*, 3(1), pp. 1–24.
Mezran, K. (2000) Morocco after Hassan II, *Middle East Intelligence Bulletin*, 2(8), www.meforum.org/meib/articles/0009_me1.htm.
Miller, R. and A. Bower (2010) The Threat from the South? The Islamist Challenge as a Factor in Euro-Moroccan Relations, 1995–2009, *Journal of Contemporary European Studies*, 18(4), pp. 499–515.
Milliken, J. (1999) The Study of Discourse in International Relations: A Critique of Research and Methods, *European Journal of International Relations*, 5(2), pp. 225–254.
Mills, G. (ed.) (2002) *Morocco and South Africa: Globalisation, Development and Pivotal States* (Johannesburg: South African Institute of International Affairs).
Ministère de l'Économie et des Finances (2007) Les relations du Maroc avec l'Union Européenne du partenariat au statut avancé.
Ministère de l'Économie et des Finances (2008) Enjeux de l'intégration maghrébine. 'Le coût du non Maghreb'.
Ministère Délégué chargé du Commerce Extérieur (2014a) Fiche-Pays: République de France.
Ministère Délégué chargé du Commerce Extérieur (2014b) Fiche-Pays: Royaume de L'Espagne.
Ministère des Affaires Étrangères-France (2014) La France et le Maroc.
Ministère des Finances et de la Privatisation (2003a) Enjeux sur le Maroc de l'élargissement de l'Union Européenne à l'Est.
Ministère des Finances et de la Privatisation (2003b) Les enjeux de l'intégration maghrébine.
Ministère des Finances et de la Privatisation (2005) Enjeux pour le Maroc de la perspective d'adhésion de la Turquie à l'Union Européenne.
Mohsen-Finan, K. (1997) *Sahara Occidental. Les enjeux d'un conflit régional* (Paris: CNRS).
Mohsen-Finan, K. (2002) The Western Sahara Dispute under UN Pressure, *Mediterranean Politics*, 7(2), pp. 1–12.
Mohsen-Finan, K. (2008) *Le Maghreb et le projet d'Union pour la Méditerranée* (IFRI).
Mohsen-Finan, K. (2010) Sahara occidental. Divergences profondes autour d'un mode de règlement, in: *L'Année du Maghreb 2009* (Paris: CNRS), pp. 553–569.
Mohsen-Finan, K. (ed.) (2011) *Le Maghreb dans les relations internationales* (Paris: CNRS).

Mohsen-Finan, K. and M. Zeghal (2006) Opposition islamiste et pouvoir monarchique au Maroc. Le cas du Parti de la Justice et du Développement, *Revue française de science politique*, 56(1), pp. 79–119.

Mokhefi, M. and A. Antil (eds) (2012) *Le Maghreb et son sud. Vers des liens renouvelés* (Paris: CNRS/IFRI).

Moon, B.E. (1995) The State in Foreign and Domestic Policy, in: L. Neack, J.A.K. Hey and P.J. Haney (eds) *Foreign Policy Analysis: Continuity and Change in its Second Generation* (Englewood Cliffs: Prentice Hall), pp. 187–200.

Mortimer, R.A. (1999) The Arab Maghreb Union: Myth and Reality, in: Y.H. Zoubir (ed.) *North Africa in Transition: State, Society, and Economic Transformation in the 1990s* (Gainesville: University Press of Florida), pp. 177–191.

Mouhib, L. (2014) EU Democracy Promotion in Tunisia and Morocco: Between Contextual Changes and Structural Continuity, *Mediterranean Politics*, 19(3), pp. 351–372.

Mundy, J. (2006) Neutrality or Complicity? The United States and the 1975 Moroccan Takeover of the Spanish Sahara, *Journal of North African Studies*, 11(3), pp. 275–306.

Mundy, J. (2007) Western Sahara between Autonomy and Intifada, *Middle East Report Online*, 16(3).

Mundy, J. and S. Zunes (2014) Western Sahara: Nonviolent Resistance as a Last Resort, in: V. Dudouet (ed.) *Civil Resistance and Conflict Transformation* (Abingdon, UK and New York: Routledge), pp. 20–44.

Naciri, H. (1994) *Les grandes solidarités culturelles dans la politique étrangère marocaine (de 1956 à 1993)*, PhD thesis, Université Hassan II Casablanca.

Najih, N.B.S. (1984) *Les acteurs de la politique étrangère marocaine. Étude de cas: Le parti de l'Istiqlal*, thesis, Université Hassan II Casablanca.

Natorski, M. (2008) *The MEDA Programme in Morocco 12 Years On: Results, Experiences and Trends* (Barcelona: CIDOB).

Neack, L., J.A.K. Hey and P.J. Haney (eds) (1995) *Foreign Policy Analysis: Continuity and Change in its Second Generation* (Englewood Cliffs: Prentice Hall).

Nonneman, G. (ed.) (2005) *Analyzing Middle East Foreign Policies and the Relationship with Europe* (Abingdon, UK and New York: Routledge).

Obiols, R. and P. Solanilla (2002) Marruecos y España. Crónica de un desencuentro, in: *Anuario internacional CIDOB 2001* (Barcelona: CIDOB), pp. 295–298.

Oficina Económica y Comercial de España en Rabat (2014) Informe económico y comercial. Marruecos.

Ouaouicha, D. and A. Aboussaid (eds) (2003) *Moroccan–Saudi Relations and the Need for Intercultural Dialogue* (Ifrane: Al Akhawayn University).

Ouaouicha, D., M.J. Willis, J. Kalpakian and A. Aboussaid (eds) (2003) *Moroccan–American Relations in the New Millennium* (Ifrane: Al Akhawayn University).

Ounaïes, A.A. (2003) Le Maghreb et l'élargissement, *Confluences Méditerranée*, 46, pp. 39–46.

Ozkececi-Taner, B. (2005) The Impact of Institutionalized Ideas in Coalition Foreign Policy Making: Turkey as an Example, 1991–2002, *Foreign Policy Analysis*, 1(3), pp. 249–278.

Pace, M. (2006) *The Politics of Regional Identity: Meddling with the Mediterranean* (Abingdon, UK and New York: Routledge).

Pardo, J.L. (2009) Potencialidades y perspectivas para Marruecos en el marco de la Política Europea de Vecindad de la UE, in: A. Morillas and I. Blázquez (eds) *La cooperación territorial en el Mediterráneo: La Política Europea de Vecindad* (Sevilla: UNIA), pp. 68–77.

Pew Research Center (2004) A Year after Iraq War. Mistrust of America in Europe Ever Higher, Muslim Anger Persists. A Nine-Country Survey (Washington, DC).
Pham, J.P. (2008) America's New Africa Command: Paradigm Shift or Step Backwards? *Brown Journal of World Affairs*, 15(1), pp. 257–272.
Pham, J.P. (2010) U.S. Interests in Promoting Security across the Sahara, *American Foreign Policy Interests*, 32(4), pp. 242–252.
Planet, A.I. (1997) España y la Unión Europea, vistas desde la élite marroquí, in: T. Desrues and E. Moyano (eds) *Cambio, gobernabilidad y crisis en el Magreb* (Córdoba: IESA/CSIC), pp. 67–79.
Planet, A.I. (1998) *Melilla y Ceuta. Espacios-frontera hispano-marroquíes* (Melilla: UNED).
Planet, A.I. and M. Hernando de Larramendi (2006) Una piedra en el camino de las relaciones hispano-marroquíes. La crisis del islote de Perejil, in: A.I. Planet and F. Ramos (eds) *Relaciones hispano-marroquíes. Una vecindad en construcción* (Madrid: Ediciones del Oriente y del Mediterráneo), pp. 403–430.
Potomac Institute for Policy Studies (2009) Why the Maghreb Matters: Threats, Opportunities, and Options for Effective American Engagement in North Africa (Arlington, VA).
Powel, B. and L. Sadiki (2010) *Europe and Tunisia: Democratization via Association* (Abingdon, UK and New York: Routledge).
Putnam, R.D. (1988) Diplomacy and Domestic Politics: The Logic of Two-Level Games, *International Organization*, 42(3), pp. 427–460.
Ramsbotham, O., T. Woodhouse and H. Miall (2011) *Contemporary Conflict Resolution: The Prevention, Management and Transformation of Deadly Conflicts* (3rd edn) (Cambridge: Polity).
Rapport Avicenne (2007) Maghreb-Moyen-Orient. Contribution pour une politique volontariste de la France.
Régragui, I. (2013) *La diplomatie publique marocaine. Une stratégie de marque religieuse?* (Paris: L'Harmattan).
Réseau Marocain Euromed des ONG (2007) Evaluation du Plan d'action Maroc/UE dans le cadre de la PEV.
Rieker, P. and N. Bremberg (2014) *The ENP as an Instrument for Building a Security Community: The Case of Morocco* (Oslo: Norwegian Institute of International Affairs).
Rifai, I. (2005) *Morocco's National Interest* (Ifrane: Al Akhawayn University).
Riziki Mohamed, A. (2005) *La diplomatie en terre d'islam* (Paris: L'Harmattan).
Riziki Mohamed, A. (2014) *Sociologie de la diplomatie marocaine* (Paris: L'Harmattan).
Rojo, P. (ed.) (2008) *El 2007 visto por los árabes* (Barcelona and Rabat: Icaria/Al Fanar).
Rollinde, M. (2002) *Le mouvement marocain des droits de l'Homme. Entre consensus national et engagement citoyen* (Paris: Karthala/Institut Maghreb-Europe).
Rosenau, J.N. (ed.) (1969) *Linkage Politics: Essays on the Convergence of National and International Systems* (New York: The Free Press).
Rosenblum, J. and I.W. Zartman (2009) The Far West of the Near East: The Foreign Policy of Morocco, in: B. Korany and A.E.H. Dessouki (eds) *The Foreign Policies of Arab States: The Challenge of Globalization* (3rd edn) (Cairo: AUC Press), pp. 319–342.
Roussellier, J. (2013) *Algiers and Rabat: Storm or Spat?* (Washington, DC: Carnegie Endowment for International Peace).
Saaf, A. (1991) Vers la décrépitude de l'État néo-patrimonial. Limites du néo-patrimonialisme comme concept et phénomène observable, in: M. Camau (ed.) *Changements politiques au Magreb* (Paris: CNRS), pp. 73–106.

Saaf, A. (ed.) (1996) *Le Maroc et l'Afrique après l'indépendance* (Rabat: Institut des Études Africaines).

Saidy, B. (2009) La politique de défense marocaine. Articulation de l'interne et de l'externe, *Maghreb-Machrek*, 202, pp. 117–131.

Santucci, J.-C. (2006) Le multipartisme marocain entre les contraintes d'un 'pluralisme contrôlé' et les dilemmes d'un 'pluripartisme autoritaire', *Revue des mondes musulmans et de la Méditerranée*, 111–112, pp. 63–117.

Sater, J.N. (2007) *Civil Society and Political Change in Morocco* (Abingdon, UK and New York: Routledge).

Sater, J.N. (2010) *Morocco: Challenges to Tradition and Modernity* (Abingdon, UK and New York: Routledge).

Schimmelfennig, F. (2000) International Socialization in the New Europe: Rational Action in an Institutional Environment, *European Journal of International Relations*, 6(1), pp. 109–139.

Schmid, D. (2003) *Interlinkages within the Euro-Mediterranean Partnership: Linking Economic, Institutional and Political Reform* (Barcelona: EuroMeSCo).

Schmid, D. (2005) Le partenariat, une méthode européenne de démocratisation en Méditerranée? *Politique étrangère*, 70(3), pp. 545–557.

Schumacher, T. (2011) The EU and the Arab Spring: Between Actorness and Spectatorship, *Insight Turkey*, 13(3), pp. 107–119.

Schumacher, T. (2012) Conditionality, Differentiation, Regionality and the 'New' ENP in the Light of Arab Revolts, in: E. Barbé and A. Herranz-Surrallés (eds) *The Challenge of Differentiation in Euro-Mediterranean Relations* (Abingdon, UK and New York: Routledge), pp. 142–158.

Sehimi, M. (2003) La política exterior de Mohamed VI, *Política Exterior*, 91, pp. 97–111.

Shelley, T. (2004) *Endgame in the Western Sahara: What Future for Africa's Last Colony?* (London: Zed Books).

Shelley, T. (2006) Natural Resources and the Western Sahara, in: C. Olsson (ed.) *The Western Sahara Conflict: The Role of Natural Resources and Decolonization* (Uppsala: Nordiska Afrikainstitutet).

Singer, J.D. (1996) Armed Conflict in the Former Colonial Regions: From Classification to Explanation, in: L. van de Goor, K. Rupesinghe and P. Sciarone (eds) *Between Development and Destruction: An Enquiry into the Causes of Conflict in Post-Colonial States* (London: Macmillan).

SIPRI (Stockholm International Peace Research Institute) (2008) *SIPRI Yearbook 2008* (Oxford: Oxford University Press).

SIPRI (Stockholm International Peace Research Institute) (2009) *SIPRI Yearbook 2009* (Oxford: Oxford University Press).

Smith, J.J. (2013) Fishing for Self-Determination: European Fisheries and Western Sahara, in: A. Chircop, S. Coffen-Smout and M. McConnell (eds) *Ocean Yearbook 27* (Leiden and Boston: Martinus Nijhoff), pp. 267–290.

Smith, L.E. (2005) The Struggle for Western Sahara: What Future for Africa's Last Colony? *Journal of North African Studies*, 10(3–4), pp. 545–563.

Solà-Martín, A. (2007) The Western Sahara Cul-de-Sac, *Mediterranean Politics*, 12(3), pp. 399–405.

Soler, E. (2006) El Mediterráneo tras la cumbre de Barcelona. La necesidad de una voluntad política ampliada (Barcelona: CIDOB).

Soler, E. (2008) Proceso de Barcelona: Unión por el Mediterráneo. Génesis y evolución del proyecto de Unión por el Mediterráneo (Madrid: Fundación Alternativas).

Sorroza, A. (2006) La Conferencia Euroafricana de Migración y Desarrollo: más allá del 'espíritu de Rabat'. (Madrid: Real Instituto Elcano).

Steinberg, G. and I. Werenfels (2007) Between the 'Near' and the 'Far' Enemy: Al-Qaeda in the Islamic Maghreb, *Mediterranean Politics*, 12(3), pp. 407–413.

Stephan, M.J. and J. Mundy (2006) A Battlefield Transformed: From Guerrilla Resistance to Mass Nonviolent Struggle in the Western Sahara, *Journal of Military and Strategic Studies*, 8(3), pp. 1–32.

Stora, B. (2002) *Algérie, Maroc. Histoires parallèles, destins croisés* (Paris: Maisonneuve et Larose).

Stora, B. (2003) Algeria/Morocco: The Passions of the Past. Representations of the Nation that Unite and Divide, *Journal of North African Studies*, 8(1), pp. 14–34.

Tazi, A. (1989) *Histoire des relations internationales du Maroc* (Mohamedia: Fédala).

Teti, A. (2004) A Role in Search of a Hero: Construction and the Evolution of Egyptian Foreign Policy, 1952–67, *Journal of Mediterranean Studies*, 14(1–2), pp. 77–105.

Teti, A. (2012) The EU's First Response to the 'Arab Spring': A Critical Discourse Analysis of the Partnership for Democracy and Shared Prosperity, *Mediterranean Politics*, 17(3), pp. 266–284.

Teti, A., D. Thompson and C. Noble (2013) EU Democracy Assistance Discourse in Its 'New Response to a Changing Neighbourhood', *Democracy and Security*, 9(1–2), pp. 61–79.

Theofilopoulou, A. (2006) The United Nations and Western Sahara: A Never-Ending Affair (Washington, DC: USIP).

Theofilopoulou, A. (2007) Western Sahara: How to Create a Stalemate (Washington, DC: USIP).

Theofilopoulou, A. (2010) Western Sahara: The Failure of 'Negotiations without Preconditions' (Washington, DC: USIP).

Theofilopoulou, A. (2012) Morocco's New Constitution and the Western Sahara Conflict: A Missed Opportunity? *Journal of North African Studies*, 17(4), pp. 687–696.

Thies, C.G. and M. Breuning (2012) Integrating Foreign Policy Analysis and International Relations through Role Theory, *Foreign Policy Analysis*, 8(1), pp. 1–4.

Tobji, M. (2006) *Les officiers de Sa Majesté. Les dérives des généraux marocains 1956–2006* (Paris: Fayard).

Torres, A. (2013) La frontera terrestre argelino-marroquí. De herencia colonial a instrumento de presión, *Historia Actual Online*, 31, pp. 7–19.

Tozy, M. (1991) Représentation/intercession, les enjeux du pouvoir dans les 'champs politiques désamorcés' au Maroc, in: M. Camau (ed.) *Changements politiques au Magreb* (Paris: CNRS), pp. 153–168.

Tozy, M. (2008) Morocco's Elections. Islamists, Technocrats, and the Palace, *Journal of Democracy*, 19(1), pp. 34–41.

Tuquoi, J.-P. (2006) *'Majesté, je dois beaucoup à votre père…'. France-Maroc, une affaire de famille* (Paris: Albin Michel).

Tuquoi, J.-P. and A. Amar (2012) *Paris-Marrakech. Luxe, pouvoir et réseaux* (Paris: Calmann-Lévy).

Vagni, J.J. (2010) *Marruecos y su proyección hacia América Latina a partir de Mohamed VI* (Sevilla: UNIA).

Vaquer, J. (2003) The Domestic Dimension of EU External Policies: The Case of the EU–Morocco 2000–01 Fisheries Negotiations, *Mediterranean Politics*, 8(1), pp. 59–82.

Vaquer, J. (2004) The European Union and Western Sahara, *European Foreign Affairs Review*, 9(1), pp. 93–113.

Vaquer, J. (2007) España y el Sáhara Occidental. La dimensión partidista, *Revista CIDOB d'Afers Internacionals*, 79–80, pp. 125–144.
Vaquer, J. (2009) Un estudio de redes en la política exterior española. Las negociaciones pesqueras con Marruecos (2000–2001), *Revista Española de Ciencia Política*, 20, pp. 49–74.
Vasconcelos, Á. (2009) Un test de la volonté et de la cohérence de l'Europe, in: *Le Maroc et l'Union européenne. Vers un statut avancé dans l'Association euro-méditerranéenne* (Barcelona: IEMed), pp. 82–85.
Védie, H.-L. (2008) *Une volonté plus forte que les sables. L'expérience du développement durable des régions sud-marocaines* (Paris: Eska).
Veguilla, V. (2010) L'articulation du politique dans un espace protestataire en recomposition. Les mobilisations des jeunes Sahraouis à Dakhla, in: *L'Année du Maghreb 2009* (Paris: CNRS), pp. 95–110.
Veguilla, V. (2012) *Politiques du poulpe à Dakhla. Action publique, ressources naturelles et dynamiques sociales*, PhD thesis, Institut d'Études Politiques d'Aix-en-Provence.
Vermeren, P. (2004) *Maghreb: La démocratie impossible?* (Paris: Fayard).
Vermeren, P. (2009) *Le Maroc de Mohammed VI. La transition inachevée* (Paris: La Découverte).
Volpi, F. (2013) Explaining (and Re-Explaining) Political Change in the Middle East during the Arab Spring: Trajectories of Democratization and of Authoritarianism in the Maghreb, *Democratization*, 20(6), pp. 969–990.
Wallihan, J. (1998) Negotiating to Avoid Agreement, *Negotiation Journal*, 14(3), pp. 257–268.
Walt, S.M. (1998) International Relations: One World, Many Theories, *Foreign Policy*, 110, pp. 29–46.
Wehrey, F. and A. Boukhars (eds) (2013) *Perilous Desert: Insecurity in the Sahara* (Washington, DC: Carnegie Endowment for International Peace).
Wendt, A.E. (1987) The Agent-Structure Problem in International Relations Theory, *International Organization*, 41(3), pp. 335–370.
Wendt, A.E. (1992) Anarchy is What States Make of It: The Social Construction of Power Politics, *International Organization*, 46(2), pp. 391–425.
Wendt, A.E. (1995) Constructing International Politics, *International Security*, 20(1), pp. 71–81.
Wendt, A.E. (1999) *Social Theory of International Politics* (Cambridge: Cambridge University Press).
White, B. (1999) The European Challenge to Foreign Policy Analysis, *European Journal of International Relations*, 5(1), pp. 37–66.
White, G. (1996) The Mexico of Europe? Morocco's Partnership with the European Union, in: D. Vandewalle (ed.) *North Africa: Development and Reform in a Changing Global Economy* (New York: St. Martin's Press), pp. 111–128.
White, G. (1997) Too Many Boats, Not Enough Fish: The Political Economy of Morocco's 1995 Fishing Accord with the European Union, *Journal of Developing Areas*, 31(3), pp. 313–336.
White, G. (2005) Free Trade as a Strategic Instrument in the War on Terror? The 2004 US-Moroccan Free Trade Agreement, *Middle East Journal*, 59(4), pp. 597–616.
White, N. (2014) Conflict Stalemate in Morocco and Western Sahara: Natural Resources, Legitimacy and Political Recognition, *British Journal of Middle Eastern Studies*, 42(3), pp. 339–357.

Willis, M.J. (2002a) Political Parties in the Maghrib: The Illusion of Significance? *Journal of North African Studies*, 7(2), pp. 1–22.

Willis, M.J. (2002b) Political Parties in the Maghrib: Ideology and Identification. A Suggested Typology, *Journal of North African Studies*, 7(3), pp. 1–28.

Willis, M.J. (2012) *Politics and Power in the Maghreb: Algeria, Tunisia and Morocco from Independence to the Arab Spring* (London: Hurst).

Willis, M.J. and N. Messari (2003) Analyzing Moroccan Foreign Policy and Relations with Europe, *The Review of International Affairs*, 3(2), pp. 152–172.

World Bank (2006) Une nouvelle vision pour l'intégration économique du Maghreb? (Washington DC)

Wunderlich, D. (2010) Differentiation and Policy Convergence against Long Odds: Lessons from Implementing EU Migration Policy in Morocco, *Mediterranean Politics*, 15(2), pp. 249–272.

Yom, S.L. and F. Gregory Gause, III (2012) Resilient Royals: How Arab Monarchies Hang On, *Journal of Democracy*, 23(4), pp. 74–88.

Youngs, R. (2001) *The European Union and the Promotion of Democracy* (Oxford: Oxford University Press).

Youssoufi, A. (2003a) Intérrogations et inquiétudes, *Confluences Méditerranée*, 46, pp. 47–56.

Youssoufi, A. (2003b) Intérrogations et inquiétudes, in: *Beyond Enlargement: Opening Eastwards, Closing Southwards?* (Toledo: Escuela de Traductores de Toledo), pp. 92–96.

Zartman, I.W. (1983) Explaining the Nearly Inexplicable: The Absence of Islam in Moroccan Foreign Policy, in: A. Dawisha (ed.) *Islam in Foreign Policy* (Cambridge: Cambridge University Press), pp. 97–111.

Zartman, I.W. (2001) Morocco, in: L.C. Brown (ed.) *Diplomacy in the Middle East: The International Relations of Regional and Outside Powers* (London and New York: I.B. Tauris), pp. 207–217.

Zartman, I.W. (2013) Morocco's Saharan Policy, in: A. Boukhars and J. Roussellier (eds) *Perspectives on Western Sahara: Myths, Nationalisms, and Geopolitics* (Lanham: Rowman & Littlefield), pp. 55–70.

Zeghal, M. (2005) *Les islamistes marocains. Le défi à la monarchie* (Casablanca and Paris: Le Fennec/La Découverte).

Zemni, S. and K. Bogaert (2010) Trade, Security and Neoliberal Politics: Whither Arab Reform? Evidence from the Moroccan Case, in: F. Cavatorta and V. Durac (eds) *The Foreign Policies of the European Union and the United States in North Africa: Diverging or Converging Dynamics?* (Abingdon, UK and New York: Routledge), pp. 88–104.

Zerhouni, S. (ed.) (2006) *L'avenir se discute: Débats sur les scénarios du Maroc à l'horizon 2025* (Rabat: FES).

Zerhouni, S. (2008) The Moroccan Parliament, in: E. Lust-Okar and S. Zerhouni (eds) *Political Participation in the Middle East* (Boulder and London: Lynne Rienner), pp. 217–237.

Zisenwine, D. (2013) Mohammed VI and Moroccan Foreign Policy, in: B. Maddy-Weitzman and D. Zisenwine (eds) *Contemporary Morocco: State, Politics and Society under Mohammed VI* (Abingdon, UK and New York: Routledge), pp. 70–81.

Zoubir, Y.H. (2000) Algerian-Moroccan Relations and their Impact on Maghribi Integration, *Journal of North African Studies*, 5(3), pp. 43–74.

Zoubir, Y.H. (2004) The Resurgence of Algeria's Foreign Policy in the Twenty-First Century, *Journal of North African Studies*, 9(2), pp. 169–183.

Zoubir, Y.H. (2007) Les États-Unis et le Maghreb. Primauté de la sécurité et marginalité de la démocratie, in: *L'Année du Maghreb 2005–2006* (Paris: CNRS), pp. 563–584.
Zoubir, Y.H. (2009) The United States and Maghreb-Sahel Security, *International Affairs*, 85(5), pp. 977–995.
Zoubir, Y.H. and L. Aït-Hamadouche (2006) Anti-Americanism in North Africa: Could State Relations Overcome Popular Resentment? *Journal of North African Studies*, 11(1), pp. 35–54.
Zoubir, Y.H. and K. Benabdallah-Gambier (2004) Morocco, Western Sahara and the Future of the Maghrib, *Journal of North African Studies*, 9(1), pp. 49–77.
Zoubir, Y.H. and K. Benabdallah-Gambier (2005) The United States and the North African Imbroglio: Balancing Interests in Algeria, Morocco, and the Western Sahara, *Mediterranean Politics*, 10(2), pp. 181–202.
Zoubir, Y.H. and L. Dris-Aït-Hamadouche (2006) The United States and the Maghreb: Islamism, Democratization, and Strategic Interests, *The Maghreb Review*, 31(3–4), pp. 259–292.
Zoubir, Y.H. and L. Dris-Aït-Hamadouche (2013) *Global Security Watch. The Maghreb: Algeria, Libya, Morocco, and Tunisia* (Santa Barbara: Praeger).
Zoubir, Y.H. and D. Volman (eds) (1993) *International Dimensions of the Western Sahara Conflict* (Westport: Praeger).
Zouitni, H. (1986) *Le Maroc dans les organisations régionales politiques (LEA, OUA, OCI)*, PhD thesis, Université Hassan II Casablanca.
Zouitni, H. (1997) Les intérêts nationaux. Entre la pratique de la politique extérieure du Maroc et les besoins d'une redéfinition par rapport au nouveau système international, in: M. Jari (ed.) *Rapport annuel sur l'évolution du système international (RAESI) 1997* (Rabat: GERSI).
Zouitni, H. (1998) *La diplomatie marocaine à travers les organisations régionales (1958–1984). Aspects de la politique extérieure du Maroc* (Casablanca: Fondation Konrad Adenauer).
Zouitni, H. (2001) Les compétences de l'exécutif et du législatif en matière de politique étrangère. L'exemple du Maroc avec une référence au cas français, *Revue Marocaine d'Administration Locale et de Développement*, 41, pp. 27–39.
Zouitni, H. (2003) La conception de la politique étrangère au Maroc, *Revue Marocaine d'Administration Locale et de Développement*, 48–49, pp. 69–80.
Zubaida, S. (1990) Débats sur l'État-nation au Moyen-Orient, in: J.-C. Santucci and H. el Malki (eds) *État et développement dans le monde arabe* (Paris: CNRS), pp. 55–66.
Zunes, S. and J. Mundy (2010) *Western Sahara: War, Nationalism and Conflict Irresolution* (New York: Syracuse University Press).

Official documents

Council of the EU (1999) Action Plan for Morocco, 11426/99, 30 September.
EMP (Euro-Mediterranean Partnership) (2005) Five Year Work Programme, Barcelona, 28 November.
EMP (Euro-Mediterranean Partnership) (2007) Agreed Conclusions of the 9th Euro-Mediterranean Meeting of Ministers of Foreign Affairs, Lisbon, 6 November.
ENI (European Neighbourhood Instrument) (2014) Single Support Framework. Morocco 2014–2017. Summary.
ENPI (European Neighbourhood and Partnership Instrument) (2007a) Morocco. Strategy Paper 2007–2013.

References

ENPI (European Neighbourhood and Partnership Instrument) (2007b) Morocco. 2007–2010 National Indicative Programme.

ENPI (European Neighbourhood and Partnership Instrument) (2011) Mid-Term Review of the Country Strategy Paper Morocco 2007–2013 and National Indicative Program 2011–2013.

ENPI (European Neighbourhood and Partnership Instrument) (2014) 2007–2013 Overview of Activities and Results.

EU (European Union) (2012) Consolidated version of the Treaty on European Union, *Official Journal of the European Union*, 26 October.

EU/Morocco (2000) Euro-Mediterranean Agreement Establishing an Association between the European Communities and their Member States, of the One Part, and the Kingdom of Morocco, of the Other Part, *Official Journal of the European Communities*, L 70/2, 18 March.

EU/Morocco (2013) Joint Declaration Establishing a Mobility Partnership between the Kingdom of Morocco and the European Union and its Member States, Luxembourg, 7 June.

EU–Morocco Association Council (2000) Draft Minutes. First Meeting of the EU–Morocco Association Council, 9 October.

EU–Morocco Association Council (2001) Déclaration du Royaume du Maroc, 9 October.

EU–Morocco Association Council (2005) EU/Morocco Action Plan, 25 July.

EU–Morocco Association Council (2007) Déclaration de l'Union européenne, 23 July.

EU–Morocco Association Council (2008a) Document conjoint UE-Maroc sur le renforcement des relations bilatérales/Statut Avancé, 13 October.

EU–Morocco Association Council (2008b) Déclaration de l'Union européenne, 13 October.

EU–Morocco Association Council (2009) Déclaration de l'Union européenne, 7 December.

EU–Morocco Association Council (2013) Projet de Plan d'Action Maroc pour la Mise en Œuvre du Statut Avance (2013–2017), 16 December.

EU–Morocco Working Group on the Advanced Status (2008) Document du Royaume du Maroc, 1st meeting, 8/16 May.

Euro-African Partnership for Migration and Development (2006a) Rabat Declaration, Rabat, 11 July.

Euro-African Partnership for Migration and Development (2006b) Action Plan, Rabat, 11 July.

European Commission (2004) European Neighbourhood Policy. Country Report. Morocco, COM(2004) 373 final, 12 May.

European Commission (2006) Communication from the Commission to the Council and the European Parliament on Strengthening the European Neighbourhood Policy, COM(2006) 726 final, 4 December.

European Commission (2011a) Action Fiche for the southern Neighbourhood region programme Support for Partnership, Reforms and Inclusive Growth (SPRING), 26 September.

European Commission (2011b) EU response to the Arab Spring: the SPRING Programme, MEMO/11/636, 27 September.

European Commission/High Representative of the Union for Foreign Affairs and Security Policy (2011a) Joint Communication: A Partnership for Democracy and Shared Prosperity with the Southern Mediterranean, COM(2011) 200 final, 8 March.

European Commission/High Representative of the Union for Foreign Affairs and Security Policy (2011b) Joint statement by EU High Representative Catherine Ashton and Commissioner Štefan Füle on Morocco's future constitutional reform, 10 March.

European Commission/High Representative of the Union for Foreign Affairs and Security Policy (2011c) Joint Communication: A New Response to a Changing Neighbourhood, COM(2011) 303 final, 25 May.

European Commission/High Representative of the Union for Foreign Affairs and Security Policy (2011d) Joint statement by High Representative/Vice-President Catherine Ashton and Commissioner Štefan Füle on the announcement of the new Constitution of Morocco, 19 June.

European Commission/High Representative of the Union for Foreign Affairs and Security Policy (2011e) Joint statement by High Representative Catherine Ashton and Commissioner Štefan Füle on the referendum on the new Constitution in Morocco, 2 July.

European Commission/High Representative of the Union for Foreign Affairs and Security Policy (2012) Joint Communication: Supporting closer cooperation and regional integration in the Maghreb: Algeria, Libya, Mauritania, Morocco and Tunisia, JOIN(2012) 36 final, 17 December 2012.

European Parliament (2011) Recommendation on the draft Council decision on the conclusion of a Protocol between the European Union and the Kingdom of Morocco setting out the fishing opportunities and financial compensation provided for in the Fisheries Partnership Agreement between the European Community and the Kingdom of Morocco, Committee on Fisheries, 29 November.

European Parliament (2012) Annual report on human rights and democracy in the world 2011 and the European Union's policy on the matter, 13 December.

Forum for the Future (2004) Chair Summary, Rabat, 11 December.

MAEC (Ministère des Affaires Étrangères et de la Coopération du Royaume du Maroc) (2002) Pour une dynamisation du Partenariat euro-méditerranéen, Rabat, 5 April.

MAEC (Ministère des Affaires Étrangères et de la Coopération du Royaume du Maroc) (2003a) Lettre datée du 21 octobre 2003, adressée au Président du Conseil de sécurité par le Représentant permanent du Maroc auprès de l'Organisation des Nations Unies, S/2003/1028, 21 October.

MAEC (Ministère des Affaires Étrangères et de la Coopération du Royaume du Maroc) (2003b) Contribution du Royaume du Maroc à la négociation d'une solution politique mutuellement acceptable de la question du Sahara, 23 December.

MAEC (Ministère des Affaires Étrangères et de la Coopération du Royaume du Maroc) (2004a) Présentation de l'accord de libre-échange entre le Maroc et les États-Unis.

MAEC (Ministère des Affaires Étrangères et de la Coopération du Royaume du Maroc) (2004b) Note sur la concertation avec le secteur privé au sujet du FTA.

MAEC (Ministère des Affaires Étrangères et de la Coopération du Royaume du Maroc) (2004c) Memorandum of the Kingdom of Morocco on the regional dispute on the Sahara, 24 September.

MAEC (Ministère des Affaires Étrangères et de la Coopération du Royaume du Maroc) (2007) Initiative marocaine pour la négociation d'un statut d'autonomie de la région du Sahara, 7 April.

MAEC (Ministère des Affaires Étrangères et de la Coopération du Royaume du Maroc) (2008) *Le Maroc et l'Union européenne. Le Partenariat Maroc-UE: vers la concrétisation du Statut Avancé.*

MAEC (Ministère des Affaires Étrangères et de la Coopération du Royaume du Maroc) (2009) Guide du diplomate marocain, May.

MAEC (Ministère des Affaires Étrangères et de la Coopération du Royaume du Maroc) (2011) Charte des valeurs du diplomate Marocain.

MAEC (Ministère des Affaires Étrangères et de la Coopération du Royaume du Maroc)/ CGEM (Confédération Générale des Entreprises du Maroc) (2001) Mémorandum de coopération entre le Ministère des Affaires Étrangères et de la Coopération et la Confédération Générale des Entreprises du Maroc.

UN General Assembly (2008) Resolution adopted by the General Assembly [on the report of the Special Political and Decolonization Committee (Fourth Committee) (A/63/408)]. Question of Western Sahara, A/RES/63/105, 18 December.

UN Security Council (2000) Report of the Secretary-General on the situation concerning Western Sahara, S/2000/461, 22 May.

UN Security Council (2001) Report of the Secretary-General on the situation concerning Western Sahara, S/2001/613, 20 June.

UN Security Council (2002a) Letter dated 29 January 2002 from the Under-Secretary-General for Legal Affairs, the Legal Counsel, addressed to the President of the Security Council, S/2002/161, 12 February.

UN Security Council (2002b) Report of the Secretary-General on the situation concerning Western Sahara, S/2002/178, 19 February.

UN Security Council (2003a) Report of the Secretary-General on the situation concerning Western Sahara, S/2003/565, 23 May.

UN Security Council (2003b) Report of the Secretary-General on the situation concerning Western Sahara, S/2003/1016, 16 October.

UN Security Council (2004) Report of the Secretary-General on the situation concerning Western Sahara, S/2004/325, 23 April.

UN Security Council (2012) Report of the Secretary-General on the situation concerning Western Sahara, S/2012/197, 5 April.

United States/Morocco (2004) United States–Morocco Free Trade Agreement, Washington, DC, 15 June.

United States/Morocco (2012) Joint Statement of the First Session of the U.S.–Kingdom of Morocco Strategic Dialogue, Washington, DC, 12 October.

Interviews

List of interviewees who did not request confidentiality, followed by the positions they held at the time of their interview, and the place and date(s) of interview.

Ministry of Foreign Affairs and Cooperation

Adghoughi, Nabil, head of the Division for the European Union, Directorate of European Affairs, Rabat, 13 February 2006.

Alj Hakim, Jaafar, director of Asian and Oceanian Affairs, Rabat, 17 February 2006.

Atrari, Abdelkhalik, head of the Division of Ceremonial and Protocol, Directorate of Protocol, Rabat, 11 June 2009.

Bichri, Saloua, head of the Spain Service, Division for Bilateral Relations with the Countries of Meditrereanean Europe, Directorate of European Affairs, Rabat, 13 February 2006.

Boufekar, Driss, head of the Training Service, Division of Training and Social Work, Department of Personnel and Training, Rabat, 17 June 2009.

De Fouad, Habib, head of the Division for Bilateral Relations with the Countries of Northern, Central and Eastern Europe, Directorate of European Affairs, Rabat, 17 February 2006.
Hami, Hassan, head of the Division for Arab and Islamic Organisations, Directorate of Arab and Islamic Affairs, Rabat, 13 February 2006.
Ifriquine, M'hamed, head of the Service for Interstate Organisations, Directorate of African Affairs, Rabat, 14 February 2006.
Moslih, Abdelkader, head of the Division for Political Affairs, Directorate of American Affairs, Rabat, 14 February 2006.
Naciri, Khalid, head of the Division for the Arab Maghreb Union, Directorate of Arab and Islamic Affairs, Rabat, 17 February 2006.

Mission of Morocco to the European Union

Abderrazaq, Nabil, minister plenipotentiary in charge of Migration Issues and EU–Africa Relations, Brussels, 23 May 2014.
Akkor, Faiçal, minister plenipotentiary in charge of Financial Cooperation, Brussels, 23 May 2014.
Belayachi, Mounir, deputy ambassador to the European Union, Brussels, 23 May 2014.
Benzekri, Narjis, counsellor in charge of Human Rights and Relations with the Council of Europe, Brussels, 23 May 2014.
Fyad, Abderrahman, minister plenipotentiary in charge of Relations with the European Parliament, Brussels, 23 May 2014.
Lahsaini, Khalid, minister plenipotentiary in charge of Sectorial Cooperation, Brussels, 23 May 2014.

Political parties and parliament

Akesbi, Moussa, local officer, Party of Progress and Socialism (PPS), Rabat, 9 October 2007.
Alaoui, Ismaïl, secretary-general, Party of Progress and Socialism (PPS), Rabat, 14 February 2006.
Ameskane, Saïd, spokesperson and member of the Political Bureau, Popular Movement (MP), Rabat, 13 February 2006.
Baha, Abdellah, deputy secretary-general and chairman/spokesperson of the parliamentary group, Justice and Development Party (PJD), Rabat, 24 February 2006.
Baraka, Nizar, member of the Executive Committee, Istiqlal Party (PI), Rabat, 24 February 2006.
Barhmi, Mustapha, head of the Division of Legislation, Commissions and Sessions of the House of Representatives, Rabat, 9 June 2009.
Benaboud, Khaled, press officer, Justice and Development Party (PJD), Rabat, 5 October 2007.
Benkhaldoun, Réda, member of the General Secretariat and MP, head of the Foreign Relations Committee, Justice and Development Party (PJD), phone interview/Rabat, 10 January 2007, 1 November 2007, 6 June 2013.
Benyahia, Mohamed, MP and former member of the Committee on Foreign Affairs, National Defence and Islamic Affairs (2002–2007), Socialist Union of Popular Forces (USFP), Rabat, 19 October 2007.

Bouqentar, El Hassane, member of the Political Bureau and the Committee on International Relations, Socialist Union of Popular Forces (USFP), Rabat, 17 October 2007, 5 June 2013.

Chatri, Abdellatif, member of the Committee on Foreign Affairs and the Youth Wing, Istiqlal Party (PI), Rabat, 30 October 2007.

Chekrouni, Nezha, member of the Political Bureau and the Committee on International Relations, Socialist Union of Popular Forces (USFP), deputy minister for Moroccans Living Abroad (2002–2007), Rabat, 12 February 2006.

Daoudi, Lahcen, member of the General Secretariat and MP, Justice and Development Party (PJD), Rabat, 17 February 2006, 1 November 2007.

Fkir, Ali, senior member, Democratic Way (VD), Mohamedia, 11 October 2007.

Grine, M'hamed, member of the Political Bureau in charge of International Relations, Party of Progress and Socialism (PPS), Rabat, 17 October 2007.

Messari, Mohamed Larbi, chairman of the Foreign Relations Committee, Istiqlal Party (PI), Rabat, 15 October 2007, 24 October 2007, 5 December 2007, 26 November 2011.

Mounib, Nabila, member of the Political Bureau, Unified Socialist Party (PSU), Casablanca, 10 October 2007.

Osman, Ahmed, president, National Rally of Independents (RNI), former prime minister (1972–1979), Rabat, 14 February 2006.

Radi, Abdelwahed, member of the Political Bureau, Socialist Union of Popular Forces (USFP), president of the House of Representatives (1997–2007, 2010–2011), minister of Justice (2007–2010), Rabat, 3 December 2007.

Sadouk, Khadija, member of the Central Committee, Unified Socialist Party (PSU), Casablanca, 18 February 2006.

Soussi, Thami, administrative officer, National Rally of Independents (RNI), Rabat, 8 October 2007.

Civil society

Abou El Aazme, Abdelghani, member of the Executive Committee, Moroccan Association in Support of the Palestinian Struggle (AMALP), Rabat, 6 November 2007.

Amine, Abdelhamid, vice-president, Moroccan Association for Human Rights (AMDH), Rabat, 31 October 2007.

Andalousi, Mohamed Benjelloune, president, Moroccan Association in Support of the Palestinian Struggle (AMALP), Rabat, 6 November 2007.

Ayouche, Mouhcine, former deputy director, General Confederation of Moroccan Entrepreneurs (CGEM, 1995–2006), Casablanca, 29 October 2007.

Drissi, Abderrazak, coordinator, Moroccan Cell against the Forum for the Future (CEMACOFA), Rabat, 11 June 2009.

El Boukili, Mohamed, member of the Central Bureau and the Administrative Committee, Moroccan Association for Human Rights (AMDH), Rabat, 20 February 2006, 22 February 2006.

Fikry, Soundouss, head of the International Department, General Confederation of Moroccan Entrepreneurs (CGEM), Casablanca, 16 October 2007.

Moussaoui, Driss, president, Collectif Démocratie et Modernité, Casablanca, 21 February 2006.

Oudouni, Aziz, member of the Political Circle and the Support Committee for the Causes of the Umma, Al Adl wal Ihsan, Casablanca, 4 December 2007.

Soufiani, Khalid, coordinator, National Action Committee in Support of Iraq and Palestine, Rabat, 25 October 2007, 26 November 2007.
Yafout, Merieme, member of the Political Circle and the Women's Section, Al Adl wal Ihsan, Casablanca, 4 December 2007.
Yassine, Nadia, leader of the Women's Section, Al Adl wal Ihsan, Salé, 5 November 2007.

Universities, thinktanks and media

Benabid, Mohamed, deputy editor-in-chief of *L'Économiste*, Casablanca, 15 February 2006, 23 February 2006.
Bouqentar, El Hassan, professor of International Relations, University Mohammed V Rabat, Rabat, 17 October 2007, 5 June 2013.
Brouksy, Omar, editor at *Le Journal Hebdomadaire* and lecturer of Political Science at the University Mohammed V Settat, Rabat, 5 October 2007, 5 November 2007.
Darif, Mohamed, professor of Political Science, University Hassan II Mohammedia, Casablanca, 30 October 2007.
El Azizi, Abdellatif, editor at *Tel Quel*, Casablanca, 23 February 2006.
El Messaoudi, Amina, professor of Political Science, University Mohammed V Rabat, Rabat, 23 October 2007.
El Ouahhabi, Othmane, PhD candidate, University Mohammed V Rabat, Rabat, 31 October 2007.
El Ouali, Abdelhamid, professor of International Law and International Relations, University Hassan II Casablanca, former member of the Consultative Commission on Regionalization (CCR), Casablanca, 7 June 2013.
Fassi Fihri, Brahim, president of the Institut Amadeus, Rabat, 6 June 2013.
Fleury, Bénédicte, development director of the Institut Amadeus, Rabat, 11 June 2009.
Ibahrine, Mohammed, assistant professor, Al Akhawayn University in Ifrane, Ifrane, 7 November 2007.
Jamaï, Aboubakr, editor-in-chief of *Le Journal Hebdomadaire*, Casablanca, 21 February 2006.
Kerdoudi, Jawad, president of the Institut Marocain des Relations Internationales (IMRI), Casablanca, 6–25 February 2006, 1–2 October 2007.
Khrouz, Driss, secretary-general of the Group of Studies and Research on the Mediterranean (GERM), Rabat, 15 February 2006.
Maalmi, Abdelwahab, professor of International Relations, University Hassan II Casablanca, Casablanca, 23 February 2006, 16 October 2007, 7 June 2013.
Madani, Mohammed, professor of Political Science, University Mohammed V Rabat, Rabat, 19 October 2007, 22 November 2011, 5 June 2013.
Sater, James N., assistant professor, Al Akhawayn University in Ifrane, Ifrane, 8 November 2007.
Sehimi, Mustapha, professor of Law, University Mohammed V Rabat, research director at the Rabat Centre for Strategic Studies (CESR), Rabat, 22 February 2006.

Others

Member of the Royal Consultative Council for Saharan Affairs (CORCAS), Rabat, 7 June 2013.

European Union

Officials of the Delegation of the European Union to Morocco, Rabat, 6 June 2013.

Konstantopoulos, Alexis, official in charge of Morocco Desk, Maghreb Division, European External Action Service (EEAS), phone interview, 6 June 2014.

Landaburu, Eneko, former ambassador and head of the Delegation of the European Union in Morocco (2009–2013), Brussels, 23 May 2014.

Planas, Luis, ambassador of Spain to Morocco (2004–2010), Rabat, 20 February 2006.

Index

Page numbers in *italics* denote tables, those in **bold** denote figures.

5 + 5 Dialogue 81, 84, 88, 95n8, 109, 130, 137
9/11 attacks 18–19, 84, 106, 189–93, 195, 210, 212; aftermath 21, 199; post-9/11 context 81, 194, 204

Abouddahab, Z. 10, 21–2, 29, 35, 178, 199
Action Plans 115, 117, 119–20, 124, 154; annexed 150; bilateral 114; ENP 132, 134, 136–7, 140, 142, 144–5, 151–2, 155; EU–Morocco 115, 121, 135; on Human Rights and Democracy 40, 145; national 116, 145; Valencia 107
Adler, E. 12–13, 105, 114, 119, 172
Africa 27, 63, 98, 125; EU–Africa Summit 85, 94; European policy towards 134; peace and security 141; South 26, 89, 92, 146; Western 42, 201, 206; *see also* North Africa
African 86, 133; AFRICOM 206–7; Arab-African Union 20; Central 31; conflicts 189; continent 92; countries 28, 63, 96, 122, 124–5; Directorate of African Affairs *25*; environment 21; Euro-African Ministerial Conference 31, 123, 181; Franco-African summits 31; governments 206; immigration 123; joint military exercises 71; migration 124; policy 22, 42, 125, 213, 215, 218; state 146; tours 31; Union 94, 125; Western 27, 31
Aggestam, L. 14, 47, 96–8, 158, 189
agricultural 142, 146; agreement 154, 184; exports 112; imports 113; market 203; productivity 199; products 111, 202; relations 99; sector 202, 204; sector reforms 117; trade 108, 137, 189

agriculture 107, 110, 112, 117, 134, 141–2, 153, 171, 175, 184, 200; Euro-Mediterranean Roadmap 113; technical cooperation 193
Al Adl wal Ihsan 43, 192, 197, 215, 217
Al Akhawayn University in Ifrane (AUI) 24, 26–7, 195, 197; Master of Arts in International Studies and Diplomacy (MAISD) 24, 26
Al Khouri, R. 111, 200
Al Qaeda in the Islamic Maghreb (AQIM) 204–5
Alami M'chichi, H. 119–20, 122–3
Albrecht, H. 19, 30, 213
Algeria 5, 9–10, 17, 29, 82, 85–7, 89, 107, 109, 129, 150, 154, 166, 169, 206, 217; absence from AU 125; Baker Plan I rejected 53, 165, 177; Baker Plan II 54–5; bilateral normalisation 91; bilateral rapprochement 93, 82, 180; bilateral relations with 37; borders 76, 83, 90, 95n7; eastern Sahara 94; French deference 131; military expenditure **92**; political disagreements 113; political liberalisation 81; relations with 43–4, 77, 93, 216; relations with Morocco 77–9; Trans-Sahara Counter-Terrorism Initiative 205; U.S. ambassador 66; U.S. partnership project 190, 199
Algerian 78, 83, 85, 94; Algerian–Moroccan High Joint Commission 86; authorities 84; border 123; foreign minister 90; founding president 93; independence 170; Moroccan–Algerian dispute 89; Moroccan–Algerian normalisation 88; Moroccan–Algerian relations 95; people 79; political crisis 76; president 53, 84–5;

Algerian *continued*
  pressure 56, 87; ruling class 91; Salafist Group for Preaching and Combat (GSPC) 204–5; tourists 82; war 81
Algerians 78, 88, 167
Algiers 70, 82–4, 87, 89, 93; alignment with Madrid 86; AMU summit 88; arms race 168; borders issue 91; French rapprochement 166; Global Counterterrorism Forum meeting 94; rivalry with Rabat 180, 191; Spanish rapprochement 175; state visit 169; U.S. rapprochement 53, 201
ALTHEA military operation in Bosnia and Herzegovina 134
Amar, A. 2, 10, 22, 40–1, 51, 162, 166–8, 186n5, 193–4, 208
Ammor, F.M. 113, 115, 122
anti-terrorist 192; intelligence collaboration 194; solidarity 87
Arab Maghreb 79, 90–1; Press (MAP) 16, 95n4; Union 9, 20, 76, 85, 88, 97, 180, 197, 199
Arab Maghreb Union (AMU) 9, 20, 76, 85, 97, 107, 180, 197, 199; cooperation with EU 83, 97; Council of Ministers of Trade 80; Directorate for the Greater Maghreb and the AMU Affairs **25**; foreign ministers 86, 93; foundation 77, 81; integration project 9; ministerial and sectoral dialogue 84; Presidential Council 88; relaunch 90, 93, 95n7, 113, 180, 199; summit 89, 93
Arab Spring 1, 68, 93–4, 100–1, 127, 146–9, 151–2, 154–5, 168, 183, 213; post Arab Spring 2, 35, 93, 146, 219; protests 2, 7, 33
Arab-African Union 20
asylum 119–21, 126n13; seekers 123, 150

Baker Plans *48*, 60, 83, 207; Baker Plan I (Framework Agreement on the Status of Western Sahara) 52–5, 86–7, 165, 177, 207; Baker Plan II (Peace Plan for Self-Determination of the People of Western Sahara) 54–61, 73, 87–9, 95n6, 165, 180–1, 201, 207
Barnett, M.N. 4, 20, 79, 189, 214
Barreñada, I. 47, 60
Bayart, J.-F. 2, 15, 212
Beau, N. 160, 163–4, 166, 186n2
Behr, T. 2, 100–1, 157
Belalami, M. 10, 22–3, 26, 29, 39, 42
Belayachi, M. 149–50, 152–4

Belgourch, A. 9–10
Belguendouz, A. 120–2, 176–7
Belhaj, A. 9–10, 15, 31, 43, 45n20, 192, 194, 196
Benaissa, M. 22–3, 26, 34, 37, 44n6, 53, 55, 57, 59, 63, 74n13, 86–9, 108, 111, 115, 124, 179, 192, 197–8, 202, 208
Benali, A. 24, 26
Benchemsi, A. 7, 218
Ben El Hassan Alaoui, M. 20, 97
Benmoussa, B. 10, 63, 200, 203
Bennani-Chraïbi, M. 17, 43
Bennis, S. 10, 187n12
Berramdane, A. 10, 189
Bicchi, F. 127–8
Biscop, S. 2, 127
Boukhars, A. 9, 72
Bouqentar, H. 10, 36, 50, 64, 70, 153, 168
Bouteflika, President A. 53, 84–8, 94, 107, 131
Bremberg, N. 132, 134, 140, 155n7, 171–2, 185
Broader Middle East and North Africa (BMENA) initiative 190, 195–6, 199, 204, 210
Brouksy, O. 31–2, 40, 60, 67, 70, 162, 168, 170, 185, 194

Calleya, S.C. 109, 113
Cantir, C. 13–14, 47, 77–8, 97–8, 104, 158, 188
Catusse, M. 16–17, 42
Cebolla, H. 102, 162, 179
Cembrero, I. 10, 35, 164–5, 177–8, 180, 219
Ceuta and Melilla 89, 123, 158, 170, 177, 179, 181–3, 185–6, 187n8
Chaarani, A. 192–4
Charillon, F. 3, 6, 9, 19, 41
Checkel, J.T. 14, 101–2, 104
Cheikh, A. 10, 45n19
Cherkaoui, M. 64, 74n4
Chirac, President J. 58, 87; bilateral crisis 164; French–Maghrebi relations 166; friendship with King Hassan II 163, 169; paternalism 186; presidency 165
Civil Concord Law 84
Clinton, H. 66–7, 209
CNDH (*Conseil National des Droits de l'Homme*) 40, 105, 149–50
coalitions 13, 184; building 7, 11, 215; cabinet 35; cross-cutting 2; FTA Business 211n10; government 33, 52, 93, 197; international 196; policy 3, 12; ruling 37, 193; War on Terror 189, 191–2, 210

Collectif Sahara-Maghreb 56, 82
Collective of Sahrawi Defenders of Human Rights (CODESA) 60, 67, 71
Colombo, S. 100, 148, 157
Comité Directeur du Rapport 41, 44, 135
Common Foreign and Security Policy (CFS) 116, 134, 141, 164
Community of Sahel-Saharan States (CEN-SAD) 86
Compés, R. 112, 154
Consultative Council on Human Rights (CCDH) 33, 40, 104–5, 142, 195
Council of the EU 63, 110, 120
Council for the Moroccan Community Abroad (CCME) 40–1
counterterrorism 79, 81, 193; efforts 194; Global Counterterrorism Forum 94; Trans-Sahara Counter-Terrorism Initiative 205
crisis 31, 47, 71, 158, 179, 183, 218; Algerian political 76; Aznar government 184; bilateral 86, 107, 164, 169, 175, 177, 186, 191; diplomatic 182; economic 153, 184; Europeanisation 124; financial 173; Laayoune 50, 67–8; management 117; migration 181, 185; MINURSO mandate 37; Moroccan–Spanish 177; Morocco–UN 209; multilateral 69–70; Perejil 23, 35, 214; political representation 38; rejection of the Baker Plan II *48*, 54, 95n6; resolving 178; storming of border fences 89, 123, 181, 185; strategic 54, 66, 73
Crombois, J.F. 200, 202–3

Dahbi, O. 10, 187n12
Dalle, I. 4, 20, 31–3, 35, 178
Daoud, Z. 15, 41
decentralisation 51, 56, 74n18, 134
Deep and Comprehensive Free Trade Area (DCFTA) 149, 154
Dekkar, T. 10, 86, 95n4
Del Sarto, R.A. 5, 96–8, 100, 106, 114
democracy 51, 116–17, 138; absence in Morocco 174; bottom-up assistance 119; building deep 127; EU assistance 43; EU promotion policies 104, 119; lack of 146; multi-party 190; Partnership 148, 151; pluralist 151; promotion 111, 118, 162, 174, 196, 200; related vocabulary 144; strong 166; transition to 149
democratisation 7, 30, 40, 56, 101, 104–5, 110–11, 133–4, 138, 144–5, 147–8, 196–7, 212–13
Desrues, T. 7, 30, 34, 38, 197, 201

détente 79, 94, 179; defensive 93
Díez Peralta, E. 111–12
Directorate-General for Studies and Documentation (DGED) 22, 30, 32–4, 63, 214
drugs 81; control 109; European Monitoring Centre 143; generic 203–4; international dealer 85; trafficking 110, 117, 178, 185

education 20, 24, 26–7, 52, 110, 116–17, 134; French-style 102, 161; higher 128; Moroccan 142, 151
educational 211n18; cooperation 161, 173
Eizenstat Initiative 77, 190, 199
El Houdaïgui, R. 3, 7, 9–10, 15, 23, 30–1, 34–5, 39, 41, 45n13, 64, 97–8, 110, 116, 134, 158, 173, 187n13, 201, 214
El Maslouhi, A. 30, 35
El Messaoudi, A. 22, 61–2, 74n18
El Othmani, S.-E. 37, 69, 93, 152, 185
El Ouali, A. 64, 66
El Qadim, N. 120–2, 134, 176
EMHRN *see* Euro-Mediterranean Human Rights Network
EMP *see* Euro-Mediterranean Partnership
ENI *see* European Neighbourhood Instrument
ENP *see* European Neighbourhood Policy
ENPI *see* European Neighbourhood and Partnership Instrument
Equity and Reconciliation Commission (IER) 40, 61
Escribano, G. 21, 111–12, 114, 200
EU (European Union) 2, 14, 22, 37–8, 44, 73, 106–7, 111, 115, 133, 143, 147; acquis 137, 141–2, 146; Advanced Status 129; Africa Summit 85, 94; agencies and programmes 135–6, 140, 143; agricultural agreement 184; assistance 122; authorities 150; cooperation with AMU 20; Council 63; Declaration 83, 121, 134, 143–4, 146; democracy assistance 43; democracy promotion policies 119; economic ties 99; expectations 91, 138; foreign policy 100, 127; High Representative 93, 147; institutions 108, 128, 163–4; irregular migrants 120–1, 123; market 122; Neighbourhood Barometers 97, *98*; Neighbourhood Info Centre 148–9, 151, 156n10; partners 164, 178; policymaking 155, 157; political support 104; Single Market 112–14, 149, 200; Structural Funds 141, 144

252 Index

EU (European Union) finance 118; assistance to Morocco 80, 113, *117*; Commissioner for Trade 204; Financial Framework 149; Financial Perspective 114, 117, 143; Single Market 112–14, 149, 200; trade with Morocco 125n3

EU (European Union) fisheries agreement 137, 175, 182, 184; with Morocco 72, 164, 175, 182, 184; negotiations with Morocco 107

EU (European Union) member states 99, 120, 128–9, 136, 140, 150, 153, 157, 163–4, 217; EU (European Union) accession 97, 108, 134, 140; membership expectations 114

EU (European Union) relations 5–6, 22, 40, 114, 129, 152, 189, 217; bilateral 109–11; foreign 102; with Mediterranean countries 105, 127; with its periphery 133; with Rabat 134, 137, 155, 168; with Tunisia 125n4; *see also* EU relations with Morocco

EU (European Union) relations with Morocco 2, 40, 42, 68, 72, 77, 81–3, 95–7, *98*, 99, 102–4, 111, 116, 118–19, 127, 129–32, 144–6, 151–3, 213, 215–16, 218; bilateral 109–11; Delegation 102–3, 138, 148, 150, 152, 155n7; economic cooperation 72, 153; financial assistance 113, *117*; fisheries agreement 72, 164, 175, 182, 184; fisheries negotiations 107; model student 6, 17–18, 96–9, 101, 103–5, 125, 132, 157, 188, 214, 218; Moroccan accession 97; Moroccan perceptions 97, *98*; partnership 140; socialisation 101, 104, 118; trade 125n3

EU/Morocco (2000) 110; (2013) 150

EU–Morocco Advanced Status 27, 40, 83, 89, 104, 135, 155, 164, 168; EU–Morocco Working Group on the Advanced Status 27, 139–40

EU–Morocco Association Council 27, 42, 83, 100, 106, 109–11, 116–17, 121, 129, 131–2, 134–7, 140–6, 151; bilateral 105–6, 116

EU–Morocco fisheries agreement 38, 72, 137, 153, 164, 175, 182, 184, 187n13; negotiations 107

Euro-African Ministerial Conference on Migration and Development 31, 123, 181

Euro-African Partnership for Migration and Development 124

Euro-Mediterranean 18, 133; Bank 107; Charter for Peace and Stability 106; Code of Conduct on Countering Terrorism 109; conferences 105–7, 109; cooperation 83, 107, 122; dynamic 130; environment 21; forum 131; free trade area 111; game 106; issues 153; Morocco's activism 106; Morocco's commitment 97; policies 96, 99, 128; region 98; relations 111, 128–9; Roadmap for Agriculture 113; University 128

Euro-Mediterranean Human Rights Network (EMHRN) 139, 150

Euro-Mediterranean Partnership (EMP) 31, 39, 81, 99, 105–11, 113–15, 117, 119, 123, 125, 127–30, 135, 137, 171, 198–9

European Commission 20, 93, 116, 119, 121–2, 124, 125n3, 127–8, 132, 135, 142–3, 147, 149–51, 154–5, 164, 182

European Economic Community (EEC) 20, 77, 97, 171; application for membership 99, 132

European Neighbourhood and Partnership Instrument (ENPI) 114, 116, *117–18*, 125n8, 143, 149

European Neighbourhood Instrument (ENI) 149, 155n9

European Neighbourhood Policy (ENP) 108, 114, 118, 125, 131, 134; Action Plan 132, 134, 136–7, 140, 142, 144–5, 151, 155; Action Plan for Morocco 115, 132; essential characteristic 133; EU Commissioner 155; follow-up report 148; framework 119, 152; launch 121; partners 143; procedures 116; progress reports 154; reports on implementation 153; review 100, 127; strengthening 135

European Parliament *48*, 72, 99, 113, 118, 124, 146–7, 153–4, 156n11, 163, 182, 184

European Security and Defence Policy (ESDP) 109, 116, 134, 136, 141

extraversion 2, 212

Fassi Fihri, B. 44, 130, 148
Fassi Fihri, T. 27, 34, 37, 57, 59, 63, 66, 81, 83, 95n8, 108–9, 115–16, 123, 130, 136–7, 139, 143, 145, 147, 167, 178, 197–8, 200, 202, 204
Feliu, L. 7, 9, 43, 174–5, 180
Fernández-Molina, I. 1, 7, 36, 39, 42, 61, 71, 105, 127, 133, 146, 184, 196, 209–10, 215, 218

Fibla, C. 179, 181
Filali, A. 23
fisheries 110, 117, 171, 175, 177, 184, 199; agreement 137, 153, 187n13; completed protocol 154; relations 99; Spanish–Moroccan relations 176; *see also* EU–Morocco fisheries agreement
Fondation Hassan II 162, 173
foreign policies 3, 5, 11–12, 120; of Arab countries 7–9, 191; Europeanised 157; Third World 7, 12
Foreign Policy Analysis (FPA) 3, 7, 9–13, 212
Forum for the Future 190, 195–7–8, 210, 210n5
Framework Agreement on the Status of Western Sahara 52; *see also* Baker Plans (Baker Plan I)
France 31, 34, 47, 51, 57–8, 60, 77, 87, 91, 100, 109, 121, 136, 150, 164, 170, 172, 174, 177, 186n4, 212, 217; alliance with 18, 186; ambassador to 33; bilateral crisis 186; bilateral relations with 10, 18, 135, 155, 157, 167, 169; deference to Algeria 131; diplomatic intervention 67; education of Moroccan elites 102; FDI in Morocco **161**; foreign ministry 137; intervention 165; media 16, 162; Moroccan delegation 62; Moroccan imports 184; Moroccan interdependence 158; Moroccan lobby 162; Moroccan migrants 173; policy towards Maghreb 166, 180; relations with 37, 163, 168; resistance 71; rivalry with U.S. 189; Security Council member 63, 71; support for Morocco 75n28, 123, 169; trade with Morocco **159, 160**; *see also* French
Franco-Spanish alliance 136, 155; harmony 164; relations 157
Free Trade Agreement (FTA) 198, 200–4, 207, 211n8, 211n14; U.S.–Morocco 199, 211n10; *see also* Deep and Comprehensive Free Trade Area (DCFTA)
French 167; ambassador 163, 169; businessmen 160; candidate 166; capital 170; citizens 162, 169; companies 160, 166–8; culture 162; deputy minister for Foreign Trade 204; Development Agency 161; diplomats 166, 168; Directorate-General for External Security (DGSE) 164;
economy 159; education model 102; embassy 16, 160, 169; government 167; groups 160; initiative 128–9, 155; investment 159, 167; lobbying 165; mediation 88; Ministry of Foreign Affairs 164, 169; NGO 169; partner 170; politics 186n5; presidency of the EU 128, 136, 163, 168; president 163–4, 167; presidential elections 166; presidential spokesperson 165; presidentialism 30; project 129; proposal 128, 130; protection 168; resistance 164; role expectations 158; state 161–2; veto 180
French justice 167; court actions 167; judge 166
French–Maghrebi relations 166
French–Moroccan alliance 163
French-Spanish firm Altadis 172
fundamental freedoms 116–117, 134, 151

G-8 196–8; BMENA initiative 190, 195, 210
Gaddafi, Colonel M. 89
Garçon, J. 30, 33
Gause, F.G. 2
GERM (*Groupement d'Études et de Recherches sur la Méditerranée*) 127
Gillespie, R. 106, 119, 128–9, 145, 171, 173, 182
Gimeno, S. 61, 68
Gourevitch, P. 11
Grimaud, N. 9, 190, 199
Group of Friends of Western Sahara 63, 71, 177, 209

Hagan, J.D. 3–5, 11–12, 19, 31, 218
Hami, H. 9–10, 15, 77
Hasenclever, A. 4, 13
Hermann, C.F. 10–11, 31, 217
Hernando de Larramendi, M. 1, 9–10, 15, 31, 35–6, 39, 41, 56–7, 59, 76, 81, 86, 93, 123, 164, 171, 174–5, 178
High-Level Working Group on Asylum and Migration 120
Hill, C. 30, 35, 40
Hinnebusch, R. 4–5, 8
Hollande, F. 75n28, 163, 170; bilateral crisis 186; presidency 169
Holsti, K.J. 5, 13, 46–7, 77, 96, 157–8
Houston Accords 49
Hudson, V.M. 11–12
human development 109, 116, 134; National Initiative (INDH) 117

human rights 60, 69, 112, 116–17, *118*, 123, 134, 151, 154, 167, 194, 198; abuses 150; associations 42, 214; Consultative Council (CCDH) 33, 40, 195; dialogue 142; Euro-Mediterranean Network 139; Inter-Ministerial Delegation 149; international NGOs 40, 68; international provisions 116; international standards 54, 56–7; judicial crises 170; of migrants 122; monitoring 34, 68, 94, 168, 186, 209; Moroccan Association (AMDH) 43, 206; Moroccan movement 42; National Action Plan 40, 145; National Council (CNDH) 40, 105, 149–50; reforms 195; Sahrawi activists 67; shortcomings 144; subcommittee 110–11, 145; UN High Commissioner (OHCH) 68, 71, 209; violations 60–1, 67, 71, 99, 118, 169, 195; Watch (HRW) 34, 68, 150, 194; Western Sahara 73, 156n11, 209–10; *see also* CODESA

ICG (International Crisis Group) 51, 60, 64, 74n8, 74n18, 199, 205
IEMed (*Institut Europeu de la Mediterrània*) 39, 95n1, 111, 134–7, 144–5, 155n4
Iglesias, M. 171, 175, 177, 183
Ihraï, S. 10, 45n19
immigration 119; combatting 123; illegal 120, 124, 126n14, 134, 150, 185; legal 150; security-based policy 120
IMRI (*Institut Marocain des Relations Internationales*) 44, 130
IMRI (*Institut Marocain des Relations Internationales*)/KAS (*Konrad Adenauer Stiftung*) 130
international recognition 2, 20, 28, 46, 60, 68, 148, 215, 219
Islamist 35; activity 199; association 197; discourse 216–17; groups 43, 81, 85, 193, 203; movement 42–3, 77, 195, 214; organisation 217; parties 37, 195, 203; political parties 207; sensibilities 218; spheres 5; terrorism 34, 191; terrorists 85; tone 189
Islamists 33, 192, 215; moderate 43, 216

Jaidi, L. 111–13, 115, *117*, 118, 129–30, 133–5, 139, 142–4, 146, 155n4, 200
Janati-Idrissi, A. 22, 35, 99
Jensen, E. 9, 49, 53, 55, 58–9, 74n6
justice 30, 109, 119–20; cooperation 116–17, 151, 182; former minister 33; French 167; reforms 134, 146, 153; Robert F. Kennedy Center 209; Special European Council 119; subcommittee 110; transitional 40, 61
Justice and Development Party (PJD) 1, 33, 35–8, 42, 56, 74n10, 93, 184, 192, 197, 203, 206–7, 216–17

Kalpakian, J. 41, 208
Katzenstein, P.J. 11
Kausch, K. 111, 119, 133–4
Khachani, M. 120, 124, 176
Khakee, A. 43, 68
King Hassan II 1, 7, 10, 19–20, 30–3, 37, 39, 41, 45n19, 49–50, 57, 61, 84, 98–9, 102, 132, 162–3, 173, 180, 194, 212–13, 218
King Mohammed VI 1–2, 4–7, 10, 15, 17–21, 23, 26, 28–33, 35–9, 41–4, 44n1, 45n10, 45n13, 49–51, 53, 55, 58–62, 67, 70–1, 73n1, 78–9, 83–9, 94–6, 99, 106, 115, 122, 124–5, 125n2, 129, 131–2, 135, 138–9, 146, 150, 157, 160, 163–70, 175–85, 186n3, 190, 192–5, 200, 202, 204, 208–10, 210n2, 212–14, 216, 218
Korany, B. 7–8
Kubálková, V. 12–13

Lannon, E. 106, 155n4
Lavenex, S. 119, 124
legalisation 2, 46, 73, 215, 219
legislative elections 33, 93, 207; free and fair development 134; Moroccan 167
Leveau, R. 30, 186n4
liberalisation 6, 21, 60, 142; of agricultural trade 112, 137; of authoritarianism 213; of exchanges 113; multilateral commitments 111; political 2–3, 5, 7, 41, 81; trade 105, 110, 113, 116, 146, 190, 199
López García, B. 33, 68, 174, 178
López Sala, A.M. 173, 181

Maalmi, A. 10, 31, 35, 37, 70, 89, 93, 110, 132–3, 153, 155n6, 209
Madani, M. 2, 36–7, 40, 47, 148
MAEC (*Ministère des Affaires Étrangères et de la Coopération du Royaume du Maroc*) 16, 22, 24, 26–7, 36, 42, 44n6, 45n10, 55, 58–9, 62, 65–6, 69–70, 73, 74n13, 75n26, 75n28–75n32, 86–91, 93–4, 95n6, 95n8, 106–9, 115–17, 123–5, 127, 136–40, 142, 145, 154, 155n5, 169, 175, 177–8, 182, 187n6, 194, 196–8, 201–6, 210, 211n17

Maghraoui, D. 7, 127
Maghreb 7, 9–10, 17, 21, 63, 76, 79, 83, 86, 90–1, 97, 119, 127, 129, 169, 217; AQIM 204–5; Arab Press (MAP) 16, 95n4; Arab Union 20, 85, 88, 197; Collectif Sahara-Maghreb 56, 82; cost of non-Maghreb 80, 95n1, 180, 215–16; countries 77, 109, 190; EU policies towards 100, 153, 157; French policy towards 166, 186n2; Greater **25**; Gulf countries 159; leaders 107; political 81; political stability 65; regional integration 93, 95; relations 96, 213; relations with US 188, 191, 199; reshaped Maghreb-Sahel region 204–6; Spanish aid 172; summit 89; *see also* Arab Maghreb
Maghreb Confidentiel 37, 44, 205, 208, 211n16
Maghrebi 77–8, 80–1, 89; counterparts 167; French–Maghrebi relations 166; policy 180; project 86; regimes 9; regional integration 17, 22, 94; regional scene 84; space 82, 95; subregional environment 213; summit 93
Martín, I. 80, 111–13, *117*, 118, 133, 135, 139, 142–4, 146, 155n4
Martinez, L. 64, 77–9, 81
Mastanduno, M. 4, 11, 15
MEDA Programmes 112–15, *117*, 120; funds 137, 143
Messari, M.L. 79, 174, 179, 182
Messari, N. 10, 189, 191
Mezran, K. 9, 49, 77, 99
migrants 23, 124; human rights 122; illegal 123; integration 120; Moroccan 162, 173; remittances 197; sub-Saharan African 89, 123, 150, 181, 185
migration 44, 81, 110, 116–18, 120–2, 124, 126n13, 177, 179, 181, 186; Conference 31, 123, 181; control 119–20, 134; cooperation 119, 143; crisis 181, 185; EU Global Approach 124, 142, 150; illegal 87, 99, 121–3, 176, 178, 182; irregular flows 78; issues 109, 119, 122, 125, 181; management 108; policies 107, 123, 150; SIVE programme 122; *see also* Euro-African Partnership for Migration and Development; High-Level Working Group on Asylum and Migration; immigration; migrants
Ministère de l'Économie et des Finances 81, 118

Ministère Délégué chargé du Commerce Extérieur 159, 172
Ministère des Affaires Étrangères-France 159–60, 162
Ministère des Finances et de la Privatisation 80, 125n6
modernisation 23, 44, 44n6, 134; diplomacy 213; economic 114, 117, *118*, 201; economic and social 135, 144; economistic and technocratic 17; institutional 145; local economy 112; Moroccan economy 110
Mohsen-Finan, K. 9, 42, 49, 53, 57, 74n10, 129, 158
Moon, B.E. 3, 7, 18n5
Moroccan 15, 26–7, 39–40, 60, 73, 212; Autonomy Plan 64–5; conflicting roles 95; decision-making 29, 32, 41; discontinuity 213; discourse 4, 157, 215; domestic management of the Western Sahara 67–8; dysfunction 22, 217; foreign minister 1, 81, 141, 152, 169; functionality 4–6, 218; head of state 131, 163; management 23; migration issues 125; monarchic implementation 30; national role conceptions 17; objectives 20; occupation 86, 173; priorities 76; representatives 69, 86, 121, 124, 136, 176, 203; referendum roadmap 59; role of the Benkirane government 36; security forces 68, 123, 144, 147, 179, 181, 185; setback 58; trade with France and Spain **159**; transatlantic rivalry 189; UN Security Council membership 219; USFP 28, 91
Moroccan Academy of Diplomatic Studies (AMED) 24, 27
Moroccan Association for Human Rights (AMDH) 43, 206, 215, 217; *see also* Morocco Subcommittee on Human Rights, Democratisation and Governance
Moroccan diplomatic service 26; campaign 64, 206; corps 34; diplomats 16, 24, 26–7, 65, 70–1, 108, 142, 149, 151, 153, 169, 186, 196; display 91
Moroccan foreign policy 1–3, 16, 43, 46–9, 96–7, 99, 214; towards the EU 14; under Mohammed VI 18–19, 39, 45n13, 78; towards Spain 158, 174, 183, 186; towards the U.S. 207
Moroccan Institute of International Relations (IMRI) 44, 130

Moroccan Interdisciplinary Centre for Strategic and International Studies (CMIESI) 44, 130–1
Moroccan relations 157; with France and Spain 157–8, **159**, 174, 183, 186; relations with U.S. 188, 207
Moroccan Royal Academy of Diplomacy (MoRAD) 24, 26–7, 45n10
Moroccan–French interdependence 162; relations 163, 165–6
Moroccan–French–Spanish meeting of deputy foreign ministers 168
Moroccan–Spanish bilateral relationship 179; cooperation 182; crisis 177; difficulties 175; organisation of the Euro-African Ministerial Conference on Migration and Development 181; relations 164, 171, 173
Morocco Inter-Ministerial Delegation for Human Rights 149
Morocco Subcommittee on Human Rights, Democratisation and Governance 111, 145
Mundy, J. 9, 47, 50–2, 57, 60–1, 207

Naciri, K. 76, 80
Najih, N.B.S. 10, 45n19
National Action Plan on Human Rights and Democracy 40, 145
National Council on Human Rights *see* CNDH
National Human Development Initiative (INDH) 117
Neack, J.A.K. 7–8
Nonneman, G. 7–9
North Africa 170; Arab spring 152; BMENA initiative 190, 195; development 198; instability 5; political reform 196; U.S. Economic Partnership 199–200
North African country 84, 99; leaders 129, 166; nationalist movements 79; stability 77; states 8; tiger 95n1

Obama, President B. 66, 71, 208; Administration 70, 72, 209
Obiols, R. 176–7
Oficina Económica y Comercial de España en Rabat 172
oil 8, 72; exploration 176–7; imports 84; Middle East 196; prices 92; reserves 200
Ouaouicha, D. 26, 195, 207

Pace, M. 99, 114
Pardo, J.L. 109, 133

Partnership for Democracy and Shared Prosperity 148, 151
paternalism 162–3, 186
Peace Plan for Self-Determination of the People of Western Sahara *see* Baker Plans (Baker Plan II)
peripheral (Third World) states 12, 18n5, 120
Pew Research Center 188, 196
Pham, J.P. 204, 206
Planet, A.I. 35, 86, 97, 164, 170, 175, 178
Polisario 47, 53, 82; congress 65; defectors 28; former leader 45n12; founders 29; Front 28, 34, 40, 49, 51, 53–4, 56–7, 60, 62, 64–6, 74n6, 82, 87, 89, 93, 165, 177, 207–8; internet battlefront 64; Moroccan prisoners of war 208; returning officials 57
political change 1, 127, 148, 154; transformations 1, 60, 93, 144
political liberalisation 2–3, 5, 7, 41, 81
Potomac Institute for Policy Studies 209
poverty reduction 116, 134, 145
Powel, B. 125n4, 178, 192, 194, 197
Presidential Council 76, 86, 88
pro-democracy 5, 218; critical sectors 215; protests 146
Putnam, R.D. 11, 188

Rabat 50, 71, 73, 133; acceptance of Baker Plan 55, 58; alignment with U.S. policies 218; authorities 2, 5, 17–18, 22, 24, 28, 43, 46, 49, 51, 57, 59–60, 66, 68, 91, 94, 119–20, 125, 144–5, 154–5, 166, 168, 177–8, 180, 187n14, 193–5, 207, 209–10, 212, 213–14, 219; demands 136–7; management 61, 67; official discourse 108, 189; overall strategy 105
Rapport Avicenne 158, 166
rapprochement 13, 82, 95, 179; with Algiers 53, 166, 175, 201, 207; attempts 86; between peoples 151; bilateral 81, 85, 87, 89, 93; budding 85; domestic costs 210; with Europe 102, 141–2; mutual 78; Spanish–Moroccan 180; visible 84, 201
referendum 52, 62, 74n11, 74n18, 147; electorate 49; final 52–7; mock 177; roadmap 51, 59; on self-determination 6, 48–9, 59, 64, 165, 209; in Western Sahara (MINURSO) 34, 49, 94, 168, 209
refugees 150; camps 28, 57, 69; United Nations High Commissioner for Refugees (UNHCR) 54

Index 257

regional construction 80, 86
Régragui, I. 4, 45n7, 192, 195
Reinforced Political Dialogue 111, 134, 141, 145
Réseau Marocain Euromed des ONG 125n7, 125n9
Riziki Mohamed, A. 9, 44n4
Robert F. Kennedy Center for Justice and Human Rights 209
Rosenau, J.N. 10–11, 31
Rosenblum, J. 10, 30, 37, 45n8
Roussellier, J. 9, 72, 94
Royal Consultative Council for Saharan Affairs (CORCAS) 40, *48*, 61–3, 67, 74n16, 181
rule of law 116–17, 127, 138, 145–6, 151, 155n9, 199

Sahrawi 28, 47, 49, 60–1, 66–8, 72–3, 153; associations 71; internal activism *48*; international strategies 94; people 171; pro-Sahrawi civic platform 177; protests 50, 57, 181; referendum 209; torture 169; tribes 62; unionist 37, 214
Sahrawi Arab Democratic Republic (SADR) 28–9, 66, 89; leader 93
Sahrawi Association of Victims of Gross Human Rights Violations Committed by the Moroccan State (ASVDH) 60–1, 67, 71
Sahrawis 47, 49, 57, 61, 68; ethnic 50, 74n11; pro-independence 72; reconciliation strategy towards 67; recruitment of 208; unionist 28, 214
Sater, J.N. 16, 50
Schimmelfennig, F. 14, 102–4, 122, 137, 158, 181
Schmid, D. 103, 105
Sehimi, M. 20, 178, 195, 198
Shelley, T. 9, 50, 72, 74n6
SIPRI (Stockholm International Peace Research Institute) 91–2; Military Expenditure Database **92**
Smith, J.J. 72, 153
Smith, L.E. 50, 56–7, 61
Social Affairs and Migration 110; working group 121
Socialist Union of Popular Forces (USFP) 28, 91
Solà-Martín, A. 61–2, 208
Soler, E. 108, 128–9, 134, 184
solidarity 43, 79, 116, 124, 184, 197; conference 94; European 164; Moroccan antiterrorist 87; movements 215

Sorroza, A. 124–5, 181
Spain 5, 10, 34, 47, 60, 63, 77, 83, 100, 137, 150, 153, 164–5, 170–1, 176, 179–82, 184–5, 212, 217; 5 + 5 Dialogue 95, 109; ambassador to 33; bilateral crisis 86, 107, 177–8, 191; bilateral relations 18, 135, 157–8, 175; cooperation 173; election to UN Security Council 186; Euro-African Ministerial Conference on Migration 123; FDI in Morocco **161**; Moroccan delegation 62; Moroccan foreign policy 174; Moroccan trade **159, 160**; negotiations on Ceuta and Melilla 183; Perejil crisis 23, 214; readmission agreement 121, 126n11; relations with 44, 67, 72, 216; resistance 71; secretary of state for EU affairs 136; separatist lobby 65; support for Morocco 74n15
Spanish 56, 62, 184; aid in the Maghreb 172–3; ambassador 74, 74n15, 181, 185; army 178, 185; attitudes 175, 177; authorities 176; cities 170; Confederation of Employers' Organisations (CEOE) 179; convicts pardoned 185; cooperation 172; coordination 120; diplomacy 180, 183; diplomats 186; former colony 46, 49; historical responsibility 171; Moroccan convergence 182; Moroccan crisis 177; naval manoeuvres 178; occupation 179; productive sector 184; resistance 165; royal visit 183; state 170, 173; territory 164, 177, 185
Spanish foreign policy 174; foreign minister 181; Ministry of Foreign Affairs 95n1, 173, 175, 177
Spanish government 28, 75n28, 122–3, 165, 174–6, 178, 181; People's Party (PP) 174; presidency 146, 164; Socialist 180; Socialist Workers' Party (PSOE) 177
Spanish investments 179; foreign direct 172
Spanish–Moroccan 123; border 124; fisheries relations 176; joint military-police unit 182; rapprochement 180; relations 123, 171
Special European Council on Justice and Home Affairs 119
Stephan, M.J. 47, 50
Stora, B. 16, 78–9, 81–3, 85, 216
sub-Saharan Africa *29*, 216, 218; immigration from 123
sub-Saharan African migrants 89, 123, 150, 181, 185

terrorism 21, 213; ATA 205; combating 116; countering 109; fight against 84, 87, 134, 196, 199, 206, 210; Interdiction Program (TIP) 205; international 178; Islamist 34, 191; security imperative 81; Suppression of the Financing 192; threat of 90; *see also* counterterrorism
terrorist 194; acts 87; Al Qaeda network 192; groups 81; Interdiction Program (TIP) 205; threat 94, 182, 206, 210; violence 192; *see also* antiterrorist; terrorist attacks; terrorists
terrorist attacks 6; 9/11 189–90, 199; in Casablanca 74n10, 179; in Paris 187
terrorists 193–4; Islamist 85
Theofilopoulou, A. 51, 53
Third World 7; states 12; *see also* peripheral states
torture 169; centres 194
Tozy, M. 22, 32, 40
Trade and Investment Framework Agreement (TIFA) 211n8
transformations 47, 50, 105, 155; bottom-up 82; democratic 127, 217; political 1, 60, 93, 144
Tuquoi, J.-P. 10, 32, 35, 57, 158, 162–6, 178

UN General Assembly 32, 59, 65, 87, 89–90, 192
UN Mission for the Referendum in Western Sahara (MINURSO) 34, 53, 66, 68, 70–1; Identification Commission 49, 54; mandate 37, 68–9, 71, 94, 168–9, 186, 209; personnel 69
UN Security Council 52–6, 58, 62–5, 68–71, 73, 74n13, 165, 168, 180, 192, 201, 207, 209; members 57, 74n13, 186, 189, 209, 219
UN Security Council 52–8, 62–5, 68–71, 73, 74n13, 165, 168, 180, 186, 189, 192, 201, 207, 209, 219
UN Settlement Plan for Western Sahara 49, 51–5, 74n6, 76, 207
UN Special Political and Decolonization Committee 89
UN's Office of the High Commissioner for Human Rights (OHCHR) 68
Union for the Mediterranean (UfM) 31, 81, 127–31, 134, 152, 155, 166
United States (U.S.) 5, 26, 31, 40, 47, 60, 70, 73, 84–5, 90, 93–4, 97, 158, 162, 164–5, 171, 177, 188, 196, 198, 200, 210, 211n16, 218; African Command (AFRICOM) 206–7; agricultural products 203; crisis *48*; demands 33, 193; Eizenstat Initiative 77, 190, 199; expectations 17, 91, 194, 219; FPA tradition 7, 13; Free Trade Agreement 38, 214; free trade negotiations 42; investment in Morocco 204; MINURSO mandate 71, 186, 209; Morocco Free Trade Agreement 189, 199; officials 63, 82, 192; representative 180; support 64, 66, 178; Trade and Investment Framework Agreement (TIFA) 211n8; training system 24
United States (U.S.) administration 70, 194–5; Assistant Secretary of State 58–9, 207; Congress 22, 206, 208; members of Congress 211n10; Secretary of State 178
United States (U.S.) diplomacy 51; ambassador 41, 66, 74n15; diplomatic cable 63; diplomatic documents 83; diplomatic intervention 67; diplomats 57, 70, 183, 207, 216; embassy in Rabat 16, 63, 66–7, 74n15, 75n23, 83, 167, 181, 183, 192, 207, 210n5; Moroccan delegation 62; UN ambassador 57, 71
United States (U.S.) fight against terrorism 33–4; offshore detention centre 193; War on Terror 6, 18, 189–93, 199, 204–5, 210, 212
United States (U.S.) military 206; army 71; invasion of Iraq 202; occupation of Iraq 197; perceived security threats 81; Sixth Fleet 194
United States (U.S.) relations 6, 18, 37, 68, 77, 82, 95, 195–6, 201, 201, 205, 215, 217; allies 18, 178, 188–91, 209–10; ambiguous backing for Morocco 208; bilateral 26, 191, 210, 216–17; courtship of Algeria 107; foreign policy 43, 191, 194, 200; with Middle East 215; rapprochement with Algiers 53; Strategic Dialogue with Morocco 209, 211n18; trade 200;
U.S.–North Africa Economic Partnership 199; *see also* Eizenstat Initiative

Vaquer, J. 72, 171, 176, 181
Veguilla, V. 49, 74n3

War on Terror 6, 18, 33–4, 189–93, 199, 204–5, 210, 212
Wendt, A.E. 12–14, 98, 102, 104, 125n5, 133, 140

Western Sahara 28, 60, 65, 67–8, 74n3, 85–6, 171, 179, 186, 188, 191, 198, 204; annexation 2, 46; Authority 54, 57; autonomy 52, 165; Autonomy Plan 40, 95n7, 206, 208–9, 214; conciliation 87; cities 61; decentralisation 51; decolonisation 158, 170; deterioration of human rights 156n11; economic privileges 74n12; exploration for oil 176; fisheries 153–4; Group of Friends 63, 71, 177, 209; human rights 210; Human Rights Watch report 34; independent 64; issue 30, 42, 51, 73n1, 78, 84, 89, 91, 93, 97, 164, 167, 186n5, 201, 218; MINURSO 49, 94, 168, 209; Moroccan control 215–16, 219; Moroccanity 4, 216; Moroccan sovereignty 20, 47, 52, 69, 73; occupied 70; Peace Plan for Self-Determination 54; reconciliation 50, 180; Resource Watch (WSRW) 72; Supreme Court 55–7; territory 50, 86, 207; UN Settlement Plan 76; waters 182
Western Sahara Baker Plans *48*, 60, 83, 207; Baker Plan I 52–5, 86–7, 165, 177, 207; Baker Plan II 54–61, 73, 87–9, 95n6, 165, 180–1, 201, 207
Western Sahara conflict 6, 9, 29, 44, 72–3, 76, 82, 88, 96, 99, 125, 133, 166, 168, 189, 204, 209–10; absent from Advanced Status negotiations 145; Algerian global approach 83; Algerian refusal to negotiate 95n6, 113; international management 5, 17, *48*; link with terrorist threat 206; mediation 69; Moroccan official discourse 43; Moroccan positions 22, 34, 39, 122, 162–3, 186, 217; Moroccan performance 46; new phase 59; price to maintain 74n8; profile raised in Brussels 153; put aside 84, 86, 91; Rabat's official positions 64; resolution 51, 77; risk to regional security 208; Spanish attitude 177, 180; spatial and scalar shift 47; U.S. position 66, 188, 209–10; win–win solution 56
White, G. 96, 100, 120, 187n13, 199–202
Willis, M.J. 10, 41, 74n11, 189, 191
Working Groups 136–7; on Asylum and Migration 120; bilateral 211; EU–Morocco 27, 139–40; joint 87, 179; on Social Affairs and Migration 121; thematic 203
World Bank 80, **159, 160**, 186n1, 187n7, 187n16
Wunderlich, D. 123

Youngs, R. 108, 119
Youssoufi, A. 35–6, 84, 107–8, 175, 178

Zartman, I.W. 10, 30, 37, 45n8, 46, 51
Zeghal, M. 42–3, 74n10
Zerhouni, S. 1, 38
Zisenwine, D. 10, 31
Zoubir, Y.H. 9, 51–2, 57, 76, 78, 84, 86, 191, 195, 199, 205, 207
Zouitni, H. 10, 15, 30, 35, 37–9
Zunes, S. 9, 47, 51–2, 57, 60

eBooks
from Taylor & Francis

Helping you to choose the right eBooks for your Library

Add to your library's digital collection today with Taylor & Francis eBooks. We have over 50,000 eBooks in the Humanities, Social Sciences, Behavioural Sciences, Built Environment and Law, from leading imprints, including Routledge, Focal Press and Psychology Press.

Choose from a range of subject packages or create your own!

Benefits for you
- Free MARC records
- COUNTER-compliant usage statistics
- Flexible purchase and pricing options
- All titles DRM-free.

Benefits for your user
- Off-site, anytime access via Athens or referring URL
- Print or copy pages or chapters
- Full content search
- Bookmark, highlight and annotate text
- Access to thousands of pages of quality research at the click of a button.

Free Trials Available
We offer free trials to qualifying academic, corporate and government customers.

eCollections

Choose from over 30 subject eCollections, including:

Archaeology	Language Learning
Architecture	Law
Asian Studies	Literature
Business & Management	Media & Communication
Classical Studies	Middle East Studies
Construction	Music
Creative & Media Arts	Philosophy
Criminology & Criminal Justice	Planning
Economics	Politics
Education	Psychology & Mental Health
Energy	Religion
Engineering	Security
English Language & Linguistics	Social Work
Environment & Sustainability	Sociology
Geography	Sport
Health Studies	Theatre & Performance
History	Tourism, Hospitality & Events

For more information, pricing enquiries or to order a free trial, please contact your local sales team:
www.tandfebooks.com/page/sales

www.tandfebooks.com